A Woman's Kingdom

Portrait of D. A. Derzhavina (1767–1842), painting by V. L. Borovinkovskii (1813). 284 cm. × 204.3 cm. State Tretyakov Gallery, Moscow (inv. 5040). © State Tretyakov Gallery. Photograph, N. Akekseev and A. Sapronenkov (1998). Reproduced with permission of the State Tretyakov Gallery.

A WOMAN'S KINGDOM

Noblewomen and the Control of Property in Russia, 1700–1861

Michelle Lamarche Marrese

Cornell University Press · Ithaca and London

First published 2002 by Cornell University Press

Printed in the United States of America

Library of Congress Cataloging-in-Publication Data
Marrese, Michelle Lamarche, 1964–
   A woman's kingdom : noblewomen and the control of property in Russia,
1700–1861 / Michelle Lamarche Marrese.
      p. cm.
Includes bibliographical references and index.
   ISBN 0-8014-3911-6 (cloth : alk. paper)
   1. Women landowners—Russia—History.   2. Inheritance and
succession—Russia—History.   3. Women—Russia—History.   I. Title.
   HQ 1662 .M367 2002
   305.4′0947—dc21   2001007531

Cornell University Press strives to use environmentally responsible
suppliers and materials to the fullest extent possible in the publishing
of its books. Such materials include vegetable-based, low-VOC inks
and acid-free papers that are recycled, totally chlorine-free, or partly
composed of nonwood fibers. For further information, visit our
website at www.cornellpress.cornell.edu.

Cloth printing   10 9 8 7 6 5 4 3 2 1

Contents

Tables

Acknowledgments

The research and writing of this book would not have been possible without generous financial support and the advice and encouragement of many friends and colleagues. The International Research and Exchanges Board (IREX) made possible two lengthy research trips to Russia, in 1992–93 and again in 1997–98. I also owe special thanks to the Social Science Research Council, for a dissertation writing fellowship in 1993–94 and a postdoctoral writing fellowship in 1997–98. Finally, a General University Research Fellowship from the University of Delaware funded a summer of research in Moscow in 1996.

This work has also benefited from the kind help of many archivists in Russia. I would like to extend special thanks to the staff of the Archive of Ancient Acts in Moscow (RGADA). At RGADA, Alexander Gamaiunov and Inna Ivanova offered research assistance and created a pleasant work environment during the many months I worked there. Evgenii Rychalovskii drew my attention to collections that proved invaluable for my work. Viktor Belikov shared his inventories and knowledge of collections on land disputes with me. I also owe thanks to the staff of the State Historical Museum (GIM) and the Central State Historical Archive of the City of Moscow (TsGIAM). For the countless productive hours I spent in the Russian State Historical Archive (RGIA), I am particularly indebted to Serafima Igorevna Varekhova, Galina Alekseevna Ippolitova, and the staff of the reading room, who did everything possible to facilitate my research. Archivists in Tver', Vladimir, and Tambov also deserve thanks for helping me gain access to much-needed documents in those cities in a timely fashion.

Many colleagues have contributed to this project over the years. First, I would like to express my gratitude to my dissertation committee at

Northwestern University. John Bushnell, David Joravsky, and Sarah Maza greatly improved the quality of this work with their thoughtful criticism. Although he did not direct the dissertation, David Joravsky generously shared his time and vast knowledge of intellectual history with me throughout my years at Northwestern. I owe my greatest debt to John Bushnell. He deserves my heart-felt thanks for his unflagging enthusiasm for this project and his willingness to read and comment on endless drafts of each chapter of the book.

Other colleagues contributed to the improvement and completion of this project. Daniel Kaiser, who read the entire manuscript at least twice, must be singled out for special appreciation; my book has greatly benefited from his sound advice. The comments of Hilde Hoogenboom vastly improved chapter 6, while Eve Levin and two anonymous readers at the *Russian Review* made significant contributions to chapter 2. Ann Kleimola, Barbara Engel, John Alexander, Elise Wirtschafter, Catriona Kelly, Lindsey Hughes, and Isabel de Madariaga read and commented on various parts of the manuscript along the way. During my years at the University of Delaware, my work greatly benefited from the advice and support of Peter Kolchin and Anne Boylan. I am particularly indebted to William Wagner and an anonymous reader at Cornell University Press for their extraordinarily careful reading of my manuscript and their detailed comments. Their advice was instrumental in improving the final product. And last, but far from least, I am grateful to John Ackerman, director of Cornell University Press, for his interest and encouragement, and to Candace Akins and Mary Babcock, whose patient editing saved me from many errors.

Chapter 2 originally appeared in the *Russian Review* in July 1999. I thank the *Russian Review* for permission to reprint the chapter.

Finally, I owe Michael Marrese more than I can repay: for assembling all the statistical tables; for reading every version of the entire manuscript and offering insightful comments (often initially rejected but later incorporated); for enduring lengthy separations for the sake of Russian noblewomen's property rights; and for his support in all my endeavors, academic and otherwise.

Glossary

assignants banknotes, introduced in 1768. The value of the assignant declined sharply in the early decades of the nineteenth century. After the monetary reform of 1839–43, the ratio of the silver ruble to the *ruble-assignant* was 1 : 3.5. [See Crisp (1976), 96.]

barshchina labor obligation of serfs.

chetvert' (*chetverti*) a land measure, equal to one-half of a *desiatina*.

desiatina a land measure, equal to 2.7 acres.

dvorianskaia opeka the Noble Board of Guardians, responsible for overseeing the estates of minor children, the insolvent, and estates belonging to landowners guilty of serf abuse and other misdemeanors.

krepostnye knigi notarial records, i.e., records of property transfers.

obrok quitrent, paid by peasants in cash or kind.

pomeshchik, pomeshchitsa (*pomeshchiki, pomeshchitsy* [pl.]) a noble landowner, i.e., owners of a *pomest'e*.

pomest'e (*pl. pomest'ia*) an estate held in service tenure.

rod clan; extended kin group, descended from a common ancestor.

terem women's quarters in Muscovite households, in which upper-class women were secluded.

uezd district.

voevoda governor of a district or province.

votchina (*pl. votchiny*) a patrimonial, or hereditary, estate, subject to different rules of disposal than service-tenure land.

Abbreviations

ch.	*chast'* (part)
d., dd.	*delo, dela* (file, files)
ed. khr.	*edinitsa khraneniia* (storage unit)
f.	*fond* (collection)
l., ll.	*list, listy* (folio, folios)
op.	*opis'* (inventory)
GARF	Gosudarstvennyi arkhiv Rossiiskoi federatsii (State Archive of the Russian Federation)
GATO	Gosudarstvennyi arkhiv Tambovskoi oblasti (State Archive of Tambov oblast)
GA Tverskoi oblasti	Gosudarstvennyi arkhiv Tverskoi oblasti (State Archive of Tver' oblast)
GAVO	Gosudarstvennyi arkhiv Vladimirskoi oblasti (State Archive of Vladimir oblast)
GIM	Gosudarstvennyi istoricheskii muzei (State Historical Museum)
GNB	Gosudarstvennaia natsional'naia biblioteka (State National Library)
OAS	Opisanie dokumentov i del, khraniashchikhsia v arkhive sviateishego pravitel'stvuiushchego Sinoda
PSZ	Polnoe sobranie zakonov Rossiiskoi imperii (Complete Collection of Laws of the Russian Empire)
RGADA	Rossiiskii gosudarstvennyi arkhiv drevnikh aktov (Russian State Archive of Ancient Acts)
RGIA	Rossiiskii gosudarstvennyi istoricheskii arkhiv (Russian State Historical Archive)
SIRIO	Sbornik imperatorskogo russkogo istoricheskogo obshchestva

SPbFIRI   Sankt-Peterburgskii filial Instituta rossiiskoi istorii RAN (St. Petersburg Branch of the Institute of Russian History of the Russian Academy of Sciences)

SZ   Svod zakonov Rossiiskoi imperii (Digest of Current Russian Law)

TsGIAM   Tsentral'nyi gosudarstvennyi istoricheskii arkhiv Moskvy (Central State Historical Archive of the City of Moscow)

A Woman's Kingdom

I believe that it happens all the time—men marry money, but the money stays with the wife.

F. M. DOSTOEVSKY, *Idiot*, in *Sobranie sochinenii*, 1957

She only breathed freely when she was alone with her business accounts
and plans, or when no one interrupted her discussions with estate managers, village elders, housekeepers.

MIKHAIL SALTYKOV-SHCHEDRIN, *The Golovlyov Family*, 1988

Introduction

The story of the Russian noblewoman, as told in literature and historical narrative, has been one of paradox. She appears in each telling as both formidable and powerless, performing by turns the role of tyrant and victim in the patriarchal family. In the historical record her prominence in public life rises and falls, peaking in the eighteenth century but dwindling after the reign of Catherine the Great. In the tales of nineteenth-century novelists her moral superiority guides the feckless nobleman who grapples with the evils of serfdom and autocracy. Neither account, however, explains how the formidable woman emerged alongside her more familiar powerless counterpart, or why the experience of Russian women has been imagined as one of such stark contradictions.

The legal status of Russian women was rife with similar incongruities. Women of all social estates were obliged to live with their husbands, and they could neither work nor travel without their permission. Divorce was virtually unattainable in the Orthodox Church, even for wives who suffered physical abuse, and legal separation became prevalent only at the end of the nineteenth century. Yet, while the burden of gender tutelage seemed to weigh more heavily on women in Russian society, Russian noblewomen enjoyed one advantage virtually unknown to their counterparts in Western Europe: from the mid-eighteenth century married women could own and dispose of property separately from their husbands.[1]

This peculiar exception to women's legal servitude excited comment among foreign visitors to Russia in the nineteenth century; it has also inspired abundant speculation on the part of scholars. No one, however, has

---

1. For a discussion of the variations in European women's property rights, see chapter 2.

explored the significance of property ownership in the lives of Russian noblewomen. Many historians have dismissed Russian women's control of their fortunes as *pro forma* and assumed that women could not administer their property within the confines of the patriarchal family. In the words of one scholar, "Noblewomen, unlike their peers in West Europe, were entitled to own and dispose of property, but their right was meaningless in a society where they were bound legally to their fathers' tutelage and, if they married, to a husband chosen or approved by him."[2] At the opposite extreme, others have made extravagant claims for the liberties Russian noblewomen enjoyed vis-à-vis their European contemporaries.[3]

The subject of this work is noblewomen's relation to property in Imperial Russia. In the opening chapters I trace the evolution of women's legal status in the eighteenth century. In the realm of both inheritance and control of property, the post-Petrine era was one of genuine change for elite women. Significantly, noblewomen themselves took part in the extension of their property rights and went on to make ample use of their legal prerogatives. Whereas historians have long maintained that married women's control of their estates in the eighteenth century derived from a tradition of feminine autonomy in Slavic culture, I argue that the elevation of women's status in property law took place as the nobility worked to secure their corporate privileges and to promote a rational legal order. The aspiration to legality was a moving force behind the advancement of Russian women's property rights in the eighteenth century. Thus, noblewomen's legal status in Russia improved in tandem with changes taking place in the wider political culture.

Women's ownership and use of property comprise the second major theme of this study. Unlike women of the European elite, Russian women controlled—and often managed—vast amounts of immovable property. The percentage of land and serfs held by women in Russia rose dramatically from the second half of the eighteenth century, until female proprietors possessed as much as a third of the estates in private hands, as well as serfs and urban real estate. Noblewomen who acquired land differed little from male proprietors in the use of their assets. In this regard as well, Russian noblewomen parted company with their counterparts in the West. Historians have iden-

2. Mary Fleming Zirin, "Introduction," in *The Cavalry Maiden: Journals of a Russian Officer in the Napoleonic Wars*, by Nadezhda Durova; trans., intro. and notes by Mary Fleming Zirin (Bloomington, 1989), xvi. For a similar appraisal, see Linda Harriet Edmondson, *Feminism in Russia, 1900–1917* (Stanford, 1984), 11.

3. Nada Boskovska, "Muscovite Women during the Seventeenth Century: At the Peak of the Deprivation of Their Rights or on the Road towards New Freedom?" in *Von Moskau nach St. Petersburg: Das russische Reich im 17. Jahrhundert*, ed. Hans-Joachim Torke (Wiesbaden, 2000), 56, 61; Natalia Pushkareva, *Women in Russian History: From the Tenth to the Twentieth Century*, trans. and ed. Eve Levin. (Armonk, N.Y., 1997), 45, 48; George G. Weickhardt, "Legal Rights of Women in Russia, 1100–1750," *Slavic Review* 55, no. 1 (Spring 1996): 19–20.

tified a discrete female value system with regard to property among women in Europe and the United States. In Russia the law of property created greater equality between the sexes; as a result, the principle of separate estates encouraged women to look after their own interests and to take active part in the market for land and serfs, as sellers and as buyers. Partible inheritance, coupled with statutory limits on testamentary freedom, furnished a further incentive for husbands and wives to work together and to distribute family assets, both personal and immovable, exclusively among their offspring. While the lives of noble men and women in Imperial Russia diverged significantly in many respects, their experience as landowners was surprisingly similar.

The significance of *A Woman's Kingdom* rests, at least in part, on a claim that the position of Russian noblewomen was unique in a European context. To be sure, Russian scholars who expounded on the legal privileges of their female compatriots often exaggerated the disabilities of women in other cultures. Many of the liberties that Russian women enjoyed were, in fact, available to some of their European counterparts: in much of Europe, the dotal system safeguarded a married woman's real estate by requiring her consent to the alienation of dowry funds and, in some cases, allowing her control of nondowry property. Scholars of such diverse cultures as medieval Ireland and early modern Turkey have brought to light the surprising legal advantages of married women—surprising, at least, in contrast to the power men wielded over the property of their wives in the Anglo-American world. Under British common law, which also governed property arrangements in the New World, married women could administer their assets only with the aid of elaborate legal devices. As a result, the revelation that women instigated property litigation in the Ottoman Empire and engaged in money lending in thirteenth-century Italy has prompted scholars to overturn traditional assumptions about women's relation to property.[4]

---

4. A small sample of this vast literature includes the following: Sandra T. Barnes, "Women, Property, and Power," in *Beyond the Second Sex: New Directions in the Anthropology of Gender*, ed. Peggy Reeves Sanday and Ruth Gallagher Goodenough (Philadelphia, 1990), 255–80; Jack Goody, "Inheritance, Property, and Women: Some Comparative Considerations," in *Family and Inheritance: Rural Society in Western Europe, 1200–1800*, ed. Jack Goody, Joan Thirsk, and E. P. Thompson (Cambridge, 1976), 10–36; Abraham Marcus, "Men, Women, and Property: Dealers in Real Estate in 18th Century Aleppo," *Journal of the Economic and Social History of the Orient* 26, part II (1983): 137–63; Margaret L. Meriweather, "Women and *Waqf* Revisited: The Case of Aleppo, 1770–1840," in *Women in the Ottoman Empire: Middle Eastern Women in the Early Modern Era*, ed. Madeline C. Zilfi (New York, 1997), 128–52; Kenneth Nicholls, "Irishwomen and Property in the Sixteenth Century," in *Women in Early Modern Ireland*, ed. Margaret MacCurtain and Mary O'Dowd (Edinburgh, 1991), 17–31; Eleanor S. Riemer, "Women, Dowries, and Capital Investment in Thirteenth-Century Siena," *Women and History* 10 (1985): 59–79; Laurel Thatcher Ulrich, *Good Wives: Image and Reality in the Lives of Women in Northern New England, 1650–1750* (New York, 1982), 35–50; Fariba Zarinebaf-Shahr, "Ottoman Women and the Tradition of Seeking Justice in the Eighteenth Century," in *Women in the Ottoman Empire: Middle Eastern*

The central thesis of this book is that women of the Russian elite were nonetheless exceptional, not only in their range of rights over property but also in making ample use of their legal prerogatives. European women enjoyed clear legal advantages vis-à-vis their English counterparts, yet their opportunities to manage and alienate their fortunes during marriage were far from extensive.[5] Thus, while women in Europe remained very much on "the margins of ownership,"[6] for noblewomen in Russia independent control of property became the rule rather than the exception. As I will argue throughout this work, the "peculiarity" of the Russian case was not the existence of separate marital estates, but that Russian lawmakers took the principle of separate property to its logical conclusion and that women, in turn, exploited their legal prerogatives to the full. More general legal rights—in particular, married women's ability to litigate in their own names and to sue their husbands—supported noblewomen's rights over property. As a consequence of their economic autonomy, Russian noblewomen wielded considerable influence in the family and society.

Contemporary Accounts of Women and Property

The stereotype of the downtrodden Russian woman originated with the narratives of European travelers.[7] Visitors to early-modern Muscovy regaled their audience with tales of wife beating and domestic misery, while depicting Russian women as ill-mannered and prone to drunkenness.[8] One of these

Women in the Early Modern Era, ed. Madeline C. Zilfi (New York, 1997), 253–63. On variations in the property rights of women in Imperial China, see Patricia Buckley Ebrey, The Inner Quarters: Marriage and the Lives of Chinese Women in the Sung Period (Berkeley, 1993), 6, 100–13, and Kathryn Bernhardt, Women and Property in China, 960–1949 (Stanford, 1999).

5. On the development of the dotal system, see Diane Owen Hughes, "From Brideprice to Dowry in Mediterranean Europe," Women and History, no. 10 (1985): 13–58. For two regional studies on the contraction of European women's property rights in the early-modern era, see Martha C. Howell, The Marriage Exchange: Property, Social Place, and Gender in the Cities of the Low Countries, 1300–1550 (Chicago, 1998) and Riemer (1985), 73–75.

6. Quoted in Leonore Davidoff and Catherine Hall, Family Fortunes: Men and Women of the English Middle Class, 1780–1850 (Chicago, 1987), 275.

7. Charles J. Halperin, "Sixteenth-Century Foreign Travel Accounts to Muscovy: A Methodological Excursus," Sixteenth Century Journal 6, no. 2 (October 1975): 89–110. For a more optimistic perspective on these accounts, see E. Iu. Artemova, "Zapiski frantsuzskikh puteshestvennikov o kul'ture Rossii poslednei treti XVIII veka," Istoriia SSSR, no. 3 (1988): 165–73.

8. Samuel Collins, The Present State of Russia (London, 1671), 8–10, 36, 114; Adam Olearius, The Travels of Olearius in Seventeenth-Century Russia, trans. and ed. Samuel H. Baron (Stanford, 1967), 168–70; Johann Georg Korb, Diary of an Austrian Secretary of Legation at the Court of Czar Peter the Great (London, 1863), 1: 206–8; John Perry, "Extracts from the State of Russia under the Present Czar," in Seven Britons in Imperial Russia, 1698–1812, ed. Peter Putnam (Princeton, 1952), 37, 40; Friedrich Christian Weber, The Present State of Russia (London, 1968), I: 136, 147–50.

accounts, written by a Frenchman in 1761, drew the ire of Catherine II. Women in Russia "enjoy even greater liberty" than women in other European nations, she retorted, and then cited women's ownership of their dowries as evidence of their superior legal standing.[9] By the end of the eighteenth century, however, lurid reports of female subjugation had given way to a new preoccupation: the power of women in the family and society, which foreigners attributed to Russian women's unusual legal and economic status.

The observations of a young English traveler at the turn of the nineteenth century are typical of these later accounts. While Catherine Wilmot, like previous visitors from Europe, exclaimed more than once about the ignorance and vulgar appearance of her female companions in Russia, she also noted that they enjoyed unusually extensive property rights. "You must know that every Woman has the right over her own Fortune totally independent of her Husband and he is as independent of his Wife," she wrote to her sister Harriet in 1806. "Marriage is therefore no Union of interests whatsoever. . . . This gives a curious sort of hue to the Conversations of the Russian Matrons which to a meek English Woman appears prodigious independence in the midst of a Despotic Government!"[10] Catherine's sister Martha remarked on this phenomenon in a journal entry from the same year: "The full and entire dominion which Russian Women have over their own fortunes gives them a remarkable degree of liberty and a degree of independence of their Husbands unknown in England."[11]

Male observers also reported on the prominence of Russian women at court and in provincial society, albeit not always with approbation. Although more concerned with Russia's political development than with social customs, August von Haxthausen indulged in several asides on the status of women. "In Russia the female sex occupies a different position from its counterpart in the rest of Europe," he began. Haxthausen compared the slothful merchant women he encountered unfavorably with German housewives, but the privileges of Russian noblewomen did not escape him. "A large part of the real estate is also in the hands of women," he related, adding that "it is easy to understand what a great influence women enjoy in society as a result."[12] Writing at the end of the nineteenth century, Anatole Leroy-Beaulieu offered another perspective on Russian women, suggesting that

9. "Antidot (protivoiadie). Polemicheskoe sochinenie Ekateriny Btoroi, ili razbor knigi abbata Chappe d'Auteroche o Rossii," *Os'mnadtsatyi vek* 4 (Moscow, 1869), 352.

10. Martha Wilmot Bradford, *The Russian Journals of Martha and Catherine Wilmot, 1803–1808*, ed. and intro. by the Marchioness of Londonderry and H. M. Hyde (London, 1935), 234.

11. Ibid., 271.

12. August von Haxthausen, *Studies on the Interior of Russia*, ed. S. Frederick Starr and trans. E. Schmidt (Chicago, 1972), 21–23. Although he did not remark on women's property rights, the Marquis de Custine noted many differences between Russian and European women. The former, he reported, were "political Amazons" who often meddled in affairs of state. Marquis de Custine, *La Russie en 1839*, 2d ed. (Paris, 1843), 3: 106–7.

among Slavic peoples "the psychological differences between the sexes are
. . . less marked. . . . If the men may sometimes be accused of a certain femi-
ninity, i.e., of something mobile, flexible, . . . or impressionable to excess,
the women, as though in compensation have, in their minds and characters,
something strong, energetical, in one word, virile."[13]

Another French observer who traveled to Russia late in the nineteenth
century believed that the freedom Russian women enjoyed in managing
their estates had a profound impact on their character. "The Russian woman
manages her property and administers her fortune in addition to caring for
her household," Juliette Adam wrote in her essay on women and philan-
thropy. "A variety of affairs . . . in her home or on her estates . . . put her in
contact with the working world, [and] with human misery." Adam was an
eloquent admirer of Russian women and their philanthropic activities, and
pronounced them the most charitable of all women.[14]

Russian contemporaries were equally aware that the legal status of the
female sex in their country was unique. Their discussion of women's property rights was often as much a commentary on Russia's political and social
development, however, as it was an appraisal of women's condition.[15] For
some, the contrast between Russia's political backwardness vis-à-vis Western
Europe and the superior legal prerogatives of Russian women was an intriguing paradox.[16] These scholars singled out separate marital property as the
primary marker of women's status. The author of one survey declared that
noblewomen in Russia enjoyed complete legal equality with men in the
matter of estate management and property ownership.[17] The historian S. S.
Shashkov also identified the right of noblewomen to control property as testimony to their enviable status in the eighteenth century.[18] Those who were
less optimistic did not deny the benefits that accrued to married women who
possessed fortunes of their own. Nonetheless, they emphasized the element
of sexual asymmetry that persisted in Russian property law, declaring that
women's disadvantages in the law of inheritance were a more accurate reflection of their position in society.[19]

13. Anatole Leroy-Beaulieu, *The Empire of the Tsars and the Russians*, trans. Zenaide A. Ragozin
(New York, 1898), 1: 217–19.

14. Mme. Juliette Edmond Adam [Juliette Lamber], *Impressions Françaises en Russie* (Paris,
1912), 198–200.

15. For an overview of the commentary of nineteenth-century legal scholars on women's property rights, see G. A. Tishkin, *Zhenskii vopros v Rossii, 50–60-e gody XIX v.* (Leningrad, 1984), 16–58.

16. See, for example, M. Ia. Ostrogorski, *The Rights of Women: A Comparative Study in History
and Legislation* (London, 1893), 231: "Russia . . . whose political institutions are the least liberal
in Europe, possesses the most liberal laws as regards the civil capacity of women."

17. V. Mikhnevich, *Russkaia zhenshchina XVIII stoletiia* (Kiev, 1895), 210.

18. S. S. Shashkov, *Istoriia russkoi zhenshchiny* (St. Petersburg, 1879), 314–17. See also Ia.
Orovich, *Zhenshchina v prave*, 2d ed. (St. Petersburg, 1896), 75–76.

19. K. D. Kavelin, *Sobranie sochinenii* (St. Petersburg, 1900), 4: 553–57, and Konstantin
Nevolin, *Istoriia rossiiskikh grazhdanskikh zakonov* (St. Petersburg, 1851), 1: 45, 61, 74–75.

The provocative appearance of women proprietors in Russian literature offers a further perspective on female landownership. During the eighteenth and nineteenth centuries, the relationship of women to property was a minor but persistent theme in English and French novels. Jane Austen's satires of the English gentry featured more than one daughter barred from inheriting an entailed estate, while French women novelists criticized marital property arrangements that placed women and their wealth at the mercy of profligate husbands.[20] By contrast, Russian authors presented women as landowners in their own right. While Saltykov-Shchedrin's Arina Golovlyova is perhaps the most notorious female proprietor in Russian literature, she is by no means the only one. A central drama in Aksakov's *Family Chronicle* revolves around his grandfather's cousin Praskovia Ivanovna, who uses her economic independence to make a disastrous marriage but later retrieves her estate from her abusive husband. In the work of Dostoevsky the authority of more than one formidable woman is underscored by her financial position, while the long-suffering heroines of Chekhov's stories appear at times in the guise of factory owners and impoverished proprietors.[21] As we will see, representations of women who control estates in Russian fiction reflected not only the visibility of female proprietors but also the conflicting attitudes among contemporaries toward landowning women.

The Idea of Property in Eighteenth-Century Russia

Two competing conceptions of property provided the context for the evolution of noblewomen's property rights. The first was associated with patrimonial forms of property, which privileged the rights of the kin group, or clan (*rod*), over those of the individual. Thus, although individuals controlled inherited property, their rights of alienation and disposal of patrimonial land were subject to numerous restrictions. Proprietors acted as custodians, rather than absolute owners, of their assets: if they chose to sell or mortgage an estate without the consent of family members, the latter enjoyed the right to redeem the estate at its purchase price.[22] Testamentary

20. Joan DeJean, *Tender Geographies: Women and the Origins of the Novel in France* (New York, 1991). See also Tim Dolin, *Mistress of the House: Women of Property in the Victorian Novel* (Aldershot, 1997).

21. Sergei Aksakov, *A Russian Gentleman* (Oxford, 1982); Fyodor Dostoevsky, *The Demons* (New York, 1994), 17; "Uncle's Dream," in *Uncle's Dream and Other Stories* (London, 1989), 124–5; Anton Chekhov, "The Cherry Orchard," in *Plays* (London, 1951), 331–98; "A Woman's Kingdom," in *A Woman's Kingdom and Other Stories* (Oxford, 1989), 97–130.

22. Clan members enjoyed the right to repurchase patrimonial land for forty years after the sale; in the mid-eighteenth century, the Senate restricted the right of redemption to three years. See M. F. Vladimirskii-Budanov, *Obzor istorii russkogo prava*, 6th ed. (St. Petersburg, 1909), 579.

freedom over patrimonial estates was also severely circumscribed. Under this regime, property was conceived as a resource to be used for family purposes and was governed by rules that provided support, however inequitable, for each of its members.[23]

Alongside the institution of patrimonial property, a competing conception of property emerged that invested far greater rights of ownership in the individual. From the early-modern era, Muscovite law codes allowed for a second notion of property—that of the acquired estate, or land purchased from members of another clan. Proprietors of acquired land could alienate such assets as they wished and enjoyed greater testamentary freedom over such property. Once acquired property was bequeathed to a family member, however, it became patrimonial and was subject to the restrictions governing lineage land. Whereas the notion of acquired property surfaced as early as the twelfth century in the expanded version of the *Russkaia Pravda*, the acquired estate as a legal category (*kuplennaia votchina*) dated roughly from the seventeenth century. Moreover, the status of acquired property (*blago-priobretennoe imushchestvo*) was confirmed only in 1785, when Catherine II issued her Charter to the Nobility.[24]

The eighteenth century witnessed a protracted struggle on the part of the nobility to clarify their property rights in relation to other family members and to the state. In 1714 Peter the Great restricted the rights of noble proprietors over their estates when he abolished partible inheritance and did away with the distinction between patrimonial and acquired property. After Peter's death in 1725, however, the nobility achieved the restoration of partible inheritance and embarked on a campaign to extend its rights over landed estates and human property. As a group, the nobility was divided over the best means to advance its material interests: while most nobles argued in favor of patrimonial property and partible inheritance, others supported greater powers of disposal over their fortunes as a means of minimizing estate fragmentation.[25] On the subject of the inviolability of noble corporate

23. On the diminution of clan rights in hereditary estates, see George G. Weickhardt, "The Pre-Petrine Law of Property," *Slavic Review* 52, no. 4 (Winter 1993): 663–79. See also Elena Pavlova, "Private Land Ownership in Northeastern Rus' and Mongol Land Laws," *Russian History* 26, no. 2 (Summer 1999): 125–44.

24. On the history of patrimonial and acquired property in Russia, see Nevolin (1851), 2: 26–36. Many legal historians argued that the notion of private property fully emerged in Russia only in the seventeenth century and was not elaborated in the law until the reign of Catherine II. See V. B. El'iashevich, *Istoriia prava pozemel'noi sobstvennosti v Rossii* (Paris, 1948), 1: 159; Vladimirskii-Budanov (1909), 579, 585. As Richard Wortman argues, however, the concept of private property was fraught with inconsistencies in Imperial Russia, as property rights remained "an attribute of privilege," rather than the foundation for political rights. See Wortman, "Property Rights, Populism, and Russian Political Culture," in *Civil Rights in Imperial Russia*, ed. Olga Crisp and Linda Edmondson (Oxford, 1989), 13–32.

25. V. N. Latkin, *Zakonodatel'nye kommissii v Rossii v XVIII st.* (St. Petersburg, 1887), 1: 303–4.

rights, however, there was little debate. The authors of proposals for reform argued unanimously against arbitrary confiscation of noble assets and in favor of elevating noble property rights at the expense of other social groups.[26] For its part, the state remained vitally concerned with checking the dissipation of noble fortunes, a goal it pursued by preserving restrictive inheritance laws, as well as through a system of guardianship for nobles who squandered their assets.

The conflict between these two conceptions of property mirrored the overarching tension between the interests of the individual and those of the family and state in Imperial Russia. Competition between these interests was central to the development of noblewomen's property rights. In pre-Petrine Russia, women's inferior inheritance rights in patrimonial property derived from their transient status in the natal family; thus, as long as property was conceived primarily in relation to the kin group, the incentive to minimize female claims to inheritance was considerable.[27] During the eighteenth century, however, the trend toward more individualized property rights worked in women's favor. After 1731 daughters and widows acquired full rights of ownership in their allotments, in contrast to their provisional tenure in many forms of property during the Muscovite era. The nobility's struggle to bolster its corporate privileges vis-à-vis the state and other social groups was also instrumental in the extension of married women's control of their estates. At the same time, the notion that property rights should be defined in familial,[28] rather than purely individual terms persisted into the nineteenth century and provided grounds for restricting women's control of property in the context of marital discord.

Methodology and Sources

The reign of Peter the Great and the emancipation of the serfs in 1861 comprise the temporal boundaries of this study. When Peter ascended the throne in 1689, he set out both to establish Russia as a military power and to impose

26. On the debate over inheritance rights, see Paul Dukes, *Catherine the Great and the Russian Nobility: A Study Based on the Materials of the Legislative Commission of 1767* (Cambridge, 1967); on the corporate rights of the nobility, see Brenda Meehan-Waters, "The Development and the Limits of Security of Noble Status, Person, and Property in Eighteenth-Century Russia," in *Russia and the West in the Eighteenth Century*, ed. A. G. Cross (Newtonville, Mass., 1983), 294–305.

27. Kavelin (1900), 4: 545–46; Vladimirskii-Budanov (1909), 481.

28. The idea that property was invested in families, rather than individuals, is implicit in the language of deeds of sale. Until the nineteenth century, deeds of purchase adhered to a given formula in which the seller sold his or her property to the purchaser, the purchaser's spouse, and his or her children and descendants. Whereas deeds of purchase recorded in my sample until 1780 used this formula, it is absent in documents recorded in 1805 and afterward.

European cultural norms on the Russian nobility.[29] According to received wisdom, women were among the first to benefit from the Petrine revolution: early in his reign, Peter put an end to the seclusion of elite women in the *terem*, ordered them to cast off their sarafans and adopt European dress, and instructed them to drink and dance at court.[30] As I will argue, the emancipation of women was not, in fact, part of Peter's agenda, and those benefits that accrued to women were the product of accident, not design. Most relevant to this work are the Petrine reforms concerning property tenure, which revised the rights of inheritance and control of property and thus spurred on the development of private property in Russia. Although Peter's successors abandoned his revisions of property law in short order, in the long run his attempt to reform the law of inheritance had a profound impact on female participation in property litigation.

At the end of this period, the abolition of serfdom marked a symbolic watershed in Russian history. The institution of serfdom had long been a potent metaphor of Russian backwardness for the autocracy and the educated public. Far from proving a remedy to Russia's economic and social ills, however, emancipation initiated decades of conflict between the autocratic state and elements of society eager to accelerate the pace of reform. Although the economic and social discontinuity that followed emancipation should not be exaggerated, 1861 marked a new chapter in the economic history of the Russian nobility and provides a logical close to the history of noblewomen's property rights.[31]

In this book I focus primarily on noblewomen, although women of the merchant and urban estates also enjoyed the right to control property during marriage. The legal definition of *nobility* was highly amorphous, particularly in the first half of the eighteenth century. Before the Petrine reforms, the nobility did not exist as a distinct corporation in Russia: in its place were various ranks of servitors to the tsar (*sluzhilye liudi* or *chinovnye*

---

29. Two important accounts of Peter's reign in English are Evgenii V. Anisimov, *The Reforms of Peter the Great: Progress through Coercion in Russia* (Armonk, N.Y., 1993), and Lindsey Hughes, *Russia in the Age of Peter the Great* (New Haven, 1998).

30. In fact, little work exists on the impact of the Petrine reforms on elite women. For three exceptions, see Lindsey Hughes, "Peter the Great's Two Weddings: Changing Images of Women in a Transitional Age," in *Women in Russia and Ukraine* ed. Rosalind Marsh (Cambridge, 1996), 31–44, and "Between Two Worlds: Tsarevna Natal'ia Alekseevna and the 'Emancipation' of Petrine Women," in *A Window on Russia: Papers from the Fifth International Conference of the Study Group on Eighteenth-Century Russia, Gargnano, 1994*, ed. Maria di Salvo and Lindsey Hughes (Rome, 1996), 29–36, and my "Women and Westernization in Petrine Russia," *Study Group on Eighteenth-Century Russia Newsletter*, Cambridge (1998): 105–17.

31. For two conflicting accounts of the fortunes of the nobility after emancipation, see Seymour Becker, *Nobility and Privilege in Late Imperial Russia* (DeKalb, 1985), and Roberta Thompson Manning, *The Crisis of the Old Order in Russia: Gentry and Government* (Princeton, 1982). Even a glimpse at notarial records leaves no doubt, however, that people from non-noble ranks of society became far more active in the market for rural real estate after 1861.

liudi). Although a few of these individuals were descended from princely and boyar families, many were of less exalted origin and had acquired serfs and estates through military service. Not until Peter's reign did a single category of nobles come into existence, which Peter, for lack of an appropriate term in Russian, christened the *shliakhetstvo*—the Polish designation for *nobility.* By the second half of the eighteenth century, the elite came to be known as the *dvorianstvo,* a name derived from the traditional Russian term *dvornye liudi,* the courtiers who served a prince.[32] Peter put an end to the tradition of awarding estates in return for military service; at the same time, he also reinforced the connection between noble status and lifelong service to the state. Thus, in 1722 he instituted the Table of Ranks to replace the traditional Muscovite hierarchy of offices. While those who failed to ascend the Table did not forfeit noble status, non-nobles who reached the fourteenth rank in military service or the eighth rank in the civil service were enrolled in the hereditary nobility and enjoyed the same privileges as members of the old nobility.

Since nobility could still be bequeathed through birth or marriage, however, rank was not always a foolproof indicator of status. Long after the reign of Peter, members of the nobility could be found in the lowliest ranks, including that of soldier.[33] Nobles also occupied the lower rungs of the civil service, working as petty officials and even as clerks.[34] Ultimately, the single characteristic that distinguished the nobility from other social estates (*sosloviia*) was the right to own land and serfs. Yet, during the first half of the eighteenth century even serf ownership was not a reliable indicator of status, since many military officials and other non-nobles inherited settled estates that they no longer enjoyed the right to own. This state of affairs was resolved only in 1754, after Elizabeth ordered a general land survey and ordered all non-nobles in control of settled estates to sell them within six months. At the same time, until 1761 membership in the nobility could be claimed if the petitioner could prove that his forebear had been the recipient of a *pomest'e,* an estate held in return for state service.[35]

Even among those whose lineage was not in dispute, a vast cultural and economic gulf separated the affluent from the indigent noble. Indeed, the latter was sometimes indistinguishable from his peasants.[36] In the eighteenth

32. A. Romanovich-Slavatinskii, *Dvorianstvo v Rossii ot nachala XVIII veka do otmeny krepostnogo prava* (St. Petersburg, 1870), 2–4.

33. Richard Hellie, *Enserfment and Military Change in Muscovy* (Chicago, 1971), 232. John P. LeDonne points out that "all officers were noblemen, but not all noblemen joining the army became officers." *Absolutism and Ruling Class: The Formation of the Russian Political Order, 1700–1825* (Oxford, New York, 1991), 44.

34. LeDonne (1991), 58–59.

35. *Polnoe sobranie zakonov Rossiiskoi imperii* (hereafter *PSZ*), 15: 11.255 (25.05.1761).

36. On state aid for poor nobles, see A. P. Boretskoi, "Zakhudaloe dvorianstvo," *Russkaia mysl'* 12 (1882): 339–53.

century more than half of the hereditary nobility owned fewer than twenty-one serfs. Wealth was concentrated in the hands of a small portion of the elite: only 17 percent of the nobility possessed more than one hundred serfs, while a scant 1 percent controlled more than one thousand.[37] Given the profound differences that divided the various strata of the noble estate, any attempt to discuss noble identity appears a futile exercise. It is my contention, however, that although the Russian nobility was by no means a class in an economic sense, it was unified as an estate by a common use of property that distinguished it from other property-holding estates, such as the merchantry. While noblewomen, both rich and poor, were distinguished by their active presence in the sale and purchase of settled estates, merchant women became visible in the market for urban real estate only in the second quarter of the nineteenth century. This discrepancy in the relation of women to property distinguished noble culture from that of other groups in Russian society until the mid-nineteenth century.

The elite of the Russian Empire was varied not only in economic status but also in ethnic background. As the boundaries of the empire expanded in the eighteenth century, the wellborn of annexed territories became incorporated into the noble estate and acquired the same privileges as their Russian counterparts. Thus, the nobility came to include members whose native tongue was Tatar, Georgian, Lithuanian, and German.[38] The most significant minority, however, was the Polish-speaking nobility, more than half of which lived in the western borderlands of Russia that had belonged to the Polish commonwealth until the seventeenth century.[39] Although the large majority of noble women and men in this study were Russian, many of those who hailed from the provinces of Chernigov and Poltava were of Polish origin. When nobles from this region came before the Senate with their disputes, their cases were judged according to the laws of the Livonian Statute, which still governed civil matters such as inheritance and guardianship, as well as women's control of property in the region.[40] While many provisions of the Livonian Statute bore close resemblance to those of the *Svod zakonov*, or the digest of current Russian law, the laws of the former were markedly less generous to women.

The danger of drawing conclusions about noblewomen as a group from the lives of women who were unusual by virtue of status and wealth cannot

---

37. Arcadius Kahan, "The Costs of 'Westernization' in Russia: The Gentry and the Economy in the Eighteenth Century," *Slavic Review* 25, no. 1 (March 1966): 45. The distinction between hereditary and personal nobility will not concern us; the phenomenon of personal nobility dates from Catherine II's reign. Personal nobles, like members of the merchant and urban classes, could own real estate but not serfs.

38. Richard Pipes, *Russia under the Old Regime* (New York, 1974), 177, 182.

39. Gary M. Hamburg, *Politics of the Russian Nobility, 1881–1905* (New Brunswick, 1984), 11.

40. For laws in Chernigov and Poltava provinces on guardianship and on the division of property in cases of divorce, see *PSZ*, 2d ser., 17: 15.532 (15.04.1842) and 17: 15.533 (15.04.1842).

be denied. To be sure, family papers exhibit a clear bias toward women of exceptional fortune; however, the women whose names appear in property transactions and inheritance disputes represent female proprietors of the middling and lower ranks, who left no evidence of their lives besides the sale of a few acres of land or a petition to the Land College to register an estate. I will tell the stories of women such as Anna Sheremeteva and Potemkin's nieces in these pages but will counter their experiences with those of many anonymous and impoverished noblewomen.

In order to represent noblewomen, in all their heterogeneity, as a group, this work draws upon a wide range of sources. Discussions of legal developments are based on inheritance disputes as well as normative legal sources. Notarial records (*krepostnye knigi*) from four districts and from Moscow furnished data on the sale and purchase of estates and serfs, not to mention wills, dowries, and deeds of separation (*razdel'nye zapisi*). My analysis of the practice of separate property derives from petitions for divorce heard in the Holy Synod, as well as from property litigation between spouses. Correspondence from family papers and a significant body of memoir literature contribute the voices of individual noble men and women and flesh out the contours suggested by statistical work. In short, this work makes use of an extensive array of archival and published sources to explore the myriad dimensions of noblewomen's—and noblemen's—relation to property in Imperial Russia.

Legal Sources and Civil Law in Imperial Russia

Civil law in Russia shared many similarities with continental legal systems, including a common descent from Roman law.[41] The concept of the rule of law was familiar in Russia from at least the seventeenth century.[42] Moreover, this familiarity was not confined to the law's practitioners: petitioners throughout the Imperial era appealed to officials, and to the ruler, to demand the resolution of their disputes in accordance with written law and in the spirit of legal justice (*pravosudie*).

Yet numerous obstacles hindered the development of a sustained legal tradition in Russia before the reforms of the 1860s. To begin, the absence of a unified legal code created considerable confusion among those who served on provincial courts and ruled on disputes. Until 1832, the single coherent source of civil law in Russia was the *Ulozhenie* of 1649, a collection of the rules of Russian customary law drawn from earlier Muscovite law codes. In the

41. Konrad Zweigert and Hein Kötz, *An Introduction to Comparative Law*, trans. Tony Weir (Amsterdam, 1977), 1: 306.
42. Valerie A. Kivelson, *Autocracy in the Provinces: The Muscovite Gentry and Political Culture in the Seventeenth Century* (Stanford, 1996), 180, 233–34.

eighteenth century, however, a flood of Imperial decrees and judicial decisions superseded the *Ulozhenie,* many of which contradicted the statutory collection and were at variance with one another. Whereas some decrees were intended to serve as guidelines for future rulings, many applied only to specific cases and established no clear norms. These laws were collected only in 1830 and published in the *Polnoe sobranie zakonov Rossiiskoi imperii* (Complete Collection of Russian Laws), at the same time that a digest of current Russian law (*Svod zakonov*) was compiled. Thus, few sources for understanding the law were available in the eighteenth century.

Until the late eighteenth century, no separate judiciary existed in Russia; instead, responsibility for dispensing justice lay in the hands of bodies whose functions were administrative as well as judicial. Property litigation fell under the jurisdiction of the Land College (*Votchinnaia kollegia*), which granted title for all land transactions and was the court of first resort for inheritance disputes. Above the Land College, the Senate stood as the highest court of appeal. In the provinces the *voevoda,* or district governor, ruled on cases, both civil and criminal. The first separate judicial organs appeared only in 1775, when Catherine II established a series of courts on the district and provincial level. Catherine's judicial reform provided separate courts for nobles, townsmen, and state peasants and set in place a system of appellate procedure: as a result, property litigation after 1775 originated in the district (*uezd*) court or in the Provincial Chambers (*Palata grazhdanskogo suda*). For all their organizational advantages, however, the new courts suffered from the absence of a legal profession. The vast majority of those who ruled over the new judicial offices were nobles who had retired from military service, lacked higher education, and served as judges for only three years. Although members of the Senate tended to be wealthier and better educated than judges for the lower courts, they also came from the ranks of former military officers and conducted their work without the benefit of formal legal training.[43]

Finally, a strong element of personal authority characterized the Russian legal process. The judicial powers of the monarch remained extensive in the pre-reform era.[44] An edict of the sovereign could take on the force of law, even if it contradicted previous rulings, and legal texts made no distinction

43. The best work on the legal process in pre-reform Russia remains Richard Wortman, *The Development of a Russian Legal Consciousness* (Chicago, 1976). For an overview of legal reform under Peter I, see Hughes (1998), 121–34. On the Catherinean legal reforms, see Isabel de Madariaga, *Russia in the Age of Catherine the Great* (New Haven, 1981), 277–91. For a discussion of legal procedure, see LeDonne (1991), 181–99.

44. As John LeDonne observes, however, the Russian ruler resembled monarchs in other ancien régime states in delegating the dispensation of justice to his officials yet reserving the right to reverse their decisions. See LeDonne, *Ruling Russia: Politics and Administration in the Age of Absolutism, 1762–1796* (Princeton, 1984), 179.

between a law (*zakon*) and an administrative ruling (*razporiazhenie*).[45] Moreover, rulers could intervene directly in the judicial process. Decisions of the
Senate took on the force of law and did not require the sovereign's confirmation; however, in cases where the senators could not reach a decision,
they would turn to the ruler to settle the dispute. The creation in 1810 of a
separate department for the receipt of petitions addressed to the emperor
further underscored the notion that the ruler was the source of justice.[46]

As a source, court records defy simple interpretation. Disputes heard in
the Land College were filed more often than not without resolutions; thus,
neither the outcome of the case nor the veracity of the litigants' tales can
be established. Records of Senate cases are more complete and generally
include resolutions, as well as a painstaking review of the decisions made in
lower courts. Whereas petitioners often lamented corruption among court
personnel, court documents reveal little of the role of patronage and corruption in a particular case. For all their shortcomings, however, property
disputes offer invaluable insight into petitioners' understanding of the law,
as well as the attempts of the central government to see that justice was
dispensed. Legal standards in Imperial Russia left much to be desired. Nonetheless, cases that reached the Land College and the Senate demonstrate
elements of a viable legal culture among the nobility in pre-reform Russia—
namely, familiarity with the fundamental laws of property, and the conviction that conflicts should be resolved in accordance with those laws. If
Russian nobles did not recognize the legal system as the "preferred means
of solving conflicts,"[47] the sheer volume of surviving property litigation attests
to their willingness to make use of the courts, for all their limitations. Some
litigants expressed their distrust in the legal process by turning to powerful
individuals to see that justice was carried out; at the same time, their
petitions brim with requests for their case to be decided according to
written law.

The problem of continuity between pre-Petrine and Imperial Russia in
regard to noblewomen's legal rights will recur throughout this work. An
abundant literature has documented variations in women's legal status
across the medieval and Muscovite centuries; the diminution of elite
women's property rights in the sixteenth and seventeenth centuries, in particular, has been warmly debated. The results of this research demonstrate

45. Wortman (1976), 16.

46. S. N. Pisarev, *Uchrezhdenie po priniatiiu i napravleniiu proshenii i zhalob, prinosimykh na Vysochaishee Imia, 1810–1910 gg.* (St. Petersburg, 1909).

47. The phrase is from Jane Burbank, "Legal Culture, Citizenship, and Peasant Jurispru-
dence: Perspectives from the Early Twentieth Century," in *Reforming Justice in Russia, 1864–1996: Power, Culture, and the Limits of Legal Order*, ed. Peter H. Solomon Jr. (Armonk, N.Y., 1997), 85.

that many daughters and wives of the tsar's servitors controlled landed property, acquired as dowry or inheritance, and enjoyed control of this property with their husbands. Moreover, as early as the twelfth century, Russian women of all social groups shared the prerogative of men to initiate litigation when their honor or economic interests were threatened. Women's legal privileges in the pre-Petrine era clearly served as the foundation for the elaboration of their rights to property in the eighteenth century.

At the same time, attention to precedent has encouraged historians to overlook genuine change. Noblewomen's access to property was greatly enhanced in the eighteenth century as daughters, regardless of marital status, gained the right to a statutory share (*ukaznaia chast'*) of their parents' estates. As married women, they acquired full control of their estates only in 1753, when their obligation to request their husbands' permission to alienate property was abolished. From the mid-eighteenth century married women were far more likely to petition the courts on their own behalf, and women as a group relied less on men to act as their representatives. The post-Petrine era also witnessed a striking development in female litigation, as noblewomen moved beyond mere defense of their legal prerogatives and pressed judicial authorities for clarification of their inheritance rights and control over their property during marriage.

The following chapters will chronicle the evolution of noblewomen's singular relation to property in Russia and recount women's persistent, resourceful, and sometimes unscrupulous use of the right to control their estates. Inevitably, this story will touch repeatedly on the interaction—and the divergence—between gender ideologies and the practice of gender in everyday life. The fascination of Western scholars with the image of the formidable woman in Russian culture is only one symptom of contrasting conceptions of gender and authority in Russia and the West. Much has been said about the formidable woman as a literary motif[48]; scholars have made few attempts, however, to locate more tangible sources of female authority in Russian society. As we will see, while the formidable woman of the literary imagination was distinguished by her moral attributes, the authority of her historical counterpart rested equally on control of her fortune.

---

48. Vera Sandomirsky Dunham, "The Strong-Woman Motif," in *The Transformation of Russian Society*, ed. Cyril Black (Cambridge, 1960), 459–83; Antonia Glasse, "The Formidable Woman: Portrait and Original," *Russian Literature Triquarterly*, no. 9 (Spring 1974): 433–53; Barbara Heldt, *Terrible Perfection: Women and Russian Literature* (Bloomington, 1987); Joanna Hubbs, *Mother Russia: The Feminine Myth in Russian Culture* (Bloomington, 1988).

CHAPTER ONE

From Maintenance to Entitlement: Women and the Law of Inheritance

The law of inheritance shaped the lives of Russian nobles, both female and male, to a degree unimaginable in the modern world. During the early-modern era the laws governing the transmission of property from one generation to the next were central to family survival; as such, they embodied contemporary assumptions about sexual difference and women's role in society. Across Europe the rules of inheritance varied widely, not only from country to country but also among regions, many of which adhered to their own version of common law. Yet, in the midst of this diversity, sexual asymmetry remained a universal feature of property law. Although all European legal codes provided for female inheritance in some form, they routinely granted women marriage portions in movable property rather than land and often barred dowered daughters from further inheritance.[1] Women who survived their husbands benefited from more generous provisions from conjugal assets. As often as not, however, these settlements restricted the widow's disposal and use of property, in the interests of her husband's heirs.

At the close of the seventeenth century, elite Russian women shared many legal disabilities with their European counterparts. Russian law codes allowed women a surprising degree of independence in matters judicial yet maintained a clear distinction between men and women's relation to property. Thus, the pre-Petrine law of property was characterized by unequal inheritance for sons and daughters, by limitations on women's use of landed estates, and by a striking failure to address some critical dimensions of female inheritance. For Russian noblewomen, however, the reforms of Peter the Great marked the starting point of an era of profound cultural and legal

1. Hughes (1985), 31–35.

change. If the impact of cultural reform was confined initially to the highest ranks of the elite and slow to extend beyond Moscow and St. Petersburg, legal innovations rapidly touched the lives of women from all strata of the nobility. Most notably, the eighteenth century witnessed the gradual expansion of women's rights to property. This was true in respect both to married women's control of their estates and to women's access to family property. While innovations in female inheritance were less dramatic than advances in women's control of their fortunes, the elaboration of women's inheritance rights in the law was emblematic of a larger process of legal change: in response to women's demands, the courts clarified important ambiguities in women's property rights and revised the law in women's favor.

The goal of this chapter is to trace the regularization of noblewomen's inheritance rights in the eighteenth century. I will argue that in the realm of inheritance, noblewomen achieved a single but significant gain over the course of the century. Namely, their inheritance rights as daughters were transformed from a maintenance portion (*prozhitok*), intended primarily to support their husbands' military service, to an entitlement (*ukaznaia chast'*), or a share of their parents' estates fixed by law. A parallel shift took place in regard to the inheritance rights of widows. In both cases, this linguistic change was not a mere textual formality but signaled a transformation in the nature and form of women's inheritance rights.

Noblewomen and the Pre-Petrine Law of Inheritance

Noblewomen's access to landed property in pre-Petrine Russia was determined in large part by their marital status and the survival of male siblings. As early as the twelfth century, the *Russkaia Pravda*, medieval Russia's chief legal code, allowed daughters to inherit immovable property in the absence of sons but ruled out female inheritance of estates when brothers survived.[2] In the form of dowry or inheritance, daughters often made due with movable goods, which were indispensable for establishing a new household but lacked the status and immutability of land in an economy based overwhelmingly on agriculture and peasant labor.[3] Historians of Russia

---

2. Vladimirskii-Budanov (1909), 480–81. For a brief period, from 1562 until 1628, daughters were barred from inheriting patrimonial estates even when no brothers survived (p. 496).

3. In the words of one scholar, the "preference for cash dowries" was a "sign of the daughter's effective disinheritance" in Western Europe. Husbands also preferred cash, since the latter "could be much more easily merged with the husband's estate." Hughes (1985), 34–35. Christiane Klapisch-Zuber argues that the dowry in Renaissance Florence was used effectively to disinherit daughters. See *Women, Family, and Ritual in Renaissance Italy*, trans. Lydia Cochrane (Chicago, 1985), 216.

attributed women's inferior inheritance rights to their transient status in the family; when a woman married, she abandoned her natal kin group, or *rod*, and joined her husband's family, taking her wealth along with her.[4]

Despite such limitations on female inheritance, medieval Russian noblewomen surface in a variety of sources as owners of land and of liquid assets.[5] By the seventeenth century, however, women's modest rights to landed property had contracted further and varied according to land tenure.[6] The *Ulozhenie*, or law code, of 1649 identified three types of patrimonial, or hereditary, estates (*votchina*): estates that had been inherited from other family members (*rodovye votchiny*), hereditary estates awarded for service (*vysluzhennye votchiny*), and the purchased hereditary estate (*kuplennaia*). A second form of land tenure was the *pomest'e*, or service estate, which appeared late in the fifteenth century and was granted by the sovereign to his servitors in return for military service.[7] Both forms of land tenure, with the exception of the purchased estate, were subject to regulations that protected clan, or family, interests at the expense of the individual. The pro-

4. In keeping with other historians, I will use the term *clan*, or *rod*, for the extended-kin group, although, as Robert O. Crummey points out, "Russian nobles belonged to lineages, not clans, since they could trace their descent from a known ancestor." See Crummey, *Aristocrats and Servitors: The Boyar Elite in Russia, 1613–1689* (Princeton, 1983), 65. On the origin of women's inferior inheritance rights, see Kavelin (1900), 4: 553–56; Vladimirskii-Budanov (1909), 481; N. F. Rozhdestvenskii, *Istoricheskoe izlozhenie russkogo zakonodatel'stva o nasledstve* (St. Petersburg, 1839), 33; Vitalii Shul'gin, *O sostoianii zhenshchin v Rossii do Petra Velikogo* (Kiev, 1850), 46–47.

5. Valerie A. Kivelson, "The Effects of Partible Inheritance: Gentry Families and the State in Muscovy," *Russian Review* 53, no. 2 (April 1994): 210; Eve Levin, "Women and Property in Medieval Novgorod: Dependence and Independence," *Russian History* 10, pt. 2 (1983): 163–65; Sandra Levy, "Women and the Control of Property in Sixteenth-Century Muscovy," ibid., 10, pt. 2 (1983): 208–11; Susanne Janosik McNally, "From Public Person to Private Prisoner: The Changing Place of Women in Medieval Russia" (Ph.D. dissertation, State University of New York at Binghamton, 1976), 33; N. L. Pushkareva, "Imushchestvennye prava zhenshchin na Rusi (X–XV vv.)," *Istoricheskie zapiski* 114 (1986): 180–224.

6. Ann M. Kleimola argues that the seventeenth century marked the nadir in women's inheritance rights. See Kleimola, " 'In Accordance with the Canons of the Holy Apostles': Muscovite Dowries and Women's Property Rights," *Russian Review* 51 (April 1992): 204–29. Daniel Kaiser points out, however, that a 1627 statute permitted testators to bequeath land to a variety of female kin in the absence of male offspring and also admitted married daughters to their father's estate, if no brothers survived. See Kaiser, "Women, Property, and the Law in Early Modern Russia" (unpublished manuscript presented at Indiana University, 1988), 6–7.

7. S. B. Veselovskii, *Feodal'noe zemlevladenie v severno-vostochnoi Rusi* (Moscow, 1947), 1: 286–87. L. V. Milov and I. M. Garskova argue that the *votchina* and *pomest'e* were not merely separate legal entities but represented "distinct forms of the feudal economy." See Milov and Garskova, "A Typology of Feudal Estates in Russia in the First Half of the Seventeenth Century (Factor Analysis)," *Russian Review* 47, no. 4 (October 1988): 375–90. Several scholars have observed that the Muscovite gentry used every means possible to convert their holdings from *pomest'ia* to *votchiny* in the seventeenth century, but the implications of this development for women's inheritance rights remain unexplored. See Crummey (1983), 108, and Hellie (1971), 56.

prietor of a patrimonial or service *votchina* could bequeath his estate only to a restricted circle of heirs, although he was free to sell or mortgage his land as he pleased.[8] By contrast, the recipient of a *pomest'e* enjoyed the use of this property during his lifetime but could neither sell the estate nor bequeath it to his children. Over time, however, noble servitors began to treat their service holdings as patrimonial property. The characteristics of *votchina* and *pomest'e* gradually converged, until Peter the Great abolished the last legal distinctions between the two forms of land tenure in favor of a single category of immovable property.[9] This development would eventually contribute to the extension of noblewomen's inheritance rights.

The *Ulozhenie* allowed for the inheritance rights of married daughters in the absence of brothers, but only when the deceased left patrimonial estates (*votchiny*). Married daughters thus enjoyed the right to inherit patrimonial land when no brothers survived, although the *Ulozhenie* stipulated that they might have to share their inheritance with their aunts, or the surviving sisters of the deceased.[10] Daughters could not, however, inherit their father's *pomest'e*, even in the absence of brothers: they were permitted only a maintenance portion (*prozhitok*) from service holdings. Any land that remained after they received their portion would be distributed to male kin of the deceased who had no service estates of their own.[11] When sons survived, daughters, both married and unmarried, were barred altogether from inheriting patrimonial land. Their inheritance was limited to the maintenance allotment, or pension,[12] taken from their father's service estates—the amount of which was mandated in the *Ulozhenie* and destined to serve as their dowry. Muscovite law held out one final possibility for female inheritance, however: purchased estates could be granted as dowry and freely bequeathed to female kin at the owner's discretion.

The widow's inheritance rights were as intricate as those of her daughters and were further circumscribed by her status as an outsider in her husband's

---

8. Although the proprietor of a hereditary or service *votchina* could sell or mortgage his estate, he was required to obtain the permission of his brothers and other male kin (although the signatures of his children and grandchildren were not required). If he failed to obtain these signatures, the male members of his clan had the right to redeem the property at its purchase price. See *The Muscovite Law Code (Ulozhenie) of 1649. Part I: Text and Translation*, trans. and ed. Richard Hellie (Irvine, Calif., 1988), 17: 27; Jerome Blum, *Lord and Peasant in Russia from the Ninth to the Nineteenth Century* (Princeton, 1961), 81.

9. *PSZ*, 5: 2.789 (23.03.1714).

10. *The Muscovite Law Code*, 17: 2.

11. The amount of the maintenance allotment depended on the circumstances of the holder's death. Widows and daughters whose husbands or fathers were killed in battle received as much as 20% and 10%, respectively; these amounts were reduced to 15% and 7.5% if the estate holder died during military service, and 10% and 5% if the servitor died at home. *The Muscovite Law Code* 16: 30, 31, 32. On widows and daughters marrying with their allotments, see 16: 17, 18, 19, 21; on inheritance of the service holdings of men without sons, see 16: 13.

12. Vladimirskii-Budanov (1909), 570–71.

family. In medieval Russia, before the creation of the *pomest'e*, widows with children had enjoyed a life estate in their husbands' property, both movable and immovable, provided they did not remarry.[13] Yet by the seventeenth century the bereaved wife was entitled only to one-fourth of her husband's movable wealth and a maintenance allotment from his service holdings, as well as the return of her dowry. As a member of another clan, the widow could inherit neither her husband's patrimonial land nor his hereditary estates granted for service (*vysluzhennye votchiny*), although purchased estates could pass freely from husband to wife.[14] Also, on a positive note, the widow enjoyed considerable power over her allotment from her husband's service-tenure estates: the record shows that she not only could bequeath her *prozhitok* but also could retrieve and redistribute such land if she saw fit. Thus, after Maria Iusupova lost her husband in the late seventeenth century, she remarried and granted her *pomest'e* first to her second husband and later to her stepson, Feodor Ushakov. Just before she entered a monastery, however, Iusupova reconsidered her gift, reclaimed half the estate from Ushakov, and signed it over to her brother, Semen Nebol'sin.[15] If a man did not own service estates when he died, his widow received a maintenance allotment from his patrimonial estates; she was not permitted to alienate this land, however, or to use it as dowry in a second marriage.[16]

For all the complexity of the *Ulozhenie*, a consistent set of assumptions about women's relation to property informed its many articles on female inheritance. The underlying logic of the law was distinctly paternalistic. Muscovite property law opted to withhold patrimonial land from women whenever possible and imposed restrictions on women's use of property.[17] Yet the state also displayed unambiguous concern for the material welfare of the widows and unmarried daughters of its servitors. As a result, the problem of female inheritance within the context of different forms of land tenure occupied a central place in the law code of 1649.

13. Aleksandr Dobriakov, *Russkaia zhenshchina v do-mongol'skii period* (St. Petersburg, 1864), 89–90. For an overview of widow's inheritance rights, see George Vernadsky, "Studies in the History of Moscovian Private Law of the 16th and 17th Centuries. Inheritance: The Case of the Childless Wife," in *Studi in Memoria di Aldo Albertoni* (Padua, 1938) 3: 433–54.

14. *The Muscovite Law Code*, 17: 1, 2.

15. *Opisanie dokumentov i del, khraniashchikhsia v arkhive sviateishego pravitel'stvuiushchego Sinoda* (hereafter *OAS*) (St. Petersburg, 1868), 1: 553–54. The Boyar Duma returned another widow's *pomest'e* to her when her son-in-law violated the terms of their agreement by exchanging the estate for another. See *PSZ*, 3: 1.341 (22.07.1689).

16. *The Muscovite Law Code*, 16: 16; *PSZ*, 2: 781 (03.12.1679). Widows who received allotments of their husbands' patrimonial land were also instructed not to bring these estates to ruin or to overburden their serfs with excessive *obrok* payments.

17. Widows and daughters who received maintenance portions from service estates could not sell or mortgage them, although they could use their portions as dowry. As we will see in chapter 2, women who sold property before 1714 referred only to *votchina* in deeds of purchase, while male sellers alienated both service and hereditary holdings.

When discussing widows' prerogatives, the articles of the *Ulozhenie* took care to consider every eventuality, distinguishing between women who had produced offspring and those who were childless. Neither the *Ulozhenie* nor the rulings that followed later in the seventeenth century, however, elaborated in a similar fashion on daughters' inheritance rights.[18] The law carefully spelled out the provisions for daughters whose fathers had died: Unmarried daughters enjoyed limited entitlement to their father's service estates, while daughters of any marital status could inherit patrimonial property in the absence of surviving male offspring. On the topic of the dowry, however, the *Ulozhenie* was virtually silent. Indeed, the articles of the *Ulozhenie* attended to the dowry only within the context of maintenance for unmarried daughters: a young woman's *prozhitok* from her father's service holdings was intended to serve as her marriage portion, which she would bring to her husband and which he subsequently registered in his own name.

The expectations for daughters who married while their fathers were living, however, were far more nebulous. The expanded *Russkaia Pravda* had instructed the brothers of unmarried sisters to dower the latter to the best of their ability (*kako si mogut*), whereas the author of the *Domostroi* advised parents to set aside property for their daughters' dowries.[19] Pre-Petrine law codes gave no instructions, however, on the percentage of family wealth a daughter could anticipate when she married. The *Ulozhenie* also skirted this question and failed to distinguish between dowry and inheritance. Custom, rather than written law, governed the granting of dowries in early-modern Russia,[20] and both the amount of the award and whether or not the dowry would include land were left entirely to the donor's discretion. In practice, Muscovite nobles often awarded generous portions to their daughters when

18. As George Weickhardt observes, however, the law code of 1649 clarified daughters' inheritance rights to a greater degree than the *Russkaia Pravda* and the law codes of 1497 and 1550. See Weickhardt, "Legal Rights of Women in Russia, 1100–1750," *Slavic Review* 55, no. 1 (Spring 1996): 13–14.

19. K. Pobedonostsev, *Kurs grazhdanskogo prava* (St. Petersburg, 1871), 2: 234; *The Domostroi: Rules for Russian Households in the Time of Ivan the Terrible*, ed. and trans. Carolyn Johnston Pouncy (Ithaca, 1994), 95.

20. Vladimirskii-Budanov (1909), 451. The *Kormchaia kniga* (the Book of the Pilot), a compendium of ecclesiastical law that preserved many tenets of Byzantine law, also touched on the subject of the dowry. As Nevolin observed, Byzantine law obliged parents to dower their daughters but did not elaborate on the amount of the dowry. For the provisions of the *Ecloga* and the *Procheiros* that were included in the *Kormchaia kniga*, see Nevolin (1851), 1: 89–94. Under the Byzantine statutes, daughters and sons inherited equal shares in their parents' estates if the latter died intestate [Weickhardt (1996), 6], but living parents could give, or bequeath, unequal shares to their children; men, as well as women, received a dowry upon marriage. See Ruth Macrides, "The Transmission of Property in the Patriarchal Register," in *La Transmission du patrimoine: Byzance et l'aire méditerranéenne*, ed. Joëlle Beaucamp and Gilbert Dagron (Paris, 1998), 179–88.

they married.[21] Yet, the law offered no recourse to noblewomen whose dowries fell short of the amount, or its cash equivalent, mandated in the *Ulozhenie* for their unmarried sisters' maintenance portions. If bestowing movable goods alone on young brides did not amount, in the words of one scholar, to "the daughter's effective disinheritance,"[22] the silence in legal texts on this dimension of female inheritance served to underscore women's vulnerable status in the law of property.

Female Inheritance and the Petrine Reforms

Despite the shortcomings that characterized female inheritance at the beginning of the eighteenth century, a significant number of Russian noblewomen could expect, at some point in their lives, to possess or enjoy the use of landed property. At the same time, women's standing in the law of inheritance was less than enviable: they enjoyed no guarantee that their dowries would include land or be commensurate with their parents' wealth, and held no further hope of inheriting when male offspring survived. It also appears, if the record of litigation can be trusted, that women's expectations were in keeping with the regulations of the *Ulozhenie*. Throughout the seventeenth century noblewomen, especially widows, took active part in property litigation, suing for the return of their dowries from their husbands' kin and defending the rights of their children. On occasion some even attempted to circumvent the laws of inheritance by claiming patrimonial land or questioning the wishes of the deceased.[23] Yet no records survive of women challenging their parents' right to determine the composition of their dowry, or

21. The extent to which land was included in dowries in early-modern Russia remains the subject of debate. In surveys of seventeenth-century dowry inventories, two scholars found that more than 50% of their samples included only movable property. See Daniel H. Kaiser, "Women, Property, and the Law in Early Modern Russia" (unpublished mss. presented at Indiana University, 1988): 17–18, and Ann M. Kleimola, "'In Accordance with the Canons of the Holy Apostles': Muscovite Dowries and Women's Property Rights," *Russian Review* 51 (April 1992), 225. My own sample of thirty-five dowries recorded in Moscow between 1703 and 1714 points to a different conclusion: in this sample, 80% (28/35) of dowries included land. See chapter 4. Valerie Kivelson also found that of the 211 women whose names appear in land documents in Vladimir-Suzdal' in the seventeenth century, 143 (68%) were landowners. Of these, however, it is not known how many received land as dowry. See Kivelson (1994), 210.

22. Hughes (1985), 34.

23. On women's litigation in Russia, see Nancy Shields Kollmann, "Women's Honor in Early Modern Russia," in *Russia's Women: Accommodation, Resistance, Transformation*, ed. Barbara Evans Clements, Barbara Alpern Engel, and Christine D. Worobec (Berkeley, 1991), 60–73. On litigation among peasants and townspeople in northern Russia in the early-modern era, see Jennifer Anderson, "Recovering Gendered Identities: Family and Community Life in Early Modern Russia" (unpublished manuscript, 2001). For two examples of women who tried to circumvent the law of inheritance, see *PSZ*, 2: 1256 (26.07.1687) and 5: 2667 (24.04.1713).

of dowered daughters claiming assets, after their parents' demise, above the amount of their marriage portion.

In the eighteenth century petitioners introduced a new element into the discourse on female inheritance, highlighting inconsistencies in the law and forcing authorities to clarify married daughters' inheritance rights. The debate over noblewomen's rights of inheritance took the form of controversy over a single issue: Did the dowry represent only an advance on inheritance or did married daughters who accepted their portion relinquish further claims to the family fortune? The controversy over the precise share women could anticipate from their parents' estates originated with the Law of Single Inheritance in 1714, became a major source of family conflict after the law's repeal in 1731, and receded from view only at the end of the century, when legislators finally agreed on consistent guidelines for female inheritance. While male inheritance rights were clearly elucidated in 1731, the notion of entitlement evolved slowly in relation to women and required decades of debate and negotiation in local and central courts, not to mention active participation in legal suits on the part of women themselves.

Since the nineteenth century, scholars have credited Peter the Great with reversing the restrictions on women's property rights that developed in the seventeenth century and restoring the privileges they had enjoyed in a previous era.[24] Ironically, the amount of property legislation generated during Peter's reign was sparse, especially in comparison with the number of supplementary decrees (*novoukaznye stat'i*) concerning property issued by his father, Tsar Alexei Mikhailovich, and by his sister, Tsarevna Sophia Alexeevna.[25] Moreover, with the exception of one ruling in 1715,[26] Petrine property legislation did not focus on women and was not intended to benefit them, but to simplify the law and enhance the profits of the state. Yet by subsuming the two forms of land tenure identified in Muscovite law codes under the rubric of immovable property in the Law of Single Inheritance, Peter effectively ended the practice of excluding women from inheriting patrimonial estates.[27]

24. Dmokhovskii, "O pravakh zhenshchiny v Rossii," *Biblioteka dlia chteniia* 172 (June 1862): 75; S. S. Shashkov, *Istoriia russkoi zhenshchiny* (St. Petersburg, 1879), 314; V. G. Shcheglov, *Polozhenie i prava zhenshchiny v sem'e i obshchestve v drevnosti, srednie veka i novoe vremia* (Iaroslavl', 1898), 91; L. N. Semenova, *Ocherki istorii byta i kul'turnoi zhizni Rossii: Pervaia polovina XVIII v.* (Leningrad, 1982), 49; Lee A. Farrow, "Peter the Great's Law of Single Inheritance: State Imperatives and Noble Resistance," *Russian Review* 55, no. 3 (July 1996): 445.

25. On the abundance of legislation regulating inheritance during Sophia's regency (1682–89), see Lindsey Hughes, *Sophia, Regent of Russia, 1657–1704* (New Haven, 1990), 106–7. One scholar of Russian law has argued that Peter's only significant legislation concerning property law was a measure on confiscation of church land, since the Law of Single Inheritance was never practiced. El'iashevich (1951), 2: 231–33.

26. See chapter 2.

27. A decree in 1712 forbade nobles who were the last in their clan to sell patrimonial property. Such nobles were required to bequeath their patrimonial estates to their closest female relations but at a degree no farther removed than granddaughters; if no such relative

Peter's most controversial innovation in the realm of property law was his attempt to impose unigeniture, or single inheritance, on the Russian nobility in 1714. Russian devotion to partible inheritance is legendary: inevitably, after centuries of dividing land equally among their sons, bequeathing estates intact to a solitary heir appeared as rank injustice to the service elite.[28] Moreover, in addition to repealing the distinction between hereditary and service estates, Peter ignored the unique status of purchased estates, over which the nobility had traditionally enjoyed greater rights of disposal. Parents were to provide for their remaining children, both male and female, by dividing their movable property equally among them.[29] From the perspective of the average noble, the Law of Single Inheritance not only violated centuries of tradition but also undermined their children's material welfare. The new regime placed an unwelcome burden on noble families, most of which were cash-poor and hard-pressed to come up with cash for marriage settlements or bequests for younger sons.[30] Even the fortunate heir to landed property faced the unpleasant prospect of immediately acquiring the livestock and grain necessary to run his estate, since the latter, as movable property, was divided among his siblings. For his part, Peter believed that the Law of Single Inheritance would prevent the fragmentation of estates and prolong the fortunes and lineage of noble families, many of whom had been ruined by the division of assets after several generations.[31] He also hoped to press younger sons into state service by depriving them of immov-

survived, the land reverted to the state. This decree was the first to ignore the distinction between *votchina* and *pomest'e*, in favor of a single category of immovable property. See *PSZ*, 4: 2471 (23.01.1712).

28. *PSZ*, 5: 2.789 (23.03.1714); on the discord within noble families generated by the decree, see Brenda Meehan-Waters, *Autocracy and Aristocracy: The Russian Service Elite of 1730* (New Brunswick, 1982), 118–22, and Farrow (1996). In cases of intestate succession, partible inheritance was not only customary but also enshrined in written law as early as the twelfth century, in the *Russkaia Pravda*.

29. On the evolution of the concept of immovable and movable property in medieval and post-Petrine Russian law, see Nevolin (1851), 2: 12–17. Real property included land, both settled and unsettled; the status of shops, houses, and factories was not determined as being immovable until late in the eighteenth century. Movable, or personal, property included all liquid assets, agricultural products, precious metals, and house serfs. The question of whether serfs who worked in agriculture were classified as real or personal property remained unsettled into the nineteenth century. See LeDonne (1991), 218–19.

30. Meehan-Waters (1982), 121–22.

31. Historians agree that European influence played a central role in Peter's inheritance reform. See S. M. Soloviev, *Istoriia Rossii v epokhu preobrazovaniia* (Moscow, 1866), 16: 198–99; Vasili Kliuchevskii, *Peter the Great* (London, 1958), 108; N. Pavlov-Sil'vanskii, *Proekty reform v zapiskakh sovremennikov Petra Velikogo* (St. Petersburg, 1897), 50–52; *Rossiiskoe zakonadatel'stvo X–XX vekov*, ed. A. G. Mankov (Moscow, 1986), 4: 303–4. In fact, the practice of primogeniture in England and on the European continent differed in crucial respects. See Joan Thirsk, "The European Debate on Customs of Inheritance, 1500–1700," in Goody, Thirsk, and Thumpson (1976), 177–91.

able property—a goal, according to contemporaries, that met with minimal success since young noblemen had to be forced to enter military service and few entertained the thought of engaging in trade.[32]

Despite noble opposition to single inheritance, Peter enforced unigeniture throughout his reign. In response, the more rebellious resorted to illegal land transactions to undermine the decree, fabricating debts and selling land in defiance of the law in order to redistribute the proceeds among their heirs.[33] The nobility's attempts to circumvent single inheritance come to light in deeds of purchase and mortgages in which seller and buyer assert that the transaction is genuine. When Lieutenant Colonel Brylkin tried to claim title to an estate in 1724, he wrote in his petition that widow Korobina had mortgaged her estate to him a year earlier for two thousand rubles. "She mortgaged [the property] to me . . . for the repayment of debts," Brylkin stated, "and not for any illegal transfer (*nepravdivago ukrepleniia bezdenezhno*) . . . to her younger sons and daughters."[34] As for nobles who played by the rules, they took care to admonish the heir to their landed estate not to shortchange his siblings.[35]

The Law of Single Inheritance attended to several dimensions of women's property rights. In regard to inheritance, however, it proved a mixed blessing for women. In one respect, the law bolstered female inheritance: if male siblings did not survive, one daughter was designated heir and inherited her father's entire estate. The import of this prerogative was somewhat diminished, however, by Article 7 of the decree, which stipulated that when the last male member of a clan left only female offspring, one son-in-law could adopt his name and inherit his immovable property. With this device, noblewomen could perpetuate their clan, but with some diminution of their rights as heiresses. Thus, Prince Romadanovskii named his daughter and son-in-law as joint legatees to his estate in 1730.[36] Article 7 passed over the question of which spouse would enjoy powers of alienation over the estate in such cases[37]; however, the prevalence of hyphenated names among the Russian

32. M. V. Danilov, "Zapiski," *Russkii arkhiv* 2, no. 3 (1883): 8.

33. G. D. Kapustina, "Zapisnye knigi Moskovskoi krepostnoi kontory kak istoricheskii istochnik (Pervaia chetvert' XVIII v.)," in *Problemy istochnikovedeniia* (Moscow, 1959), 7: 234; A. Romanovich-Slavatinskii, *Dvorianstvo v Rossii ot nachala XVIII veka do otmeny krepostnogo prava* (St. Petersburg, 1870), 251–52.

34. Rossiiskii gosudarstvennyi arkhiv drevnikh aktov (hereafter RGADA), f. 1209 (Arkhiv prezhnikh votchinnykh del), op. 79, ed. khr. 10, l. 53.

35. See the will of B. P. Sheremetev from 1718: Rossiiskii gosudarstvennyi istoricheskii arkhiv (hereafter RGIA), f. 1088, op. 1, ed. khr. 14, l. 2.

36. P. Baranov, ed., *Opis' vysochaishim ukazam i poveleniiam kraniashchimsia v Sankt-Peterburgskom Senatskom arkhive za XVIII vek* (1725–1740) (St. Petersburg, 1875), 2: no. 3750.

37. A supplement to the Law of Single Inheritance later stipulated that if a husband who had assumed his wife's name along with her estate survived her, yet had no children, the property should remain in his hands. The property would only revert to the state if he, too, died childless. See *PSZ*, 7: 4722 (28.05.1725), art. 7.

nobility hints that Romadanovskii was not alone in his preference for male heirs.[38]

Another positive development was that the Law of Single Inheritance confirmed women's control of their dowries. Significantly, there was no discussion in the text of the administration of women's property during marriage. Instead, Article 8 addressed the problem of maternal inheritance in the context of remarriage. While the law implied that spouses with children from a single marriage would choose the same heir for their immovable estates, it also emphasized that men could appoint heirs only to their own estates and not to those of their wives. In cases of intestate succession, a woman's dowry villages would pass to her eldest son or daughter, and her personal property would be divided among her remaining children. In practice, however, the status of maternal inheritance would remain highly ambiguous throughout the eighteenth century: the testimony of wills and dowries strongly suggests that some spouses treated their assets as a common unit, rather than scrupulously dividing their respective estates among each of their children.[39]

The Law of Single Inheritance and a subsequent decree in 1716 made the status of widowhood more palatable for women. The notion of maintenance, however, rather than entitlement, informed Peter's rulings on widows' allotments and restricted their rights of alienation. Thus, the Law of Single Inheritance stated that a childless widow could enjoy the use of all her husband's immovable property until she remarried or died, after which the estate would revert to her husband's clan. Peter later acknowledged that this decree made no provision for widows with children, and in 1716 he added the proviso that a widow, with or without children, might claim outright one-fourth of her husband's immovable and personal property, along with the obligation to assume one-fourth of his debts. The remaining three-fourths would then pass to the couple's children or to the husband's clan. Husbands could make similar claims on the estates of their wives.[40] Although the 1716 ruling stated that widows would hold their allotments "in perpetuity" (*v vechnoe vladenie*) and did not prohibit widows from selling or bequeathing such land, widow's powers of alienation over their husbands' property were not explicitly formulated. In 1725, Catherine I stated that widows were free to appoint heirs to their inherited share of their husbands' property, but said nothing about their right to sell or mortgage this land. In practice, however, widows sold and mortgaged their allotments long before the 1725 decree.[41]

---

38. Inheritance disputes also feature husbands who had adopted their wives' names. See RGADA, f. 1270 (Musiny-Pushkiny), op. 1, ed. khr. 86; RGIA, f. 1330 (Obshchie sobraniia departamentov Senata), op. 3, ed. khr. 23. In these cases the wives survived their husbands and went on to challenge other heirs for independent control of the family estate.

39. See chapter 5.

40. *PSZ*, 5: 3.013 (15.06.1716).

41. See chapter 4, Table 4.15.

Female Litigation and the Law of
Single Inheritance

Despite bolstering women's status as heiresses and widows, the Law of Single Inheritance introduced one setback for women that would have far-ranging consequences: the decree prohibited parents from granting dowry villages to their daughters. The Petrine dowry consisted entirely of chattel and personal property—household items, clothes, and jewels—and might include a sum of money earmarked for the purchase of villages by the young bride and her husband. Noblewomen could still acquire real estate if they purchased it with dowry funds.[42] Nonetheless, by prohibiting the conveyance of land through the dowry the Law of Single Inheritance eliminated an important source of female landholding.

In keeping with medieval precedent, the Law of Single Inheritance made no attempt to clarify the legal status of the dowry vis-à-vis inheritance. The law failed to specify a fixed amount for the dowry and passed over the inheritance rights of married daughters. Moreover, by refusing to include land in the marriage award, the Law of Single Inheritance not only fostered discord between brothers but also encouraged women to sue kin of both sexes if they felt they had been shortchanged in the division of family assets. Indeed, the most enduring legacy of Peter's vain attempt to overturn centuries of tradition was the astonishing visibility of noblewomen in property disputes after 1714: in the eighteenth century, 57.5 percent of suits recorded in the Land College involved litigants of both sexes, while another 9 percent involved female litigants alone.[43] Thus, although Muscovite women had been no strangers to the legal process, the Law of Single Inheritance ushered in a new era for women in the realm of property litigation. For decades after repeal of the law, men and women appealed to the courts on the grounds that they or their parents had been born "during the points" (*v punkhtakh*)—that is, while the Law of Single Inheritance was in force—and had been cheated of their share of family wealth.

From the moment their access to landed property was restricted, noble-

---

42. In fact, the right of women married to younger sons to purchase land was left in doubt until 1725: in 1714, Peter prohibited younger sons (*kadety*) from purchasing real estate until they had served seven years in the army or ten in the civil service. When Catherine I revised this provision in 1725, allowing younger sons to purchase land as soon as they entered state service, she also specified that women married to younger sons were free to purchase real estate, as long as their husbands complied with the law. See *PSZ*, 5: 2.796 (14.04.1714); 7: 4.722, art. 15.

43. RGADA, f. 1209, op. 79 (Zemel'nye dela). The official inventory for this collection of more than two hundred disputes lists the cases according to the district in which they originated and makes no mention of the names of the litigants. I am grateful to Victor Iurevich Belikov for allowing me to use the inventory he compiled, in which he recorded the participants in each case.

women exploited ambiguities in the Law of Single Inheritance to present themselves as legitimate heirs to their fathers' estates. After the death of his father and uncle, Nikolai Treskin found himself embroiled in a dispute with his four aunts, each of whom interpreted the Law of Single Inheritance in her own favor. In a petition submitted to the Land College in 1722, Treskin argued that he was the sole heir to the landed estates of his father and uncle, who had recently died. Three of his father's sisters had received dowries in movable property when they married. As for his father's fourth sister, Marfa, ". . . my grandfather and father and uncle, seeing her commitment and desire to take holy orders, purchased a cell for her in Moscow in the Monastery of the Passion, and a sum of money was given to the monastery." Marfa had enjoyed the financial support of her brothers for many years, but now, for reasons unknown to Treskin, his aunt wanted to renounce her vocation and aspired "to be heir to her father and mother and brothers." Upon the death of her second brother, Treskin's uncle, Marfa had arrived in Treskin's village and "seized all of his property from his house— money and clothing and silver utensils . . . and . . . horses and equipment . . . and carried them off to Kashirskii district to the house of her sister." Treskin's three other aunts submitted petitions in turn: each claimed to be the sole legitimate heir to their father's estate on the grounds that they had received nothing when they married, and protested that the other sisters had already received their portion, while all brushed aside the claims of their nephew.[44]

As is so often the case, the ruling of the Land College in the dispute between Nikolai Treskin and his aunts has not survived. What is known is that the College had no grounds for confirming the claim of Marfa Treskina or her sisters; in the seventeenth century, a ruling had already established that aunts had no right to share in an inheritance with their nephews.[45] Yet each of these women believed—or claimed to believe—that her status as direct heir to her father's estate after the death of her brothers took precedence over the claims of her nephew. Moreover, each used some element of the Law of Single Inheritance to support her demand. Marfa Treskina argued that her father had bestowed an inheritance upon her brothers before "the points" of 1714, while she had remained at home; her father, she maintained, had intended that she would inherit the rest of his estate. Marfa's sister, Matrena, asserted that she, as the eldest, was entitled to inherit. Meanwhile, everyone involved in the case shared the assumption that daughters who left their father's house with property in hand automatically renounced any claim to further inheritance. Although every provision of the Law of Single Inheritance pointed to Treskin as the only

44. RGADA, f. 1209, op. 79, ed. khr. 4, ll. 1–4; ed. khr. 7, ll. 15–23.
45. *PSZ*, 2: 700 (10.08.1677), sect. 2, art. 9.

possible heir, the law's failure to articulate the inheritance rights of married daughters allowed Treskin's aunts to fashion a plausible defense.

The volume of litigation generated by the Law of Single Inheritance inspired Peter's spouse and successor, Catherine I, to clarify some of the law's ambiguities. One of the articles in the decree of 1725 sought to address the question of married daughters' inheritance rights. Here, the law mandated that if a man was survived by unmarried daughters, the eldest would inherit his estate, while the remaining sisters would divide his movable property. If some of his daughters were married, then the eldest unmarried girl would inherit the land and her unmarried sisters would divide his movables. His married daughters would receive nothing, however, since they would have received dowries when they married. Finally, if all his daughters were married, the eldest would inherit the landed property, while the rest divided his movable estate.[46] Although Catherine's decree represented a valiant attempt to clarify the inheritance rights of married daughters vis-à-vis their unmarried siblings, her ruling failed to put an end to litigation on this topic.

Inheritance after 1731

The passage of time failed to reconcile the nobility to the practice of unigeniture. As a result, when Anna Ivanovna ascended the throne in 1730, one of her first acts was to revoke the Law of Single Inheritance. In a report to the empress on December 9, 1730, the Senate contended that providing an inheritance in movable property for younger sons had only accelerated the fragmentation of estates that Peter had tried to avoid. The senators also observed that providing dowries in movable property was a drain on family assets, and argued in favor of resuming the practice of granting dowry villages to daughters when they were given in marriage. Far from suffering a loss, parents who gave their daughters dowry villages would eventually be compensated with land from other families when their sons married.[47]

Three months later, in 1731, the empress issued an edict that maintained some elements of the Law of Single Inheritance but also satisfied noble demands for a return to partible inheritance. The empress confirmed the abolition of service and hereditary estates in favor of a single category of immovable property. At the same time, deferring to the Senate's wishes, she reinstated the rules of intestate inheritance outlined in the *Ulozhenie* of 1649, albeit with some variations on the law of female inheritance. Partible inheritance of both landed and movable property between sons was restored. Widows also benefited from the ruling: henceforth, spouses were to receive one-seventh of the other's immovable property and one-fourth of their

46. *PSZ*, 7: 4722 (28.05.1725), art. 2.
47. *PSZ*, 8: 5.653 (09.12.1730).

movable goods; widows would also receive any dowry property they had brought to the marriage. Although one-seventh of her husband's immovable property represented a decline from the one-fourth she had received under the Law of Single Inheritance, the bereaved wife held this property in perpetuity and could freely bequeath, mortgage, or sell her portion. In contrast to the inheritance rights of daughters, widows' dower rights were established conclusively in 1731 and were not the subject of further debate, although widows were often compelled to file suit against in-laws who refused to deliver their portion.[48]

Following medieval and Petrine tradition, the repeal of the Law of Single Inheritance discussed the inheritance rights of widows at length but summarized daughters' entitlements in a few terse lines and offered no guidelines for distinguishing dowry from inheritance.[49] The empress ruled in her 1731 decree that parents must divide their property among their children according to the *Ulozhenie*. On the subject of daughters' inheritance rights, however, the decree simply stated that dowries were to be awarded to daughters "as before" (*za docher'mi v pridaniia davat' po prezhnemu*), meaning before implementation of the Law of Single Inheritance. The ruling further stipulated that when male offspring survived, daughters of parents who died intestate could expect half of their mothers' entitlements—in other words, one-fourteenth of the landed estate and one-eighth of liquid assets (*a docheriam pri brat'iakh . . . protiv materi, ili machikhi vpoly*)—while daughters without brothers would become the sole heirs.[50] As the historian Got'e observed, the new provisions for daughters and widows in the 1731 edict represented a compromise between the principles governing their previous entitlements to *pomest'ia* and *votchiny*—in other words, henceforth women could inherit patrimonial estates, but their entitlements were in keeping with seventeenth-century regulations on inheritance of service-tenure land.[51] What Got'e did not note, however, was that the 1731 ruling introduced a crucial variation: although the revised law drew on the *Ulozhenie* to determine the amount of property women might claim, it nonetheless replaced the notion of maintenance (*prozhitok*) with the language of entitlement (*ukaznaia chast'*). The post-Petrine law of property thus not only expanded noblewomen's rights of inheritance in landed property but also invested women with greater powers over the estates in their possession.[52]

48. In a survey of eighteenth-century property disputes, 24% (11/45) involved women and relations by marriage. Most of these cases involved the widow's portion from her husband's estate.

49. This ambiguity in regard to daughters' inheritance rights was also evident in medieval regulations. See Levin (1983), 165.

50. *PSZ*, 8: 5.717 (17.03.1731).

51. Iu. V. Got'e, *Ocherki istorii zemlevladeniia v Rossii* (Sergiev Posad, 1915), 105.

52. Rozhdestvenskii emphasized that the term *prozhitok* implied provisionary ownership, and suggested that lawmakers believed that women were more likely to attend to the productivity of estates held in perpetuity. Rozhdestvenskii (1839), 73.

Defining the Dowry

Nineteenth-century legal scholars abandoned their analysis of noble-women's inheritance rights with the repeal of the Law of Single Inheritance,[53] assuming that the 1731 decree conclusively established women's claim to the family estate. These scholars acknowledged variations in the control women exercised over their fortunes, but considered the problem of entitlement to have been solved in 1731. However, the record preserved in inheritance disputes heard in the Land College (*Votchinnaia kollegia*) and the Senate throughout the eighteenth century points to a very different conclusion. It should come as no surprise that married women's control of property continued to provoke acrimonious suits between husband and wife. More striking, however, is the volume of litigation concerning the inheritance rights of daughters and their descendants. By failing to stipulate in 1731 whether dowered daughters were automatically barred from further inheritance, lawmakers inadvertently offered married women the chance to sue for a larger share of family assets—an opportunity they exploited in full. The 1731 edict contributed further to this ambiguity by saying nothing about the obligation of parents to dower their daughters.[54]

On the surface, the inheritance rights of sisters vis-à-vis brothers were not open to interpretation and not an obvious source of family conflict. Direct male heirs were always favored over female siblings in the division of family property. As mandated in 1731, in cases of intestate succession each daughter could claim only one-fourteenth of her parents' immovable property and one-eighth of movable assets, after which her brothers shared the remaining land and other property equally. Yet when this rule was applied to married daughters it was unclear whether one-fourteenth pertained to their share of the family estate at the time of marriage or at the time of their parents' demise. The kind of property women might claim was also at issue. Although the edict of 1731 restored the right of parents to grant dowry villages, in a subsequent ruling Anna Ivanovna introduced an important variation on her earlier decree. Noble donors might award their daughters immovable property when they married, but only if the land in question was acquired or inherited from another clan: patrimonial property was not to

53. See Kavelin (1900), 4: 580–81; Nevolin (1851), 3: 444; Pobedonostsev (1871), 2: 242, 250; Vladimirskii-Budanov (1909), 506.

54. European observers noted the distinction between female inheritance and dowry: in the words of a Swedish diplomat, who lived in St. Petersburg in 1735–36, "According to Russian law, daughters do not receive an inheritance, but only a dowry, the size of which her father determines. If he dies before his daughter's marriage, she also receives a share of the inheritance, but less than that of her brothers." See Karl Reinkhold Berk, "Putevye zametki o Rossii," in *Peterburg Anny Ioannovny v inostrannykh opisaniiakh*, ed. Iu. N. Bespiatykh (St. Petersburg, 1997), 202.

be awarded as dowry.[55] Dowry agreements throughout the eighteenth century violated this decree, but the ruling was designed to discourage parents from partitioning villages to marrying daughters, despite the restoration of pre-Petrine customs of inheritance. Parents who wished to do so were free to give their daughters only movable property in lieu of dowry villages—an option that many dowry donors preferred.[56]

The ambiguous status of daughters' inheritance rights soon drew the attention of the courts. As a result, one of the most prominent themes in eighteenth-century inheritance disputes was the problem of defining a "sufficient" dowry.[57] This ambiguity stemmed from the language of the Senate's report in 1730 and the subsequent ruling of 1731: the former suggested that the dowry was traditionally a matter of parental discretion (*otsy i pri zhivote svoem detei delili, i v pridanye za docher'mi derevni davali po svoei vole*),[58] whereas the latter simultaneously guaranteed daughters an entitlement of one-fourteenth of their fathers' immovable estates. Although the second provision clearly pertained to unmarried daughters, lawmakers struggled until the end of the century with the question of whether the dowry was only an advance on inheritance and should be supplemented if it fell short of the allotted one-fourteenth, or whether daughters must be content with the property they received when they married.[59] The uncertainty surrounding the precise nature of married daughters' inheritance rights was further underscored by the language of petitioners, who routinely maintained that the woman at the center of the dispute had been given in marriage with a "sufficient dowry" (*vydana v zamuzhstvo s dovolnym nagrazhdeniem*), usually without specifying the precise amount of the award.

With astonishing regularity, petitioners, both male and female, argued throughout the eighteenth century that rival female claimants to family property had no right to inherit because they had received an adequate dowry when they married and, having accepted their portion, tacitly ceded further claims to the family estate. The motif of the sufficient dowry was not the only recurring element in these suits. The composition of kin who engaged in disputes over married daughters' inheritance rights was another commonality. Indeed, the configuration of litigants not only underscores the power of hierarchies of gender and generation in eighteenth-century Russia

---

55. *PSZ*, 8: 5.880 (17.11.1731).

56. See chapter 4.

57. Women in Renaissance Italy also had the right to a "suitable" dowry, but the size of the dowry was not specified. See Thomas Kuehn, "Some Ambiguities of Female Inheritance Ideology in the Renaissance," *Continuity and Change* 2, no. 1 (1987): 11–12.

58. *PSZ*, 8: 5653 (09.12.1730), stated in the *doklad*.

59. For a discussion of the dowry as an advance on inheritance, see Robin Bisha, "The Promise of Patriarchy: Marriage in Eighteenth-Century Russia" (Ph.D. dissertation, Indiana University, 1993), 131–33.

but also demonstrates how these hierarchies shaped women's participation in the legal process. Men infringed on the property rights of every type of female kin; however, women filed suit selectively against family members.

Overwhelmingly, the participants in disputes over daughters' inheritance rights were not brothers and sisters, but aunts and their nieces and nephews, or female siblings. Thus, in a sample of forty-five inheritance disputes heard in the Land College and the Senate in the eighteenth century, only 7 percent (3/45) involved brothers and sisters. By contrast, disputes between sisters comprised 16 percent (7/45) of the total, while suits between aunts and nieces or nephews made up 20 percent (9/45) of the sample.[60] Timing was another crucial element. Married women rarely litigated to augment their inheritance immediately after their parents' demise. Instead, with few exceptions, the death of a brother supplied the catalyst for the dispute. Eighteenth-century noblewomen were reluctant to take action against their brothers while they were living,[61] but did not hesitate to maintain that their rights had been violated vis-à-vis their brothers' children. As for nephews and nieces, respect for the authority of elderly kin went by the wayside when questions of property were at stake. Rivalry between sisters, however, was expressed during their lifetime. Distance and obstacles to communication encouraged women to "conceal" the existence of siblings when they petitioned the Land College to register estates, or to lie about their marital status, claiming to be single and maintaining that they, not their married sisters, should inherit their parents' estates.[62]

The petitions that survive recount the same quarrel time and again: the aunt asserts her claim to a larger portion of her father's estate, while her nieces and nephews maintain that their aunt had received an adequate dowry when she married. "In 1702 . . . my brother gave me in marriage . . . with the smallest dowry (s samym malym pridanym) from our father's movable estate," Fedosia Shatilova stated when she challenged the Land College in 1743 for a share of her father's immovable property. Shatilova was moved to petition the court, however, only after her brother died and his widow and daughter inherited all the estates that had once belonged to her father.[63] Solomonida Obasheva went to Moscow in 1741 to plead for part of her father's estate after the death of her brother, to which her nephew

<hr />

60. See appendix 2.

61. For exceptions that prove this rule, see RGADA, f. 1209, op. 84, ch. 14, ed. khr. 327 (1741–42); f. 1209, op. 79, ed. khr. 241 (1758); f. 1209, op. 84, ch. 14, ed. khr. 1509 (1775). Note that ed. khr. 327 involves a brother and sister litigating jointly against their half-brothers and sisters; ed. khr. 241 does not concern inheritance rights. See also V. P. Alekseev, *Dvoriane Salovy iz Sosnovki* (Briansk, 1993), 37–38, for a suit by a woman against her brother in 1757, in which the former claims she was married without a dowry.

62. RGADA, f. 1209, op. 84, ch. 14, ed. khr. 252, ll. 33–42; continued in ed. khr. 268, ll. 3, 23 (1736), and *PSZ*, 15: 11.210 (16.02.1761); *OAS* (1879), 2: no. 385 (1722).

63. RGADA, f. 22, op. 1, ed. khr. 94, l. 1.

responded that she had accepted a dowry in movable property in lieu of her statutory share (*ukaznaia chast'*) when she married, and had no right to change her mind at this late date.[64] Princess Elena Shcherbatova was incensed when her aunt inherited the widow's portion of her mother, Shcherbatova's grandmother. Her aunt had already received a dowry of twenty-four serfs, Shcherbatova argued, as well as a thousand rubles worth of movable property and another thousand rubles in cash for the purchase of an estate. In response, Shcherbatova's aunt did not deny that she had received a portion in excess of what the law decreed, but observed that her mother had violated no law with her generous bequest, since her brother, Shcherbatova's father, had consented to the transaction.[65]

To make matters more complicated, the composition of the "sufficient" dowry was a matter of interpretation for both donors and lawmakers. In marriage contracts, donors often referred to the dowry as something composed only of movable goods and cash. Thus, one resident of Tambov and his wife relinquished one hundred *chetverti* of land to their son-in-law in place of a dowry (*vmesto pridanogo deneg i plati'ia*) when he married their daughter in 1718.[66] Female petitioners also distinguished between the dowry, composed of movable assets, and the remuneration (*voznagrazhdenie*) owed them from their father's estate, which must include land. Tatiana Chemoduova made this distinction when she asserted that she had been married without remuneration (*bez vsiakogo voznagrazhdeniia*) and had been given a dowry only in movable property (*dav v pridanoe tol'ko dvorovykh liudei . . . a takzhe raznye pozhitki*). The receipt of the latter, she implied, fell far short of what she should expect from her father's estate.[67] Elena Varpakhovskaia also alleged that she had wed without property (*bez nagrazhdeniia*) when, to her brother's dismay, she petitioned for her share (*ukaznaia chast'*) of her father's estate in 1775.[68]

The battle to define the sufficient dowry and clarify female inheritance rights was played out repeatedly in the Land College and Senate in the eighteenth century.[69] Simply stated, the debates over married daughters'

---

64. RGADA, f. 1209, op. 84, ch. 14, ed. khr. 499, ll. 1–2.
65. RGADA, f. 1209, op. 79, ed. khr. 51, ll. 9, 11, 26–34, 58.
66. RGADA, f. 615, op. 1, ed. khr. 11254, ll. 64–65.
67. Alekseev (1993), 37–38.
68. RGADA, f. 1209, op. 84, ch. 14, ed. khr. 1509, l. 1. Varpakhovskaia's brother produced a dowry agreement, drawn up in 1758, in which his mother awarded her land and serfs; however, the dowry was taken from her mother's estate, not her father's.
69. Other disputes concerning the problem of the "sufficient dowry" include the following: RGADA, f. 248, op. 13, kn. 687, ll. 115–130 (1726–27); f. 1209, op. 79, ed. khr. 9, l. 3 (1724); f. 1209, op. 79, ed. khr. 400, ll. 1–2 (1768–71); f. 1209, op. 79, ed. khr. 417, l. 12 (1769–77); f. 1209, op. 79, ed. khr. 514, l. 4 (1778–79); f. 1209, op. 83, ed. khr. 82, ll. 1–5, 15–17 (1740–41); f. 1209, op. 84, ch. 14, ed. khr. 252, ll. 36–37 (1736); f. 1209, op. 84, ed. khr. 327, l. 1 (1741–72); f. 1209, op. 84, ed. khr. 354, l. 1 (1742); f. 1209, op. 84, ed. khr. 1322, ll. 1–4 (1769); f. 1209, op. 84, ed. khr. 1509, l. 1 (1775); RGIA, f. 1330, op. 1, ed. khr. 76, ll. 514–15, 535 (1797–1800); *PSZ*, 13: 9.728 (29.03.1750).

entitlements concerned the right of the latter to claim the difference between her dowry and the full portion of the family estate promised her by law. What each dispute underscored, however, was female vulnerability in the law of inheritance. As formulated in the law of 1731, the dowry represented a gift rather than an entitlement, and its size depended on the donor's discretion. Married daughters enjoyed no guarantee that their dowries would comprise the equivalent of one-fourteenth of their parents' landed wealth. Moreover, despite explicit instructions on the inheritance rights of unmarried daughters, in practice the latter often found themselves dependent on the goodwill of male kin. Thus, Corporal Eremeev of Tambov divided his village, serfs, and movable property between his sons in 1753 and admonished his two daughters not to petition for a portion of his estate after his death. His sons bore the responsibility, when the young women married, "to endow them to the best of their ability with movable property (*nagradit' po vozmozhnosti dvizhimym imeniem*)."[70] Such arrangements left women with little recourse if their brothers elected to give them a dowry that fell short of the one-fourteenth allotted them by law.

A number of disputes that reached the Senate highlight the difficulty lawmakers faced in determining whether women could claim a fixed share of family assets or whether they must be satisfied with paternal (or maternal) largess. For several decades after Anna's ruling, the courts maintained that simply accepting a dowry implied women's renunciation of further inheritance. In a typical example, in 1731 the Land College rejected a petition from Avdotia, the daughter of Prince Shakovskii, who argued that she, as the eldest of three daughters, was entitled to inherit the estate of her father, who died while the Law of Single Inheritance was still in force. The Land College denied Avdotia's request, not only on the grounds that she had been unmarried at the time of her father's demise and yet failed to petition for the estate, but also because she had renounced further claims by accepting a dowry when she married. "Leaving her father's estate, she married with the above-mentioned dowry in movable property," the summary of the case read, "and by accepting a dowry and by her marriage she herself renounced any part of the immovable property."[71] One year later, the Land College questioned its interpretation, admitting that the 1731 decree had not explicitly excluded married daughters from taking part in the division of their parents' estates.[72] By contrast, later in the eighteenth century the Senate increasingly came to insist on married daughters' entitlement to the full one-fourteenth desig-

70. RGADA, f. 615 (Krepostnye knigi mestnykh uchrezhdenii XVI–XVIII vv.), op. 1, ed. khr. 11418, ll. 12–13. This instruction from Eremeev is reminiscent of the formula that appears in the *Russkaia Pravda*, in which brothers of unmarried daughters were to give the latter in marriage with property *kako si mogut*.

71. RGADA, f. 1209, op. 79, ed. khr. 27, l. 162.

72. *PSZ*, 13: 9.728 (29.03.1750).

nated by law. In their new formulation, the senators agreed that dowered daughters were no longer automatically barred from inheritance unless they signed a document upon receiving their dowry in which they waived their right to their portion. It required several decades, however, before the senators settled on this interpretation.

During the reign of Catherine the Great, legislators wavered between adherence to a literal reading of the 1731 ruling, which implied that the size of the dowry depended on the donor's discretion, and their own deep-seated conviction, as expressed in their rulings, that families should not be given license to shortchange their daughters. The result was a series of decisions that appear at first glance to be highly variable but in fact were founded on consistent reasoning on the part of the senators. Two rulings in the 1770s defended married women's right to a fixed share of their fathers' assets. When the senators upheld Anna Somova's demand for her full portion in 1770, they contended that she was entitled to one-fourteenth of her father's immovable property because she had married when the Law of Single Inheritance was still in force and at that time had received a dowry solely in movable property.[73] The Senate went on to rule in 1772 that Daria Lavrova was entitled to one-fourteenth of her deceased father's estate since her dowry consisted only of house serfs when she married in 1712.[74] Both rulings suggested that married daughters should consider the dowry no more than an advance on their inheritance when the award fell short of one-fourteenth of their parents' landed estates, or the equivalent in movable property.

With an abrupt about-face in 1789, however, the Senate conveyed a con-flicting message to women dissatisfied with their marriage portion. Follow-ing the death of State Councillor Molchanov, his daughter, Princess Avdotia Vadbol'skaia, went before the Senate to declare that she had received a meager dowry (ves'mo malo), and asserted her right to one-fourteenth of her father's considerable estate. Vadbol'skaia's stepmother and siblings coun-tered by pointing out that she had received a dowry worth 2,378 rubles, as well as 2,000 rubles in cash, with which she had purchased villages and 102 serfs. Although the Land College had ruled in Vadbol'skaia's favor, the Senators overturned the decision, arguing that the 1731 ruling had provided for the bestowal of dowries but had not established a precise amount for the award. The granting of dowries, they declared, "has always depended on the will of the parents and on the agreement of those people to whom they are giving their daughters in marriage." The Senate therefore concluded that Vadbol'skaia had no legal grounds for sharing in the inheritance, and rejected her suit.[75]

73. *PSZ*, 19: 13.520 (25.10.1770).
74. *PSZ*, 19: 13.750 (30.01.1772).
75. *PSZ*, 23: 16.769 (19.05.1789). The Senate stated the following: "... a so vremeni ulozhenia po togdashnim zakonam ne bylo predpisaniia, kakoe kolichestvo pridanago dolzhen

Far from acting arbitrarily, the Senate operated according to a concept of justice that was consistent, on the one hand, with a tradition of partible inheritance that provided for daughters as well as sons, yet was also in keeping with women's secondary status in the law of property. In the first two cases, the women in question either had married under the Law of Single Inheritance—a measure that the nobility vehemently opposed—or had clearly been deprived of a reasonable portion of family wealth. By contrast, Vadbol'skaia's plea drew attention to the ambiguity of the 1731 ruling yet offered the senators no grounds for questioning or revising the rules governing the granting of dowries. Vadbol'skaia had not been ill-treated when she married, despite failing to benefit from her father's wealth to the full extent. In short, the senators agreed that Vadbol'skaia's family had transgressed neither written law nor accepted practice when they refused to let her share in the division of her father's assets.

By the close of the century, a new element entered into the Senate's decision making, as its members placed greater emphasis on written contracts between donors and recipients. In cases where women had not signed a document waiving their inheritance when they received a dowry, they could be confident that the courts would uphold their rights. Such contracts were not unheard of earlier in the century: Natalia Iakovleva renounced any future inheritance upon receiving a dowry worth fifty rubles from her mother in 1739.[76] These agreements were the exception, however, until late in the eighteenth century. Over time, lawmakers came to apply such waivers separately to the estates of both parents, as a suit that came before the Senate in 1797 reveals. The plaintiff, the wife of Lieutenant Akhlestyshev, filed suit against her stepmother and stepsiblings. She demanded that the latter hand over her mother's dowry, which consisted of 10,762 rubles in movable property, as well as 6,000 rubles for the purchase of villages. Not surprisingly, Anna Akhlestysheva's stepmother refused to comply, arguing that Akhlestysheva had received a sufficient dowry. Reviewing the case, the Senate established that Akhlestysheva had indeed signed a contract in which her father stipulated that her dowry was well in excess of her entitlement and represented her total inheritance. The Senate nonetheless ruled without hesitation in Akhlestysheva's favor, maintaining that although she had waived her right to inherit from her father, she had made no such agreement with her mother, and that she was fully entitled to the latter's estate.[77]

Significantly, both the motif of the "sufficient" dowry and uncertainty over

---

otets davat' vydavaemym v zamuzhestvo docheriam svoim, i siia dacha pridanago vsegda zavisila ot voli roditelei i ot soglasiia tekh liudei, za koikh docheri ikh vydaiutsia . . ." and went on to say that when Vadbol'skaia accepted her dowry, she automatically lost her right to take part in any further division of her father's estate.

76. Gosudarstvennyi istoricheskii muzei (hereafter GIM), f. 47, ed. khr. 1, l. 13.

77. RGIA, f. 1330, op. 1, ed. khr. 1, ll. 4–5. See also *PSZ*, 32: 25.576 (27.04.1814).

married daughters' inheritance rights disappeared in the opening decades of the nineteenth century. Noblewomen filed suit against male siblings when the latter did not deliver their requisite portion,[78] but the entitlement of daughters to a fixed share of the family estate and the necessity of their consent to the dowry contract were no longer at issue. The *Svod zakonov* (the digest of Russian laws), first compiled in 1830, defined the dowry simply as property apportioned to daughters or female kin on the occasion of marriage. It stipulated that dowered women could be excluded from inheritance only if they had willingly signed away their right to their legal portion; in the absence of written proof, daughters were to take part in the division of the family estate.[79] The courts later ruled that even if the allotment of property to a daughter had not taken the form of a dowry, but a deed of separation (*otdel'naia zapis'*), unless the young woman had signed away her rights, she could not be barred from further inheritance.[80] The *Svod zakonov* also confirmed women's right to one-fourteenth of the immovable estate, except when there were so many daughters that their brothers would receive less than that amount.[81]

The record of litigation in the Senate demonstrates that officials took the inheritance rights of daughters seriously and, when the need arose, instructed male kin in no uncertain terms to hand over their share of family wealth. Indeed, the most striking feature of inheritance disputes between siblings in the first half of the nineteenth century is the very absence of cases concerning the dowry. Siblings squabbled over the precise division of assets[82] or failure to relinquish land and serfs once an agreement had been reached.[83] Brothers objected when sisters inherited shares above their legal entitlement, even when the property in question was acquired and the bequest was clearly the wish of the deceased; others tried to prevent their sisters from alienating family property.[84] For noblewomen willing to defend their rights, however, the "insufficient" dowry was a thing of the past. Despite the persistence of disagreements among siblings, by the beginning of the nineteenth century the entitlement of married daughters to family assets was firmly established.

78. See, for example, the dispute among the Golitsyns in 1848. RGIA, f. 1330, op. 6, ed. khr. 14, ll. 5–18, 340–51. See also RGIA, f. 1330, op. 4, ed. khr. 369, ll. 1–22; *PSZ*, 35: 27.299 (17.01.1818).

79. *Svod zakonov Rossiiskoi imperii* (hereafter *SZ*) 10, pt. 1 (1900), arts. 1001–3.

80. *Zhurnal Ministerstva Iustitsii* 13 (June 1862): 90–91.

81. *SZ*, (1913) 10, art. 1131.

82. RGIA, f. 1330, op. 5, ed. khr. 1806, ll. 2–3, 24–25, 75–90.

83. RGIA, f. 1330, op. 6, ed. khr. 1285, ll. 68–80, 323, 563.

84. RGIA, f. 1330, op. 1, ed. khr. 307 (1799); f. 1330, op. 4, ed. khr. 655, ll. 2–4, 147–152 (1820); f. 1330, op. 4, ed. khr. 983 (1825); f. 1330, op. 6, ed. khr. 447, ll. 12–33; f. 1555, op. 1, ed. khr. 300, ll. 1–2 (1826); Gosudarstvennyi arkhiv Rossiiskoi federatsii (hereafter GARF), f. 109, 2-aia eksp., op. 75, ed. khr. 188, ll. 10–11 (1845).

The status of Russian noblewomen in the law of inheritance should not be overstated. The temptation to exaggerate feminine prerogatives in the realm of inheritance has proved irresistible to some historians who question why women "fared so well in Russian law in the seventeenth and eighteenth centuries" in comparison with elite women in Western Europe.[85] A statutory share of 7 percent for daughters in their parents' land, or the cash equivalent, can hardly be considered the height of generosity; furthermore, this rule applied only to patrimonial land, and proprietors of both sexes were free to devise their acquired estates to whomever they pleased, if they had the foresight to make a will.[86]

For all its advances over the course of the eighteenth century, the law of female inheritance in Russia displayed only marginal superiority over European legal codes. In regard to widows, Russian property law was distinguished less by generous dower provisions than by the absence of measures to limit women's autonomy.[87] The portion allotted to a noble widow in Russia was considerably smaller than that enjoyed by her bereaved European counterpart;[88] on the other hand, the property in her possession was not limited to a life interest but was held outright. Moreover, it assimilated into her patrimonial estate, reverting to her clan, not that of her husband, if she died without issue.[89] A Russian widow thus could freely dispose of property inherited from her husband's estate, rather than settle for the lesser privilege of

85. Weickhardt (1996), 20. As the legal historian I. G. Orshanskii observed, although the link between landownership and government service was severed early in the eighteenth century, noblewomen's inheritance rights never exceeded the modest one-fourteenth they received from their fathers' service-tenure estates in the seventeenth century. See Orshanskii, *Issledovaniia po russkomu pravu semeinomu i nasledstvennomu* (St. Petersburg, 1877), 367.

86. Catherine II's Charter to the Nobility guaranteed nobles testamentary freedom over their acquired estates. *PSZ*, 22: 16.187 (21.04.1785), sect. A, art. 22.

87. French law restricted the amount of property a widow might bestow on her second husband and treated widows as minors until the age of twenty-five; Portuguese law permitted authorities to take property from widows who mismanaged their estates. See Barbara B. Diefendorf, "Widowhood and Remarriage in Sixteenth-Century Paris," *Journal of Family History* 7, no. 4 (Winter 1982): 379; DeJean (1991), 123; Alida C. Metcalf, "Women and Means: Women and Family Property in Colonial Brazil," *Journal of Social History* 24, no. 3 (Spring 1991): 280.

88. According to common law, English widows could claim a life estate in one-third of their husbands' immovable assets; French and Dutch widows were entitled to the use of one-half of their husbands' property, as well as the use of community property acquired during marriage. See Eileen Spring, *Law, Land, and Family: Aristocratic Inheritance in England, 1300–1800* (Chapel Hill, 1993), 40–65; Susan Staves, *Married Women's Separate Property in England, 1660–1833* (Cambridge, 1990); Diefendorf (1982): 384–85; Sherrin Marshall Wyntjes, "Survivors and Status: Widowhood and Family in the Early Modern Netherlands," *Journal of Family History* 7, no. 4 (Winter 1982): 399. Polish widows also were allowed the lifetime use of some of their husbands' property but without the right to dispose of it. Bogna Lorence-Kot, *Child-Rearing and Reform: A Study of the Nobility in Eighteenth-Century Poland* (Westport, Conn., 1985), 47–48.

89. *PSZ*, 18: 12.830 (01.1767); 24: 19.100 (08.1799).

having the use of the income from his property during her lifetime. In award-ing widows possession, rather than use, of their husbands' estates, Russian law presumed a certain degree of confidence in female administration of property. For Russian widows who inherited meager estates, however, access to half of their husbands' property may have been a happier prospect than independent control of their own modest fortunes.[90]

The inheritance rights of daughters in Russian law were also commensu-rate with those of women in European legal codes. Both east and west of the Elbe, nobles preferred male heirs and exhibited varying degrees of gen-erosity toward their daughters. Throughout Europe, however, it was more common than not for women to inherit landed estates in the absence of brothers; the provisions of English common law, which entailed immovable estates to collateral male kin, were less widespread on the continent.[91] In the provinces of France that adhered to Roman law, parents were legally obliged to dower their daughters, and women could file suit if they suffered a loss by accepting a dowry in lieu of inheritance.[92] Whereas many European noblewomen were compelled to accept the cash equivalent of their portion of the family estate, Russian women enjoyed a slight advantage in being able to claim immovable property; however, depending on the number of sur-viving daughters, women in Poland and Hungary could anticipate a larger share of family wealth than their Russian counterparts.[93] Thus, both as

90. Widows did have the option of relinquishing their one-seventh in favor of a life estate in their husbands' property, but this was possible only if the latter made this arrangement while living. Granting spouses a life estate became more common in the nineteenth century. See chapter 5.

91. In the absence of male heirs, women could succeed to landed estates in several French provinces; Dutch and Castilian women could also inherit if they had no brothers. See E. Glasson, *Histoire du droit et des institutions de la France* (Paris, 1896), 7: 466–70; Sherrin Marshall, *The Dutch Gentry, 1500–1650: Family, Faith, and Fortune* (Westport, Conn., 1987), 40; J. P. Cooper, "Patterns of Inheritance and Settlement by Great Landowners from the Fifth to the Eighteenth Centuries," in *Family and Inheritance: Rural Society in Western Europe, 1200–1800*, ed. Jack Goody, Joan Thirsk, and E. P. Thompson (Cambridge, 1976), 240–41. On English law, see Spring (1993), 9–17. The entail of estates to collateral male kin was more widespread among gentry families in England than among the aristocracy. Nonetheless, in a study of landowners in East Yorkshire, Barbara English found that between 1530 and 1910, daughters succeeded to their fathers' estates in only 5.5% of recorded successions. See English, *The Great Landowners of East Yorkshire, 1530–1910* (New York, 1990), 99–100.

92. Cooper (1976), 267; Robert Forster, *The Nobility of Toulouse in the Eighteenth Century: A Social and Economic Study* (Baltimore, 1960), 135–36; Paul Viollet, *Histoire du droit civil français*, 2d ed. (Paris, 1893), 795. In the region of Paris, the eldest son inherited up to two-thirds of his parents' estates, but all remaining sons and daughters had equal inheritance rights. See Barbara B. Diefendorf, *Paris City Councillors in the Sixteenth Century: The Politics of Patrimony* (Princeton, 1983), 254.

93. In both Hungary and Poland, the daughters' share consisted of one-fourth of their parents' estates; however, this amount did not increase with the number of daughters, and in Hungary, it was always paid in cash. Polish women could claim their inheritance in immovable property if their brothers did not pay their dowries in the allotted time. See Charles D'Eszlary,

heiresses in their own right and when they shared the family fortune with brothers, Russian women stood on roughly equal footing with their European counterparts. The revised rules of inheritance at the end of the eighteenth century represented a genuine advance for noblewomen; nonetheless, inequalities in the law of inheritance would draw the ire of reformers until the end of the Imperial era.[94]

By addressing significant absences and ambiguities in the realm of female inheritance, eighteenth-century Russian lawmakers bolstered noblewomen's standing in the law of property. The courts offered women protection from rapacious family members and set limits on the abuse of authority within the patriarchal family. Thus, they denied men the option of disinheriting their wives, sisters, and daughters without sufficient cause,[95] as in the case of Katerina Podlutskaia, whose father left his entire estate, both patrimonial and acquired, to his sons. The senators agreed that Podlutskaia's father acted within his rights when he devised his acquired property to his sons, but instructed Podlutskaia's brothers to relinquish their sister's entitlement from the patrimonial estate.[96] Women such as Podlutskaia did not hesitate to protect their economic interests, despite the modest allowance made for them in the law.

While the inheritance rights of men remained stationary from the repeal of the Law of Single Inheritance, the rights of women were the subject of negotiation and debate, prompting lawmakers to reinterpret the import of

"Le Statut de la femme dans le droit Hongrois," *Recueils de la Société Jean Bodin pour l'histoire comparative des institutions* (hereafter *Recueils de la Société Jean Bodin*) 12 (1962): 432; Erik Fügedi, "Some Characteristics of the Medieval Hungarian Noble Family," *Journal of Family History* 7, no. 1 (Spring 1982): 32; Stanislaw Roman, "Le Statut de la femme dans l'Europe orientale (Pologne et Russie) au moyen âge et aux temps modernes," *Recueils de la Société Jean Bodin* 12 (1962): 399. On the preference for cash dowries and bequests, see Hughes (1985): 13–58; Paul Ourliac and Jean-Louis Gazzaniga, *Histoire du droit privé français de l'an mil au Code Civil* (Paris, 1985), 321–28; Gregory W. Pedlow, "Marriage, Family Size, and Inheritance among Hessian Nobles, 1650–1900," *Journal of Family History* 7, no. 4 (Winter 1982): 349; Jean Portemer, "Le Statut de la femme en France depuis la reformation des coutumes jusqu à la redaction du Code Civil," *Recueils de la Société Jean Bodin* 12 (1962): 463. The legacies of daughters and younger sons in early-modern England were highly unequal, and fathers had the option of disinheriting children altogether. See Susan Staves, "Resentment or Resignation? Dividing the Spoils among Daughters and Younger Sons," in *Early Modern Conceptions of Property*, ed. John Brewer and Susan Staves (London, 1995), 194–218. Among Portugese families in seventeenth-century São Paulo, married daughters received dowries in excess of their brothers' portions; this came to an end in 1761, however, when female inheritance was temporarily outlawed: Muriel Nazzari, *Disappearance of the Dowry: Women, Families, and Social Change in São Paulo, Brazil (1600–1900)* (Stanford, 1991), 15–19, 150–51.

94. William Wagner has shown how the attempts of the reformed courts after 1861 to equalize the inheritance rights of daughters met with defeat. See Wagner, *Marriage, Property, and Law in Late Imperial Russia* (Oxford, 1994), 333–34.

95. Russian law permitted parents to disinherit children on grounds of "disobedience" (*nepochtenie*) and for committing serious crimes. Rozhdestvenskii (1839), 82–82.

96. *PSZ*, 35: 27.229 (17.01.1818); see also 11: 8.190 (30.06.1740) and 23: 16.993 (16.10.1791).

a few crucial decrees enacted at the beginning of the century. Ironically, when men engaged in inheritance disputes, female antecedents were often at the root of the conflict, as the claims of direct descendants through the female line competed with those of plaintiffs descended from male kin further removed. In such cases Russian lawmakers upheld the claims of female heirs and their descendants versus those of collateral male kin, and consistently ruled against men who attempted to seize the property of nieces or female cousins.[97] Despite claims to the contrary, Russian noblewomen may not have been much better off than their eighteenth-century European counterparts in regard to inheritance, and they were at a clear disadvantage in the nineteenth century.[98] Yet there can be no doubt that by the end of the eighteenth century noblewomen enjoyed far greater security in the law of property than their Muscovite predecessors. The elevation of noble-women's standing in the law of inheritance set the stage for women's increasing visibility in the legal process, as well as their growing participation in economic life. It was in the realm of control of property, however, that Russian women were to make their most striking advance and to enjoy clear superiority vis-à-vis their European counterparts.

97. The competing rights of nieces and aunts and uncles were at the heart of many property disputes. RGIA, f. 1330, op. 2, ed. khr. 6, l. 7 (1801). See also Lee A. Farrow, "Inheritance, Status, and Security: Noble Life in Eighteenth-Century Russia" (unpublished manuscript, 2000), 160–63; LeDonne (1991), 228. The direct descendants of women, bearing the name of another clan, were preferred to more remote male relations, even when the latter belonged to the clan of the deceased. See *PSZ*, 19:13.428 (15.03.1770); *SZ*, 10 (1913), art. 1132.

98. The Civil Code of 1804 in France equalized the inheritance rights of sons and daughters. See M. Ia. Ostrogorski, *The Rights of Women: A Comparative Study in History and Legislation* (London, 1893), 208. The nineteenth century witnessed the equalization of male and female inheritance rights in many European states. The adoption of equal inheritance rights took place in Sweden in 1845, in Norway in 1854, and in Denmark in 1857: B. J. Hovde, *The Scandinavian Countries, 1720–1865: The Rise of the Middle Classes* (Boston, 1943), 2: 688.

The Enigma of Married Women's Control of Property

In his recital of the symptoms of moral decline at the eighteenth-century Russian court, Prince M. M. Shcherbatov drew particular attention to a 1753 decree granting married women control of their property. The impact of this innovation, he claimed, had been no less than "to loosen the bonds of matrimony." Shcherbatov represented the ruling as a radical break with tradition and went on to explain the deplorable change in women's legal status as a consequence of imperial favoritism. "Count Pyotr Ivanovich Shuvalov needed to buy an estate, belonging to a certain Countess Golovin . . . who lived apart from her husband, and hence could not secure his consent." At Shuvalov's suggestion, Shcherbatov alleged, "a decree was drawn up" that did away with "this sign of female subjugation. He bought the estate and thus gave occasion for women to leave their husbands at will, to ruin their children, and having left their husbands, to ruin themselves."[1]

Remarkably, with the exception of Shcherbatov, contemporaries passed over the 1753 ruling in silence. In striking contrast to Western Europe, where lawmakers adopted the married women's property acts only after prolonged and violent public debate, in Russia the transformation of women's relation to property took place without commentary on the part of the elite. Over time, however, Russian scholars came to celebrate the legal status of women in their country, noting the ironic contrast between Russia's archaic political and economic institutions and the relative emancipation of Russian women. Married women in much of Western Europe waited well into the nineteenth century before they were judged capable of controlling their

---

1. Prince M. M. Shcherbatov, *On the Corruption of Morals in Russia*, ed. and trans. A. Lentin (Cambridge, 1969), 219–21.

assets.[2] By contrast, Russian noblewomen freely disposed of their fortunes after 1753 and became active participants in the market for land and serfs.

Inspired by debates over the "woman question," nineteenth-century Russian historians wrote extensively on the topic of married women's property rights. They speculated at length about the origin of this curious exception to the rule of gender tutelage and warmly disputed its implementation in practice. By far the most striking feature of this literature, however, is the failure of scholars to account satisfactorily for the development of married women's control of property. The legal historian I. G. Orshanskii called the separation of property in marriage the "sphinx of Russian law," admitting that "we do not know of one serious attempt to explain [this phenomenon]."[3] Authors advanced a variety of theories to explain this divergence between Russia and Europe. Some attributed the Russian tradition of separate property in marriage to the influence of Byzantine legal culture on the development of ecclesiastical and property law.[4] Others maintained that women's unique status in Russia could be traced to the ancient customs of Slavic tribes. The author of one influential survey, M. F. Vladimirskii-Budanov, rejected the thesis of foreign influence, arguing that separate marital estates were an exclusively Slavic phenomenon that reached its full potential only in eighteenth-century Russia. According to his account, the 1753 ruling represented the culmination of earlier trends in Russian law that favored women.[5] A third school awarded Peter the Great the decisive role in extending women's property rights—a tradition that persists in contemporary scholarship.[6] Inevitably, at least one author speculated that the female

2. Lee Holcombe, *Wives and Property: Reform of the Married Women's Property Law in Nineteenth-Century England* (Toronto, 1983), 4; Claire Goldberg Moses, *French Feminism in the Nineteenth Century* (Albany, 1984), 18–19, 138, 167, 171. For a survey of married women's property rights in nineteenth-century Europe, see Ostrogorski (1893), 208–32.

3. Orshanskii (1877), 155. As late as 1910, V. I. Sinaiskii also maintained that legal scholars had failed to explain this feature of Russian property law. See *Lichnoe i imushchestvennoe polozhenie zamuzhnei zhenshchiny v grazhdanskom prave* (Iur'ev, 1910), 236.

4. D. N. Dubakin, *Vliianie khristianstva na semeinyi byt russkogo obshchestva* (St. Petersburg, 1880), 92–93; Nevolin (1851), 2: 97. See also Weickhardt (1996), 20–21. The Byzantine woman could freely dispose of nondowry property (*parapherna*) during marriage; her dowry was returned to her after her husband's demise, but the law stated that during marriage "the husband has the control and benefit of the dower." See Georgina Buckler, "Women in Byzantine Law about 1100 A.D.," *Byzantion: Revue Internationale des Études Byzantines* 11 (1936): 408–9. Even when a woman in Byzantium consented to alienation of her dowry goods, the transaction was considered null and void if she had not been instructed in her rights. See Macrides (1998), 180–81.

5. Vladimirskii-Budanov (1909), 374, 446, 456. Pobedonostsev argued that separate estates in marriage had been a feature of Russian law from time immemorial, while N. N. Debol'skii claimed that married women suffered no legal incapacity under pre-Petrine law. See Pobedonostsev (1871), 2: 102, and Debol'skii, *Grazhdanskaia deesposobnost' po russkomu pravu do kontsa XVII veka* (St. Petersburg, 1903), 12, 21–22.

6. Dmokhovskii (1862), 75; Shashkov (1879), 314; Shcheglov (1898), 91; Semenova (1982), 49; Farrow (1996), 445.

sex in Russia owed its legal status to the empresses who dominated the throne in the eighteenth century.[7]

For all the attention scholars lavished on the history of separate property in Russia, none of their scenarios explained why Russian women gained control of their estates during marriage more than a century before women in Western Europe came to enjoy similar privileges. Vladimirskii-Budanov and his contemporaries managed to avoid the question by glossing over the crucial distinction between the establishment of separate estates in marriage and women's active control over their fortunes. All European law codes offered women some protection by limiting the rights of men to dispose of their wives' property, and by requiring return of the dowry when wives became widows. But this security came as part of a larger package of gender tutelage that prohibited married women from behaving as economic actors in their own right and allowed them few, if any, powers of alienation. While Russian historians composed a reliable chronicle of the evolution of separate property, they fell back on tradition to account for noblewomen's right to control their estates. For their part, recent scholars have skirted the issue by dismissing women's control of property as strictly *pro forma* and arguing that women, in fact, could not exercise their prerogatives within the confines of the patriarchal family.[8]

This chapter offers a new interpretation of the development of married women's control of property in Russia. In contrast to other historians, I argue that the elevation of women's status in the law of property cannot be studied in isolation but should be located within the broader context of noble property rights in the eighteenth century. I contend that the nobility's acquiescence to laws that potentially undermined the subordination of wives to husbands speaks volumes about the state of property rights in the Imperial era. Far from being mere coincidence, the absence of public dissent in the wake of the 1753 ruling demonstrates the depth of noble concern for the establishment of corporate rights; for the elevation of individual, as opposed to family, interests in property; and for the development of a rational legal culture. Moreover, as the following chapters will demonstrate, although women were not the real focus of new laws governing their control of property, they reaped tangible benefits from the transformation of their legal status.

Separate Estates in Pre-Petrine Russia

From the late medieval era, both law and custom in Russia distinguished between the property of husband and wife. The tradition of separate estates

---

7. D. I. Meier, *Russkoe grazhdanskoe pravo* (St. Petersburg, 1861), 2: 522–523.
8. Edmondson (1984), 11; Wagner (1994), 66; Zirin (1989), xvi.

in Russian property law, combined with evidence from non-normative sources, has encouraged twentieth-century scholars to identify a pattern of feminine economic autonomy in Russia: they maintain that married women in Novgorod and Muscovy managed their own assets and, in some cases, invested in real estate and trade. In fact, noblewomen in early-modern Russia took part in a wide range of property transactions, purchasing and selling land, mortgaging estates, and making charitable bequests to monasteries.[9]

The appearance of female signatories on donations and deeds of sale goes only so far, however, in illuminating the real import of separate property in Muscovite women's lives. Pre-Petrine legal codes approached the topic of married women's control of property obliquely, at best, and attended primarily to two central problems: the protection of property women brought to marriage, and the fate of women's property if they died without heirs. With regard to the first, the law set clear bounds on men's power over their wives' estates and required husbands to obtain their wives' consent to alienate dowry land. Nonetheless, male encroachments on female property compelled lawmakers repeatedly to address the problem until the end of the seventeenth century. In three separate decrees in 1676 and 1679 the Boyar Duma prohibited men from selling their wives' patrimonial property without the latter's consent; the Duma further admonished husbands that women must give their consent freely and not be beaten into submission.[10] The status of women's property after their husbands died also featured prominently in early-modern law codes. Childless widows could expect to recover their dowries in full—a provision that suggests husbands enjoyed the use of their wives' property during marriage but were obliged to account for the use of those assets. Widows were then at liberty to appoint legatees to their dowry estates.[11]

The pre-Petrine law of property offered ample protection to wives for any patrimonial land they brought to marriage. The service holdings (*pomest'e*) a woman used as dowry, however, comprised a crucial exception to the rules of separate property. Unlike patrimonial property, service holdings were registered in the name of the groom, who was required to petition for registration of his bride's *pomest'e* before they were married[12] and who would make use of the land to support his military service. This exception further

9. Alexandre Eck, "La Situation juridique de la femme russe au moyen âge," *Recueils de la Société Jean Bodin* 12 (1962): 406–13, 415–17; Levin (1983), 166; Levy (1983), 204–5; Pushkareva (1986); Pushkareva (1997), 48; Weickhardt (1996), 8–10.

10. *PSZ*, 2: 650 (20.06.1676); 2: 751 (21.02.1679); 2: 762 (19.07.1679).

11. Levin (1983), 164–65; Levy (1983), 210; Veselovskii (1947), 44–45. The *Sudebnik* of 1589 explicitly stated that the dowry should revert to women upon their husbands' death. See Kleimola (1992), 208. Widows could not freely bequeath all the property in their possession, however: if their dowry estates were patrimonial (*pridanyia votchiny*), the latter could only be inherited by sons. See *PSZ*, 2: 674 (24.01.1677).

12. *The Muscovite Law Code*, 16: 20.

circumscribed the rights of married noblewomen, since they were far more likely to receive service-tenure land as dowry than to inherit patrimonial estates.[13] During her husband's lifetime, a wife could not stop her husband from selling or exchanging her *pomest'e*, nor could she alienate such property herself. Upon her husband's death, however, a woman could anticipate the return of her *pomest'e*, and, if she died without issue, her husband was obliged to return three-fourths of the estate, or its cash value, to her kin.[14]

Clearly, some continuity between noblewomen's prerogatives in early-modern property law and the evolution of women's control of property in the eighteenth century cannot be denied. By the close of the seventeenth century the inviolability of married women's estates was a time-honored tenet of Russian property law. At the same time, the pre-Petrine law of property barely alluded to women's control of their assets during marriage, and only fragmentary evidence survives of married women acting independently of their husbands. Even the most optimistic historians of pre-Petrine women acknowledge that widows predominated in property transactions and that they acted more often than not with sons or other male relations. Moreover, in the early-modern era women did not take part in the same range of property transactions as did their male counterparts.[15] Taken in sum, both law and practice point to an inescapable conclusion: until the eighteenth century, Russian noblewomen experienced the benefits of separate property primarily after their husbands' demise. Although founded on medieval precedent, the elimination of gender tutelage in marital property relations was a real innovation in eighteenth-century Russia.

The European Context

The elimination of gender tutelage not only marked an advance in the rights of eighteenth-century Russian noblewomen vis-à-vis their predecessors but also was unusual in the wider context of European property law. Russian scholars, admittedly, were inclined to exaggerate the degree of subjugation suffered by European women in property relations; nonetheless, elite

13. Kaiser (1988), 14–15; Kleimola (1992), 225.

14. *PSZ*, 2: 1008 (25.04.1683).

15. Eve Levin notes that land deals by women usually included participation by husbands or sons. See Levin (1983), 166. In a survey of 104 donation charters in the fourteenth and fifteenth centuries, N. Pushkareva found that 50% of donations were made by women independently, while the remainder were carried out jointly with male kin, or on behalf of the latter. Her survey does not note, however, what percentage of married women engaged in these transactions. See Pushkareva, *Zhenshchiny drevnei Rusi* (Moscow, 1989), 118. Elena Pavlova notes that although women in Northeastern Rus' in the fifteenth century made donations of land to monasteries, she found no examples of women purchasing or exchanging land. See Pavlova (1999), 126–27.

women both east and west of the Elbe suffered varying degrees of legal incapacity. At one extreme, the tradition of coverture in English common law
vested men with the authority to manage their wives' real property and to
dispose of their personal assets as they saw fit. Englishwomen could retain
control of some part of their fortune if their fathers drew up the appropriate prenuptial agreement, but such arrangements were the exception rather
than the rule.[16] Adding insult to injury, Englishwomen who received an
allowance, known as pin money, were not at liberty to spend it as they wished.
Pin money was to be spent on clothing and household items; any real property a woman purchased with her allowance came under her husband's
control, and money she saved was also considered to be his.[17] These restrictions actively discouraged women from investing in immovable property and
were no doubt an incentive to the very extravagance and conspicuous consumption that middle-class commentators deplored among women of the
aristocracy.

On the continent, the dowry system, or *régime dotal*, protected the assets
of married women. Statutory law safeguarded women's fortunes by requiring their consent to alienation of dowry funds, as well as the return of dowry
property to the wife or her surviving heirs upon her husband's death. While
the marriage endured, however, men generally enjoyed the right to administer the dowry, as well as any property that their wives inherited in the course
of their marriage.[18] Moreover, for all that the dowry was considered a

16. Mary Murray, *The Law of the Father? Patriarchy in the Transition from Feudalism to Capitalism*
(London, 1995), 66–67. Under a system of law that evolved in the seventeenth century, called
the Law of Equity, trusts could be set up for a married woman and property reserved for her
separate use. Yet these arrangements benefited only the wealthy, since the Law of Equity did
not apply when a woman's fortune was only two hundred pounds, or ten pounds per annum.
Joan Perkin maintains that in the nineteenth century only 10% of wives had separate
incomes—a figure that hardly suggests widespread economic independence among elite
Englishwomen. See Perkin, *Women and Marriage in Nineteenth-Century England* (London, 1989),
71, 74. On the limitations of separate estates, see Amy Louise Erickson, *Women and Property
in Early Modern England* (London, 1993), 107, and Mary Poovey, *Uneven Developments: The
Ideological Work of Gender in Mid-Victorian England* (Chicago, 1988), 71. Englishwomen often
compared their property rights with those of women on the continent and lamented their
disadvantages. Thus, Lady Mary Wortley Montagu noted with envy that the property of
Austrian noblewomen remained at their disposal during marriage: *The Complete Letters of Lady
Mary Wortley Montagu. Vol. I: 1708–1720* (Oxford, 1965), 273–74. English feminists in the eighteenth century also made much of the economic independence of Dutch women. G. J. Barker-
Benfield, *The Culture of Sensibility: Sex and Society in Eighteenth-Century Britain* (Chicago, 1992),
129.

17. Susan Moller Okin, "Patriarchy and Married Women's Property in England: Questions
on Some Current Views," *Eighteenth-Century Studies* 17, no. 2 (Winter 1983/84): 136; Staves
(1990), 135.

18. Viollet (1893), 795. Castilian husbands administered not only their wives' dowries but
also any property their wives inherited or otherwise acquired during marriage. David S. Reher,
Perspectives on the Family in Spain, Past and Present (Oxford, 1997), 48–49.

woman's property, more often than not she required her husband's consent if she wished to sell or mortgage her land.[19] In much of Europe, as in Russia, the laws that governed dowry property were in place to prevent men from squandering the assets of a woman's natal family rather than to promote women's economic autonomy.

The dotal regime allowed for considerable variation across the continent. At least until the eighteenth century, women in southern France were free to dispose of nondowry funds (*peripheraux*) during marriage.[20] The laws of Holland were more generous still, allowing married women to choose between the regime of community property, in which husbands managed family assets, and the rule of separate property, in which married women retained all the prerogatives of single women.[21] Among the gentry, however, men were usually the administrators of their wives' fortunes.[22] Further east, the legal status of women was also highly variable, and a gap may be discerned between written law and everyday practice. Hungarian noblewomen could sell nonpatrimonial land without their husbands' consent,[23] but their financial autonomy was limited. As one scholar of the Hungarian nobility observed, "Expenditures . . . wives wished to make beyond normal household or purely personal ones required [their] husbands' specific approval."[24] Married women in medieval Poland maintained control of immovable property that comprised their dowry[25]; from the sixteenth century, however,

19. Viollet (1893), 292.

20. Leon Abensour, *La Femme et le féminisme avant la Revolution* (Paris, 1923), 14; Barbara B. Diefendorf, "Women and Property in Ancien Regime France: Theory and Practice in Dauphine and Paris," in *Early Modern Conceptions of Property* ed. John Brewer and Susan Staves (London, 1995), 176. Ourliac and Gazzaniga [(1985), 271] state that women in the Midi eventually lost control of nondowry funds, while Diefendorf [(1995), 175] observes that the husband's consent to the alienation of his wife's property was included in legal contracts even when it was not technically required.

21. Linda Briggs Biemer, *Women and Property in Colonial New York: The Transition from Dutch to English Law, 1643–1727* (Ann Arbor, 1983), 1–3.

22. Marshall (1987), 50–51. This rule held true in the New World as well: although married women descended from Dutch settlers in colonial New York could retain control of their property through an antenuptial agreement, only a minute percentage elected this option. David E. Narrett, *Inheritance and Family Life in Colonial New York City* (Ithaca, 1992), 77–82. Married women among the gentry of South Carolina enjoyed a similar prerogative in regard to slave ownership, but, again, fewer than 2% of women who married between 1785 and 1810 executed such contracts. See Marylynn Salmon, "Women and the Law of Property in South Carolina: The Evidence from Marriage Settlements, 1730 to 1830," *William and Mary Quarterly*, 3rd ser., 39 (1982): 655–85.

23. Charles D'Eszlary, "Le Statut de la femme dans le droit Hongrois," *Recueils de la Société Jean Bodin* 12 (1962): 433.

24. Rebecca Gates-Coon, *The Landed Estates of the Esterházy Princes: Hungary during the Reforms of Maria Theresia and Joseph II* (Baltimore, 1994), 14–15.

25. Roman (1962), 397.

husbands administered their wives' dowries, as well as any property they acquired during marriage.[26]

In short, until the nineteenth century and the advent of the Napoleonic Code, the laws that regulated married women's control of property in Europe exhibited bewildering variety. This survey of the spectrum of married women's rights nonetheless reveals striking similarities between the law of property in pre-Petrine Russia and the *régime dotal* in continental Europe[27]: separate estates were designed to protect family interests, not individual women; as a result, women benefited from the institution of separate property primarily as widows. Although legal authorities took pains to restrict men's use of their wives' property, married women enjoyed limited opportunities at best to make use of their assets during their husbands' lifetime.

Extending Women's Powers of Alienation, 1700–53

In Russia, the formal separation of property in marriage dated at least from the late medieval era and provided the necessary foundation for the extension of noblewomen's control of their estates. Yet the eighteenth century witnessed a new and striking development: in matters of property, elite women acquired a fully separate identity in marriage. Noblewomen's liberation from gender tutelage should not be read as an attempt on the part of Imperial authorities to enhance the autonomy of wives vis-à-vis their husbands or, as Shcherbatov claimed, to undermine the institution of marriage. Instead, the elevation of women in the law of property was part of a larger campaign on the part of lawmakers to define the rights of individual nobles in relation to the claims of family members and the state, and to defend those rights against the abuses of local and central authorities. Noblewomen

26. *Grazhdanskie zakony gubernii tsarstva Pol'skogo. Tom 1: Grazhdanskoe ulozhenie 1825 goda* (St. Petersburg, 1875), arts. 192–93. Men could not alienate their wives' immovable property without permission, however, and women had the right to revoke their husbands' power over their property if they could prove that their estates were poorly managed: see art. 199.

27. Swedish law recognized both community and separate property in marriage. Under the law code of 1734, husbands were prohibited from selling their wives' immovable property without permission of the latter, and neither spouse was responsible for the debts of the other. However, a woman could not sell or manage property that she held in common with her husband. The law invested women with some rights of disposal over community property if they were in need while their husbands were absent or had abandoned them; however, in such cases, women were obliged to consult with their parents before alienating property. See Raoul de la Grasserie, *Les Codes Suédois de 1734* (Paris, 1895), 16: 1–7. Swedish women acquired control over their earnings only in the 1870s, when the regime of community property in marriage was abolished. Donald Meyer, *Sex and Power: The Rise of Women in America, Russia, Sweden, and Italy* (Middletown, Conn., 1987), 171.

were the unintentional but indisputable beneficiaries of the struggle to define the parameters of private property.

A single act of legislation, in 1753, entitled noblewomen to alienate their estates without their husbands' consent. The 1753 ruling, however, was not simply the whim of the sovereign but the product of a new conception of women's relation to property that gradually evolved among the nobility in the first half of the eighteenth century. Just as revisions in the law of property under Peter the Great inspired legal authorities to clarify the inheritance rights of women, these same innovations encouraged noblewomen to press for greater proprietary powers and led the courts ultimately to decide in their favor.

By far the most notable innovation during Peter's reign in regard to women's property was a Senate decree in 1715 affirming women's right to draw up deeds of purchase and mortgages in their own names.[28] Russian scholars traditionally identified this ruling as the turning point in women's progression toward independent control of their property. But the 1715 decree was never intended to authorize women to act without their husbands' consent and, indeed, made no mention of women trying to do so. The true significance of the ruling was not that it permitted women to act independently or to take part in property transactions for the first time, but that it established their right to engage in property transactions involving former service-tenure estates. Noblewomen purchased and sold patrimonial estates throughout the seventeenth century, albeit rarely and overwhelmingly as widows. Notarial records demonstrate that before 1715 noblewomen took part in less than 5 percent of estate sales and purchased land or serfs on infrequent occasions; moreover, while men's transactions involved both service-tenure and hereditary estates, women bought and sold only the latter.[29] The Senate decree of 1715 specified that women could now engage in transactions involving both *pomestia* and *votchiny*; in short, the ruling concerned the type of land that women might sell, not women's right to dispose of their assets.

Both the wording of the act and subsequent practice reveal that the 1715 decree did not relieve women of the obligation to obtain their husbands' permission for sales of property. During the first half of the eighteenth century, not only were married women less likely than widows to take part in land transactions,[30] but also they routinely stated in deeds of sale that they

28. *PSZ*, 5: 2.952 (04.11.1715).

29. See RGADA, f. 1209, op. 4, ch. 1, ed. khr. 2624 (Pomestnyi prikaz, 1701–3); f. 1209, op. 4, ch. 1, ed. khr. 2920 (Vladimirskii stol, 1699–1701). Female buyers and sellers are also underrepresented in published sources. See, in particular, *Akty iuridicheskie, ili sobranie form starinnogo deloproizvodstva* (St. Petersburg, 1838), *Akty, otnosiashchiesia do iuridicheskogo byta drevnei Rossii* (St. Petersburg, 1864), vol. 2, and the appendix to Debol'skii (1903), 416–30.

30. See chapter 4, Table 4.3.

sold or mortgaged their estates with their husbands' consent (*s vedoma moego muzha*) and produced letters from their husbands when the transaction took place. On some occasions the contents of these letters are reproduced in the notarial records. When the wife of Lieutenant Polivanov sold her dowry estate of forty serfs in 1751, she presented the following letter from her husband: "My dear (*svet moi*), Ustinia Feksistovna, greetings! The dowry village of Cheblakovo in Erenskii district that you mortgaged with my knowledge to Titular Counselor Kudriavstov for four hundred and fifty rubles cannot be redeemed (*vykupom neispravit'sia*). If you wish to sell this village to someone, I permit it and will not object, since this village is your dowry and we, as you yourself know, are not without need of money. Your husband, Mikhail Polivanov."[31] In another transaction later that year, the wife of Ensign Selevachev sold the property she had inherited from a previous husband for one hundred rubles and also produced evidence of her husband's consent to the transaction. "Maria Petrovna, greetings! If you are in need of money, then I allow you to sell property from your holdings in Iaroslavskii district . . . and will not dispute the sale."[32]

Men's power over their wives' persons and property was in no way undermined by Peter's decree authorizing women to take part in real estate transactions. Legal authorities acknowledged that in practice, married men made no distinction between their own and their wives' property.[33] Women continued to defer to their husbands in property affairs, as in all other matters. When the widow Lomanita contracted herself to the service of Daria Kishkina, she did so only with the permission of Daria's husband, Stolnik Kishkin.[34] Another woman in Vladimir district sold her dowry serf in 1717 because her husband ordered her to do so (*po prikazu muzha*),[35] whereas Marfa Surmina accepted the conditions of her mother's will in 1736 "with the knowledge" of her husband, Roman Vorontsov.[36] Comparing the inheritance laws of several European nations with Russian customs during Peter's reign, an official in the Chancellery of Foreign Affairs (*Posol'skii prikaz*) observed that in Scotland a husband and wife could draw up a contract between them that did not conform to the rules of intestate succession. By contrast, he noted, Muscovite law precluded any agreement "of a wife with

31. RGADA, f. 282 (Iustits-kollegiia), op. 1, ed. khr. 394, ll. 403–4.

32. RGADA, f. 282, op. 1, ed. khr. 394, ll. 575–76. See also ll. 854–57.

33. A decree in 1740 allowed for recruits to be levied from the villages of a retired officer's wife as well as his own, "since husbands use their wives' villages as they use their own, and for this reason they are required, upon retirement, to declare openly their own as well as their wives' dowry villages." Quoted in A. S. Paramonov, *O zakonodatel'stve Anny Ioannovny* (St. Petersburg, 1904), 161–62.

34. RGADA, f. 615, op. 1, ed. khr. 1956, l. 3 (Vladimir, 1717).

35. RGADA, f. 615, op. 1, ed. khr. 1956, l. 21.

36. P. I. Shchukin, *Sbornik starinnykh bumag* (Moscow, 1901), 9: 49.

her husband" at the time of marriage, because in Russia "husbands rule absolutely over their wives (*vo vsem vlastvuet zhenoiu muzh*)."[37]

The Registration of Dowry Property

Despite the persistence of men's authority over their wives' property affairs, during the first half of the eighteenth century the courts slowly reinforced the boundary separating men's and women's property in marriage. A close reading of notarial practice reveals that limitations on the separation of property in marriage persisted from the seventeenth century yet eventually gave way to a new conception of women's relation to property among both legal authorities and the nobility as a group. By far the most compelling evidence of this change comes from the registration of dowry estates: without any prompting from above, in the 1740s the courts gave up the practice of registering dowry land under the name of the groom and elected instead to register such property in the bride's name.

In theory, the 1714 Law of Single Inheritance should have put an end to petitions from men for registration of their wives' dowry estates. When Peter the Great eliminated the distinction between patrimonial (*votchina*) and service (*pomest'e*) estates, he also severed the link between landholding and military service that had worked to restrict women's property rights.[38] Under the new regime, the *pomest'e* disappeared and women's dowries were no longer intended to finance their husbands' service obligations; hence, the practice of men petitioning for ownership of their wives' dowries, logically, should have come to an end. Yet notarial practice followed slowly in the wake of normative legal change. Husbands continued to petition the Land College for registration of their wives' dowry property, and women themselves offered petitions in support of their husbands' claims. Over time, however, these petitions died out and were replaced by petitions from noblewomen requesting registration of dowry estates on their own behalf.[39]

The persistence of male requests for registration of dowry land underscores the limits of married women's control of property before midcentury.

37. RGADA, f. 181 (Rukopisnoe sobranie biblioteki MGAMID), ed. khr. 162, l. 9.

38. On the impact of this development on women's property rights, see Weickhardt (1996), 21–22.

39. These petitions survive in the records of the Land College. See RGADA, f. 1209, op. 84, ch. 14. For petitions from men requesting registration of their wives' dowries, see f. 1209, op. 84, ch. 14, ed. khr. 14, 52, 58, 84, 154, 158, 171, 193, 409. The last of these petitions dates from 1744. Other examples appear of women petitioning for registration of their dowries in their husbands' names: see f. 1209, op. 84, ch. 14, ed. khr. 58 (1715), 158 (1723), 520 (1748). For petitions from women requesting registration of dowry estates in their own names, see f. 1209, op. 84, ch. 14, ed. khr. 545, 630, 636, 642, 875, 986, 1543. The first of these petitions dates from 1749; the last, from 1776.

Not surprisingly, Russian noblemen proved reluctant to relinquish control of their wives' dowries, even as the category of service land fell out of use. Indeed, some male petitioners assumed that the repeal of service holdings had by no means put an end to their control of their wives' dowries but actually extended their rights over any land their wives brought to marriage. A few petitioners maintained that they had married "before the points" (*do punktov*) of 1714 and alluded to their right to the service allotments (*prozhitochnoe pomest'e*) their wives had brought to marriage.[40] In 1718, however, Captain Podkhomskii explicitly requested registration to him of his wife's "dowry service and patrimonial estates" (*pridanyia pomestia i votchiny*).[41] The majority of male petitioners after 1714 ignored the old distinctions and simply requested registration of their wives' "immovable property" (*nedvizhimoe imenie*) when they married.[42]

By the mid-eighteenth century, a striking change appears in the records of the Land College: officials no longer accepted husbands' petitions for the registration of their wives' dowries but insisted that women's dowry estates should be registered under their own names. While husbands initially may have submitted requests for dowry property to be registered to their wives,[43] the overwhelming pattern was for women themselves to petition the Land College on their own behalf. Thus, Avdotia Iablonskaia petitioned the Land College in 1749, stating that her father had awarded her a dowry that year of twenty *chetverti* of land with peasants. She presented a copy of the dowry agreement and requested that the college register the estate to her (*onoe nedvizhimoe imenie za mnoiu . . . spravit'*).[44] After 1753, this pattern intensified and the Land College expressed dwindling interest in husbands' petitions. One petitioner, Sergeant Tokmachev, waited fourteen years after his marriage to clarify the status of his wife's dowry. His request in 1757 was accompanied by an appeal from his wife, Irina, who wrote that she had found, among her personal papers (*mezhdu domashnikh svoikh pisem*), the documents proving her claim to the estate. The Land College responded by registering the estate in Irina Tokmacheva's name; in their discussion of her right to

40. RGADA, f. 1209, op. 84, ch. 14, ed. khr. 58, l. 1 (1715); f. 1209, op. 84, ch. 14, ed. khr. 193 (1729); f. 1209, op. 84, ch. 14, ed. khr. 52 (1714); f. 1209, op. 84, ch. 14, ed. khr. 154 (1722).

41. RGADA, f. 1209, op. 84, ch. 14, ed. khr. 84, l. 1 (1718).

42. RGADA, f. 1209, op. 84, ch. 14, ed. khr. 171, l. 1 (1726); f. 1209, op. 84, ch. 14, ed. khr. 409 (1744).

43. Lee Farrow gives two examples of men petitioning for registration of dowry property to their wives. See Farrow (2000), 115–16, and RGADA, f. 1209, op. 84, ch. 14, ed. khr. 352 (1742); f. 1209, kn. 14640, ed. khr. 2, ll. 16–17 (1754). Examples of fathers, mothers, and brothers petitioning for registration of dowry property to female kin after 1753 include the following: RGADA, f. 1209, op. 84, ch. 14, ed. khr. 793 (1756; petition from brother); f. 1209, op. 84, ch. 14, ed. khr. 837 (1757; petition from mother); f. 1209, op. 84, ch. 14, ed. khr. 1539 (1776; petition from father); f. 1209, op. 84, ch. 14, ed. khr. 1744 (1785; joint petition from father and daughter, in which the daughter also renounces any further inheritance).

44. RGADA, f. 1209, op. 84, ch. 14, ed. khr. 545, l. 1.

the land, however, they ignored her husband's petition altogether.[45] Sadly, we can draw no conclusions about the use of property during marriage from this development. Nonetheless, the recognition of married women as legal entities and owners of dowry property independent of their husbands marked a significant break with seventeenth-century arrangements and was an important precursor to the 1753 ruling.

Noblewomen's Demands for Control of Property

The overwhelming majority of eighteenth-century noblewomen offered no resistance to constraints on their financial independence. Yet sufficient numbers of women actively sought more power over their holdings to encourage lawmakers to reinterpret the 1715 decree. Thus, in the interest of preventing fraudulent sales of property, the Senate ruled in 1733 that when a representative carried out a transaction, the original deed of purchase should be kept in the notarial office (*krepostnaia kontora*) and the representative should take an oath that the letter he presented was genuine. The deed then was to be recorded in a register, and a copy of the document given to those who took part in the transaction. Significantly, female misbehavior prompted this ruling on bureaucratic procedure: a number of men had complained to the courts that their wives had sold property without their consent. The Senate cited the example of Matrena Griaznova, who sold her dowry villages to Captain Kolychev for one thousand rubles and slyly claimed that the letter from her husband had been lost. An incensed Midshipman Griaznov wrote to his son-in-law, Prince Viazemskii, that he had no debts and was not in need of capital; consequently, he had given his wife neither written nor verbal permission to sell her villages. Griaznov instructed his son-in-law to take the necessary steps to recover the estate, adding that his wife deserved any punishment meted out to her. Another woman, Anna Durnova, mortgaged her estate for five hundred rubles, also with the help of a buyer willing to overlook her failure to produce a letter from her husband. Since proprietors of both sexes could alienate property through representatives, opportunities to forge deeds of sale were abundant. The new procedural rules thus were designed to minimize fraud. As a member of the Justice College acknowledged, however, sales carried out on the basis of "letters from husbands to wives, and from wives to husbands" figured prominently in fraudulent transactions.[46]

As noblewomen persisted in their attempts to alienate property without their husbands' consent, the Senate wrestled more than once with the

45. RGADA, f. 1209, op. 84, ch. 14, ed. khr. 857, ll. 1, 7, 21.
46. *PSZ*, 9: 6.487 (21.09.1733).

dilemma of married women's control of property. The debate was resolved at last in women's favor in 1753, in the case reviled by Prince Shcherbatov. Aksinia, the wife of Major Ivan Golovin, instigated the suit, complaining to the Senate that she wished to sell her house serfs but that the Justice College in Moscow refused to register the sale without her husband's consent. Golovina explained that she did not get along with her husband, and since they did not live together, she could not obtain his consent to the sale. She argued that the Justice College had acted in violation of the 1715 ruling, which had explicitly authorized women to execute deeds of purchase in their own names (*v protivnost' ukazu 715 goda, po kotoromu tochno ot zhenskikh person kreposti pisat' dozvoleno*), and petitioned the Senate to instruct the college to register the sale.

After lengthy debate the Senate ruled in favor of Golovina. The senators began by reviewing decisions made by the Justice College in 1744 and 1752 to prohibit women from executing deeds of purchase without their husbands' knowledge, admitting that in neither case had the Senate responded to a plea from the college to pass a resolution on the legality of such sales. The Justice College had reported that it was well aware of the 1715 decree on sales of property by women, but hesitated to implement the ruling without confirmation from the Senate (*tokmo de Iustits-Kollegiia onago soboiu uchinit' ne smeet*). Next, the senators considered the problem of fraudulent transactions that had culminated in the 1733 ruling on procedures for the registration of sales through representatives. They then produced evidence in favor of women's status as independent owners of property, such as a 1677 decree which stated that widows could reclaim patrimonial property sold by their husbands without their knowledge, and rulings in 1679 that forbade husbands to sell their wives' property or to force their wives to part with their assets. Another ruling in 1680 had established further that the sale of a woman's dowry *votchina* was legal if it bore the signatures of both husband and wife, or of the wife alone. The senators surveyed restrictions on the sale of immovable property that Peter the Great had enacted, all of which applied to sellers of either sex. They also touched more than once on the oft-cited 1715 decree, which they argued had already empowered women to sell their dowries and other immovable property in their possession. At last, the Senate concluded that none of these previous rulings had explicitly required women to obtain their husbands' consent to property transactions. In short, Golovina, and henceforth all married women, could sell her property without permission from her husband.[47]

The senators' curious disregard for gender is the most noteworthy feature of the 1753 ruling. Their discussion focused exclusively on bureaucratic procedure and made no reference to female subordination in marriage as ratio-

47. *PSZ*, 13: 10.111 (14.06.1753).

nale for restricting their property rights, as was often the case in European legal codes. Moreover, their willingness to accept the 1715 ruling as evidence for women's autonomy in property relations marked a clear departure from the judgments of their predecessors. The senators reasoned that since they could not identify a single ruling that explicitly forbade women's unrestricted disposal of property in Russian law, there were no grounds not to allow it. They chose instead to focus on two key issues: the protection of women's property from their husbands (which had been affirmed in the seventeenth century) and existing restrictions on the sale of immovable property (none of which distinguished between the sexes). Since seventeenth-century decisions and Peter's ruling in 1715 had singled out women's signatures to deeds of sale not only as necessary, but sufficient, to prove the legality of the transaction, there were no legal grounds to require women to obtain consent for the sale of their own estates (*na sobstvennoe ikh imenie*).

This pragmatic approach stands in sharp contrast to the attitude of Western European lawmakers, who believed that property relations should mirror the hierarchical relationship of husband and wife and that separate property violated the very essence of marriage.[48] Ironically, at the same time Russian legislators ruled in favor of granting women financial autonomy, lawmakers in at least two Western European countries confronted a similar dilemma—and decided that eliminating gender tutelage in property relations was, in the words of one scholar, "intolerable."[49] Legal innovations in eighteenth-century England provided for separate trusts for women but stopped short of allowing married women control over their capital.[50] In France, when the revolutionary government overturned the laws of the old regime, it pronounced married women independent agents in matters of property. By 1804, however, the Napoleonic Code gave gender tutelage a new lease on life, not only in France but also in nations that fell within the empire's sphere of influence.[51]

Unlike their European counterparts, Russian lawmakers took the principle of separate property to its logical conclusion and awarded married

48. See Diefendorf (1995), 175, and Poovey (1988), 73–74.

49. Susan Staves, "Pin Money," in *Studies in Eighteenth-Century Culture*, ed. O. M. Brack Jr. (Madison, 1985), 14: 64. The laws governing married women's control of property became more restrictive after women used their limited financial independence to invest in stocks during the height of the South Sea Bubble. In 1685, 20% of shareholders in the East India Company were women. See Catherine Ingrassia, "The Pleasure of Business and the Business of Pleasure: Gender, Credit, and the South Sea Bubble," in *Studies in Eighteenth-Century Culture* (Baltimore, 1995), 24: 191–210, and John Carswell, *The South Sea Bubble* (London, 1960), 11.

50. Staves (1990), 222.

51. Jennifer Birkett, "'A Mere Matter of Business': Marriage, Divorce, and the French Revolution," in *Marriage and Property: Women and Marital Customs in History*, ed. Elizabeth Craik (Aberdeen, 1984), 133–34. Not only could Frenchwomen not dispose of their property during marriage but also they were forbidden to claim an inheritance without their husbands' permission. See also Ostrogorski (1893), 208–32.

women full powers of alienation over their estates. Russian legislators did not discuss how changes in property relations might affect the institution of marriage. Instead, they reviewed all previous statutes that established the separation of property in marriage and eliminated the single contradiction in their implementation, thus introducing an important divergence in the history of women's property rights in Russia and the West.

Noble Reaction to Women's Control of Property

Virtually no record exists of contemporary reaction to the monumental change in married women's property rights. From the beginning of the eighteenth century, Russian nobles were preoccupied with matters of property and expressed open displeasure with those dimensions of property law that did not meet their approval. In particular, nobles had vehemently opposed Peter the Great's Law of Single Inheritance, which they circumvented through illegal land transactions. Delegates to the 1767 Legislative Commission aired their grievances over laws governing provisions for widows from their husbands' estates, as well as a wide variety of restrictions on the alienation of immovable property.[52] Among the many complaints about property arrangements recorded during the meetings of the commission, however, only one objection appears to the law allowing married women to dispose freely of their property. A legislator from Kostroma province complained that too many noblewomen sold or mortgaged serfs to support their extravagant lifestyle, with the result that their husbands inherited nothing when they died. To prevent women from squandering their estates, the legislator proposed that they should be forbidden to dispose of property without their husbands' consent.[53]

The delegate from Kostroma was not alone in objecting to noblewomen's economic autonomy. The deputies appointed by Catherine the Great in 1770 to compile a new law code would have turned back the clock and granted husbands the power to manage their wives' dowries during marriage, "for the overall benefit of the family," with the routine proviso that neither spouse might sell or mortgage the property of the other; on another occasion, they added that wives should be forbidden to sell their estates if this conflicted with the interests of the family.[54]

Despite these objections to women's new legal status, a significant portion

---

52. Wilson R. Augustine, "Notes toward a Portrait of the Eighteenth-Century Nobility," *Canadian Slavic Studies* 4, no. 3 (Fall 1970): 396–97; *Sbornik imperatorskogo russkogo istoricheskogo obshchestva* (hereafter *SIRIO*) (1896), 4: 419, 424; (1871), 8: 539–540.

53. *SIRIO*, (1869), 4: 284.

54. RGADA, f. 342, op. 1, ed. khr. 220, ch. 2, ll. 21, 106. Neither of these proposals were adopted.

of the nobility displayed surprising receptivity to the extension of women's property rights. Notarial practice offers compelling evidence that, far from being imposed from above, the increasing separation of property in marriage reflected the preferences of the elite. In particular, the language of dowry agreements argues in favor of a transformation of women's relation to property: by the second half of the eighteenth century many noble families chose to view the dowry as a contract between parents and daughters, rather than with prospective sons-in-law. The shift in dowry conventions did not come about in response to a decree from a legislative body but emerged gradually in the wake of the 1753 ruling.

Dowry agreements in the seventeenth century followed a given formula in which a father gave his daughter in marriage and bestowed her portion upon his son-in-law. The consent of daughters to the arrangement was so irrelevant that their signature to the document was not required. In one typical agreement, drawn up in 1695, Boyar Feodor Lopukhin married his daughter to Prince Kurakin and made over a portion of his patrimonial estate and one hundred serfs to the prince.[55] The boyar's daughter did not figure in this document in any way, aside from the fact of being given in marriage by her father to her future husband. Until the mid-eighteenth century most donors adhered faithfully to this pattern: in essence, the dowry was a contract between parents and sons-in-law, and therefore bore the signature of the latter. When young women were given in marriage, property was relinquished on their behalf, but it was bestowed on their husbands to be managed for the common good of the family. The opening lines of the dowry contract articulated noble assumptions about women's relation to property and underscored the real purpose of separate estates. Although the latter were sacrosanct, they existed to protect family interests rather than to allow married women independent control over their fortunes.

From the mid-eighteenth century, however, the conventions governing dowry agreements showed signs of change. For the first time noble families began to conceive of the dowry as an agreement between parents and daughters. This development was by no means universal: in the notarial records of the Justice College in Moscow, the old formula persisted into the nineteenth century.[56] Yet dowry contracts from provincial *krepostnye knigi* and from family papers offer an intriguing contrast. In many of the contracts recorded in the provinces, daughters signed the agreement themselves or, if they were illiterate, asked a representative to sign for them. Clearly, in the eyes of many families responsibility for adhering to property arrangements had shifted from the groom to the bride.

55. *Arkhiv kniazia F. A. Kurakina*, ed. M. I. Semevskii (St. Petersburg, 1894), 6: 161–64.
56. See, for example, the dowries recorded in Tsentral'nyi gosudarstvennyi istoricheskii arkhiv Moskvy (hereafter TsGIAM), f. 50, op. 14, ed. khr. 2100 (1810).

The recasting of the dowry as an agreement between parents and daughters was manifest from the opening sentence of the contract. Donors now granted the deed to their daughters, rather than to their sons-in-law, and invoked the former's responsibility for collecting taxes, supplying serf recruits, and carrying out other obligations as the owners of land and serfs.[57] Thus, whereas in 1742 Anna Nelidova drew up an agreement in which she made over her daughter's dowry to her son-in-law, Lieutenant Aleksandr Sukhotin, in 1771 Avdotia Trusova granted her daughter a dowry of thirty-four serfs "in perpetual and hereditary possession."[58] Lieutenant Andrei Saburov acknowledged in 1771 that he had received in full all of the property described in the dowry agreement of his wife, Maria Zubareva, but the contract specified that Zubareva bore responsibility for all taxes on her dowry estate of fifty-six serfs. Zubareva also signed the contract in the presence of six witnesses.[59] By 1845, when Sofia Mikhailovna Vorontsova married Count Andrei Shuvalov, the groom received only a brief mention in the document: Vorontsova's dowry was devised as a contract solely between her parents, her brother, and herself.[60]

The gradual, albeit partial, transformation of notarial practice, unlike Senate and Imperial decrees, underscores the evolution of noblewomen as legal entities in their own right and goes far in illuminating noble attitudes toward female property ownership. The 1753 Senate ruling by no means overturned traditional property relations: families continued to look upon the dowry as property destined for family maintenance, and as often as not, husbands went on to manage their wives' dowry estates. At the same time, the willingness of individual nobles to act according to the spirit of the 1753 decree signaled a countervailing trend. Rather than resisting the elevation of women's legal status, these nobles took the law a step further when they affirmed the legal accountability of their daughters and created a more distinct boundary between the estates of husband and wife. The abundance of dowry agreements signed by women, or made out in their names, after 1753 reveals that a significant group within the nobility was receptive to the extension of women's property rights. By refashioning the dowry as a contract

57. For some examples of this practice, see RGADA, f. 615, op. 1, ed. khr. 4220, l. 42 (Kashin, 1753); f. 615; op. 1, ed. khr. 2045, l. 72 and 81 (Vladimir, 1776); f. 615, op. 1, ed. khr. 5565, l. 1 (Kursk, 1775); f. 615, op. 1, ed. khr. 11237, l. 77 (Simbirsk, 1777); f. 615, op. 1, ed. khr. 11578, ll. 8–9; f. 615, op. 1, ed. khr. 11592, l. 36 (Tambov, 1777, 1779); f. 1278 (Stroganovy), op. 1, ed. khr. 579, ll. 1–2 (1800); f. 1274 (Paniny-Bludovy), op. 1, ed. khr. 1318, ll. 1–2 (1868); RGIA, f. 840 (Batiushkovy), op. 1, ed. khr. 31, ll. 5–6 (1753); f. 942 (Zubovy), op. 1, ed. khr. 35, l. 1 (1821); f. 1088 (Sheremetevy), op. 1, ed. khr. 756 (1808); Gosudarstvennyi arkhiv Tverskoi oblasti (hereafter GA Tverskoi oblasti), f. 668, op. 1, ed. khr. 6444, ll. 33–34; f. 668, op. 1, ed. khr. 6447, ll. 52–53 (Kashin, 1806, 1808).

58. RGIA, f. 840, op. 1, ed. khr. 31, ll. 4, 7.

59. RGIA, f. 1044 (Saburovy), op. 1, ed. khr. 578 (1771).

60. GIM, f. 60, op. 1, ed. khr. 434, ll. 1–2.

between brides and dowry donors, these nobles chose to enhance women's control over their estates without any prompting from above.

In the nineteenth century, this trend culminated in the gradual disappearance of the dowry. By midcentury, parents no longer drew up marriage agreements but elected instead to transfer property to their daughters through deeds of gift (*darstvennye zapisi*) or deeds of separation (*otdel'nye zapisi*).[61] These documents surface on frequent occasions in notarial records at the same moment that the number of dowries diminished; moreover, while sons were sometimes recipients of such gifts, daughters were far more likely to benefit from this type of transfer.[62] The transition from dowry to gift was the logical outcome of placing the dowry in women's hands, and with it married women's control of their estates was reinforced.[63]

Women's Property and the Insecurity of Property

Establishing the receptivity of Russian nobles to the extension of women's property rights raises as many questions as it answers. Why, in a society as patriarchal as that of eighteenth-century Russia, were noblemen willing to allow women the option of parting with their dowries without male sanction? The institution of separate property already offered women ample protection for the assets they brought to marriage and safeguarded the interests of women's natal families. By extending women's powers of alienation over their estates, however, the state moved beyond the protection of family interests and recognized the property rights of women as individuals. In doing so, Russian lawmakers acted well in advance of their counterparts in Western Europe.

To begin, a comparison with the evolution of Anglo-American women's

61. In her study of marriage in eighteenth-century Russia, Robin Bisha [(1993), 136] noted that she found no dowries dated after 1845. According to Gaby Donicht, who is writing a dissertation on marital discord in late Imperial Russia, the absence of dowry agreements in the second half of the nineteenth century worked to the benefit of men; she argues that husbands expected parents to hand over the dowry to them and objected vehemently when their wives asserted their right to their property. The cases she cites, however, overwhelmingly concern cash rather than landed property. See Donicht, "The Idea of Morality in the Russian Noble Family of Late Imperial Russia, 1870–1914" (paper presented at the Third Carleton Conference on the History of the Family, May 15–17, 1997).

62. *Sanktpeterburgskie senatskie ob"iavleniia po sudebnym, rasporiadiitel'nym, politseiskim i kazannym delam* (St. Petersburg, 1859), #1082, 1084, 1101, 1102, 1109, 1513, 1865, 1867, 1868, 1980, 1981, 2005, 2032, 2374, 12180, 14591. In this publication, I found no dowry agreements. Daughters who received gifts of property were not automatically excluded from inheritance unless they waived their right to inherit.

63. Discussions by lawmakers of the status of women's property in marriage focused exclusively on the dowry; there was no question of men enjoying legal power over property that women inherited before or during the course of marriage.

legal status is instructive. Historians of married women's property in England and the United States have argued that separate estates appeared in response to the shift from an economy in which landed property was central to one based on stocks, bonds, and other forms of personal property.[64] They also have observed that creating separate estates provided a means for families to avoid financial ruin when men declared bankruptcy. Although Russian legal specialists never invoked the financial interests of the nobility to explain women's property rights, August von Haxthausen offered this interpretation in an account of his sojourn in Russia. Commenting on the amount of real estate concentrated in the hands of women, Haxthausen went on to say:

> The entire development of social life has been leading up to this. Nowhere does property change hands as frequently as in Russia. In public service, in commerce, in manufacturing, and in the trades large fortunes are quickly amassed but are lost just as quickly. . . . Poor business ventures (and at bottom the Russian is a gambler) destroy the merchant and manufacturer. In such cases the families are completely ruined. This occurs all too frequently, and from the outset the husband has to prepare for such probabilities by providing the family with a financial reserve. He puts a part of the property, specifically the house and the land, in his wife's name; at the beginning it is more *pro forma*, but after a time it becomes a legally binding arrangement. In this way the moveable property has come to belong to the husband, whereas the wife holds the real property. The latter remains even after her husband's property has been scattered to the four winds.[65]

Haxthausen could have applied his argument to the nobility with similar effect, as noblemen took abundant advantage of separate estates to elude their creditors in the nineteenth century. As a rationale for the appearance of women's control of property in the mid-eighteenth century, however, it misses the mark. The 1753 ruling did not make explicit provision for absolving wives from responsibility for their husbands' debts; indeed, women's accountability for their husbands' financial misdemeanors comprised a murky area of property law throughout the century. In the seventeenth century, the *Ulozhenie* held a widow responsible for her husband's debts if she inherited any part of his estate; later rulings specified that a widow's dowry was not liable to her husband's creditors.[66] The problem of female

---

64. Norma Basch, *In the Eyes of the Law: Women, Marriage, and Property in Nineteenth-Century New York* (Ithaca, 1982), 114; Okin (Winter 1983/84), 125; Carole Shammas, "Re-assessing the Married Women's Property Acts," *Journal of Women's History* 6, no. 1 (Spring, 1994): 25.

65. Haxthausen (1972), 23.

66. *The Muscovite Law Code*, 10: 132, 207; *PSZ*, 1: 210 (25.07.1657). Nevolin argued that canon law forbade creditors to hold women responsible for their husbands' debts; as a result, from the medieval era creditors could not seize women's dowries. By contrast, Vladimirskii-Budanov believed that women escaped liability for their husbands' debts only in the late seventeenth

accountability for male profligacy remained a point of contention in the eighteenth century. Nonetheless, the principle that the wives of debtors should not sacrifice their dowry property was followed with little variation[67] and long predated the 1753 ruling on married women's control of property. Thus, Haxthausen not only overlooked the fact that the separation of assets in Russian law predated women's active control of their estates, but also failed to acknowledge that noble (and merchant) interests could have been equally well served without allowing women power to alienate their property. The experience of women in England and America demonstrates that separate estates were not necessarily accompanied by women's prerogative to dispose of their assets. More often than not, a guardian—male kin, or even husbands—controlled the estate, presumably for women's own good.[68]

In a critique of the emergence of separate estates in early-modern England, one scholar has argued that families in sixteenth- and seventeenth-century England became concerned with protecting their daughters' fortunes precisely because "personal, as opposed to real, property was becoming an increasingly important part of the fortunes of daughters." A variety of devices already existed to prevent husbands from disposing of their wives' real estate; movable property, however, could not be entailed and, according to common law, came under a husband's power as long as the marriage endured.[69] In antebellum Virginia, where the law of coverture was not revoked until 1877, separate estates were an anomaly before 1810. As Suzanne Lebsock has demonstrated, however, between 1821 and 1860 almost six hundred separate estates were established in the town of Petersburg, Virginia. Yet Lebsock does not imagine that families set up separate estates to encourage female autonomy. "The growth of separate estates constituted a major advance for women of the middle and upper classes, but it began in expediency, a response to the failures of scores of individual men," she argues. Only one-fourth of the agreements Lebsock surveyed permitted

century. See Nevolin (1851), 1: 101–7; Vladimirskii-Budanov (1909), 454–56. In both early-modern and Imperial Russia, authorities held the heirs of the deceased responsible for his debts; the ambiguity surrounding a widow's liability to her husband's creditors hinged on whether or not she could be considered her husband's heir. Since spouses were not related by kinship, although widows received one-seventh of their husbands' estates, they were not considered their heirs. See Wagner (1994), 229–30.

67. In 1758, for example, the Senate decreed that if an official was found guilty of stealing from the state treasury and could not repay the money, the estate of his father could be held liable, but the assets of his wife and mother should not be touched: *PSZ*, 15: 10.789 (09.01.1758). See also *PSZ*, 14: 10.238 (18.05.1754). The property of merchants' wives was subject to seizure according to the Statute on Bankruptcy of 1740 [*PSZ*, 11: 8.300 (15.12.1740)]; however, by 1800, the property of merchant wives was exempt, as long as the latter did not take part in their husbands' business affairs: *PSZ*, 26: 19.692 (19.12.1800) (*Ustav o bankrotakh*).

68. Suzanne Lebsock, *The Free Women of Petersburg: Status and Culture in a Southern Town, 1784–1860* (New York, 1984), 57–67; Okin (1983/84), 124–25.

69. Okin (1983/84), 124–25.

women to sell their property, and less than a fifth allowed women to make a will disposing of their assets.[70]

The context in which Russian noblewomen gained control of their fortunes bore little resemblance to the social and economic environment of their Anglo-American counterparts. Eighteenth-century Russia did not witness a transition in capital formation or the structure of the economy, as was the case in England. Nor did financial depression prompt legal innovation on the part of Russian lawmakers, as it would in antebellum America. The imperatives that lay at the heart of the transformation of Russian women's legal status were, by contrast, purely political. In short, the efforts of the nobility to bolster the security of private property in the eighteenth century culminated in the reconfiguration of married women's property rights.

Significantly, the 1753 ruling that granted women control of their fortunes was passed at a moment when the nobility had begun to press for estate privileges similar to those of their European counterparts.[71] Insecurity of person and property was an inescapable fact of life for the eighteenth-century Russian nobility. Until the reign of Catherine the Great, Russian nobles lacked the corporate rights enjoyed by European elites and risked losing their estates if they fell out of favor or were suspected of treason; indeed, a whole series of misdemeanors warranted seizure of noble property.[72] One scholar's assertion that confiscation of property for political crime was a rare occurrence may be a valid point,[73] but it fails to appreciate the psychology of a nobility traumatized first by Peter the Great's attempts to ride roughshod over the sacred custom of partible inheritance and later by the spectacle of mass exile and executions during the reign of Anna Ivanovna.[74] Through-

70. Lebsock (1984), 57–67.

71. Carol S. Leonard, *Reform and Regicide: The Reign of Peter III of Russia* (Bloomington, 1993), 49–50. Delegates at the Legislative Commission in 1767 proposed that the privilege of owning settled estates should be restricted to hereditary nobles and forbidden to officers who achieved noble rank through military service. See *SIRIO* (1869), 4: 209.

72. The *Ulozhenie* and subsequent rulings in the eighteenth century threatened confiscation on such grounds as treason and evasion of military service. *The Muscovite Law Code*, 2: 5; 7: 20; 16: 51; 17: 39, 42. Peter III's Manifesto on the Freedom of the Nobility liberated noblemen from state service but also specified that nobles who failed to educate their children or who refused to return from abroad when recalled risked confiscation of their estates. See Leonard (1993), 41.

73. George G. Weickhardt, "Was There Private Property in Muscovite Russia?" *Slavic Review* 53, no. 2 (Summer 1994): 532–34.

74. Quoting the findings of T. Chernikova on arrests and exiles during the reign of Anna Ivanovna, Evgenii Anisimov absolves the latter of excessive brutality but also admits to the "tradition of political repression" at the Russian court. Evgenii V. Anisimov, "Empress Anna Ivanovna, 1730–1740," in *The Emperors and Empresses of Russia: Rediscovering the Romanovs*, ed. Donald J. Raleigh (Armonk, N.Y., 1996), 61–62. See also T. V. Chernikova, "Gosudarevo slovo i delo vo vremena Anny Ioannovny," *Istoriia SSSR*, no. 5 (1989): 155–63. Lee Farrow notes that P. N. Baranov's inventory of Senate decrees between 1725 and 1762 reveal more than two hundred references to confiscated property. See Farrow (2000), 219.

out the eighteenth century the Russian nobility remained vitally concerned with the limits of security of its status and property.[75]

The specter of confiscation haunted the proposals of noble reformers into the nineteenth century, and with good reason.[76] Although Catherine II's Charter to the Nobility in 1785 stipulated that noblemen could not be deprived of their estates without trial, it stopped short of guaranteeing the inviolability of noble status or property; moreover, the charter defined the crimes meriting confiscation as broadly as possible.[77] Nobles who indulged in deeds "irreconcilable with . . . noble dignity"[78] forfeited their status and could be subject to corporal punishment and exile. Thus, in 1800 the wife of Major Tatarinov was stripped of her nobility, beaten with a knout, and dispatched to Siberia after harboring brigands.[79] Arbitrary state action against noble property also persisted after the Charter to the Nobility was issued.[80] As late as 1834, Nicholas I decreed that Russian citizens who left the country without permission would forfeit their property. One victim of the ruling, Admiral Chichakov, wrote in his last will and testament that he had left Russia in 1834 and acquired British citizenship, after "the arbitrary measures of Emperor Nicholas, which deprived the Russian nobility of its privileges, property rights, and individual liberty."[81]

While confiscation of estates was a rare occurrence by the end of the eighteenth century, the state employed other means to restrict the property rights of nobles guilty of treason, or of far less subversive offenses, such as poor estate management or insolvency.[82] In 1792 Catherine II placed the

---

75. Pipes (1974), xxi–xxii, 66; Brenda Meehan-Waters, "The Development and Limits of Security of Noble Status, Person, and Property in Eighteenth-Century Russia," in *Russia and the West in the Eighteenth Century*, ed. A. G. Cross (Newtonville, Mass., 1983), 294–305.

76. See Marc Raeff, ed., *Plans for Political Reform in Imperial Russia, 1730–1905* (Englewood Cliffs, N.J., 1966), 75–76, 79.

77. Meehan-Waters (1983), 300. The charter established that noble status could be forfeited on grounds of "violating an oath," "deceitful conduct," and "crimes that by law entail deprivation of honor and corporal punishment." See *PSZ*, 22: 16.187 (21.04.1785), sect. A, art. 6.

78. *PSZ*, 22: 16.187 (21.04.1785), sect. A, art. 6.

79. RGIA, f. 1345 (Piatyi departament Senata), op. 98, ed. khr. 477, ll. 2, 17. The vast majority of nobles who lost their status in the nineteenth century were male. They were deprived of nobility for theft of state or private property, abuse of office, and murder. See RGIA, f. 1343, op. 56. The names of a few noblewomen appear in this inventory; of these, most lost their status after killing illegitimate children.

80. For some examples, see *PSZ*, 34: 26.780 (09.04.1817); RGIA, f. 1330, op. 5, ed. khr. 516, ll. 14, 23, 47. See RGIA, f. 1101, op. 1, ed. khr. 344, ll. 1–2, for a letter chronicling the extent of confiscations among the local nobility in Ukraine after an uprising in 1816. According to Nikolai Kaznakov, the military governor of Kiev, at least 850 estates of Polish landowners, comprising two and a half million desiatins, were confiscated in Kiev province after the uprising of 1863. RGIA, f. 948 (Kaznakovy), op. 1, ed. khr. 55, ll. 69–70.

81. RGIA, f. 1101, op. 1, ed. khr. 585, ll. 1–2.

82. On the sequestration of estates for serf abuse, insolvency, and other misdemeanors, see chapter 7.

estate of Princess Varvara Shakhovskaia in guardianship after the princess married her daughter to a nobleman who had taken part in the French Revolution. Shakhovskaia lost the right to manage or alienate her holdings, although she still received any profits that remained after her debts were paid. The empress further decreed that Shakhovskaia's daughter would forfeit her inheritance altogether if she failed to return from France to Russia when her mother died.[83] The estates of the Decembrists, unlike those of earlier offenders, were not confiscated and eventually were passed on to their heirs; nonetheless, their assets were sequestered during their lifetime, and those who took part in the uprising could no longer make decisions relating to the use of their property. The letters of the bailiff of the Volkonskii family include more than one reference to the difficulties of providing for the exiled Prince Sergei Volkonskii, who could no longer enjoy the use of, or even the income from, his holdings.[84] By contrast, Anna Rozen, the wife of another exiled Decembrist, continued to conduct her property affairs while in Siberia with her husband.[85]

The evolution of married women's property rights must be viewed within the context of the insecurity of property that persisted well into the nineteenth century, despite the state's attempts to guarantee that innocent noblewomen were not bereft of the means of subsistence. As early as 1718, Peter the Great had ruled that women's dowries should not be subject to confiscation when their husbands' property was seized by the state.[86] In practice, however, officials did not scruple to deprive women of their assets. Writing in 1732, the wife of the English ambassador to Russia, Lady Rondeau, noted that when nobles were convicted of treason, they were stripped of their rank and they and their families lost their estates.[87] As a result, the sovereign was compelled to deal with cases on an individual basis in response to women's pleas that they had been robbed of their last crust of bread because of the crimes of male relations. Appealing to the 1718 ruling, Empress Elizabeth consistently ruled in favor of returning confiscated estates to these women, as long as they had not shared in their husbands' misdeeds.[88]

83. *PSZ*, 23: 17.033 (24.03.1792).

84. RGIA, f. 914 (Volkonskie), op. 1, ed. khr. 27, ll. 12, 15–16. Sergei Volkonskii's wife, Maria Nikolaevna, was entitled to her dowry and one-seventh of her husband's property after his "civil death"; however, since she chose to share his exile, she was permitted to receive only ten thousand rubles (assignants) annually. See S. M. Volkonskii, *O dekabristakh (po semeinym vospominaniiam)* (St. Petersburg, 1998), 61 (first published 1922).

85. See her letter granting her aunt power of attorney during a division of family property in 1832. RGIA, f. 1101, op. 1, ed. khr. 451, l. 1.

86. *PSZ*, 5: 3204 (26.05.1718).

87. Mme. Rondeau, *Pis'ma ledi Rondo, suprugi angliiskogo ministra pri Rossiiskom dvore, v tsartsvovanie Imperatritsy Anny Ioannovny* (St. Petersburg, 1836), 41.

88. RGADA, f. 22, op. 1, ed. khr. 99, ll. 1–8; f. 22, op. 1, ed. khr. 124, ll. 1–5; f. 22, op. 1, ed. khr. 136, ll. 11–13.

A decree issued in May 1753—one month before the Senate's decision in favor of Golovina—reveals a possible connection between the extension of married women's property rights and the security of noble property. Both the *Ulozhenie* of 1649 and the *Voinskii ustav* of 1716 had called for the confiscation of all property, both immovable and personal, belonging to the families of nobles found guilty of treason or insulting the sovereign. As the 1718 ruling failed to prevent authorities from acting according to these previous regulations, in 1753 new guidelines were introduced. These guidelines stipulated not only that the dowry of an innocent wife should not be confiscated but also that a certain portion of the guilty husband's property should be set aside to support his wife and children.[89] The combined rulings of 1753 ensured that women would not suffer for the crimes of their husbands and moreover, that they would not become a burden on their families or the state. The wives of exiled noblemen thus could maintain their property and manage their fortunes without restraint.

Perhaps the most compelling commentary on the vital link between the evolution of private property and married women's property rights can be found in a later attempt, in 1826, to restrict women's financial autonomy. Over the course of the eighteenth century, separate estates had evolved to protect family property and to prevent innocent women from bearing the consequences of their husbands' misdemeanors. With time, however, noblemen took advantage of their wives' legal privileges to conceal the true extent of their own holdings by transferring assets into their wives' names and avoiding full payment of debt. As the abuse of separate property became more common, officials debated whether they should restrict women's property rights in the interest of forcing men to discharge their financial obligations.

Yet when the emperor proposed a law in 1826 that would subject the acquired property of wives to their husbands' creditors, Senator N. S. Mordvinov objected on the grounds that Russian law was renowned precisely for making no distinction between men and women in regard to property. By violating the principle of separate estates, which Russians had observed "for centuries," the proposed law threatened the very institution of private property. On the one hand, Mordvinov argued that the law would have little impact. Men resorted to a variety of means to evade their creditors: they could easily sell their holdings to a third party and conceal the proceeds, as well as transfer ownership of an estate to their wives. He went on to warn of the possible dangers of undermining women's property rights: "A wife, having purchased an estate from her husband, will never freely administer it, for who would wish to buy such an estate from her?" Consequently,

---

89. *Proekty Ugolovnogo ulozheniia 1754–1766 godov: novoulozhennoi knigi chast' vtoraia. O rozysknykh delakh i kakie za raznye zlodeistva i prestupleniia kazni, nakazaniia i shtrafy polozheny* (St. Petersburg, 1882), chap. 2, arts. 1 and 2, p. 76; chap. 21, art. 1, p. 78.

Mordvinov concluded that the benefits of the proposed law would be minimal and—more crucially—it would undermine the very existence of "the laws of property" (*prava sobstvennosti oslabeiut*) in Russia.[90] This opinion was well in keeping with Mordvinov's lifelong mission to bolster the status of the nobility and the security of individual property rights.[91] Later, in 1846, the Senate finally set forth new rules regulating women's culpability for the debts of their husbands: the only assets vulnerable to seizure were properties given to wives by their husbands, or purchased with their capital, in the decade preceding bankruptcy. These measures effected a compromise between the inviolability of women's separate property (and, by association, private property) and the potential for abuse.[92]

Mordvinov's observation that the principle of separate estates was integral to the larger concept of private property in Russia highlights a crucial connection between the experience of noblewomen and changes in Russian political culture. Ironically, the long tradition of despotic government and corrupt officialdom in Russia created possibilities for female autonomy that did not exist in the more liberal regimes of Western Europe. In Russia, as in Europe, lawmakers perceived the family as a microcosm of the state and drew an explicit parallel between patriarchy and autocratic government. When members of the Senate undermined the rule of husbands by upholding women's property rights, their goal was not to do away with the patriarchal order but to restrain despotic rule in Russia and defend the broader principle of the inviolability of private property. The campaign to extend their rights over property was central to the nobility's struggle for greater corporate privileges in the second half of the eighteenth century; thus, noble legislators used their powers of interpretation against the arbitrary exercise of power on the part of the state and its representatives, and in favor of estate and individual rights. As part of their struggle for individualized property rights, however, Russian lawmakers took the more surprising step of recognizing the individual rights of married women.

Neither the financial woes of noblemen nor the disappearance of service holdings explain the enigma of married women's control of property in

90. *Arkhiv grafov Mordvinovykh* (St. Petersburg, 1903), 8: 101–7.

91. See, for example, Mordvinov's proposals to the government for ameliorating the burden of debt of the nobility. RGIA, f. 994 (Mordvinovy), op. 2, ed. khr. 221, ll. 7–8. Mordvinov by no means set up a dichotomy between the autocratic state and the institution of private property. Indeed, he perceived the state as the origin of private property in Russia, implying that central authority was the sole defense against the exercise of arbitrary power. See RGIA, f. 994, op. 2, ed. khr. 575, ll. 1–2. On Mordvinov's interest in property rights, see Susan P. McCaffray, "What Should Russia Be? Patriotism and Political Economy in the Thought of N. S. Mordvinov," *Slavic Review* 59, no. 3 (Fall 2000): 572–96.

92. *PSZ*, 2d ser., 21: 20.138 (17.06.1846).

Russia. As many historians have argued, Peter the Great may be said to bear responsibility for the extension of women's property rights in the eighteenth century. His contribution was no single decree elevating women's legal status, however, but the introduction of European values and legal norms to nobles who once viewed themselves as humble servants of the sovereign. As they struggled to undermine arbitrary rule and secure noble property, lawmakers used the legal status of women to bolster individual property rights. In the final analysis, Russian women escaped the full burden of gender tutelage because their husbands and fathers worked to undermine the tutelage of the state.

CHAPTER THREE

Marriage and the Practice of Separate Property

"You must know that every Woman has the right over her Fortune totally independent of her Husband and he is as independent of his wife," Catherine Wilmot marveled in a letter from Russia to her sister Harriet in 1806. "Marriage therefore is no union of interests whatsoever, and the Wife if she has a large Estate and happens to marry a poor man is still consider'd rich while the Husband may go to Jail without one farthing of her possessions being responsible for him! This gives a curious sort of hue to the conversations of the Russian Matrons which to a meek English Woman appears prodigious independence in the midst of a Despotic Government!"[1]

By the time Catherine Wilmot arrived in Russia, the status of Russian noblewomen in the law of property had improved substantially in the realm of inheritance and control of their assets. European visitors to early-modern Russia had singled out the subjugation of women as a defining trait of "backward" Muscovite society; by contrast, foreigners in the nineteenth century noted the extensive legal privileges of Russian women with astonishment. Despite the undeniable tendency of travelers from abroad to misinterpret or exaggerate what they saw, their accounts highlight the eighteenth century as one of genuine change for noblewomen. Yet even the most insightful testimony of European visitors barely touched on the question of how Russian women experienced the transformation of their legal status. For their part, historians have identified the legal benchmarks in the enhancement of women's property rights with relative ease. They have made no attempt, however, to evaluate the significance of separate property in practice, in the daily lives of Russian men and women, or the real scope of

---

1. Bradford (1935), 234.

women's control of their fortunes. Was separate property merely a legal device that had no impact on how families administered property? Did husbands and wives keep track of the assets they invested in each other's estates or did they think purely in terms of family interest? In the absence of evidence to the contrary, scholars have assumed that women's control of their fortunes was nominal and that men were the *de facto* administrators of joint marital property. As William Wagner has argued, "Legal norms were accorded little intrinsic value by either state officials or society generally and in any case appear often to have been poorly known [and] unevenly enforced. . . . The degree to which the rights formally enjoyed by married women under Imperial law were observed in practice therefore remains uncertain."[2]

This chapter will examine the pivotal but elusive problem of the practice of separate property in marriage. In the pages that follow, I consider the impact of separate property on relations between husbands and wives, as well as noblewomen's opportunities to exercise their proprietary power after 1753. To begin, I present attendance at property transfers as one manifestation of women's active administration of their assets during marriage. I go on to explore debates over property ownership that surface in marital disputes, which reveal that separate estates were an active concept for noble families. Breaking with received wisdom, I argue that noblewomen's control of property was far more than a legal convention; in particular, the willingness of the courts to uphold the rights of dispossessed women illuminates the potential significance of separate property in noblewomen's lives. For all its limitations, the law of separate property offered Russian noblewomen a margin of liberty not readily available to their Western counterparts: the chance for some to protect their holdings against their husbands' encroachments, and, for others, to escape intolerable abuse.[3]

The Historical Debate: Family Law versus the Law of Property

From the mid-eighteenth century, a fundamental contradiction characterized married women's legal status and gender relations in Russia. At the heart of this contradiction lay the tension between married women's status in family law and their standing in the law of property. Custom, family law,

---

2. Wagner (1994), 66.

3. As Lawrence Stone observes, "even after a judicial separation," English husbands enjoyed full power over the income and personal assets of their wives. See Stone, *Broken Lives: Separation and Divorce in England, 1660–1857* (Oxford, 1993), 13. In eighteenth-century France, an unhappy wife might achieve a separation of property if she could prove that her husband was squandering her fortune, yet she could not sell the property she had brought to marriage without the latter's consent. See Diefendorf (1983), 244.

and religious ideology unanimously prescribed women's personal subjugation to their husbands. Authorities, both civil and ecclesiastical, decreed that a wife must live with her husband and submit even to his abusive behavior. At the same time, the law of property defined married women as autonomous agents and guaranteed them full control over any property in their possession. It should come as no surprise that these principles could clash, and often at the expense of female autonomy. Or, as one observer of Russian social customs astutely remarked, "'Tho a married Woman has compleat power over her Fortune she has not over her person."[4]

Clearly, noblewomen's control of their holdings was a reality only to the extent that the courts were willing to reconcile these extremes and defend married women's entitlements.[5] With few exceptions, however, historians since the nineteenth century have maintained that women's freedom to alienate property was a legal fiction, a privilege that could not be realized within the constraints of marriage in Imperial Russia. The scholar N. V. Reingardt declared that since the authority of husbands over wives was unlimited in Russian civil law, women's economic independence was "only a fiction."[6] Reingardt stated that there were no obstacles to prevent husbands from obtaining a power of attorney from their wives and managing their estates to their own advantage. In response to those who believed that Russian women's legal status was superior to that of women in Western Europe, Reingardt responded that West European law guaranteed women more personal freedoms and that the law of community property offered women greater protection from their husbands' misuse of their property. The scholar admitted that Russian women sometimes were able to protect their assets from their husbands, but only when they succeeded in circumventing the law.[7] Furthermore, he observed that the principle of separate estates held true only when it did not conflict with state interests. In consequence, the wives of officials were forbidden to engage in trade, and women who did not engage in trade in their own right were forbidden to sign promissory notes without their husbands' consent.[8]

Other authors contested Reingardt's pessimistic assessment. In his influential survey, M. F. Vladimirskii-Budanov argued that eighteenth-century

---

4. Bradford (1935), 232.

5. In early-modern England, the establishment of separate estates for wives as a means of protecting their property was pronounced a failure, since husbands easily convinced their wives to conform to their wishes. Staves (1990), 84.

6. N. V. Reingardt, *O lichnykh i imushchestvennykh pravakh zhenshchin po russkomu zakonu* (Kazan, 1885), 7. See also I. V. Gessen, "Vliianie zakonodatel'stva na polozhenie zhenshchin," *Pravo*, no. 51 (1908): cols. 2837–38; I. G. Orshanskii, "O pridanom," *Zhurnal grazhdanskogo i torgovogo prava*, no. 12 (1872): 985–1045; A. Zagorovskii, "Lichnye i imushchestvennye otnosheniia mezhdu suprugami," *Russkaia mysl'*, no. 4 (1897): 66.

7. Reingardt (1885), 11–12.

8. Ibid., 10.

Russian law was noteworthy for the absence of statutes concerning the relation of husband to wife, which belonged to the realm of religious ideology. He pointed out that rulings prohibiting spouses from living separately had been adopted when Imperial authorities began to resettle peasants and were intended to prevent the breakup of peasant families. Moreover, he continued, Peter the Great had explicitly absolved women of all social estates of the obligation to follow their husbands into exile, which demonstrated that the state had set definite limits on the authority of husbands over their wives.

Vladimirskii-Budanov also remarked on the dearth of eighteenth-century rulings concerning the duty of wives to obey their husbands. A decree in 1782 was the first to explicitly prescribe feminine obedience in civil law; moreover, it was only in 1830 that the compilers of the *Svod zakonov* added that this obedience should be unlimited. If this law were implemented, he concluded, it would impinge not only on women's property rights but also on the prerogative of wives to file suit against their husbands. At no time, however, had Russian law restricted women's rights in this regard.[9] By contrast, K. D. Kavelin believed that the article mandating female obedience was not a mere recommendation but had the force of law; inevitably, marriage severely restricted women's personal freedoms.[10] The historian Karamzin was convinced that foreign influence had inspired the new emphasis on women's subjugation in Russian law, and accused the statesman Mikhail Speranskii of imitating the Napoleonic Code when he introduced this provision on wives' obedience in the *Svod zakonov*.[11]

The glaring discrepancy between married women's personal and property rights in Russian law not only garnered growing attention from legal specialists from the mid-nineteenth century but became even more marked as the Imperial era drew to a close. Members of the commission for a new codification of Russian law in the 1880s discussed the troubling contradictions in women's legal status at length, and most spoke in favor of limiting the authority of husbands over their wives. According to one representative, the institution of marriage in Russia was still governed by the principles laid out in the *Domostroi* in the sixteenth century, which precluded married women's active control over their property. The courts found themselves in an impossible position when disputes between spouses over dowry ownership arose: although property law guaranteed women independent ownership of their fortunes, the representative claimed, it was not uncommon for legal authorities to distort the law's meaning by declaring that during mar-

---

9. Vladimirskii-Budanov (1909), 445–46. Nevolin made similar observations in his history of Russian civil law. See Nevolin (1851), 1: 76.

10. Kavelin (1900), 4: 1063.

11. Tishkin (1984), 29. On the role of the Civil Code and Speranskii in enhancing the authority of husbands, see also Sinaiskii (1910), 116–17, 124, 158, 162, 185–87.

riage husbands were the custodians of their wives' dowry.[12] Among legal scholars and officials with experience of legal practice, the prevailing view was that married women stood little chance of administering their assets unless their husbands permitted them to do so.

Separate Property and Notarial Practice

Much of the evidence on the significance of separate property derives, inevitably, from marital disputes. For that reason, notarial practice offers a crucial perspective on the role separate estates played in more harmonious unions, as well as drawing attention to the nobility's keen observance of legal formalities. A survey of men's and women's signatures to property transactions demonstrates that noblewomen's control of property during marriage was far more than a mere article of the law. The presence of transactors was by no means required when estates were sold, or in any other type of property transaction: nobles of both sexes frequently sent representatives to sign deeds and documents in their place. When manumitting serfs, for example, proprietors almost never appeared in person at the notarial office but dispatched a bailiff or peasant elder to carry out the business.

If women's property ownership was no more than a formality, however, one might expect to find significant differences in the attendance of men and women at sales of real estate. There was no pressing reason for women to show up at the notarial office when they sold or purchased property: wives could easily appoint their husbands to act as representatives rather than appear themselves. Indeed, this would be only fitting if, as scholars have assumed, women relinquished decisions about estate management to their husbands or male kin. Signatures to deeds of purchase reveal, however, that husbands and wives were faithful to the spirit, as well as to the letter, of the law of separate property. Both as buyers and as sellers, women and men attended property sales at almost identical rates. In the eighteenth century, landowners of both sexes witnessed in person almost 90 percent of sales and purchases of estates in this sample (Table 3.1). Furthermore, when women's participation rates declined in the nineteenth century, they did so in tandem with the rates for men. Within each district and across time, the behavior of women conformed remarkably with that of their male counterparts: women were just as reluctant as men to entrust representatives with matters involving real estate.

The composition of signatories for illiterate noblewomen further underscores the desire of spouses to affirm the formal separation of their estates. Until the nineteenth century, many noblewomen could not sign the deeds

12. *Zamechaniia o nedostatkakh deistvuiushchikh grazhdanskikh zakonov* (St. Petersburg, 1891), no. 109.

TABLE 3.1 Attendance of Noble Women and Men at the Sale of Their Estates, 1750–1860*

	Vladimir		Kashin		Tambov		Moscow		All Regions	
	W	M	W	M	W	M	W	M	W	M
1750–55	95	91	100	80	90	93	94	95	94	94
	(20)	(11)	(25)	(5)	(31)	(28)	(243)	(202)	(319)	(246)
1775–80	89	94	82	75	83	93	90	86	87	86
	(28)	(17)	(76)	(20)	(92)	(54)	(267)	(352)	(463)	(443)
1805–10	46	45	96	88	71	100	83	91	64	63
	(147)	(85)	(27)	(16)	(7)	(3)	(88)	(54)	(269)	(158)
1855–60	65	73	—	—	—	—	—	—	65	73
	(85)	(30)							(85)	(30)
All periods	60	60	88	80	84	93	90	88	82	84
1750–1860	(280)	(143)	(128)	(41)	(130)	(85)	(598)	(608)	(1,136)	(877)

* W = women, M = men. Each value is the percentage of women or men who attended the sale of their estate. The number of sales is in parentheses.
Source: See appendix 1.

that they witnessed.[13] Yet, surprisingly, the signatures of husbands and male kin did not predominate in property deeds of illiterate women: while an average of 22 percent of women asked their husbands to sign deeds for them in the eighteenth century, women were far more likely to appeal to a priest or official to witness their documents (Table 3.2). Notarial records reveal that illiterate women might request the signature of an official even when their husbands were transacting business at the same time. Ensign Izvolskii was present in the notarial office in Tambov in 1777 when his wife mortgaged thirty serfs; Izvolskii himself had mortgaged twenty desiatins of land and together the couple raised fifteen hundred rubles, presumably to pay off their debts. Izvolskii signed his own mortgage deed but not that of his wife, Elena, who asked a clerk to witness her deed.[14] Furthermore, nobles of both sexes proved disinclined to ask their spouses to transact business for them when the alienation of property was at stake.[15] Spouses clearly shared

13. For a discussion of female literacy, see chapter 7, Table 7.1.
14. RGADA, f. 615, op. 1, ed. khr. 11579, ll. 5–6.
15. In this sample of approximately six thousand sales and mortgages of estates and serfs, I found only nine cases in which men acted as representatives for their wives. See RGADA, f. 615, op. 1, ed. khr. 11576, ll. 32–33; f. 615, op. 1, ed. khr. 11578, l. 7; f. 615, op. 1, ed. khr. 11579, ll. 14–15; f. 615, op. 1, ed. khr. 11581, ll. 36–37; f. 615, op. 1, ed. khr. 11592, l. 35 and ll. 54–55; Gosudarstvennyi arkhiv Vladimirskoi oblasti (hereafter GAVO), f. 92, op. 5, ed. khr. 21, ll. 194–95 and ll. 309–10; f. 92, op. 2, ed. khr. 682, ll. 62–63. For examples of men sending their wives as representatives, even though several of these women were illiterate, see RGADA, f. 282 (Iustitskollegiia), op. 1, ed. khr. 394, ll. 354–356 and ll. 227–231; f. 615, op. 1, ed. khr. 2045, ll. 64–65; f. 615, op. 1, ed. khr. 11569, l. 11; f. 615, op. 1, ed. khr. 11577, ll. 22–23; f. 615, op. 1, ed. khr. 11578, l. 7; Gosudarstvennyi arkhiv Tambovskoi oblasti (hereafter GATO), f. 67, op. 1, ed. khr. 27a, ll. 29–30; GAVO, f. 92, op. 5, ed. khr. 21, ll. 50–51; f. 92, op. 2, ed. khr. 682, ll. 77–78.

TABLE 3.2 Signatories for Illiterate Noblewomen, 1750–1860*

	Vladimir			Kashin			Tambov			Moscow			All Regions		
	H	M	O	H	M	O	H	M	O	H	M	O	H	M	O
1750–55	14	7 (14)	79	20	5 (20)	75	15	4 (27)	81	25	11 (115)	64	22	8 (176)	69
1775–80	57	14 (7)	29	27	8 (37)	65	14	5 (42)	81	17	17 (46)	59	21	11 (132)	66
1805–10	13	13 (8)	75	0	0 (3)	67	0	0 (0)	0	0	50 (2)	50	8	15 (13)	69
1855–60	0	0 (0)	0	—	—	—	—	— (0)	—	—	—	—	0	0 (0)	0
All periods 1750–1860	24	10 (29)	66	23	5 (60)	68	15	4 (69)	81	23	13 (163)	63	21	9 (321)	68

* H = husband, M = male kin, O = official or priest. All signatories not falling in the H, M, or O categories were female relatives. The value in each category is the percentage of illiterate women represented by that type of signatory. The number of illiterate women involved in estate sales is given in parentheses.
Source: See appendix 1.

a common interest in their financial well-being, if only for the sake of their children, but they were far more likely to turn to a third party to oversee their affairs when they could not attend in person. These features of notarial practice leave little doubt that married noblewomen were expected to act as representatives of their own affairs, if only to the extent of appearing in person during property transactions.

Serf Ownership and the Problem of Serf Marriage

For all the protection the institution of separate estates offered married women and their natal families, maintaining the boundary between the property of husband and wife created a host of legal dilemmas for the Russian courts. Significantly, legal battles over the clarification of the status of property belonging to husband and wife were predominantly an eighteenth-century phenomenon that originated early in the century and intensified after the ruling of 1753 that awarded married women control of their estates. Although early-modern Russian law acknowledged married women's ownership of the dowry, the administration of marital property was traditionally a joint affair. As we have seen, until the second quarter of the eighteenth century, dowry donors made their property over to the groom. In the early-modern era, spouses alienated dowry property together and awarded marriage portions to their daughters from their joint assets (*iz obshcha*). Moreover, both wives and children bore responsibility for the debts of their husbands and fathers.[16]

As rights of property increasingly came to be invested in individuals, rather than families, legal authorities in eighteenth-century Russia encountered new problems in implementing the law of separate property. Long before women won the right to control their fortunes, noble families were all too conscious of the risk of being swindled by kin-by-marriage. Throughout the eighteenth century their awareness took the form of obsessively detailed dowry inventories, which not only listed the amount of land and number of serfs that had been relinquished on behalf of the bride, but also included lengthy descriptions of icons, dresses, household items, and corsets. Such inventories proved indispensable in property disputes in which ownership of every last feather pillow and kitchen utensil was a point of contention. As a typical example, in 1761 Lieutenant Colonel Svechin presented an eight-page inventory of his wife's dowry to the Senate after accusing her of adultery and attempting to gain control of her estate. Svechin itemized every item in his wife's dowry and stated whether it was at the moment in his possession or in hers. If it had been sold, he noted by whom. A number of items, including several undergarments and a fox-fur coat, Svechin declared, had been "worn out" by his wife (*iznoshena zhenoiu*).[17]

Infinitely more complex than the division of chattel, however, was determining serf ownership when peasants who belonged to spouses married and produced children. The problem of serf ownership exemplifies the problems inherent in maintaining separate marital property on a day-to-day basis. It also reveals that in order to reap the benefits of separate property, noblewomen were compelled to assume responsibility for guarding the legal boundaries between their own estates and those of their husbands. A series of legal conventions, including registration of dowry villages and the tedious accounting of the contents of the dowry, ensured that men and women could not ignore the separation of their assets; at the same time, husbands more often than not managed both estates and married their own peasants to serfs belonging to their wives. Women's failure to keep close watch on their holdings, however, could lead to considerable loss for themselves and for their children.

Serf women were routinely included in dowry contracts, and inevitably

16. For examples, see *Akty iuridicheskie* (1838), no. 71, X; no. 357. Vladimirskii-Budanov argued that a form of community property existed in Russia from the fourteenth through the seventeenth centuries, whereas V. I. Sergeevich maintained that separation of property coexisted with a system of community property. See Vladimirskii-Budanov (1909), 449–56; V. I. Sergeevich, *Lektsii i issledovaniia po drevnei istorii russkogo prava*, 2d ed. (St. Petersburg, 1899), 366–69.

17. RGADA, f. 22 (Dela sudnye), op. 1, ed. khr. 53, ll. 22–29.

marriages took place between serfs belonging to married couples. This arrangement disturbed no one while the serf owners' marriage endured; when one spouse died, however, a serious complication arose. The *Ulozhenie* of 1649 forbade serf owners to separate wives from their husbands. Since married serfs could not be parted, the surviving serf owner confronted an awkward dilemma: which spouse was now the owner of the couple and their offspring?

The widow Akulina Voeikova insisted that she was the owner when she brought her suit to the Land College in 1737. Following her husband's death in 1735, Voeikova entered into a lengthy dispute with her son-in-law, Prince Nikanor Meshcherskii, over the division of her husband's estate. Voeikova did not contest her daughter's right to six-sevenths of the estate, but she insisted on her entitlement to a full one-seventh of her husband's immovable property, as well as the return of her dowry. According to Voeikova, Meshcherskii had left her with less than one-tenth of the property, and he had taken all of the skilled serfs for himself, leaving her with "the poorest, and the crippled and the dead (*samykh nishchikh, i uvechnykh i mertvykh*)." He had also included in his share all of her serf women, whom her husband had married to peasants in his own villages.

Voeikova presented her case to the Senate in 1744, after the Land College ruled that her serf women would be returned to her, but their husbands and children would be considered part of her maintenance portion, thus diminishing the amount she would inherit from her husband's estate. In contrast, the Senate found that the ruling of the Land College contradicted an article in the *Ulozhenie*, which stipulated that when a woman died without issue, her serf women should be returned to her family. If female serfs had been given in marriage, the husbands must accompany their wives, regardless of their original ownership. Voeikova thus was entitled to claim her own serf women and their families as her original dowry, the Senate decreed, in addition to one-seventh of her husband's estate.[18]

Similar disputes over ownership of married serfs who belonged to different spouses recurred on a regular basis in the eighteenth century. The widow Akulina Koverina petitioned the Land College in 1751, claiming that her husband had married several of her serf women to his own peasants and requesting the return of her women and their families. Her brother-in-law responded with an indignant petition, arguing that Koverina had brought no serf women to the marriage. Furthermore, his brother had married ten of his own serf women to her serfs, all of whom were now in his sister-in-law's possession.[19] A series of petitions from both parties ensued; two years

18. *PSZ*, 12: 9.095 (19.12.1744).
19. RGADA, f. 1209, op. 79, ed. khr. 167, ll. 11–12.

later, the Land College ruled in Koverina's favor, awarding her one-seventh of her husband's estate, as well as all of her serf women and their offspring.[20]

Until the mid-eighteenth century, noble widows clearly benefited from the courts' interpretation of their right to reclaim their serf women, as well as their families. This state of affairs proved much less satisfactory to men who felt they had been deprived of their full inheritance. In 1767, noble assemblies brought their complaints to the attention of Catherine II, asserting in their petitions that under the present rules men suffered a loss in serf ownership and that the owner of the serf husband should be allowed to claim the entire family when a division of property took place.[21]

Members of the Senate echoed the logic of the provincial nobility in subsequent rulings on serf ownership. During the second half of the eighteenth century, as lawmakers revised their conception of women's relation to property, they also withdrew much of the protection they had previously offered propertied wives. Having invested women with full rights of ownership in 1753, the Senate was compelled to re-examine the problem of serf ownership by married couples.

As it reviewed a case presented in 1799, the General Session of the Senate discussed the principles that guided previous decisions on serf ownership in 1744 and 1762. The Senate had ruled in favor of the wife (and her relatives) in 1744 because "in previous times the dowry estate was registered not only in the name of the woman who was marrying, but in the name of her husband, and for this reason the husband, considering himself the owner of his wife's estate, could give her women serfs in marriage to his serfs." To prevent the loss of property to the wife and her clan, the Senate had ruled that serf women and their offspring were to be returned to the wife and her family. But after 1744, the Senate continued, new customs governed the registration of dowries. Officials now registered the dowry estate in the name of the wife alone, and women administered and disposed of their property without their husbands' permission, so men could no longer appropriate their wives' estates. Consequently, the Senate argued, it was unfair to replace one serf woman with an entire family, and they offered new guidelines to regulate the future division of assets. When husbands and wives agreed to marry their serfs to one another, the following principle was henceforth to apply: in a division of property, the serf family belonged to the owner of the serf husband. Therefore, if a husband married his serf women to his wife's peasants, the wife would be considered the owner, and vice versa.[22] In short, once women acquired the right to control their estates, they also took

20. RGADA, f. 1209, op. 79, ed. khr. 365, ll. 86–90. See also RGADA, f. 1209, op. 84, ch. 14, ed. khr. 1507, ll. 1–2.

21. *SIRIO* (1869), 8: 419, 424; (1871), 8: 539–40.

22. *PSZ*, 26: 19.250 (19.01.1800).

on the burden—willingly or not—of protecting their fortunes from their husbands' encroachments.

Transactions between Husband and Wife

Determining serf ownership was not the only quandary the courts faced in regulating property relations between husband and wife from the mid-eighteenth century. In keeping with their convenient assumption that women, in reality, could now determine how they would use their assets, law-makers gradually withdrew the protection they had once extended to wives who were coerced to part with their fortunes. Having spelled out the consequences for spouses who chose to marry their serfs to one another, the courts then struggled with the question of whether husbands and wives might sell or mortgage property to each other. Legal authorities did not object to this practice on the grounds that husband and wife were one entity and therefore could not execute contracts with one another, as was the case in parts of Western Europe. Their dilemma derived instead from women's obligation to obey their husbands—a duty that was originally a tenet of ecclesiastical law and later articulated as well in civil codes. With good reason the courts initially expressed apprehension that husbands would exploit their wives' weakness and force the latter to part with their assets on unfavorable terms. By the nineteenth century, however, official solicitude for vulnerable wives gradually gave way to a firm conviction that married women must defend their own interests.

Despite the relatively small number of property transactions between husband and wife that surface in notarial records, the question of whether spouses might sell real estate to one another vexed the Senate into the nineteenth century. The courts had long been sensitive to the potential for forced sales of land by abused wives. In the interest of minimizing this danger, during the seventeenth century sellers of both sexes were examined in court when they executed deeds of purchase, mortgaged property, or registered wills.[23] The surveillance of the wife's natal family was, however, the most powerful check on a husband's inclination to transfer his wife's assets into his own name. A ruling in 1679 that forbade men to sell their wives' patrimonial estates referred to the relatives of "widows and maidens", who alleged that their kinswomen had been tormented until they agreed to alienate their holdings.[24] Only much later, in the eighteenth century, did women

---

23. Originally, the law required sellers to be examined in court; later, the signature of the seller or that of a relative of the seller was considered adequate. See *PSZ*, 2: 763 (19.06.1679); 2: 909 (05.04.1682).

24. *PSZ*, 2: 751 (21.02.1679).

turn regularly to the courts on their own behalf with tales of abuse and dispossession.

It was not until the second half of the eighteenth century, after women had gained control of their fortunes, that the legality of transactions between husband and wife loomed large in debates within the Senate. Tellingly, the first discussion in the Senate in 1763 on the status of such transactions was not instigated by an ill-used wife, but by descendants involved in a quarrel over the right to repurchase the estate. The summary of the case dwelled primarily on the right of members of one clan to sell property to another; however, the Senate finally ruled that the sale of property by husbands to wives was unacceptable on the basis of a 1748 decree which forbade spouses to claim their inheritance of one-seventh of the other's estate during each other's lifetime. The sale of property by wives to husbands was more objectionable still, the senators reasoned, since a woman could not dispute her husband's decision and might relinquish her property at his insistence.[25]

In subsequent rulings legislators focused at times on the murky legal status of property transactions between spouses, while on other occasions they highlighted the need to protect wives from greedy husbands. Ironically, women emerged as the losers both when they purchased real estate from their husbands and when they were defrauded of their holdings. When Natalia Sukhotina tried to register an estate she had purchased from her husband with the Land College in 1780, the latter refused to grant her request. The authors of the ruling maintained that neither the *Ulozhenie* nor later statutes explicitly permitted transactions between spouses. In accordance with the Senate's previous decision in 1763, the Land College stated that it could not register any transfers of property between husband and wife. There was no discussion, however, of whether Sukhotina's husband would return the sum she had paid him for the estate.[26] Similarly, in 1805 the wife of Titular Counsellor Ivanov immediately filed suit against her husband when he failed to repay the two thousand rubles he had borrowed from her. Yet the Senate refused to hand over the estate Ivanov had mortgaged to his wife, declaring that on the basis of the 1763 ruling, the transaction had been illegal. On the other hand, the Senate allowed Ivanova to sue her husband for recovery of the sum she had lent him.[27]

Although penalizing women for engaging in property transactions with their husbands, legislators did not completely lose sight of female vulnerability. In 1801 the senators heard the case of a noblewoman in Tambov who had mortgaged her estate to her husband for ten thousand rubles. The Senate eventually ruled in favor of Maria Mosaleva's cousins, on the grounds

25. *PSZ*, 16: 11.764 (26.02.1763).
26. *PSZ*, 20: 15.022 (25.06.1780).
27. *PSZ*, 27: 21.926 (30.09.1805).

that Mosaleva herself had instigated a suit against her husband before she died, claiming that he had forced her to execute the mortgage deed and then seized her estate without payment.[28] Mosaleva's predicament was far from atypical for noblewomen, many of whom, like her, did not survive to see justice done.

Petitions from women for divorce in the eighteenth century were replete with similar accusations: in agonizing detail, these women described how their husbands repeatedly beat them senseless, dragged them across the floor by their hair, and deprived them of food, all in the interest of forcing them to part with their assets.[29] In one horrifying account, written in 1758, Uliana Golovnina described how her husband not only beat her black and blue but also arrived in her village one evening and threatened to break her arms and legs and set her house on fire if she refused to sign over her estate to him.[30]

While the Senate debated the legal niceties of allowing spouses to transact business, property transactions continued to take place between husbands and wives in the provinces, beyond the reach of central authorities. Finding it impossible to stop the practice, the Senate finally reversed its earlier decisions on the grounds that the resolution of the 1763 dispute merely represented a ruling on a particular case, not a general principle, and that no foundation existed in Russian law to prohibit the sale of property between spouses.[31] The final debate took place in the Senate in 1825 between the minister of justice and members of the Committee on the Codification of Law. In their discussion, most of the senators skirted the problem of men's authority over their wives altogether and maintained that the 1763 edict had never been invested with the status of law. The minister of justice strongly objected, pointing out that the Land College had set forth its opinion as a guide for ruling on all future transactions between spouses. Committee members countered the minister's reservations with their own interpretation: the issue was not, they maintained, whether the sale of property between spouses was beneficial or harmful to the parties involved, but whether any principle in Russian law existed to prohibit these transactions. Having reviewed the regulations in the *Ulozhenie* and the Charter to the Nobility, the committee concluded that no rationale could be found for

28. *PSZ*, 26: 20.021 (25.09.1801). See also *PSZ*, 30: 23.685 (04.06.1809).

29. See, for example, petitions from women for divorce in RGIA, f. 796 (Kantseliariia Sinoda), op. 52, ed. khr. 278a, ll. 1–2 (1771); f. 796, op. 58, ed. khr. 261, ll. 1–2 (1777); f. 796, op. 61, ed. khr. 216, l. 1 (1780); f. 796, op. 78, ed. khr. 440, l. 2 (1797); N. P. Rozanov, *Istoriia Moskovskogo eparkhial'nogo upravleniia so vremeni uchrezhdeniia Sviateishego Sinoda* (Moscow, 1869), 2/1: 117 (1743); ibid. (Moscow, 1870), 2/2: 114 (1765).

30. RGIA, f. 796, op. 39, ed. khr. 71, l. 2 (1758).

31. Transactions between spouses before the mid-nineteenth century were rare, but they appear on occasion in notarial records. See chapter 4, Table 4.17.

preventing the transfer of property between spouses. After long debate, with virtually no reference to feminine vulnerability, three of the four senators at the General Session agreed that transactions between husbands and wives should be permitted henceforth.[32]

Keeping in mind that previous decisions had rested, at least in part, on the conviction that wives should be protected from abusive husbands, this was an ironic conclusion.[33] Yet the ruling was consistent with the general tone of Russian property law in extending minimal protection to women. From the mid-eighteenth century the law made few distinctions between men's and women's use of their assets. Placing an equal burden on both sexes to defend their interests was the logical corollary of elevating women's status in the law of property. Thus, in the early nineteenth century Russian officials confronted a paradox that bedevils lawmakers to this day: gender neutrality in the law by no means translated into equal opportunities for women to exercise their legal rights.

Marital Discord and Separate Property

As a result of the tension between women's status in the law of property and the ideology of feminine subjugation that dominated all other dimensions of women's existence, the principle of separate property was put to the test primarily in the context of marital discord.[34] Litigation between spouses therefore provides vital insight into the potential impact of separate estates on the relationship between husband and wife. To be sure, property suits between spouses were not an everyday occurrence: relatively few cases of disputes between husbands and wives survive from the civil courts in the eighteenth century. Although property ownership was a crucial source of marital discord, evidence of such disputes survives primarily in petitions for divorce, in the records of the Holy Synod. Divorce petitions provide, on the one hand, a remarkable record of relations between husbands and wives and the

32. *PSZ*, 37: 30.472 (31.08.1825).

33. The diminishing attention to coercion on the part of husbands in Russian property law shares a parallel with developments in the United States during the same period. Marylynn Salmon traced the growing popularity of separate estates for married women in the early nineteenth century and argues that in the eyes of lawmakers, "a woman with a separate estate did not warrant the same kind of protection as a woman without one." See Salmon, *Women and the Law of Property in Early America* (Chapel Hill, 1986), 107–8.

34. The topic of marriage and marital discord among the nobility has garnered remarkably little attention from scholars of pre-reform Russia. For three exceptions, see Bisha (1993); Gregory L. Freeze, "Bringing Order to the Russian Family: Marriage and Divorce in Imperial Russia, 1760–1860," *Journal of Modern History* 62, no. 4 (December 1990): 709–46; Jessica Tovrov, *The Russian Noble Family: Structure and Change* (New York, 1987).

sources of marital breakdown and, on the other, the attitude of authorities toward male and female misbehavior.

By contrast, from the end of the eighteenth century noblewomen turned more frequently to civil authorities and proved ever more willing to sue husbands who appropriated their estates. In a survey of property disputes between kin heard in the Land College and the Senate between 1700 and 1861, only 4 percent (2/45) of eighteenth-century suits involved spouses; the proportion increased to 16 percent (11/71) in the nineteenth century.[35] A striking pattern emerges in records that survive from courts, both ecclesiastical and civil: when property ownership alone was at stake, the authorities invariably upheld women's claim to their assets. When male litigants introduced questions of immorality, however, women's prerogatives proved far more tenuous. Although representatives of church and state frowned on male adultery, women faced far more serious consequences when they violated their marriage vows. Moreover, solicitude for the well-being of children often prompted authorities to restrict women's freedom to alienate their property. Family interest frequently overshadowed the interests of individual noblewomen.

As is so often the case, the evidence inherited by historians overwhelmingly concerns unhappy families—a state of affairs that risks distorting our picture of how the "typical" noble family conceived of property ownership. Many noblewomen trusted their husbands to administer their separate holdings for their mutual benefit, as well as in the interests of their children. Yet, as the following dispute reveals, this arrangement by no means always worked to their children's advantage if the presumption of common interests broke down. In 1809 Court Counsellor Stepan Rakhmaninov petitioned the Senate to recover his inheritance, much of which he lost when his mother died. He recounted how, when his parents married, his father had owned only thirty serfs, while his mother brought a dowry of three hundred peasants. Throughout their marriage the elder Rakhmaninov had managed his wife's serfs at his discretion, collecting dues and purchasing immovable property with the proceeds in his own name. "During her lifetime my

---

35. See appendix 2. The eighteenth-century cases in this sample date from the 1790s. It should be noted that this sample consists only of property litigation between spouses found in the records of the Land College (RGADA, f. 1209) and of the Senate (RGIA, f. 1330), of which I completed a systematic survey. These figures do not include disputes found in the *Polnoe sobranie zakonov* (*PSZ*) that are cited in the text. I have also not included property disputes between spouses found in other collections: for example, RGADA, f. 248, op. 13, kn. 691, ed. khr. 69, ll. 350–51 (1727); RGIA, f. 1556, op. 1, ed. khr. 163 (1827); and GARF, f. 109, 2-aia eksp., op. 75, ed. khr. 482 (1845); f. 109, 2-aia eksp., op. 77, ed. khr. 328 (1847). The many cases of marital discord found in TsGIAM, f. 380 (see chapter 7) are also not included here. Thus, these figures are meant to be representative and do not embrace all the cases of marital disputes available in archival records.

mother, having borne children with him, had no reason to object and considered that the property belonged in common to both of them (*pochitaia vse to obshchim*)," the hapless Rakhmaninov explained. His father remarried and passed away in short order, leaving Rakhmaninov with a stepmother and stepsiblings, all of whom expected a share of the property that had once belonged to Rakhmaninov's mother. The Senate did not dispute the justice of Rakhmaninov's claim but nonetheless upheld the decision of the lower courts to include his mother's estate in the general division of assets, rather than granting the property to Rakhmaninov and his brothers alone. In short, lack of vigilance on the part of Rakhmaninov's mother resulted in a diminished inheritance for her children.[36]

When conflict erupted between husband and wife, far from viewing their assets as property held in common for the welfare of the entire family, each spouse demanded a strict accounting from the other. Ivan Musin-Pushkin claimed that the upkeep of his wife's villages had ruined him when she sued him for divorce in 1750. He had spent thousands of rubles to supply their houses in her villages. He had also sunk ponds, planted gardens, and established factories on the estates she now claimed, not to mention buying grain to augment the inadequate harvest from her fields.[37] In another divorce case in 1806, Major Petr Belgard stated that he had paid the mortgage on his wife's estates, and used six thousand rubles of his own capital to build a house in her village, purchasing furniture, a carriage, china, and indeed, "everything necessary for properly running a household."[38] The nobility of Vologodskii district maintained that separate ownership could influence how one spouse managed the estates of the other, particularly if they had no children. In their petition to the Legislative Commission in 1767, the nobles asserted that "... it often happens ... that a husband during his wife's lifetime tries to improve his own villages, and to ruin those of his wife; there are also wives who ruin their husbands' villages in this fashion."[39]

Divorce, Morality, and Women's Property

Strictly speaking, property litigation fell under the purview of civil law and could be decided only in civil courts. Nonetheless, bickering over property was a staple feature of marital discord, and ecclesiastical authorities in the

36. RGIA, f. 1330, op. 4, ed. khr. 262, ll. 2–3, 35.
37. RGADA, f. 22 (Dela Sudnye), op. 1, ed. khr. 39, l. 52.
38. RGIA, f. 1346, op. 43, ch. 1, ed. khr. 414, l. 4.
39. *SIRIO* (1875), 14: 459–60. Memoirs also offer examples of women who displayed no interest in their husbands' estates. See M. M. Bardakova, "Iz vospominanii o Tsarskom sele," *Russkaia starina* 148, no. 11 (1911): 331; A. N. Kupreianova, "Iz semeinykh vospominanii," *Bogoslovskii vestnik* 1, no. 4 (1914): 651.

eighteenth century were hard-pressed to convince indignant spouses that they could rule only on spiritual matters. This confusion had its roots in the pre-Petrine era, when the church adjudicated property disputes between spouses.[40] Petitioners of both sexes routinely accused each other of spendthrift habits and neglect of their estates, if not outright theft of their belongings, and demanded justice from whatever institution would consent to hear their case. As a result, eighteenth-century divorce cases illuminate the prominent role conflicts over property played in precipitating family breakdown. By the first decade of the nineteenth century, the boundary between civil and ecclesiastical law had become clear at last to both officials and petitioners, and discussions of property in petitions for divorce gradually tapered off. In the eighteenth century, however, the overwhelming majority of requests for divorce heard in the Synod were entangled with property claims.

Divorce cases not only make for grim reading but also highlight the vulnerability of women married to abusive husbands and their dependence on male kin or other protectors to escape mistreatment.[41] The petitions of noblewomen recount, almost without exception, years of intolerable abuse at the hands of their husbands. Indeed, a survey of petitions to the Synod reveals a striking difference in the goals of men and women who appealed to the Church: if men were far more likely to request divorce with an eye to obtaining permission to remarry, the majority of women asked for nothing more than permission to live separately from their husbands and to return to their families or to take holy orders.[42] By and large these women appealed to ecclesiastical authorities in vain, since, from the mid-eighteenth century, the Orthodox Church refused to accept even the most severe physical mistreatment as pretext for dissolving marriage. Until late in the nineteenth century, the Church sanctioned divorce only in the most extreme circumstances: desertion and Siberian exile, for example, were the most common circumstances that ecclesiastical authorities recognized as grounds for divorce.[43] When noblemen requested divorce, however, their usual strategy was to accuse their wives of adultery, which they substantiated either with their wives' own confessions (which women often later retracted, claiming

40. The Holy Synod repeatedly instructed petitioners to bring their property disputes to the civil courts. For two examples, see RGIA, f. 796, op. 41 (1760), ed. khr. 299, l. 5; f. 796, op. 50 (1769), ed. khr. 124, l. 96. On property disputes between spouses in the pre-Petrine era, see Nevolin (1851), 1: 86–7, and A. S. Pavlov, *Kurs tserkovnogo prava* (St. Petersburg, 1902), 402.

41. On the role of male kin in defending women from abusive husbands in the seventeenth century, see Kollmann (1991), 70–71.

42. In her dissertation on marriage in eighteenth-century Russia, Robin Bisha states that she found only one case of a woman initiating divorce proceedings in the records of the St. Petersburg Consistory. See Bisha (1993), 238. My own investigation of petitions heard by the Synod in the eighteenth century revealed that women initiated at least 25% of all cases.

43. In the first half of the eighteenth century, the Church accepted far broader grounds for divorce. See Freeze (1990), 715, 733, 743.

that they had been coerced) or with the testimony of house serfs. Accusations of adultery played an equally prominent role in property disputes between spouses in the civil courts.

In his indictment of the Russian court in the era of empresses, Prince Shcherbatov repeatedly denounced the dissolute behavior of noblewomen, alleging that the reign of Elizabeth marked the "beginning of the period when women began to desert their husbands."[44] Whatever the truth of Shcherbatov's allegations, ecclesiastical and civil authorities continued to demand a high standard for marital fidelity and moral rectitude on the part of women. Predictably, in the eighteenth century both Church and State displayed greater leniency for male misdemeanors, while punishing female adultery—often on the basis of slender evidence—with a life sentence in a monastery. Ecclesiastical authorities proved far less willing to indict men on the basis of women's tales of their husbands' dalliances with serf women or seductive neighbors.[45] More striking, however, is the discovery that women who broke their marriage vows not only lost their freedom of movement but also forfeited the right to control their property.[46] Even in civil suits, husbands could be confident that when they introduced evidence of adultery, abandonment, or loose behavior, their wives' legal rights would take second place to their moral transgressions. By contrast, eighteenth-century male proprietors could indulge in a wide range of misdeeds without fear of losing control of their fortunes.[47]

Despite the failure of civil law to address the relationship between

44. Shcherbatov (1969), 227.

45. Although Gregory Freeze ([1990], 738) argues that there is no evidence that the Orthodox Church "regarded female infidelity as more serious than that of males," eighteenth-century divorce cases contradict his findings. In my survey of divorce petitions from 1700 to 1860, I found only one case in which the Synod imposed penance on a nobleman who acknowledged that he had fathered illegitimate children with a serf woman. See RGIA, f. 796, op. 50 (1769), ed. khr. 137, l. 3. Moreover, only two cases appear in which the Synod granted women a divorce on the grounds that their husbands had committed adultery. See RGIA, f. 796, op. 114 (1833), ed. khr. 594, ll. 1, 31–32, and f. 796, op. 136 (1855), ed. khr. 558, ll. 1, 3–4, 7–8. Local consistories and the Synod proved far more willing to accept male accusations of their wives' sexual misdemeanors and to dispatch the latter to a monastery, while permitting their husbands to remarry. See Rozanov 2/2: 368, no. 3 (1769); OAS (1878), 2/2: 263 (1722); RGIA, f. 796, op. 47 (1766), ed. khr. 179, l. 7; f. 796, op. 50 (1769), ed. khr. 124; f. 796, op. 50 (1769), ed. khr. 294; f. 796, op. 64 (1783), ed. khr. 125; also, N. L. Pushkareva, *Chastnaia zhizn' russkoi zhenshchiny: nevesta, zhena, liubovnitsa (X–nachalo XIX V)* (Moscow, 1997), 240. However, this discrepancy in no way invalidates Freeze's argument that the church rarely accepted adultery as grounds for divorce for either sex.

46. Hungarian noblewomen also lost the right to control their property if they were convicted of adultery. See D'Eszlary (1962), 433.

47. In this survey of divorce and property suits, I found only one case in which a husband signed an agreement that forbade him to sell or mortgage that part of his estate intended for his daughters' inheritance; his wife signed a similar agreement. See the account of the divorce of Iakov and Ekaterina Sivers (1779) in *Arkhiv kniazia Vorontsova* (1882), 26: 284.

feminine morals and property rights, male petitioners and legal authorities shared the common assumption that women who trespassed moral boundaries should relinquish control of their assets. As early as 1745, Empress Elizabeth deprived the widow Praskovia Nosova of the care of her daughter and control of her estate, both personal and immovable, after Nosova's father-in-law complained of her sinful lifestyle.[48] Adultery therefore not only furnished one of the few grounds that the Orthodox Church accepted for divorce (albeit rarely), but also provided a pretext—legitimate or not—for preventing married women from exercising their property rights. With this goal in mind, in 1761 Lieutenant Colonel Svechin presented a litany of accusations against his wife Maria in a petition to the Senate. According to Svechin, he had lodged complaints against his wife both in the Novgorod Consistory (*dukhovnaia konsistoriia*) and in civil court, for committing adultery with her cousin, Collegiate Councillor Ozerov; for leaving his house and taking his daughter with her; and adding insult to injury, for squandering her own assets as well as his on gifts to Ozerov. Svechin then produced a document from the Novgorod Consistory, which had allegedly ruled that Svechin's daughter should be returned to her father and that Maria Svechina's estate should be placed in her husband's hands for safekeeping.

As is so often the case, the dispute between the Svechins was filed without a resolution. The Novgorod Consistory claimed no knowledge of the ruling Svechin brought to the Senate, and the latter decreed that if Svechin wished to pursue the case, he must resubmit his petition. For her part, Maria Svechina denied betraying her husband and accused him of seizing her dowry and abandoning her in Moscow with nothing but her travelling costume.[49]

Svechin was far from unique in presenting a tale of betrayal in order to wrest property from his wife. In 1779, Collegiate Assessor Kolokoltsov informed the Synod that his wife had run away to Penza to join her lover and was running her estates into the ground. In order to preserve the inheritance of his six children, he asked the Senate to forbid her to sell or mortgage any more of her assets. Elizaveta Kolokoltsova denied that she had betrayed her husband; nonetheless, for the sake of preserving peace in her household, she agreed to sign over her estate to her children and to allow her husband use of all of the estate's income, with the exception of an annual allowance of twelve hundred rubles. Kolokoltsov was obviously content with a compromise so clearly in his favor: he made no further references to his wife's alleged moral transgressions once he had gained full use of the income of her estate, nor did he object if she wished to live apart from him in one of her villages.[50] The husband of Natalia Koltovskaia gained

48. *PSZ*, 12: 9.142 (04.04.1745).
49. RGADA, f. 22, op. 1, ed. khr. 53, ll. 2–35. See also Rozanov, 1/3: 534.
50. RGIA, f. 796, op. 60, ed. khr. 388, ll. 1–2, 13, 47–49 (1779).

control of his wife's estate with even less effort. Koltovskaia made no secret of her loathing for her husband or of her infidelity: she declared that she was willing to sacrifice her fortune and abandon her children, rather than return home. "I hand over my entire estate to you . . . to manage as you see fit," she wrote in 1798. "Only, for your own sake, forget me."[51]

The rhetoric of family and financial interest figured prominently in marital disputes, as petitioners of both sexes acknowledged that an appeal on behalf of their heirs would carry more weight with the courts than mere self-interest. Thus, a favorite device of antagonistic spouses was to level charges of mismanagement at one another. In a typical example, Lieutenant General Dedenev claimed that his wife's feeble intellect and indecent conduct rendered her incapable of managing her estate. As their quarrels escalated, Dedenev petitioned the empress in 1766 to appoint a trustee to the estate and, for their children's sake, to forbid his wife from selling her holdings. The empress decided in Dedenev's favor and relieved Avdotia Dedeneva of control of her property.[52] A decade earlier, Prince Vasilii Meshcherskii accused his wife of mortgaging his serfs and using the proceeds to lead a wild life in St. Petersburg. He made his appeal in the name of his three poverty-striken young children, which prompted the empress to summon Natalia Meshcherskaia to appear before her.[53] Only noblewomen of impeccable morals, however, could make use of the same strategy with any success. In 1779, for example, the Senate came to the defense of Ekaterina Sivers: she was absolved of any guilt in the breakdown of her marriage, and the Senate vowed to put a stop to her husband's attempts to prevent her from administering her estate.[54] By contrast, the guardian of the adulterous Natalia Koltovskaia accused her husband of mismanaging her property, with no results.[55]

Legal authorities agreed wholeheartedly with noblemen, such as Prince Meshcherskii, who argued that when their wives abandoned them and squandered their fortunes, the result was to impoverish their children. When women leveled similar charges, however, the same principle did not necessarily apply. Thus, Alexandra Voeikova appeared before the Senate in 1789, recounting how her husband and his mistress had run his estate into the ground and squandered more than one hundred thousand rubles in the last two years. For the sake of their children, she begged the Senate to hand over the estate to a board of guardians. Although the lower courts had ruled in Voeikova's favor, the Senate overturned their decision on the grounds that none of Captain Voeikov's natal kin had complained that he was misman-

51. RGIA, f. 1330, op. 1, ed. khr. 58, ll. 186, 207, 268.
52. RGADA, f. 8 (Kalinkin dom), op. 1, ed. khr. 212, ll. 1–12.
53. RGADA, f. 22, op. 1, ed. khr. 148, ll. 6–13, 46.
54. *Arkhiv kniazia Vorontsova* (1882), 26: 307.
55. RGIA, f. 1330, op. 1, ed. khr. 58, ll. 174–75 (1798).

aging his estate. The senators also remarked that no precedent could be found for depriving a nobleman of his estate at the request of his wife. "From Voeikova's petition, it is obvious that she would like to be not her husband's wife, but his mother," they declared, and went on to say that pure self-interest, rather than maternal solicitude, had prompted Voeikova's request.[56] The Senate granted Voeikova an allowance from her husband's estate but forbade her to leave her village in Riazan or to plague them with further petitions.

Throughout the eighteenth century, the tension between married women's entitlement to their separate property and their duty to uphold the sanctity of marriage resulted in a series of highly ambiguous decisions on the part of the courts. Some petitions from noblewomen hint at decisions taken at the provincial level that blatantly violated their property rights.[57] In the eyes of the sovereign and the Senate, however, the law of property often outweighed women's moral shortcomings. In 1745, for example, Efim Saburov accused his wife, Elena Trusova, of committing adultery. Denying any wrongdoing, Trusova launched a series of petitions in which she alleged that her husband and father-in-law had subjected her to beatings and confinement in order to seize control of her villages. The Moscow Consistory initially ruled in Saburov's favor, granted him custody of their daughter, and dispatched Trusova to a monastery near her villages. With the help of her uncle, however, Trusova persisted in her defense, and in 1748 the Senate instructed the Synod, on behalf of Empress Elizabeth, to release Trusova from exile and to return her daughter and all of her property to her. The empress declared that relinquishing Trusova's estate to her husband violated the law of property; until her death, Trusova was to maintain full control of her fortune, although the decree stipulated that she could neither sell nor mortgage any part of the estate so that it would remain intact for her daughter.[58] The empress reached a similar conclusion in 1750, when Ivan Musin-Pushkin charged his wife, Tatiana, with abandoning him and giving their daughter in marriage without his consent. When she countered her husband's charges, Tatiana Musina-Pushkina claimed that the latter had slept with his serf women and that his abusive treatment had driven her from their home. As she had done in Trusova's case, Elizabeth placed the estate and the couple's young son in Musina-Pushkina's care, but with the provisio that she could not sell or mortgage her immovable assets.[59]

56. RGADA, f. 7 (Razriad VII), op. 2, ed. khr. 2749, ll. 23–36.

57. See the petition from Sofia Maslova, who wrote in 1797 that the Zaraiskii district court refused to instruct her husband to return her dowry to her, on the grounds that wives had no right to demand the return of their personal property from their husbands. The Senate later overturned this decision. RGIA, f. 796, op. 78, ed. khr. 676, l. 2.

58. RGADA, f. 22, op. 1, ed. khr. 106, ll. 1–9; Rozanov (1869), 1/2: 327.

59. RGADA, f. 22, op. 1, ed. khr. 39; f. 248 (Zhurnaly i protokoly Senata, 1750), op. 131, ed. khr. 2615, l. 579; *OAS* (1907), 26: 429–31 (1746).

Princess Natalia Golshtein-Bek fared better than either Trusova or Musina-Pushkina. While the latter, despite having been absolved of wrong-doing, were subject to restrictions on their use of property, Golshtein-Bek suffered no constraints when she regained control of her estate. Responding to the complaints of Prince Golshtein-Bek about his wife's neglect of their daughter, in 1762 Peter III ordered that the princess's estate be placed in the care of her husband until their daughter came of age.[60] Later that year, however, the Senate revoked the emperor's decree and decided to return the estate to Princess Golshtein-Bek, on the grounds that no precedent existed either in the *Ulozhenie* of 1649 or in any other law code for handing over a woman's estate to her husband, and that the latter was entitled only to one-seventh of his wife's property after her death.[61] It is conceivable that Peter III's fall from the throne influenced the senators' decision; nonetheless, the appeal to law and precedent in their decision should not be dismissed as merely perfunctory.

Far from ruling on marital disputes arbitrarily, legal authorities at the highest level were acutely aware of the disparity between noblewomen's standing in family law and in the law of property. One case in particular, heard in the Senate in 1779, reveals that lawmakers never lost sight of their obligation to treat women's property rights with great care, even after women had compromised their virtue and no longer merited control of their assets. The acrimonious dispute between Nikita and Sofia Demidov highlights the conflict the courts faced when weighing women's standing in the law of property—a purely civil affair—with feminine duty to respect the sanctity of marriage.

When he appeared before the Senate in 1779, Nikita Demidov claimed he had invested all of his capital in an estate of more than five thousand serfs for his wife, and that she had repaid his generosity by twice committing adultery. Having endured years of her dissolute behavior, Demidov wished to divorce his wife and demanded the return of his estate. Demidova's mother and brothers all testified in her husband's favor, substantiating his claim that she had run off with another man. Although Sofia Demidova protested that her husband's abuse had driven her to the brink of suicide, the Senate accepted the testimony of her husband and family: in their review of the dispute, the senators declared that the statement of Demidova's mother had been instrumental in their decision and appealed to the "sacred" nature of a mother's testimony. After lengthy consideration, the Senate ruled that henceforth Demidova should live under the guardianship of her mother and brothers and transferred ownership of the estate back to Demidov.

60. *PSZ*, 15: 11.419 (28.01.1762).
61. *Senatskii arkhiv* (St. Petersburg, 1904), 11, kn. 102, ll. 120–22.

In their commentary on the Demidov case, however, the senators admitted that the law of property was, in fact, on Sofia Demidova's side. "This is a genuine example of the truth that there are cases that pass out of the realm of the law (*vykhodiat inogda iz zakonov*) and depend more on their moral content (*zavisiat bolee ot nravstvennogo o nikh poniatiia*)," they argued. "Who here is it more befitting to pity and defend from oppression: the husband, who . . . with love and good deeds attempted to correct the depraved morals of his wife, purchasing for this purpose a large village in her name, . . . Or should the wife be compensated for the estate which was purchased in her name?" The senators agreed that according to the law, Demidova was the legal owner of the estate (. . . *zakon, veliashchii krepostnomu byt po krepostiam*), but if they granted her the estate, they were trespassing divine law and providing Demidova with the means to continue her depraved life. They also agreed that it was unjust to deprive Demidov of his wealth, since he had given the estate to his wife in the belief that they would enjoy its use together until the end of their lives.

By far the most curious feature of the Demidov dispute is that although there was no dearth of witnesses, including her own family, to testify against Sofia Demidova, the members of the Senate by no means assumed that Demidova's forfeiture of her property was a foregone conclusion. Instead, they felt compelled to discuss at length the legal status of the property purchased by Demidov in his wife's name, and carefully considered the articles of the law that argued in favor of Demidova's continued ownership of the estate. The senators were convinced that they had established Demidova's moral guilt beyond question, yet in their report to the empress, they acknowledged that if they had abided strictly by the rules of property, the estate would have remained in Demidova's possession.[62]

The Demidov dispute was hardly unique in its juxtaposition of matters of property with strictures on feminine conduct. Yet the intricate commentary on the case underscores the dilemma that authorities faced when weighing married women's control of property with crimes against morality. Noblemen also could be deprived of control of property for moral transgressions. When, for example, the Senate indicted Andrei Neledinskoi in 1769 for flogging his mother and sister, Neledinskoi was sent to a monastery for one year, while his mother received control of his estate.[63] Nonetheless, prevailing gender conventions permitted men greater latitude than women in the realm of marital indiscretions. The result of this asymmetry was that the courts were far more likely to impose restrictions on noblewomen's exercise of their legal prerogatives when they were suspected of moral misdemeanors.

62. *PSZ*, 20: 14.886 (01.06.1779). This case also appears in *Arkhiv kniazia Vorontsova* (1888), 34: 406–34.

63. *PSZ*, 18: 13.262 (23.03.1769).

On the other hand, despite their unforgiving response to women who deceived or abandoned their husbands, legal authorities refused to allow men free reign over their wives' fortunes. In some cases, the sovereign intervened on the behalf of women, such as Elena Trusova, to prevent the courts from handing women's property over to their husbands. More often, even when the courts pronounced women unfit to administer their assets, they placed women's estates in the hands of guardians and imposed significant restrictions on men's use of their wives' fortunes.

Marital Discord and Civil Law

If, during the eighteenth century, evidence of marital conflict over property emerged primarily in petitions for divorce, by the nineteenth century women turned increasingly to the civil courts to defend their property rights. The growing number of wives filing suit against husbands in civil court, not to mention the decision of the courts to uphold their rights, serves as vivid testimony to the transformation of women's status in the law of property. Litigation by women on their own behalf against errant husbands was unusual in early-modern Russia.[64] By the late eighteenth century, however, women gradually became more willing to defend their interests and relied less on male kin to carry out the job for them.

Not surprisingly, female enthusiasm for bringing their husbands to court evolved slowly and became more common only in the last two decades of the eighteenth century. One early example of a noblewoman asserting her rights against her spouse appears in 1738, when Anna Barteneva accused her husband of mortgaging her estate for thirty-five rubles without her consent. Despite numerous decrees from the Senate to the Land College instructing the latter to invalidate the mortgage, the deed was not revoked. At last, citing an article in the *Ulozhenie* that forbade anyone to sell or mortgage land belonging to another clan, the Senate ordered the Land College in no uncertain terms to return the estate to Barteneva and to reimburse her for income lost during the years her estate had been mortgaged.[65]

From the turn of the nineteenth century, noblewomen turned to civil authorities with greater regularity in order to lodge complaints against husbands who failed to respect the law of separate property. Although ecclesiastical courts refused to grant women divorce even when extreme physical

64. In her work on female litigation in Muscovy, Nancy Kollmann cites several cases of wives suing husbands for abandonment, assault, and theft. In most of the cases she describes, however, male kin took on the task of litigating on behalf of injured wives. See Kollmann (1991), 70–71.

65. *PSZ*, 10: 7.651 (04.09.1738). See also a case in which a man forced his wife to make a will in his favor. This case came to the attention of Empress Elizabeth, who ordered the husband to be brought, under guard, to St. Petersburg. RGADA, f. 22, op. 1, ed. khr. 140 (1751).

abuse could not be denied, the civil courts displayed far less tolerance for husbands who sold their wives' property or spent their dowry funds. Noble-women thus discovered that crimes against property were more likely to elicit the sympathy of the courts than crimes against their persons. Moreover, unlike Nikita Demidov, in the nineteenth century husbands who transferred assets into their wives' names found that they could not retrieve their property when their affections cooled.

Both local and central authorities ruled consistently in favor of women when they could prove that their husbands had appropriated their fortunes. Countess Ekaterina Devier petitioned the Senate in 1799 to force her husband to return her dowry of ten thousand rubles, which he had squandered. The Senate found in favor of the countess, although recovering the sum proved to be complicated, since Devier had already mortgaged much of his own estate to fund his extravagant lifestyle. The senators ruled that the remaining property should be sold and the proceeds handed over to Countess Devier.[66] Similarly, Princess Natalia L'vova pursued her claim against her husband for more than fifteen years. The Senate decided finally in 1815 that Prince L'vov had indeed sold his wife's estate and spent her dowry, and instructed him to repay her with interest. Like Countess Devier, however, Princess L'vova found it no easy task to extract even part of what was owed her from her impoverished spouse.[67]

Although husbands continued to introduce questions of morality into property suits, the Senate proved less inclined to accept such evidence as having any bearing on property litigation, particularly when the welfare of children was not at stake. In a dispute heard initially in the St. Petersburg Office of Public Order (*Uprava blagochiniia*), the wife of Collegiate Assessor von Rittikh, Iulianna Gedovius, took her former husband to court when he failed to repay a debt of over one thousand rubles, which he had promised to pay after the death of his father. Von Rittikh and Gedovius were divorced in 1823; when von Rittikh's father died twenty years later, Gedovius had not forgotten the sum her husband still owed her. Von Rittikh brought his case to the Senate, arguing first, that he had never borrowed the alleged sum from his ex-wife and that they had drawn up the document in question so that his wife would inherit some of his father's capital if von Rittikh were to die during his military service; and second, since he had obtained his divorce on the grounds of his wife's immoral behavior, she did not deserve the money. The Fourth Department of the Senate ruled in von Rittikh's favor, arguing that Iulianna Gedovius had failed to respect the sanctity of marriage and brought dishonor to her husband by her depraved life. Consequently, they concluded, von Rittikh was absolved of any obligations to his

66. RGIA, f. 1346, op. 43, ch. 1, ed. khr. 254, ll. 3, 7, 30–32.
67. RGIA, f. 1330, op. 4, ed. khr. 337, ll. 1, 12–17.

former wife. Iulianna Gedovius persisted, however, and the General Session of the Senate decreed that the Office of Public Order must review the case strictly on the grounds of the laws governing the statute of limitations on the payment of debt.[68]

Other marital wrangles featured husbands who, having purchased property in their wives' names, litigated for the return of their assets. These men soon discovered that the law did not allow for a change of heart, as the following case reveals. In 1809, Nikita Gavrilov filed suit against his wife, claiming that in 1788 he had purchased a house for twelve thousand rubles in her name. At the time he had been fighting in the navy, and he bought the house so that his wife would not be left penniless if he were to die in battle. He had saved her from dire poverty, since she had come to his household without a dowry and encumbered with a mother, two small children, and a mother-in-law. When Gavrilov returned from service, their relationship deteriorated through no fault of his own, and not only did his wife refuse to live with him, but, in his words, she "took over the house and forced me out of it." According to Gavrilov, his wife alleged that she had purchased the house with money inherited from her first husband. Gavrilov pronounced this a lie and petitioned the Senate to return his house to him. The Senate proved unsympathetic to Gavrilov's sad tale, however, and decreed that since the deed of purchase had been drawn up in Elena Gavrilova's name, she was the legal owner of the house.[69]

As was the case in the eighteenth century, the decisions of the courts were intended, above all, to benefit the couple's heirs. Yet when authorities refused to allow women to manage their estates, they nonetheless stopped short of handing their holdings over to their husbands. The solution in such cases was to appoint guardians who would either administer the estate themselves or at least require a strict accounting when the husband gained some control. Such was the outcome in a dispute initiated by Varvara Mezhakova against her husband in 1797. Mezhakova pleaded before a series of courts that her husband physically abused her and had wrested control of her estate of more than seven hundred serfs. Aleksandr Mezhakov dismissed his wife's charges as patent nonsense inspired by her depraved nature, which he had been unable to correct during the course of their eighteen-year marriage. Initially, Mezhakova won the right to live apart from her husband, but she prolonged her battle when he proposed to give her an annual allowance of only two thousand rubles. Mezhakova's appeal finally reached the Senate in 1808, in which she recounted in full how her husband had forced her to sell her estate to their minor children. The senators ultimately decreed that Mezhakova should be allowed to reclaim her estate, but that she must

68. RGIA, f. 1330, op. 6, ed. khr. 278, ll. 36–50 (1850).
69. RGIA, f. 1330, op. 4, ed. khr. 107, ll. 2–3, 40. See also RGIA, f. 1330, op. 3, ed. khr. 119, ll. 92–106, 189–91 (1806).

appoint a guardian to oversee the estate with her, since her children would remain with their father. They also stipulated that Mezhakova was responsible for relinquishing half of the proceeds from her estate and her factory to her ex-husband for her children's maintenance.[70]

As these cases make clear, the Senate consistently defended women's property from the encroachments of their husbands; at the same time, legal authorities stopped short of restoring married women's full control over their estates when the welfare of children was at stake. Moreover, most marital disputes did not reach the Senate, and the record of rulings at the provincial level remains uncharted territory. Stories of women impoverished by spendthrift husbands are legion in nineteenth-century memoirs and novels: for every woman who filed suit against her husband, many more quietly returned to their families or retreated to remote dowry villages. Yet the very fact that married women litigated against their husbands in increasing numbers from the end of the eighteenth century demonstrates their faith that the authorities would rule according to the laws of property. Men's infringements of their wives' property rights long predated the nineteenth century in Russia. Unlike their predecessors, however, noblewomen from the end of the eighteenth century were less inclined to depend on male kin to defend their prerogatives and proved more likely to bring their grievances before judicial authorities. Of these, the most persistent eventually received satisfaction.

From the point of view of Imperial legislators, family interest and the welfare of children took precedence over the rights of individuals, and they interpreted the law in light of these preoccupations. Although legal scholars often boasted that Russian property law made no distinction between the rights of men and women, during the eighteenth century women were held to a higher standard as custodians of their children's inheritance and forfeited at least some measure of control of their fortunes when their virtue was called into question. On the other hand, when the courts based their decisions on the rules of property alone, women could reasonably hope for a decision in their favor. Whereas the Orthodox Church proved reluctant to take action against abusive husbands, the civil courts chose to honor the principle of separate property and to deny men unbridled dominion over their wives.

Marital Discord and Noblewomen's Financial Autonomy

Independent property ownership also served women well outside the courtroom. The Holy Synod refused to grant divorces even when both partners

70. RGADA, f. 7, op. 2, ed. khr. 3065, ll. 1–7, 16–18, 38–39, 81–82; RGIA, f. 1330, op. 4, ed. khr. 69, ll. 11–17; f. 1346, op. 43, ch. 1, ed. khr. 451.

were eager to put an end to their union[71]; however, informal separation was widespread, if not epidemic in the eighteenth century. Many contemporaries noted the propensity of noble couples to lead separate lives, with or without the sanction of the Church. "Informal divorces (*samovol'nye razvody*) . . . were extremely common," maintained Andrei Bolotov in his lengthy memoir of provincial noble life in the late eighteenth century.[72] In an account of estate life early in the nineteenth century, Arkadii Kochubei recalled dining at the home of a neighboring landowner and discovering that all of the guests at the dinner had been divorced.[73] Prince Shcherbatov was convinced that married women's economic freedom encouraged them to indulge in adulterous relationships.[74] During her lengthy sojourn in Russia, Martha Wilmot hinted at this possibility as well when she wrote of Marie Bakhmeteff, who "quitted her husband (a woman's fortune in Russia is always at her disposal) and attach'd herself to Count Alexis O[rloff]."[75]

Undoubtedly, women's property ownership facilitated such arrangements and permitted them a greater measure of freedom to leave their husbands. In their report to the 1767 Legislative Commission, the nobility from Kolomenskii district observed that it was not uncommon among the nobility for an unhappy wife to abandon her husband and to "live in her villages or with her relatives"; indeed, it was so common that the nobility requested legislation to regulate property settlements in these cases.[76] Aggrieved husbands, such as Collegiate Assessor Petr Bakhteiarov, went before the Synod to complain that their wives had abandoned them and gone to live on their own estates. Bakhteiarov stated in his petition that his wife had taken advantage of a trip to Moscow in 1742 to leave him and return to her ancestral village in Rzhevskii district, where she had built a house with money stolen from him. Having accused her husband of committing adultery with his serf women, Maria Bakhteiarova instructed her own serfs to kill him if he ventured into her village.[77] Despite repeated appeals, Bakhteiarov never

71. Until 1730, the Orthodox Church permitted divorce when both spouses agreed to separate. Despite the prohibition of informal divorce after 1730, the practice continued until the mid-eighteenth century. See A. Lebedev, "O brachnykh razvodakh po arkhivnym dokumentam Khar'kovskoi i Kurskoi dukhovnykh konsistorii," in *Chteniia v Imperatorskom obshchestve istorii i drevnostei rossiiskikh*, 2/1 (Moscow, 1887), 27–29 and Freeze (1990), 714–15.

72. Quoted in A. Levshin, "Zhenskie nravy i vospitanie proshlogo veka (Istoricheskie kartiny)," *Kolos'ia: Zhurnal nauchno-literaturnyi*, no. 1 (January 1887), 160.

73. Arkadii Vasil'evich Kochubei, *Semeinaia khronika. Zapiski, 1790–1873* (St. Petersburg, 1890), 238–39.

74. Shcherbatov (1969), 219–21.

75. Bradford (1935), 345.

76. *SIRIO* (1869), 4: 338.

77. RGIA, f. 796, op. 45, ed. khr. 164, ll. 6–9, 15–19. See Prince Meshcherskii's declaration that his wife, having left him, was living on the proceeds of an estate he had purchased in her name. RGADA, f. 22, op. 1, ed. khr. 148, l. 18.

received satisfaction from the courts, and the case was closed only in 1770 when both Bakhteiarovs had died.

When husbands petitioned the Synod, it was often to demand the return of runaway wives. Not only aristocratic women but also those of more modest means utilized their resources to flee unhappy marriages, even when the Church instructed them to return. Elena Khvoshchinskaia recalled that after her father had an affair, her mother left their estate in Tambov province and took their three daughters to a village of her own in Penza.[78] On the other hand, the wife of Matvei Karniolin-Pinskii eluded her husband and his demand for a divorce for several years by using her wealth to purchase the protection of local officials.[79]

The decision to abandon a husband and the comforts of life on his estate was far from easy. One noblewoman recounted that her mother's sister, after enduring many unhappy years with her husband, took her daughter to live on her dowry estate. Her voluntary exile dragged on for years in a remote village "where snow covered the roof and wolves howled under the windows."[80] Khvoshchinskaia imagined her mother's state of mind when she determined to leave her father: "My mother . . . abandoned Saltyki [their estate] with a heavy heart. . . . The prospects which lay before her were scant means, loss, loneliness, depression, and unaccustomed labor."[81]

As well as providing the means to escape a husband's worst abuses, property ownership elevated women's status within the family in more happy circumstances. Recalling his childhood in Ukraine, one petty nobleman described the balance of power in his family's household in the following words: "Grandfather . . . was considered the official head of the family, but in reality . . . my grandmother held the reins of domestic government in her plump little hands. This was not only because the house and the little plot of land . . . were her (and not his) property, but also a result of her innate business and management abilities."[82] Martha Wilmot noted the link between separate marital property and domestic harmony when she observed that "here a Woman's powers to dispose of her own wealth is a great check on her husband's inclination to forsake her or to Tyrannize."[83]

Married women's control of property was far from absolute in Imperial Russia. When conflict arose between spouses over the administration of women's assets, women had no guarantee that the courts would uphold their

78. Elena Iur'evna Khvoshchinskaia, *Vospominaniia* (St. Petersburg, 1898), 45–49.
79. Quoted in Wortman (1976), 189.
80. Kupreianova (1914), 662.
81. Khvoshchinskaia (1898), 46.
82. F. V. Volkhovskii, "Otryvki odnoi chelovecheskoi zhizni," *Sovremennik* 4, no. 4 (1911): 257.
83. Bradford (1935), 271.

rights or even that their families would take their side. But it is equally inaccurate to assume that separate marital property played no part in ameliorating the subordinate position of women in the noble family. In a memoir recounting her family history before Emancipation, Countess Bludova maintained that the tradition of separate property in Russia had shaped the character of Russian women and had a profound impact on the relationship of spouses. She introduced this theme by quoting a letter from her father to her mother concerning one of the latter's serfs. "Not only according to law, but also to custom, which is often more powerful than law, a married woman or unmarried girl was owner and administrator of her property in her own right," Bludova told her readers. "Even in the most . . . affectionate families . . . the husband found it necessary that the relationship of his wife with her serfs, the local authorities, and bailiffs on her estates was completely independent—not only in fact, but in the eyes of everyone who did business with her."[84] As a result of the regime of separate property, noblewomen of means preserved a separate identity and legal autonomy vis-à-vis their husbands in the realm of economic relations. If not an antidote to the rigid hierarchy of the patriarchal family, control of property allowed married women the chance to circumvent the absolute obedience prescribed for them in family law.

84. A. D. Bludova, "Zapiski grafini Antoniny Dmitrievny Bludovoi," *Russkii arkhiv*, kn. 1, no. 4 (1874): 872.

A *Desiatina* of Her Own: Gender and the Culture of Noble Property

"In front of every house in Moscow and St. Petersburg is a sign with the name of the owner," August von Haxthausen remarked in his account of Russian life in the 1840s. "In walking along the streets, one can be certain to find the name of a woman before every third house. This is also the case with real estate in rural areas; perhaps one-fifth to one quarter of this property is in the hands of the female sex."[1]

Like so many visitors from abroad, Haxthausen was intrigued by the spectacle of property-owning women in Russia. Both the fact of married women's economic independence and the scale of women's holdings surprised foreign observers and inspired speculation on differences between women in Russia and in the West. Haxthausen was unique, however, in venturing an estimate of the amount of property concentrated in women's hands, and his appraisal has never been put to the test. The first part of this study mapped the gradual erosion of gender asymmetry in the realm of property law. It remains to be seen if legal parity translated into real economic gains for women. Given the miserly portion most daughters could anticipate from family holdings, we might anticipate that the majority of noblewomen possessed only negligible allotments of land, incapable of bestowing real economic independence on their owner. Historians of the Russian economy have not overlooked the occasional female serf owner or factory proprietor, but—in their defense—they have had no grounds to believe that substantial female proprietors were anything but a marginal phenomenon.

In this chapter I will chart women's visibility as property owners and analyze the dimensions of women's economic activity. The problems that

---

1. Haxthausen (1972), 23.

demand scrutiny are, on the surface, fairly simple ones. Were noblewomen active participants in Russian economic life? How much real estate was, in fact, in the hands of noblewomen? Did women of other social estates also take part in economic transactions or was property ownership the exclusive domain of the wellborn? And, finally, how did the economic behavior of women compare with that of their male counterparts? With these questions in mind, I move beyond investigation of women's legal status to take a closer look at the culture of noble property.

Sources and Methodology

In this chapter, with its geographical and temporal scope, I represent the diversity and changing fortunes of the Russian nobility. My discussion extends over five districts during the century and a half bracketed at one extreme by the reign of Peter the Great and at the other by the emancipation of the serfs. Approximately eight thousand property transactions drawn from the *krepostnye knigi*, or provincial notarial records, form the basis of this analysis.[2] An abundant and underutilized source for investigating economic life in both the provinces and the capitals, the *krepostnye knigi* document a wide variety of economic transactions. These include the sale of estates and individual serfs, manumission of serfs, mortgages, rental of land, and the sale of property in town, not to mention a scattering of wills, dowries, and deeds of separation (*razdel'nye zapisi*). In addition to citing the amount of property sold and the purchase price, each entry sets forth the marital status of female participants, how the property being sold was originally acquired, and if the participants were kin, how the two were related. Far from merely documenting the absence or presence of women landowners, evidence from the *krepostnye knigi* allows a comparison of several dimensions of women's and men's use of property.

As part of a larger campaign to centralize government administration and increase state revenue, Peter the Great established the *krepostnaia kontora*, or notarial bureau, in 1701, with detailed instructions on how transfers of property should be documented and the amount of duty to be collected on each transaction. The difficulty of enforcing the new law, however, prompted Peter and his successors to reassign jurisdiction over notarial affairs on several occasions. In the provinces, the new notarial offices fell first under the control of the *voevoda*, the provincial governor, but in 1706 were transferred to the local town council (*ratusha*); later, after 1719, the Justice College oversaw the registration of deeds and collection of duties on the transactions. In Moscow registration of deeds of purchase took place in the

2. For a more detailed discussion of the methodology used for this chapter, see appendix 1.

Justice College itself, while property transfers in provincial capitals and other towns took place initially in the local civil courts (*nadvornye sudy*). From 1731, however, provincial and district governors assumed responsibility for overseeing transfers of property. Following Catherine II's reform of provincial government in 1775, the Justice College was abolished, and all property transactions henceforth were recorded in courts at the district or provincial level.[3]

The records available in the Archive of Ancient Acts in Moscow dictated the choice of districts surveyed in this work. This archive holds notarial records for districts throughout Russia; very few districts, however, provide a continuous run of data from the beginning to the end of the eighteenth century. Pursuing transactions recorded after Catherine II's reforms proved more complicated still, since nineteenth-century notarial documents are located in provincial archives and many have not survived. As a result, complete data for all districts and all variables could not be assembled. Nonetheless, for all their gaps and inconsistencies, the surviving transactions reveal unmistakable trends in women's participation in economic life.

Two districts in this survey, Vladimir and Kashin (in Tver' province), are located near Moscow and were settled as early as the sixteenth century. Many powerful noble families owned estates in this region, which despite the poor quality of the soil was considered desirable for its proximity to Moscow.[4] Tambov and Kursk, in the fertile black-earth region, were colonized primarily by petty servitors in the seventeenth century and attracted great numbers of settlers as the threat of Tatar raids diminished. By the end of the eighteenth century, nobles vied for control of estates in both districts.[5] The fifth, and final, sample is drawn from the records of the Justice College in Moscow. While transactions registered in provincial notarial offices primarily concerned property located in the region, in Moscow the surviving estate sales encompass every province in Russia. The contrast between the records that survive in district *krepostnye knigi* and those in the Justice College

3. For an overview of the history of the *krepostnaia kontora*, see Kapustina (1959), 217–22. Initially, transactions of any value could be recorded in Moscow and the provincial capitals; in other provincial towns, only transactions of less than one hundred rubles could be registered. Petrine Russia consisted of eleven *gubernii*, or provinces, which were further subdivided into forty-nine provinces (*provintsii*). Moscow, Vladimir, and Tambov were provincial capitals from 1719. See Iu. V. Got'e, *Istoriia oblastnogo upravleniia v Rossii ot Petra I do Ekateriny II.* (Moscow, 1913), 103. Catherine II's provincial reform of 1775 created new territorial subdivisions and allowed provincial agencies a greater role in dispensing justice and overseeing transfers of property. See Madariaga (1981), 277–91, and Robert E. Jones, "Urban Planning and the Development of Provincial Towns in Russia, 1762–1796," in *The Eighteenth Century in Russia*, ed. J. G. Garrard (Oxford, 1973), 327.

4. Dukes (1967), 11.

5. On the settlement of Tambov province, see E. N. Shchepkina, *Starinnye pomeshchiki na sluzhbe i doma* (St. Petersburg, 1890), 95–97.

(or, after 1775, the Moscow Civil Court) not only illuminates striking differences between the economic activity of nobles in the provinces and in Moscow but also highlights one crucial similarity. As we will see, the number of estate sales in the provinces was meager in contrast to the brisk trade in all forms of property in Moscow. A further disparity appears in the size of the estates that were sold and the value of the property transacted. These widely varying property markets were both characterized, however, by the unequivocal prominence of noblewomen after the mid-eighteenth century.

The Russian Economy before 1861

As in most preindustrial societies, access to land was a key constituent of economic power in Imperial Russia. Russian nobles calculated their wealth on the basis of serf ownership rather than landholding.[6] Nonetheless, the circulation of unsettled land, much of it in small parcels, reveals that nobles seized every opportunity to expand and consolidate their holdings and exploit their natural resources. Indeed, by the second half of the eighteenth century the nobility made a valiant attempt to exclude members of other social estates from rural land ownership.[7] During the implementation of the General Land Survey in the 1770s, when the state offered Treasury Land for sale to the nobility, the latter responded by purchasing almost three million acres.[8] Land hunger was inevitable in a society that lacked liquid assets and that could boast only the most primitive banking system.

Agriculture was not the sole source of wealth for the nobility in the eighteenth century. After 1714 government servitors of all ranks received annual salaries and pensions; however, until the reign of Catherine II these salaries were paid sporadically, and the more savvy members of the nobility wisely invested their funds in landed estates. Despite government subsidies to encourage noble participation in manufacturing, trade and industry were dominated by the merchant class and by peasant entrepreneurs into the nineteenth century.[9]

While acknowledging the significance of landed wealth for the nobility, many historians have argued that an active market for real estate in Russia did not develop until after 1861.[10] The evidence of the *krepostnye knigi* points

6. Blum (1961), 367; Dukes (1967), 11; Kahan (1966), 42.

7. Leonard (1993), 51–52.

8. L. V. Milov, *Issledovanie ob "ekonomicheskikh primechaniiakh" k general'nomy mezhevaniiu (k istorii russkogo krest' ianstva i sel'skogo khoziaistva vtoroi poloviny XVIII v.).* (Moscow, 1965), 28.

9. Arcadius Kahan, *The Plow, the Hammer, and the Knout: An Economic History of Eighteenth-Century Russia* (Chicago, 1985), 134–36.

10. Peter Gatrell, *The Tsarist Economy, 1850–1917* (New York, 1986), 106; Michael Confino, "Histoire et psychologie: Á propos de la noblesse russe au XVIII siécle," *Annales: Économies, sociétés, civilisations* 22, no. 6 (November–December 1967): 1185.

to a more active market than scholars have suspected. During the eighteenth century relatively few sales of estates were recorded in the northern provinces, but an average of six to eight hundred sales of both settled and unsettled estates took place annually in Moscow. A brisk trade in land and serfs was also the rule in the black-earth district. Between 1775 and 1780, for example, at least one hundred sales of estates, settled and unsettled, were recorded each year in Tambov. Reflecting the social composition of the district, many sellers and buyers were lower military officials or freeholders (*odnodvortsy*), rather than nobles. Other types of transactions, such as the manumission and sale of individual serfs, appear in far greater numbers than the sale of estates in the eighteenth century. Although its scope would increase substantially in subsequent decades, the market for rural real estate in Russia was far from stagnant in the era before emancipation.

Noblewomen and Estate Ownership

For all of their interpretive differences, historians have portrayed Russian economic life as predominately, if not exclusively, a male phenomenon. On those rare occasions when the names of women landowners appear, they are passed over without comment. The scope of female landholding, as well as women's activities in provincial economic life, remains uncharted territory.

Since the nineteenth century, the notion that Russian noblewomen exercised considerable economic power from the medieval era has become an article of faith.[11] And yet in the realm of property ownership as well as in the legal domain, historians have emphasized continuity at the expense of change. Documents that survive from pre-Petrine Russia demonstrate that although individual women controlled estates and took part in urban and rural economic life, women as a group were poorly represented as landowners. Elite women in early-modern Russia enjoyed some financial autonomy, but little more than their European counterparts and far less than their eighteenth-century descendants. Thus, a land cadastre compiled in Novgorod in 1582–84 included the names of sixty-four women, comprising 2.3 percent of all landholders. The names of ninety-one women, or 5.5 percent of estate owners, appeared in a later survey in 1626–27. Both of these figures exceed the proportion of female slaveholders cited in surviving deeds

11. The amount of land controlled by women in pre-Petrine Russia has been the subject of numerous studies. The most optimistic assessment of women's landownership in Muscovy can be found in Kivelson (1996), 106–8, 116–20. See also Daniel H. Kaiser, "Women's Property in Muscovite Families, 1500–1725" (paper presented at Kent State University, 1988); Kleimola (1992): 225; Levin (1983), 164; Levy (1983), 205–6.

of purchase. According to these records, only 2 percent of elite women owned slaves.[12]

While these sources may well underestimate the extent of women's estate ownership, they fall short of demonstrating that women in medieval and early-modern Russia were singularly fortunate in their access to property. Notarial records reveal that women took part in less than 5 percent of property transactions recorded in Moscow and in Vladimir before 1715; in Riazan from 1706 to 1711, women do not appear to have been either sellers or purchasers of estates.[13] The absence of women in the market for real estate does not necessarily prove that they did not possess land of their own. These figures nonetheless underscore the limitations of women's power over their assets; the law allowed women to sell hereditary estates (*votchiny*) but prohibited them from alienating service-tenure land (*pomestia*) in their possession. Once women gained the right to dispose of *pomestia* in 1715, as well as patrimonial land,[14] their visibility as sellers of property grew more pronounced than in the records of 1699–1711.

Noblewomen's economic position in the opening decades of the eighteenth century, viewed through the lens of notarial records, was characterized above all by limited participation in property transactions. No census survives to reveal the precise amount of property controlled by women. There can be little doubt, however, about the extent of female participation in the market. The percentages vary from district to district (Table 4.1): In Kashin, for example, women appeared as sellers of estates in 25 percent of recorded transactions and took part in a further 3 percent with male kin. Female property owners were less evident in Kursk, where their names showed up in only 11 percent of surviving deeds of sale. Inevitably, the largest sample comes from records collected in Moscow, where women comprised approximately 18 percent of sellers of estates between 1715 and 1720. All in all, in the districts surveyed, women accounted for 17 percent of sellers of estates on their own and 3 percent of estates sold with male kin.

The absence of women as purchasers of estates (Table 4.2) provides more eloquent testimony to the limits of women's economic autonomy in the early eighteenth century. In Vladimir, not a single woman purchased property

12. Richard Hellie, *Slavery in Russia, 1450–1725* (Chicago, 1982), 611. Elsewhere, Hellie notes that the number of female slave owners rises to 7.7% if one includes dowry agreements, which list both husband and wife as the owner. See Hellie, "Women and Slavery in Muscovy," *Russian History* 10, pt. 2 (1983): 227. See also *Real Estate Transfer Deeds in Novgorod, 1609–1616*, text and comm. Ingegerd Norlander (Stockholm, 1987), 63. The deeds recovered for the early seventeenth century mention six hundred persons, of whom about sixty are women.

13. RGADA, f. 1209, op. 4, ch. 1, ed. khr. 2624 (Pomestnyi prikaz, 1701–3); f. 1209, op. 4, ch. 1, ed. khr. 2920 (Vladimirskii stol, 1699–1701); f. 1209, op. 4, ch. 1, ed. khr. 2935 (Riazanskii stol, 1706–11). The transactions in ed. khr. 2624 consist entirely of sales and mortgages of property; in ed. khr. 2920 and 2935, sales comprise a minority of the transactions.

14. See chapter 2.

TABLE 4.1 Sale of Estates by Noblewomen, Alone or in Conjunction with Male Kin, 1715–1860*

	Vladimir		Kashin		Tambov		Kursk		Moscow		All Regions	
	Alone	+Kin	Alone	+Kin	Alone	+Kin	Alone	+Kin	Alone	+Kin	Alone	+Kin
1715–20	5	5	25	3	21	9	11	2	18	0	17	3
	(20)		(93)		(43)		(102)		(136)		(394)	
1750–55	45	3	37	2	31	3	30	1	34	1	34	1
	(31)		(57)		(80)		(98)		(401)		(667)	
1775–80	45	0	55	0	28	1	40	3	34	3	36	2
	(69)		(80)		(202)		(78)		(436)		(865)	
1805–10	35	3	38	0	33	0	—	—	41	3	36	2
	(195)		(37)		(120)				(137)		(489)	
1855–60	46	2	50	0	41	3	45	2	47	2	46	2
	(137)		(127)		(217)		(186)		(467)		(1,134)	
All periods 1715–1860	39	2	42	1	33	2	33	2	37	2	37	2
	(452)		(394)		(662)		(464)		(1,577)		(3,549)	

* +Kin = with male kin. Each value represents the percentage of women who sold estates, either alone or with male kin. The number of available transactions by both women and men is given in parentheses.
Source: See appendix 1.

TABLE 4.2 Purchase of Estates by Noblewomen, 1715–1860*

	Vladimir	Kashin	Tambov	Kursk	Moscow	All Regions
1715–20	0	9	4	0	7	5
	(19)	(81)	(47)	(96)	(144)	(387)
1750–55	34	36	18	22	33	30
	(29)	(58)	(87)	(96)	(378)	(648)
1775–80	22	57	31	45	31	34
	(72)	(81)	(200)	(71)	(413)	(837)
1805–10	46	50	41	—	39	43
	(166)	(32)	(119)		(123)	(440)
1855–60	51	31	42	44	44	43
	(85)	(100)	(174)	(164)	(452)	(975)
All periods	39	34	32	29	34	33
1715–1860	(371)	(352)	(627)	(427)	(1,510)	(3,287)

* Each value represents the percentage of women who sold estates. The number of available transactions by both women and men is given in parentheses.
Source: See appendix 1.

according to the recorded transactions, whereas in Kashin, 9 percent of those who bought land were women. Overall, the proportion of female purchasers between 1715 and 1720 averaged 5 percent. The sporadic appearance of female investors is all the more striking in the context of the Law of Single Inheritance, which was still in effect during these years and which allowed parents to grant dowries only in cash and movable property. We can only speculate on the role women's dowries played in the family economy; however, the figures on women's investment early in the eighteenth century suggest that noblemen made use of their wives' capital to purchase assets in their own names. Impressionistic evidence supports this reading; thus, in a will composed in 1735, Princess Anna Iusupova gave instructions concerning a village that her husband had purchased in his name, with her own money.[15] Noblewomen's failure to convert cash dowries into land points to men's appropriation of their wives' movable wealth, if not for the purchase of estates then to pay off debts or to fund family consumption. As investors, elite women had tenuous ties to the market at best.

The marital status of women who bought and sold property (Table 4.3) in the Petrine era underscores the sad fact that marriage severely constricted women's participation in the market. As widows or spinsters, women were far more likely to part with or acquire assets. Between 1715 and 1720, 62 percent of women who alienated estates were widows, whereas a further 18 percent reported they were unmarried. By contrast, only 20 percent of female sellers were married women. Despite the prolonged absence of men

15. RGADA, f. 1290, op. 1, ed. khr. 39, l. 1.

TABLE 4.3 Marital Status of Noblewomen Participating in Property Transactions, 1715–1860*

	All Regions: Sellers		All Regions: Buyers	
1715–20	Widows (N = 49)	62	Widows (N = 8)	44
	Wives (N = 16)	20	Wives (N = 7)	39
	Maids (N = 14)	18	Maids (N = 3)	17
	(79)		(18)	
1750–55	Widows (N = 108)	46	Widows (N = 56)	30
	Wives (N = 107)	46	Wives (N = 120)	63
	Maids (N = 18)	8	Maids (N = 13)	7
	(233)		(189)	
1775–80	Widows (N = 141)	43	Widows (N = 85)	30
	Wives (N = 154)	47	Wives (N = 174)	62
	Maids (N = 31)	10	Maids (N = 21)	8
	(326)		(280)	
1805–10	Widows (N = 50)	27	Widows (N = 17)	9
	Wives (N = 102)	55	Wives (N = 133)	70
	Maids (N = 34)	18	Maids (N = 40)	21
	(186)		(190)	
1855–60	Widows (N = 122)	22	Widows (N = 34)	8
	Wives (N = 342)	63	Wives (N = 320)	77
	Maids (N = 79)	15	Maids (N = 63)	15
	(543)		(417)	
All periods	Widows (N = 470)	34	Widows (N = 200)	18
1715–1860	Wives (N = 721)	53	Wives (N = 754)	69
	Maids (N = 176)	13	Maids (N = 140)	13
	(1,367)		(1,094)	

* Each value is the percentage of available property transactions involving women of each marital status. The number of available transactions is given in parentheses.

Source: See appendix 1.

on military service, it appears that wives rarely sacrificed their resources, even while their husbands were away. Conversely, when women were on their own, they proved far more likely to convert immovable assets into cash. This pattern held true for female purchasers as well, if not to such an extreme. Thus, 44 percent of women recorded as purchasing estates were widows and 17 percent were spinsters, while a less impressive 39 percent were wives.

Several additional variables substantiate noblewomen's marginal status as property owners early in the eighteenth century. Women sold and manumitted serfs (Table 4.4) in roughly the same percentages as they sold estates. In Vladimir, 17 percent of serf owners who manumitted peasants were women, and of these 84 percent were widows; 19 percent of the serfs manumitted in Kursk were owned by women. Few sales of serfs were recorded in the provinces in 1715–20—of these, 14 percent of the sellers were women acting on their own, and 5 percent were women acting with male kin (Table 4.5). Among proprietors in Vladimir who rented out land to peasants (Table

TABLE 4.4 Manumission of Serfs by Noblewomen, 1715–1810*

	Vladimir	Kashin	Tambov	Kursk	All Regions
1715–20	17 (190)	—	—	19 (48)	17 (238)
1750–55	25 (197)	20 (385)	29 (24)	—	22 (606)
1775–80	30 (139)	41 (330)	40 (70)	—	38 (539)
1805–10	—	49 (71)	—	—	49 (71)
All periods 1715–1810	23 (526)	31 (786)	37 (94)	19 (48)	28 (1,454)

* Each value is the percentage of available manumission transactions. The number of transactions by both women and men is given in parentheses.
Source: See appendix 1.

TABLE 4.5 Sale of Serfs by Noblewomen, Alone or in Conjunction with Male Kin, 1715–1810*

	Vladimir		Kashin		Tambov		All Regions	
	Alone	+Kin	Alone	+Kin	Alone	+Kin	Alone	+Kin
1715–20	18 (11)	0	—	—	13 (31)	6	14 (42)	5
1750–55	33 (43)	5	55 (44)	5	43 (63)	2	43 (150)	2
1775–80	21 (80)	0	43 (100)	0	37 (301)	0	35 (481)	0
1805–10	44 (174)	1	36 (148)	0	38 (58)	3	40 (380)	1
All periods 1715–1810	36 (308)	1	41 (292)	0	36 (453)	1	37 (1,053)	1

* +Kin = with male kin. Each value is the percentage of available transactions involving the sale of serfs by noblewomen. The number of available transactions by both women and men is in parentheses.
Source: See appendix 1.

4.6), 13 percent were women; in Kashin, 27 percent of those who let land were women. In both districts, the overwhelming majority of women taking part in these dimensions of economic life were widows.

In the cash-poor environment of the early eighteenth century, women were sometimes compelled to borrow money but were rarely in a position to act as lenders (Table 4.7).[16] During 1715–20, women in Vladimir and

16. These findings are well in keeping with those of Daniel Kaiser's study of indebtedness in early-modern Russia. Kaiser points out that women cited fewer creditors, and far fewer debtors, in their testaments than did men; the size of their debts was also much less than that of men's debts. See Daniel H. Kaiser, "'Forgive Us Our Debts . . .': Debts and Debtors in Early Modern Russia," in *Forschungen zur osteuropäischen Geschichte* (Berlin, 1995), 168–69.

TABLE 4.6 Rental of Land by Noblewomen, 1715–1810*

	Vladimir	Kashin	All Regions
1715–20	13	27	24
	(23)	(90)	(113)
1750–55	44	21	25
	(18)	(99)	(117)
1775–80	63	33	37
	(8)	(60)	(68)
All periods	33	26	27
1715–80	(49)	(249)	(298)

* Each value is the percentage of available transactions involving the rental of land by women. The number of available transactions by both women and men is given in parentheses.
Source: See appendix 1.

TABLE 4.7 Mortgages by Noblewomen, 1715–1810*

	Vladimir		Kashin		Tambov		All Regions	
	B	L	B	L	B	L	B	L
1715–20	27	2	38	4	—	—	31	2
	(45)	(64)	(26)	(28)			(71)	(92)
1750–55	44	11	40	25	—	—	42	20
	(9)	(9)	(15)	(16)			(24)	(25)
1775–80	36	11	50	43	23	23	33	18
	(45)	(45)	(6)	(7)	(26)	(26)	(77)	(78)
All periods	32	6	40	16	23	23	33	11
1715–80	(99)	(118)	(47)	(51)	(26)	(26)	(172)	(195)

* B = borrowers, L = lenders. Each value is the percentage of available transactions involving mortgages. The number of available transactions by both women and men is in parentheses.
Source: See appendix 1.

Kashin accounted for 31 percent of the recorded transactions for borrowing from other landowners. Nobles of both sexes seemed loath to borrow more than thirty rubles, yet a few required more considerable sums. One woman mortgaged her estate in 1717 for three hundred rubles—a sum far greater than the value of an average estate in Vladimir province.[17] A sole female lender appeared in Vladimir that same year with her son and daughter, handing over the astronomical sum of twenty-five hundred rubles in silver.[18] In Kashin, women featured as borrowers in 38 percent of transactions involving nobles (alone in six, with male kin in four), but as lenders

17. RGADA, f. 615, op. 1, ed. khr. 1956, ll. 93–94.
18. RGADA, f. 615, op. 1, ed. khr. 1956, ll. 22–23.

their names appeared in a scant 4 percent of transactions. Ekaterina Miliukova, unmarried, lent ninety-five rubles to an enterprising peasant for the construction of a mill.[19]

For the opening decades of the eighteenth century, several trends are apparent. Regardless of the variable, noblewomen's participation in the market for land and serfs was limited, and the transactions recorded in notarial records indicate that women possessed only modest amounts of either movable or immovable wealth. Women who inherited or received land and serfs as dowry rarely parted with their property during marriage, whereas wives who obtained cash dowries proved reluctant to invest in landed estates. These patterns may simply mirror family strategies for exploiting women's wealth during marriage rather than the actual amount of property in female hands. If any theme unites all of these trends, however, it is the peripheral role of noblewomen in the seigneurial economy. In the absence of fixed entitlements, daughters received a bare minimum of the family estate in movable wealth, which most failed to convert into landed estates. Widowhood provided greater opportunities for women to dispose of their assets or invest on their own, but even widows made a poor showing as independent actors in the early eighteenth-century economy.

To put Russian women's market activity into a wider context, a comparison with property holding among women in Western Europe is instructive. Regrettably, a strictly chronological comparison is impossible in the absence of any studies of female landownership in Europe in the seventeenth and eighteenth centuries. Indeed, the studies that exist on women and property are devoted overwhelmingly to the medieval era—the highpoint of women's economic power in the West. David Herlihy analyzed thousands of charters and contracts from several regions in Western Europe from the eighth through the twelfth centuries, and found that women appeared as alienators of property in a significant percentage of documents. Spanish women acted as alienators of property in as many as 18 percent of charters dating from the eleventh and twelfth centuries; in southern France, they figured in 9 to 13 percent of the documents. On the basis of these figures, Herlihy argued that the medieval woman had come "to play an extraordinary role in the management of family property in the early Middle Ages, and social customs as well as economic life were influenced by her prominence."[20]

Seen from this perspective, the economic standing of Russian noblewomen in the early eighteenth century was marginally superior to that of

19. RGADA, f. 615, op. 1, ed. khr. 4190, l. 4.

20. David Herlihy, "Land, Family and Women in Continental Europe, 701–1200," *Traditio* 18 (1962): 89. See also Suzanne Fonay Wemple, *Women in Frankish Society: Marriage and the Cloister, 500–900* (Philadelphia, 1981), 106–23. For a more skeptical view of the meaning of statistics on women as alienators of property, see Penny Schine Gold, *The Lady and the Virgin: Image, Attitude, and Experience in Twelfth-Century France* (Chicago, 1985), 116–44.

their European counterparts, albeit in an earlier era. Yet to argue for the extraordinary role of women—in either Russia or Western Europe—is unconvincing when female proprietors controlled less than 20 percent of landed wealth, rarely appeared as investors or lenders, and participated in the market primarily as widows. Early in the eighteenth century, married women in Russia supervised their husbands' holdings while they were away on military service, yet carried out few property transactions in their own names. As both daughters and widows, women anticipated limited opportunities to inherit land. It was only in the wake of legal change, which enhanced women's access to and control of property, that the amount of wealth concentrated in female hands began to rise dramatically. After the Law of Single Inheritance was abolished in 1731, noblewomen's claim to a fixed portion of the family estate translated into a rapid increase in their participation in the market. Moreover, once married women were no longer required to appeal to their husbands to alienate land, they assumed a central role as investors in real estate.

The Ascent of Noblewomen's Economic Power

By the mid-eighteenth century noblewomen achieved remarkable gains in the market for provincial real estate. Indeed, the contrast between women's economic activity in 1715–20 and their visibility thirty years later highlights the first half of the eighteenth century as an era of genuine change in the relation of women to property. By 1755 women appeared as alienators of property, on average, twice as often as they had in 1715–20 (see Table 4.1). The difference in Vladimir, where female sales of estates increased from 5 to 45 percent, was particularly dramatic and derives, no doubt, from the very small sample of transactions. Yet substantial, if less spectacular, leaps in other districts confirm women's new presence in the seigneurial economy. Petty female proprietors in Tambov and Kursk selling small parcels of unsettled land accounted for 30 to 31 percent of land transactions, whereas noblewomen in Moscow, who had far more wealth at their disposal, featured in 34 percent of all sales. Despite enormous differences in wealth and standing, noblewomen of all ranks could claim tangible benefits from innovations in the law of property. By the mid-eighteenth century, noblewomen as a group were twice as likely to sell immovable assets as they had been before the Law of Single Inheritance was revoked. The revised law of inheritance may have failed to abolish gender asymmetry in regard to inheritance, but it initiated a palpable rise in noblewomen's economic power.

In keeping with this trend, women's propensity to invest in land and serfs advanced dramatically by 1755 (see Table 4.2). Once again, the consistency of change across districts reveals that noblewomen at all levels were quick to exploit their new legal prerogatives: women were just as likely to purchase small, inexpensive parcels of land in the black-earth region as they were to invest in costly settled estates. Whereas a miserly 5 percent of land sales in all districts included female purchasers in 1715–20, at mid-century 30 percent featured women. As serf owners (see Table 4.4) women also made their presence known: female proprietors carried out 22 percent of the manumission transactions in Vladimir, Kashin, and Tambov. It is worth noting, however, that women were twice as likely to sell (see Table 4.5) as to manumit peasants after 1750: women on their own transacted 43 percent of the serf sales recorded in these districts. To be sure, the discrepancy between female manumission of serfs and their sale of peasants is puzzling. We might conclude that women saw serfs as a source of ready cash: lacking other income, women may have been more inclined than men to part with individual serfs. Furthermore, as we will see, while land was not freely bestowed on daughters who married, serfs featured in almost every woman's dowry.

Although the large majority of women who figure in deeds of purchase took part in only one transaction, others sold or invested in land on repeated occasions after the mid-eighteenth century. The widow Elena Postel'nikova invested in almost seven hundred rubles worth of land and serfs in Tambov in 1776. Two years later she purchased three more parcels of land and sold one of these for a profit later the same year.[21] In Kashin, Countess Anna Vorontsova purchased serfs from five different proprietors in 1772.[22] Countess Razumovskaia of Vladimir acquired serfs and land in five separate transactions in 1806.[23] If these women were the exception rather than the rule, in this respect they were identical to their male equivalents. Noblemen, too, surface overwhelmingly in single transactions, which tells us little about their economic standing, much less what prompted them to buy or sell their holdings.

Women not only invested in estates after the mid-eighteenth century but also put their property to other uses. Nobles of both sexes rented portions of their land to state peasants (see Table 4.6). Contracts for land rentals are not abundant, perhaps because they brought little profit: contracts ranged from one to fifteen years, and peasants paid a few rubles in rent annually to the proprietors. Indeed, this practice seems to have been common only in the north, and even there it occurred on a limited scale.[24] Nonetheless, the contracts that survive feature landowners of both sexes and also demonstrate an increase in women's landholding. On other occasions, noblewomen

21. RGADA, f. 615, op. 1, ed. khr. 11566, ll. 63–64, 67–68, 69–70, 73–74; f. 615, op. 1, ed. khr. 11581, ll. 57–58, 63–65, 73.

22. RGADA, f. 615, op. 1, ed. khr. 4242, ll. 67–70, 72–73.

23. GAVO, f. 92, op. 5, ed. khr. 21, ll. 245–53.

24. These findings support Kahan's assertion that the market for rental of unsettled land was inconsiderable until the nineteenth century. See Kahan (1966), 42.

themselves leased fields from proprietors. In remote Syzran, the wife of Captain Golovin augmented her holdings in this way in 1753, paying a respectable forty-eight rubles for the use of land in a village owned by her Tatar neighbors.[25]

Although women did not have sufficient liquid assets at their disposal to lend money—or chose not to use their capital in this manner—they now controlled sufficient real estate to raise money on their own, and represented 33 percent of borrowers in Vladimir, Kashin, and Tambov in 1775–80 (see Table 4.7). The small number of transactions does not allow for a systematic comparison of male and female indebtedness. Impressionistic evidence, however, leaves no doubt that women were just as prone as their male counterparts to live beyond their means and fall into debt. Advertisements for the sale of estates by bankrupt proprietors in *Senatskie vedomosti* betray no gender bias. References to debt abound in family papers and noble correspondence, revealing the trouble even the wealthiest noblewomen had in making ends meet. A friend wrote to Elizaveta Glebova-Streshneva in 1786 of being badgered by creditors, after she ran up debts of two thousand rubles in St. Petersburg.[26] Writing in 1796 to her kinsman, Prince Aleksandr Mikhailovich Golitsyn, Anna Aleksandrovna Golitsyna described how the burden of maintaining several households and her husband's penchant for card playing had forced them to borrow eighty thousand rubles. She went on to say that she would spend summer and autumn in the country, adding that, God willing, they would be able to manage their affairs so that they would not be forced to sell any part of their estate.[27]

None of these districts offer abundant examples of money lending among the nobility. On rare occasions, female proprietors extended loans to neighbors or kin: Marfa Griboedova lent five hundred rubles to her brother in 1776, accepting his considerable estate as collateral; Princess Dashkova made a loan of 1,880 rubles to her brother in 1775, at a time when she was still consolidating her own fortune.[28] Noblewomen also petitioned the Land College for the registration of estates in their name when borrowers failed to meet their obligations. Overall, however, money lending played a negligible role in the lives of noble proprietors, at least in the provinces. Nobles of both sexes were reluctant to act as private lenders, yielding this role to merchants and townsmen.[29]

25. RGADA, f. 615, op. 1, ed. khr. 11184, l. 39.

26. GIM, f. 47, op. 1, ed. khr. 6, ll. 92.

27. "Poslednie dni tsarstvovaniia Ekateriny II (Pis'ma kniagini Anny Aleksandrovny Golitsynoi)," *Istoricheskii vestnik* 30 (October 1887): 91.

28. RGADA, f. 615, op. 1, ed. khr. 2045, l. 14; GIM, f. 60, op. 1, ed. khr. 183, l. 2.

29. Arcadius Kahan [(1985), 314] argues that by the end of the eighteenth century the nobility deposited their savings in state savings institutions, preferring "security combined with some income to high risk and high return from private lending." A survey by N. B. Golikova of provincial notarial records from the first quarter of the eighteenth century supports my findings and

By the mid-eighteenth century, women not only bought and sold estates in far greater numbers but increasingly made use of their assets during marriage. While widows and spinsters were traditionally more in evidence as economic actors, married women moved to the fore as the number of female buyers and sellers swelled (see Table 4.3). Unmarried women comprised 80 percent of female sellers of estates in 1715–20; at midcentury, their proportion dwindled to 54 percent, as the proportion of married sellers rose to 46 percent. Married women also figured prominently as investors, accounting for 63 percent of all purchases in 1750–55. The greater visibility of married women highlights the transformation in the role of women in the family economy: far from acting purely as dependents, married women were now more inclined to use their dowries and inheritance as productive assets. Again, this shift must be viewed within the context of changes in the law of property: after 1753, married women's liberty to dispose of property without their husbands' consent encouraged them both to invest in estates and to alienate their assets in greater numbers.

By the mid-eighteenth century, noblewomen had moved from the periphery of the seigneurial economy toward the center. In the ensuing decades they consolidated their hold in the market: as sellers of real estate, women's activity remained stable at 36 percent into the first decade of the nineteenth century. As investors, however, their numbers edged higher, until women accounted for 34 percent of estate purchasers in 1775–80 and reached a plateau of 43 percent in the nineteenth century. Women's prominence as sellers of property on the eve of Emancipation was even more arresting. By 1860, female sellers took part alone in a full 46 percent of documented transactions and acted with male kin in a further 2 percent. In keeping with earlier trends, it was married women who dominated the market both as buyers and as sellers; the activity of widows slipped precipitously until they accounted for only 8 percent of female investors in 1855–60 (see Table 4.3).

A glimpse at women's economic activities in England and the United States—the only available studies on women and property holding in the West—throws these figures into more dramatic relief. Of more than four hundred landowners in the county of Suffolk, England, women comprised only 4 percent of the total in the eighteenth century and held most of their land in small parcels.[30] For all of Britain, not a single woman could be found

Kahan's argument. See "Rostovshchichestvo v Rossii nachala XVIII v. i ego nekotorye osobennosti," in *Problemy genezisa kapitalizma* (Moscow, 1970), 247–48. By contrast, N. I. Pavlenko demonstrates that nobles comprised 44.8% of private lenders recorded in Moscow in 1732. See "O rostovshchichestve dvorian v XVIII v. (k postanovke voprosa)," in *Dvorianstvo i krepostnoi stroi Rossii XVI–XVIII vv.* (Moscow, 1975), 269.

30. Davidoff and Hall (1987), 276. On the basis of a land survey carried out in 1870, Jill Liddington estimates that 7% of the land in England was owned by women. See Liddington, *Female Fortune: Land, Gender, and Authority: The Anne Lister Diaries and Other Writings, 1833–36* (London, 1998), 245, 284.

in an inventory of the largest landowners in the nineteenth century; by contrast, 28 percent of the wealthiest proprietors in Russia were female.[31] A mere 8.4 percent of real estate owners in Petersburg, Virginia, were women in 1790; this number increased to 14 percent in 1814 and reached 28.7 percent in 1860.[32] American women made significant gains as property holders in the nineteenth century, as the married women's property acts extended women's control over their wealth, but they failed to match the numbers of women from noble or merchant estates engaging in urban real estate transactions in Russia during the same era.[33] Indeed, one scholar estimates that women and children possessed only 7.2 percent of all wealth in the United States in 1860.[34]

Evaluating Noblewomen's Economic Activity

To summarize, by the nineteenth century noblewomen featured in roughly 40 percent of real estate transfers, as sellers and investors, throughout Russia—a figure, as far as we know, that greatly exceeded female property holding in other European countries. Measuring female participation in the real estate market is a relatively straightforward task; evaluating the significance of this figure, however, proves more complex. How can we account for Russian noblewomen's prominence as landowners in the Imperial era? Do changes in women's market activity reflect the actual quantity of property in female hands, or do they indicate a greater inclination on the part of women to use their holdings as productive assets? In other words, to what degree did women's use of property depend on a new conception of women's relation to property among the nobility?

In particular, the pattern of estate sales may be interpreted either as a sign of noblewomen's increasing wealth or as a measure of their need for ready cash. During property transfers sellers routinely recorded how they acquired their assets; what they failed to declare was the reason for the sale. Women's alienation of their estates may well have been prompted by the need to discharge their debts, rather than to invest in more profitable holdings. In this regard, however, they were in good male company. On rare occasions, sellers such as Andrei Zykov, who sold a portion of the service estate he had inherited from his father in 1715, announced that he relinquished his land in order to pay his parents' debts.[35] When asked why Arina Golovlyova's son

---

31. Dominic Lieven, *The Aristocracy in Europe, 1815–1914* (New York, 1992), 42, 56.

32. Lebsock (1984), 129–30.

33. For the impact of the married women's property acts on the magnitude of women's wealth, see Shammas (1994), 9–30.

34. Quoted in Shammas (1994), 20.

35. RGADA, f. 615, op. 1, ed. khr. 4186, l. 9.

had sold his house in Moscow, one character in Saltykov-Shchedrin's *The Golovlyov Family* could only respond, "To pay off his debts. . . . You don't go selling up for any good cause!"[36] On the other hand, as we will see, evidence on the acquisition of property (see Table 4.15) demonstrates that from the late eighteenth century, proprietors of both sexes were more inclined to sell land with the goal of acquiring other estates, either for profit or for convenience. Catherine Wilmot, writing to her sister in 1806, related her surprise when she heard of a noblewoman traveling to her estate in Ukraine with the goal of "selling it from the extreme inconvenience of the distance which separated it from [the estate of her husband]."[37] Memoirs and the correspondence of noblewomen offer similar accounts. Natalia Divova sold several villages in 1754 with an eye to purchasing others near a kinswoman.[38] Letters also reveal female proprietors on the lookout to purchase profitable estates.[39]

If estate sales are an unreliable index of noblewomen's economic independence, however, they are not an isolated measure of women's participation in the market. Female proprietors not only parted with their assets, they also invested in land and purchased serfs in growing numbers. Furthermore, their tendency to manumit serfs and rent land increased in tandem with the figures on the sale of estates. There is, moreover, no reason to believe that women's indebtedness increased steadily in relation to men's from the mideighteenth century, or that husbands compelled their wives to sacrifice their estates in ascending numbers. While the figures on women's participation in the market may not be a foolproof measure of their economic power, they clearly demonstrate that noblewomen came to possess a growing percentage of wealth in the wake of inheritance reform in 1731.

Again, a comparative framework underscores the anomaly of Russian noblewomen's economic activities vis-à-vis their counterparts in the West. According to one scholar, under English common law, in which primogeniture was the rule and daughters divided the estate in the absence of sons, nearly 42 percent of women would have been heiresses. In practice, English landowners used the rules of strict settlement to favor male relations over daughters, reducing the scope of female inheritance in the seventeenth and eighteenth centuries to 13 percent.[40] By contrast, Russian noblewomen's visibility in property transactions more closely mirrored the demographic

36. According to John Habakkuk, in eighteenth-century England payment of debt "played a major part in the great majority of sales." See Habakkuk, *Marriage, Debt, and the Estates System: English Landownership, 1650–1950* (Oxford, 1994), 396–97.

37. Bradford (1935), 234–35.

38. Sankt Peterburgskii filial Instituta rossiiskoi istorii RAN (hereafter SPbFIRI), kol. 238, I, 23, op. 2, ed. khr. 298/50.

39. See a letter to E. P. Saltykova from another woman, in which the latter describes the advantages of purchasing an estate belonging to a bankrupt proprietor. RGIA, f. 1048, op. 1, ed. khr. 43, ll. 1–2 (1851).

40. Spring (1993), 10–12, 15.

probability that they would inherit. Property regimes in many European countries either undermined female inheritance or placed the use of women's assets in their husbands' hands. In Russia, however, the possibility of female property ownership came far closer to reaching its full potential, and the law actively encouraged women's participation in the market. In other words, Russian noblewomen's visibility in the seigneurial economy was as much a product of culture as it was of demographics. The transformation of women's legal standing during the eighteenth century thus translated into tangible economic gains for women.

Estimating Women's Wealth

Russian noblewomen scored real advances in the market as buyers and sellers of property in the eighteenth and nineteenth centuries. At the same time, women's rate of participation in the market is by no means an accurate reflection of the amount of wealth in their possession. Women indeed may have appeared as buyers and sellers in as many as 40 percent of the recorded transactions in this sample, and yet—possessing only modest portions—have owned far less than 40 percent of the estates in the provinces.

In the absence of reliable land surveys, probate inventories, or tax returns, determining the actual percentage of real estate in women's hands presents a challenge. Before the General Land Survey began in the 1770s, Russian monarchs made periodic attempts to document the number of nobles living in various provinces and the serfs they controlled. A census compiled for Petersburg province in 1766 listed 226 nobles, of whom 32 (14 percent) were women. The same census reveals, however, that female proprietors controlled a modest 9 percent of the serf population in the province.[41] The most complete data on land ownership can be found in the collection of the General Land Survey, which took place in the 1770s and 1780s. Yet even these data defy a precise calculation of the amount of land in the hands of individual owners of either sex. Surveyors did not inventory the amount of property belonging to individual landowners but measured settlements and parcels of land (*pomest'nye dachi*), which, as a result of partible inheritance, often had two or more owners.[42]

Be that as it may, a rough calculation can be made by comparing the number of male and female landowners listed in the index of surveys for each district and the average number of plots held by both sexes. The land survey of Vladimir was completed in 1775 and listed 304 proprietors, of

41. Gosudarstvennaia Natsional'naia Biblioteka (hereafter GNB), Otdel rukopisei. f. Ermitazhnoe Sobranie, no. 243/1, ll. 1–13.

42. Milov (1965), 21–22.

whom 119 (39 percent) were women. While male proprietors owned an average of 4.3 holdings, women controlled 3.3 holdings, or 32 percent less than their male counterparts.[43] Simply stated, according to the General Land Survey noblewomen in Vladimir controlled 33 percent of the estates in private hands in 1775.

A similar pattern emerges in Kashin in 1776. Of 458 landowners inventoried, 192 (42 percent) were women. In Kashin, however, the discrepancy between men's and women's holdings was less marked: on average men held 4.2 villages or fields, while women claimed 3.9, or 8 percent less than their male counterparts. Thus, according to the survey, approximately 41 percent of the estates in Kashin were owned by female proprietors.[44] In a third district, Ruza, in Moscow province, a topographical survey published in 1812 revealed that 41 percent of the estate owners were female.[45] Inventories of Lipetsk and Lebedianskii districts (Tambov province) in 1814 yielded totals for female proprietors of 43 percent and 47 percent, respectively.[46]

Estate inventories not only provide evidence of the ratio of male to female landowners, however. They also reveal an important attribute of noble landowning in the late eighteenth century. More often than not, proprietors of both sexes held land in small parcels, scattered throughout the district, and controlled a mere handful of serfs. While the inventory of holdings in the index demonstrates that these parcels were often in close proximity, they were rarely contiguous. Only the fortunate few possessed consolidated holdings. One Agrafena Miasoedova owned a single village in Vladimir, but it consisted of 92 male serfs and their families settled on 954 desiatins of land, and included a house and garden for the proprietor.[47] Princess Anna Belosel'skaia ruled over 371 desiatins and 99 male serfs in Kashin; the surveyor also noted a house on her property, located on "the left side of the river."[48] The estate of Fekla Almazova included 167 male serfs, several acres of forests, and a number of houses and churches.[49] Estate owners such as Almazova were the rare exception, however. The vast majority of nobles owned fields and serfs in several locations, and—as often as not—shared ownership of their villages with other proprietors.

Historians have made much of the relative poverty of the Russian nobility and argued that the poor financial standing of the elite undermined their

43. RGADA, f. 1355 (Ekonomicheskie primechaniia k general'nomu mezhevaniiu), op. 1, ed. khr. 43, ll. 5–10.

44. RGADA, f. 1355, op. 1, ed. khr. 1700, ll. 7–14.

45. Leonard (1993), 68.

46. RGIA, f. 1549 (Reviziia senatora L'vova A. L. Tambovskoi gubernii, 1814–1815 gg), op. 1, ed. khr. 202, ll. 24–39, 108–15.

47. RGADA, f. 1355, op. 1, ed. khr. 43, l. 53.

48. RGADA, f. 1355, op. 1, ed. khr. 1700, l. 23.

49. RGADA, f. 1355, op. 1, ed. khr. 1700, l. 34.

influence in the ruling process.[50] We might well expect that if male nobles, with their superior inheritance rights and salaries from state service, faced the prospect of penury, then the fortunes of noblewomen would be still more modest. As I will demonstrate, however, the value of assets sold by women was commensurate with that of their male counterparts. Men and women also fell into identical patterns of distribution in regard to the size of the estates and the number of serfs they alienated. In short, from the mid-eighteenth century the scope of men and women's landholding was surprisingly similar.

The ruble value of estates sold (Table 4.8) provides one perspective on the relative fortunes of male and female proprietors. Although discrepancies appear in the average value of estates sold by men and women, no single trend emerges with regard to the sex of the owner, either within districts or at particular points in time. Indeed, the most dramatic variations concern the contrast between sales in the provinces and those recorded in Moscow. Early in the eighteenth century, noblewomen may have sold far fewer properties than men, but on average the value of their estates was almost double that of male sellers—a pattern which suggests that property holding among Petrine noblewomen was characteristic only among the wealthiest of the elite (see Table 4.8). As property ownership became more extensive among women, the gap between the average price of estates sold by both sexes narrowed dramatically. The relative wealth of men and women, if estimated by the value of estates sold, fluctuated over time, moving slightly in men's favor in 1775–80, then more dramatically so—particularly in Moscow—on the eve of Emancipation.[51] Yet, averaged over time, the price of estates that noblewomen brought to the market proved slightly higher—by about 6 percent—than the price of estates sold by their male counterparts.

Another means of comparing the wealth of both sexes is to consider the distribution of the size of estates each sold, or the number of serfs on the estates they alienated. Data on both the size of estates and the number of serf households are fragile at best; until the nineteenth century, sellers were as likely to describe the boundaries of their holdings in deeds of sale as they were to cite the number of desiatins sold. Similarly, sellers would casually mention the presence of serfs on their holdings, seemingly unaware of the number of peasants they owned. In Moscow, however, clerks reported on the precise size of estates and the number of serfs with greater regularity, allowing for a coherent picture of the range of men's and women's holdings.

Just as nobles of both sexes alienated estates of commensurate value, men

50. The classic statement of this position is from Pipes (1974), 179.

51. For a discussion of inflation after 1760, which clearly affected the price of land, see Boris N. Mironov, "Consequences of the Price Revolution in Eighteenth-Century Russia," *Economic History Review* 45, no. 3 (1992): 457–78.

Table 4.8 Average Value, in Rubles, of Estates Sold by Noble Women and Men, 1715–1860*

	Vladimir		Kashin		Tambov		Kursk		Moscow		All Regions	
	W	M	W	M	W	M	W	M	W	M	W	M
1715–20	27	34	57	41	14	12	7	6	308	148	123	65
	(2)	(18)	(26)	(70)	(13)	(32)	(11)	(91)	(25)	(110)	(77)	(321)
1750–55	174	66	39	38	22	23	19	14	562	595	357	370
	(14)	(16)	(22)	(36)	(25)	(54)	(32)	(67)	(140)	(263)	(233)	(436)
1775–80	653	285	50	50	209	217	43	38	2,246	2,784	1,202	1,537
	(30)	(37)	(44)	(36)	(59)	(145)	(33)	(46)	(157)	(289)	(323)	(553)
1805–10	1,128	1,396	85	80	2,923	4,808	—	—	13,762	13,151	5,464	5,263
	(74)	(125)	(14)	(23)	(40)	(80)			(60)	(81)	(188)	(309)
1855–60	3,273	2,894	5,228	6,837	5,034	5,669	4,379	4,815	13,966	17,907	8,517	10,289
	(66)	(70)	(63)	(62)	(96)	(126)	(87)	(101)	(229)	(245)	(541)	(604)
All periods 1715–1860	1,729	1,464	1,983	1,902	2,632	2,591	2,350	1,605	7,304	6,508	4,490	3,991
	(186)	(266)	(169)	(227)	(233)	(437)	(163)	(305)	(611)	(988)	(1,362)	(2,223)

* W = women, M = men. Estates refer to any land, with or without serfs. The number of transactions is in parentheses.
Source: See appendix 1.

and women who registered sales in Moscow (Table 4.9) parted with relatively small holdings. The size of an estate was not always a reliable measure of its value: the fertility of land in the north was much less than in the black-earth region; moreover, the presence of a forest on an estate contributed significantly to its value. If we examine the distribution of the size of estates sold by men and women, however, we find that both male and female proprietors rarely parted with vast tracts of land. More striking still, as the percentage of men selling larger estates increased, the number of women disposing of estates of similar size rose in tandem.

After the mid-eighteenth century, noble proprietors not only possessed estates of greater value but also controlled holdings of far greater size. Although inflation may account for the rising cost of land in the eighteenth century, the tendency of nobles to offer larger estates for sale points to the concentration of wealth in the hands of a smaller percentage of the nobility.[52] This fluctuation of noble fortunes did not, by any means, discriminate against women: the patterns of economic behavior for both women and men were strikingly similar. Proprietors who sold land in 1750–55 were clustered on the low end of the spectrum. Thus, estates of fewer than 50 desiatins comprised 85 percent of holdings sold by women and 88 percent of those sold by men. In subsequent decades, the percentage of petty landowners declined, however, and proprietors of both sexes brought greater amounts of land to the market. Throughout the eighteenth century, women were absent among those major landowners who alienated holdings of more than 1,000 desiatins; yet in 1805–10, 7 percent of the estates sold by women were larger than 1,000 desiatins, and this percentage increased to 16 percent in 1855–60. In other words, the distribution of the size of estates sold follows the same pattern as the average ruble value of estates: very little discrepancy appears between the size of estates sold by women and men. Furthermore, over time noblewomen became marginally more likely to alienate estates larger than those held by men.

Women and Serf Ownership

Since serf ownership was the primary means of calculating wealth in Russia, we might expect to find a wider gap in the ratio of male to female serf owners, or to discover that women possessed far fewer laborers than male proprietors. In addition to figures on the sale of individual serfs by noblewomen, evidence of serf manumissions and the sale of settled estates under-

---

52. N. M. Shepukova arrives at a similar conclusion in "Ob izmenenii razmerov dushevladeniia pomeshchikov evropeiskoi Rossii v pervoi chetverti XVIII–pervoi polovine XIX v." *Ezhegodnik po agrarnoi istorii vostochnoi Evropy. 1963 g.* (Vilnius, 1964), 388–419.

TABLE 4.9 Size of Estates Sold in Moscow by Noble Women and Men, 1750–1860*

	<50 des.		51–100 des.		101–500 des.		501–1,000 des.		1,001–10,000 des.		>10,000 des.	
	W	M	W	M	W	M	W	M	W	M	W	M
1750–55 (W = 41) (M = 110)	85	88	5	7	10	5	0	0	0	0	0	0
1775–80 (W = 46) (M = 113)	52	57	24	20	22	16	2	3	0	4	0	0
1805–10 (W = 14) (M = 19)	57	63	14	21	22	11	0	0	7	5	0	0
1855–60 (W = 199) (M = 219)	13	7	10	11	44	47	15	21	16	14	2	<1
1750–60 (W = 300) (M = 461)	31	41	12	13	35	28	10	10	11	8	1	<1

* W = women, M = men, des. = desiatins. Each value is the percentage of transactions by noble women or men. The numbers in parentheses in the left column represent the number of transactions involving women and men.
   Source: See appendix 1.

scores women's visibility in the seigneurial economy: noblewomen's participation in the sale of serfs parallels their activity as sellers of real estate. As
women took more active part in the market for land, they also engaged more
frequently in the traffic of serfs, on whom the productivity of their estates
depended. In the early part of the eighteenth century women were no more
likely to own serfs than land, and they appear independently as sellers of
peasants in only 14 percent of the recorded transactions in three districts,
and appear with male kin in another 5 percent. Three decades later their
numbers swelled to 43 percent of the total, dropping to 35 percent at the
end of the century and rising again to 40 percent in 1805–10 (see Table 4.5).

The pattern of women's serf ownership recurs in the figures on manumissions. Indeed, the sheer volume of documents on serf manumission in
the eighteenth century eliminates any doubt about the presence of women
proprietors in the provinces. Among the nobility, it was common practice to
manumit serf women who wished to marry on neighboring estates. On more
rare occasions, in gratitude for their years of service, noble proprietors
would release individual serfs and permit them to enroll in the state peasantry. Neither men nor women released serf women to other estates for economic gain, since they received only nominal compensation of a few rubles
when the transaction took place; for this reason, the data on serf manumissions provide an important measure of women's serf ownership. In this
sample, the proportion of transactions involving the manumission of serfs
by women increased from 17 percent in 1715–20 to an unspectacular 22
percent in 1750–55 (see Table 4.4). The percentage of women who owned
peasants continued to grow, however, until women represented 38 percent
of proprietors who manumitted serfs in 1775–80, and 49 percent in one district in 1805–10.

In the nineteenth century, the historian Semevskii estimated that 84
percent of the serf-owning nobility in 1777 owned fewer than one hundred
serfs—the minimum number required for a noble to eke out a precarious
living on an estate.[53] Much later, in 1858–59, an official census revealed that
79 percent of the nobility fell below this poverty line, while 20 percent held
between one hundred and one thousand peasants. Only 1.1 percent quali-
fied as grand seigneurs, those who possessed over one thousand souls.[54] An
examination of the number of serfs sold on estates in Moscow (Table 4.10)
bears out Semevskii's conclusions. Until the nineteenth century, between 76
and 80 percent of proprietors sold estates with fewer than one hundred serfs
(see Table 4.10). By the mid-nineteenth century a smaller proportion of proprietors sold estates with fewer than twenty serfs; nonetheless, female pro-

53. V. I. Semevskii, *Krest'iane v tsarstvovanie Imperatritsy Ekateriny II* (St. Petersburg, 1881), I:
30.
54. See Pipes (1974), 178.

TABLE 4.10 Number of Serfs Sold on Estates in Moscow by Noble Women and Men, 1750–1860*

	<20 serfs		21–100 serfs		101–500 serfs		501–1,000 serfs		>1,000 serfs	
	W	M	W	M	W	M	W	M	W	M
1750–55 (W = 25) (M = 32)	40	25	40	53	20	22	0	0	0	0
1775–80 (W = 51) (M = 85)	45	39	33	37	18	20	2	2	2	2
1805–10 (W = 38) (M = 48)	29	29	39	42	29	25	3	2	0	2
1855–60 (W = 184) (M = 182)	22	20	53	54	21	23	3	3	1	<1
1750–1860 (W = 298) (M = 347)	28	26	47	48	22	23	2	2	1	1

* W = women, M = men. Each value is the percentage of transactions by noble women or men. The numbers in parentheses in the left column represent the number of transactions involving women and men.

Source: See appendix 1.

prietors in the middling ranks still comprised only 22 percent of the total, while 1 percent alone could be counted among those who sold estates possessing more than one thousand souls. For the men the same situation held true, with roughly 1 percent of their number in possession of substantial wealth in human property.

Proprietors of both sexes were also far more likely to sell individual serfs without land than to part with many households. Admittedly, the behavior of men and women was not identical in every respect. Overall, women were marginally more likely to sell female serfs than their male counterparts, whereas men more often sold male serfs (Table 4.11). When selling entire families or several households, however, men and women behaved in similar ways. Among both male and female proprietors from 1715 to 1810, a total of 11 percent of all serf transactions without land involved two or more families of peasants. Clearly, conservative economic behavior was a function of limited means for both sexes, rather than the product of gender difference.

A survey of the sale of settled estates (Table 4.12) offers a final perspective on serf ownership among men and women. Until the nineteenth century, female proprietors proved more likely than their male equivalents to sell settled estates, which were defined as any parcel of land sold with serfs.

TABLE 4.11 Serfs Sold without Land by Noble Women and Men, by Type of Transaction, 1715–1810*

	1		2		3		4		5	
	W	M	W	M	W	M	W	M	W	M
1715–20 (W = 6) (M = 33)	17	30	50	30	17	30	17	9	0	0
1750–55 (W = 65) (M = 82)	32	32	31	41	26	21	8	5	3	1
1775–80 (W = 170) (M = 311)	41	35	28	27	21	23	9	10	1	5
1805–10 (W = 151) (M = 223)	43	40	26	30	21	23	7	5	4	2
1715–1810 (W = 392) (M = 649)	40	36	27	30	22	23	8	8	3	3

* 1 = single female serf, with or without children; 2 = single male serf, with or without children; 3 = a single family of serfs; 4 = two to four families of serfs; 5 = five or more families of serfs; W = women; M = men. Each value is the percentage of transactions by noble women or men. The numbers in parentheses in the left column represent the number of transactions involving women and men.
Source: See appendix 1.

TABLE 4.12 Percentage of Estates Sold with Serfs by Noble Women and Men, 1715–1860*

	Vladimir		Kashin		Tambov		Moscow		All Regions	
	W	M	W	M	W	M	W	M	W	M
1715–20	0 (2)	5 (19)	19 (26)	10 (70)	0 (13)	0 (34)	60 (25)	36 (111)	30 (66)	21 (234)
1750–55	67 (15)	18 (17)	41 (22)	14 (36)	7 (27)	5 (55)	64 (140)	41 (264)	54 (204)	32 (372)
1775–80	48 (31)	45 (38)	16 (44)	6 (36)	29 (59)	18 (146)	64 (159)	49 (289)	48 (293)	37 (509)
1805–10	50 (74)	51 (126)	21 (14)	9 (23)	40 (40)	38 (80)	72 (60)	69 (81)	53 (188)	49 (310)
1855–60	42 (66)	46 (71)	56 (64)	60 (63)	50 (96)	50 (127)	85 (230)	82 (245)	68 (454)	66 (506)
All periods 1715–1860	48 (186)	44 (271)	35 (170)	24 (228)	35 (235)	28 (442)	72 (614)	55 (990)	56 (1,205)	44 (1,931)

* W = women, M = men. The number of transactions is given in parentheses.
Source: See appendix 1.

Once again, the contrast between Moscow and the provinces is highlighted by a much higher percentage of sales of settled estates in the former: over time, as much as 72 percent of sales in Moscow by women comprised settled estates, compared to 48 percent in Vladimir and 35 percent in Kashin and Tambov. In all regions, however, women's tendency to sell populated land duplicated that of men, rising in the mid-eighteenth century and leaping again on the eve of Emancipation to as much as 68 percent for women and 66 percent for men.[55] Taken in sum, the pattern of female serf ownership, viewed across time and geographic boundaries, diverged little from that of male proprietors.

Women and Urban Real Estate

A third asset available to noblewomen, as well as to women of other social categories was urban real estate. While the nobility alone enjoyed the right to own serfs, members of all social estates in Russia could invest in houses, shops, and parcels of land in town. As a result, unlike the data available on ownership of estates, the data on sales of urban property allow a comparison of women of different social estates. Precious little is known of the lives of merchant women: a comparison of their role in the market for urban real estate with that of noblewomen, however, points to a vital difference in the relation of women to property among the nobility and the merchantry.

From the mid-eighteenth century, representatives of all property-owning estates could be found engaging in a brisk trade in urban property. Noblewomen were active as well in this sphere of the economy, appearing as buyers and sellers in over 40 percent of the transactions recorded in Moscow (Table 4.13). Far from being a negligible asset, urban property comprised an important component of noble wealth: stone houses with gardens and adjoining buildings, plots of land, and commercial property sold for thousands of rubles.[56] Noblewomen such as Elizaveta Tutolmina acquired a steady income from renting out apartments in St. Petersburg.[57] Princess Dashkova recounted in her memoirs how she put off the expense of buying a house in St. Petersburg for as long as possible, living for months at a time on her estate in the country or in rented quarters. When Catherine II asked her

55. These findings contradict Kahan's assertion that "it was principally in the second half of the [eighteenth] century that rentals and sales of land without serfs occurred to any extent." Kahan (1966), 42.

56. In the second half of the nineteenth century, urban property ownership became an important source of income for the nobility. See A. M. Anfimov, *Krupnoe pomeshchich'e khozi-aistvo evropeiskoi Rossii (konets XIX-nachalo XX veka)* (Moscow, 1969), 274–75.

57. See three contracts executed by Tutolmina in 1858: RGIA, f. 1067, op. 1, ed. khr. 24, ll. 1–7.

TABLE 4.13 Sale and Purchase of Urban Property in Moscow by Noblewomen, 1750–1860*

| | Sales | | Purchases |
	Alone	With Male Kin	Alone
1750–55	33	2	32
		(52)	(62)
1775–80	33	6	46
		(87)	(93)
1805–10	—		—
1855–60	52	0	52
		(182)	(149)
All periods	44	2	46
1750–1860		(321)	(304)

* Each value is the percentage of available transactions. The number of available transactions involving noble women and men is given in parentheses.
Source: See appendix 1.

why she had not purchased a house of her own, Dashkova replied, "The purchase of a house is as serious a matter as the choice of a husband; one must think it over not once but many times."[58]

Merchant women lagged behind their noble counterparts as dealers in urban real estate. In this small sample, until the mid-nineteenth century the behavior of merchant women resembled that of noblewomen in the early part of the eighteenth century (Table 4.14). As investors in real estate in Moscow, women alone accounted for 13 percent of the transactions involving merchants in 1750–55 and 23 percent in 1775–80. A merchant's widow engaged in the most valuable transaction of 1778, purchasing one-tenth of a factory for thirty thousand rubles.[59] Such examples were unusual, however: only on the eve of Emancipation did the visibility of merchant women in the market correspond to that of noblewomen. Moreover, while they became more active, merchant women were considerably more likely to sell property than to invest in it. Thus, in 1855–60 women accounted for 47 percent of sales of urban property among the merchantry in Moscow and only 30 percent of the recorded purchases.[60]

58. Ekaterina Romanovna Dashkova, *The Memoirs of Princess Dashkova*, trans. and ed. Kyril Fitzlyon, with intro. by Jehanne M. Gheith (Durham, 1995), 197.
59. RGADA, f. 282, op. 1, ed. khr. 529, l. 249.
60. Similar results appear in provincial towns. In a survey of transactions for 1855–60, merchant women took part in 36% of sales in Vladimir (n = 66), 20% of sales in Tambov (n = 30), and 13% of sales in Kursk (n = 13). For recorded purchases, merchant women took part in 28% in Vladimir (n = 61), 19% in Tambov (n = 36), and 26% in Kursk (n = 27). By contrast, noblewomen accounted for 63% of sales in Vladimir (n = 84), 59% of sales in Tambov (n = 94), and 55% of sales in Kursk (n = 38). Of recorded purchases, noblewomen took part in 65%

TABLE 4.14 Sale and Purchase of Urban Property in Moscow by Merchant Women, 1750–1860*

	Sales		Purchases
	Alone	With Male Kin	Alone
1750–55	13	4	13
		(69)	(67)
1775–80	18	7	23
		(82)	(105)
1805–10	—		—
1855–60	47	0	30
		(120)	(149)
All periods	30	3	24
1750–1860		(271)	(321)

* Each value is the percentage of available transactions. The number of available transactions involving merchant women and men is in parentheses.
Source: See appendix 1.

The modest role of merchant women as investors in urban property points to a significant divergence in the culture of property among nobles and merchants. Although contemporaries wrote with conviction of the "terrible fate of women in merchant families,"[61] misogyny by no means accounts for the discrepancy in the relation of women to property among the two estates. A variety of legal ambiguities clearly inhibited merchant women's active role in trade and as investors in real estate. Indeed, merchant women's belated appearance in the housing market was no doubt, at least in part, a consequence of a delay in the application of the rules of separate property to the assets of merchant spouses. The edict of 1753 that permitted married noblewomen to dispose of their assets without their husbands' consent referred only to "female persons" (*zhenskie persony*) and failed to clarify the relevance of the ruling to women outside the nobility. Moreover, only in 1800 did the Statute on Bankruptcy explicitly deny creditors the right to claim the assets of the wives of bankrupt merchants or others engaging in trade.[62] Noblewomen, by contrast, had enjoyed such immunity since the late seventeenth century.

in Vladimir (n = 55) and 57% in Tambov and Kursk (n = 89 and n = 40). *Meshchanki*, or townswomen, took part in 44% of sales in Vladimir (n = 90), 37% of sales in Tambov (n = 57), 36% in Kursk (n = 56), and 59% in Moscow (n = 86). In purchases recorded by townspeople, women featured in 30% in Vladimir (n = 33), 37% in Tambov (n = 48), 46% in Kursk (n = 37), and 57% in Moscow (n = 70). For sources, see appendix 1.

61. The quote is from Alfred J. Rieber, *Merchants and Entrepreneurs in Imperial Russia* (Chapel Hill, 1982), 120.

62. *PSZ*, 26: 19.692 (19.12.1800), ch. 1, otd. II, art. 43. The statute of 1740 had subjected the assets of wives to creditors. *PSZ*, 11: 8.300 (15.12.1740), art. 28.

Other legal uncertainties worked to restrain the economic liberty of merchant women. In particular, while unmarried women enjoyed the right to register as traders, married women confronted considerable obstacles to independent participation in trade, as the following story reveals. When Epistimiia Konenkova requested permission to register as a member of the second merchant guild separately from her husband in 1853, the Kharkhov Revenue Department (*kazennaia palata*) granted her request. Once the ruling of the Revenue Department reached the Ministry of Finance in St. Petersburg, however, the ministry ordered the department to instruct Konenkova to cease trading in her own name, since, according to the Statutes on Trade, she had no grounds for registering independently of her husband. Konenkova submitted another petition in which she argued that her request was founded on a precise interpretation of the law, which granted membership in the merchantry to women who married into that estate. She went on to justify her desire to trade independently of her husband, pointing out that she had inherited her capital from her parents and enjoyed full rights of disposal over that property. She also sought to allay any suspicions on the part of the court by stating that her request did not derive from marital conflict, but from logistics: Konenkova's property was in Kharkhov, and her husband conducted trade in Berdiansk; thus it was physically impossible for him to supervise her business affairs as well as his own.

When Konenkova's case reached St. Petersburg in 1856, members of the Senate admitted that the law was contradictory. On the one hand, the law stipulated that married women could not issue promissory notes without their husbands' permission; on the other hand, the law also stated that husbands and wives enjoyed the right to manage their property independently of one another. The senators finally concluded that Konenkova could register independently in the merchant guild, since the law was ambiguous and no clear grounds existed for refusing her request.[63] In light of such legal constraints, it comes as no surprise that merchant women represented a relatively small percentage of registered traders: their proportion ranged from no more than 2 percent of merchants in the first guild in St. Petersburg in 1858, to 15 percent in the third guild.[64]

Female Entrepreneurs

Since many factories in Russia were located on noble estates, women also controlled and supervised various types of industrial production. During the first half of the eighteenth century, despite the urging of Peter the Great,

---

63. RGIA, f. 1330, op. 6, ed. khr. 1004, ll. 6–8, 14–15, 22–23.

64. Catriona Kelly, "Teacups and Coffins: The Culture of Russian Merchant Women, 1850–1917," in *Women in Russia and Ukraine* ed. Rosalind Marsh (Cambridge, 1996), 65.

few nobles could be found among the ranks of factory owners. Only in the post-Petrine era did the nobility begin to perceive the economic benefits of fostering industrial production on their estates.[65] The privilege of owning serf labor comprised a significant advantage for the nobility in this respect and remained a point of contention between merchants and nobles into the nineteenth century. Noble men and women oversaw the production of cloth, paper, rope, and metal on their estates, albeit usually on a small scale. Three hundred peasants worked in the cloth factory of the *pomeshchitsa* Voikova early in the nineteenth century. Factories employing more than one thousand serfs were rare, although an inventory from 1803 reveals that nine thousand serfs labored in the cloth factory of Countess Potemkina in Kursk province.[66] The nobility also enjoyed a monopoly on alcohol distilling; a distillery was a common fixture on the estates of noble men and women. Among the eight biggest suppliers of alcohol in 1765 was Agrafena Apraksina; the widow of P. Chernyshev was also a major supplier in 1779–83.[67]

The wives and daughters of merchants also owned and managed enterprises, sometimes employing hundreds of workers. In the Morozov family, the active role of women in factory management was a veritable tradition. While Elisei Morozov wrote tracts on the coming of the anti-Christ, his wife Evdokia ran the family dye-works in the 1840s. Elisei's grandson, Vikyl Morozov, set up a spinning mill in 1872 and appointed his wife to the board of directors. Varvara Morozova not only expanded her husband's paper factory but also found time to improve the living conditions of her workers. The Morozov family was not unique, however, in exploiting feminine energy and business acumen: when Kapitolina Simonova inherited her father's linen factory, she put her husband in charge of the firm's commercial activities, while she supervised its day-to-day management.[68]

One obvious contrast between men and women in the realm of production is that women inherited firms from their husbands and fathers, rather than initiating enterprises with their own capital. There is some evidence, however, of an entrepreneurial spirit among women of both the noble and the merchant estates. The wife of Major Griboedov purchased an estate of 777 serfs in 1816, which she anticipated would bring her an income of four hundred thousand rubles a year. When her peasants refused to pay their

---

65. M. Tugan-Baranovskii, *Russkaia fabrika*, 6th ed. (Moscow, 1934), 15, 84; Mironov (1992), 465.

66. Tugan-Baranovskii (1934), 87, 93.

67. Kahan (1966), 62–63.

68. Ch. M. Ioksimovich, *Manufakturnaia promyshlennost' v proshlom i nastoiashchem* (Moscow, 1915), 18–20, 37; part II, 28. See also Muriel Joffe and Adele Lindenmeyr, "Daughters, Wives, and Partners: Women of the Moscow Merchant Elite," in *Merchant Moscow: Images of Russia's Vanished Bourgeoisie*, ed. James L. West and Iurii A. Petrov (Princeton, 1998), 102–4.

obrok in full, she resolved to cut her losses and to build a glass factory on the estate. Unfortunately for Griboedova, her serfs also declined to fulfill their labor requirements and refused to work in the factory.[69] In 1814, the wife of Aulic Councilor Belavin petitioned the Senate to convert her silk mill into a more profitable linen works.[70] Merchant women were also anxious to make the most of their commercial concerns. When Matrena Pavlova inherited her father's failing cotton plant in 1892, she managed to restore the firm's fortunes by updating the machinery in the factory.[71] To be sure, for women of all social estates, inheritance of land or capital comprised the source of their fortunes; as we will see, however, the fortunes of men also rested largely on inheritance, and women proved as likely as their male counterparts to grasp the value of a good investment.

The Acquisition of Property

In regard to use of property, the similarities of men's and women's economic behavior far outweighed their differences. Women controlled the same range of assets as men and engaged in a variety of transactions on a similar scale. A comparison of how women and men acquired their fortunes reveals less uniformity, however, in their relation to property, as well as highlighting the transformation of women's economic and legal status in the post-Petrine era. When alienating immovable assets, sellers generally provided some account of how they originally acquired the property—in some cases providing a lengthy genealogy of the estate. A survey of the sources of wealth for nobles of both sexes on the one hand illuminates the significance of inheritance as the mainstay of noble fortunes; on the other, it underscores the increasingly vital role women played in the family economy after the mid-eighteenth century. The patterns that emerge also demonstrate gradual convergence in the way women and men acquired estates.

At the beginning of the eighteenth century, noblemen in the provinces relied overwhelmingly on land inherited from their fathers (Table 4.15). When men declared how they acquired their wealth, they affirmed women's marginal role in the economy during the Petrine era: none of the men in this survey sold estates that they had inherited from their mothers or wives; in 5 percent of the deeds recorded, husbands sold their wives' dowries. All told, 77 percent of male sellers in 1715–20 alienated estates inherited from their fathers; another 14 percent received land from deceased siblings or uncles. Not only inheritance, but inheritance from male kin, was the single

69. *Krest'ianskoe dvizhenie v Rossii v 1796–1826 gg.: Sbornik dokumentov*, ed. S. N. Valk (Moscow, 1961), 476.

70. Tugan-Baranovskii (1934), 100.

71. Ioksimovich (1915), 87.

TABLE 4.15 How Estates Being Sold Were Originally Acquired, 1715–1860*

Source of Acquisition	Vladimir		Kashin		Tambov		Kursk		Moscow		All Regions	
	W	M	W	M	W	M	W	M	W	M	W	M
1715–20	N = 2	N = 11	N = 16	N = 21	N = 5	N = 12	N = 12	N = 70	N = 14	N = 24	N = 49	N = 138
Inherit from father	—	64	25	67	20	67	42	96	43	46	33	77
Inherit from mother	—	—	6	—	—	—	—	—	—	—	2	—
Inherit from spouse	100	—	50	—	40	—	58	—	36	—	49	—
Inherit from other	—	9	13	24	—	25	—	4	—	25	4	14
Dowry	—	27	6	—	40	8	—	—	21	4	12	5
Purchase	—	—	—	9	—	—	—	—	—	21	—	4
1750–55	N = 16	N = 11	N = 19	N = 26	N = 26	N = 42	N = 25	N = 43	N = 138	N = 205	N = 224	N = 327
Inherit from father	25	37	37	69	65	50	84	93	30	46	40	54
Inherit from mother	6	18	5	15	—	9	12	—	5	9	4	9
Inherit from spouse	38	—	26	4	15	—	—	5	24	3	23	2
Inherit from other	25	18	11	8	12	24	4	—	14	17	13	16
Dowry	6	9	—	—	4	—	—	—	8	—	6	—
Purchase	—	18	21	4	4	17	—	2	19	25	14	19

	N = 31	N = 34	N = 42	N = 37	N = 57	N = 119	N = 22	N = 30	N = 171	N = 296	N = 323	N = 516
1775–80												
Inherit from father	13	41	21	38	14	37	18	50	24	38	21	39
Inherit from mother	16	15	21	8	11	5	14	7	15	16	15	12
Inherit from spouse	16	12	15	3	26	—	18	3	16	5	18	4
Inherit from other	23	17	26	27	12	16	5	10	6	14	11	15
Dowry	16	—	—	—	12	—	5	—	8	—	8	—
Purchase	16	15	17	24	25	42	41	30	31	27	27	30
	N = 63	N = 111	N = 12	N = 20	N = 14	N = 36	N = 0	N = 0	N = 58	N = 76	N = 147	N = 243
1805–10												
Inherit from father	35	32	8	20	—	36	—	—	21	30	24	31
Inherit from mother	16	28	17	20	14	22	—	—	19	16	17	23
Inherit from spouse	9	6	17	5	36	8	—	—	7	1	12	5
Inherit from other	5	6	25	25	22	—	—	—	10	21	10	11
Dowry	8	—	—	—	14	—	—	—	7	—	7	—
Purchase	27	28	33	30	14	33	—	—	36	32	30	30
	N = 53	N = 55	N = 0	N = 0	N = 0	N = 0	N = 0	N = 0	N = 0	N = 53	N = 53	N = 55
1855–60												
Inherit from father	17	31	—	—	—	—	—	—	—	17	17	31
Inherit from mother	17	13	—	—	—	—	—	—	—	17	17	13
Inherit from spouse	11	4	—	—	—	—	—	—	—	11	11	4
Inherit from other	8	20	—	—	—	—	—	—	—	8	8	20
Dowry	2	—	—	—	—	—	—	—	—	2	2	—
Purchase	45	33	—	—	—	—	—	—	—	45	45	33

* W = women, M = men. Each value is the percentage of available transactions. The number of available transactions, N, is given for each time period.
Source: See appendix 1.

most important means by which men acquired land in the early eighteenth century. Significantly, only 4 percent of all male sellers had originally purchased the property they now sold—a figure that testifies to a quiescent land market in the early part of the century.

For women, the acquisition of immovable property may have been one of the joys of widowhood. Almost 50 percent of women who sold land in 1715–20 indicated that they had inherited their estates from their husbands—a finding well in keeping with the marital status of most female sellers in the early part of the century. A surprisingly small number of women brought dowry estates to the market—an average of 12 percent for all the districts surveyed—while 33 percent alienated land that had originally belonged to their fathers. And if men had little purchased property at their disposal, women had none at all: not a single woman announced the sale of a purchased estate in this sample. In short, a comparison of how men and women acquired property in the first two decades of the eighteenth century confirms noblewomen's place on the periphery of the seigneurial economy.

Three decades later, the sources of wealth for both sexes were more diverse. Men still relied heavily on property passed on by their fathers; almost half of the land that men sold, however, derived from other origins. For both men and women, the sale of purchased estates represented the most significant shift in economic behavior: in the regions surveyed, 14 percent of the estates sold by women had been acquired. Acquired estates comprised 19 percent of estates sold by men, whereas the number of estates inherited from fathers decreased to 54 percent. Equally noteworthy is the appearance of women as the original owners of property: in 9 percent of estate sales, men recorded selling their mothers' bequests. Women, on the other hand, still relied disproportionately on maintenance portions from their husbands' holdings. These accounted for a striking 23 percent of all women's sales. At the same time, land received from their fathers and other kin assumed greater significance. Across all regions, 6 percent of sales by women involved dowry land, while men ceased to sell their wives' dowries altogether—an indisputable consequence of the greater control their wives' enjoyed over their property.

The trends that appear in women's and men's acquisition of wealth in the mid-eighteenth century intensified over the following decades. Two patterns in particular deserve further discussion: First, as women became more active in the real estate market, their assets assumed greater significance in their children's inheritance. Second, nobles of both sexes were increasingly likely to alienate purchased property, rather than inherited estates. Women also became less dependent on their husband's assets to take part in the market, and both men and women sold fewer estates inherited from their fathers. As the opportunities for nobles to acquire property grew more diverse, the acquisition of property by women grew more similar to that of their male counterparts.

From the late eighteenth century until the eve of Emancipation, nobles of both sexes could accede to property at several points during their lifetime. While succeeding to the family estate remained crucial, both sexes inherited from an array of kin, who were as likely to be female as male. Investment in land grew until sales of acquired land represented 45 percent of sales by women and 33 percent of those by men.[72] Far from being more conservative than their male counterparts, Russian noblewomen responded to the changing economic climate by selling land and reinvesting their capital. Women sometimes parted with their estates in order to satisfy their creditors, but these figures demonstrate that they also sold with the goal of consolidating their holdings or acquiring more valuable land when it came on the market. In this respect, female proprietors in nineteenth-century Russia parted company with American women who owned real estate in the antebellum South. Having acquired property, American women rarely sold their assets. In the words of one scholar, "For women as a group, the watchword was caution. They invested in land, but as the deeds show, they tended to hang on to it."[73] Among Russian noblewomen, no discrepancy appears between their tendency to buy and sell.

An additional source of wealth for the nobility was the gift of land and serfs from the sovereign as a mark of favor or reward for service. The historian S. S. Shashkov maintained that during the reign of empresses women were frequently recipients of settled estates, "thanks to which they could live entirely independent lives."[74] Catherine II bestowed estates and other property on Princess Dashkova as a reward for her faithful service.[75] Catherine's male successors also granted estates to women. Emperor Paul awarded two thousand desiatins of land and an unspecified number of serfs to Matriona Serdiukova in 1798, in return for her sacrifices during the Turkish war—a reference, presumably, to the loss of male kin in battle.[76] The wife of Lieutenant Brunner received three hundred desiatins in 1824, although the deed offered no explanation for the grant.[77] These examples were more the exception, however, than the rule. Noblemen remained far more likely than women to reap tangible benefits on a large scale in return for government

72. The only data available on how estates were acquired in 1855–60 are from Vladimir district. While the absence of data for other districts is an obvious weakness in this sample, the trends apparent in Vladimir are a logical continuation of those for all regions in 1805–10.

73. Lebsock (1984), 126. William Chester Jordan also observes that women in early-modern Europe were not "risk takers" and that they invested in real estate rather than trade. See Jordan, *Women and Credit in Pre-Industrial and Developing Societies* (Philadelphia, 1993), 77.

74. Shashkov (1879), 314–15.

75. Dashkova (1995), 196–99.

76. RGIA, f. 1350, op. 56, ed. khr. 20, l. 3.

77. RGIA, f. 1350, op. 56, ed. khr. 567, l. 4; see also f. 1350, op. 56, ed. khr. 19, l. 3.

service. Of 105 recipients of crown lands between 1700 and 1749, for example, only 12 were women.[78]

The Dowry and Female Fortunes

Oddly enough, dowry estates were negligible assets for noblewomen who alienated land, even in the early part of the eighteenth century. Dowry donors were far more inclined to grant their daughters capital and movable assets, which women then converted into real estate. Indeed, while noblemen received salaries and pensions for their years of state service,[79] most noblewomen enjoyed access to only two sources of capital: cash received as dowry or inheritance, and the revenue generated by their estates. Historians have traditionally contended that land was part of the marriage bargain and an occasion for the circulation of estates among the nobility.[80] This assumption is not borne out, however, either in deeds of sale or in dowry contracts that survive in notarial records. By and large, two types of donors bestowed immovable property on female kin: nobles who had few assets at their disposal and could muster nothing more than part of a village for their daughters, and at the opposite extreme, those who could well afford a generous dowry in every form of property—real estate, chattel, and cash.

The Law of Single Inheritance marked a sea change in dowry composition. Before 1714, donors bestowed immovable property on female kin as a matter of course. Of thirty-five dowries recorded in Moscow in 1703 and 1714,[81] twenty-eight (80 percent) included land and only seven (20 percent) consisted solely of chattel and house serfs.[82] Moreover, the value of dowries recorded in Moscow was far from inconsiderable: the average value of movable property included in dowries in 1703 was 542 rubles; in 1714, the mean had reached 1,240 rubles. Dowry contracts registered after 1731, however, rarely included land. Despite the vehement protests of the nobility that they could not provide for their daughters without fragmenting their

78. E. I. Indova, *Dvortsovoe khoziaistvo v Rossii: Pervaia polovina XVIII veka* (Moscow, 1964), 66–78.

79. Peter the Great put an end to the practice of awarding estates to state servitors, and paid officers and civil servants a salary instead. Indeed, most nobles inherited no estates and were dependent on the state for their earnings. See S. M. Troitskii, *Russkii absoliutizm i dvorianstvo v XVIII v.* (Moscow, 1974), 266. The exception among women were those who served at court.

80. E. P. Karnovich, *Zamechatel'nye bogatstva chastnykh lits v Rossii* (St. Petersburg, 1874), 210–12, 294, 334–35; Meehan-Waters (1982), 79.

81. This sample includes dowries recorded before the Law of Single Inheritance was issued on March 23, 1714.

82. RGADA, f. 282, op. 1, ch. 1, ed. khr. 541 (1703), ll. 41, 44, 47–49, 55, 57–58, 60, 72–73, 77, 84, 88–89, 94–95, 100–101, 105–7, 110, 113, 116–17, 139; f. 282, op. 1, ch. 1, ed. khr. 543 (1714), ll. 40, 42, 45, 49–54, 57, 101.

estates, by 1731 dowry donors had adapted to the new state of affairs. Of sixty-one dowries recorded in the Justice College in Moscow in 1731, 1750, 1760, and 1780, a single dowry included real estate: upon her marriage to Nikolai Bakhmetev in 1760, Sofia Miloslavskaia received an estate of 246 serfs in remote Arzamas district from her widowed mother, as well as movable property worth forty-five hundred rubles.[83] Miloslavskaia's dowry was highly unusual, however; the remaining brides in Moscow made due with chattel, cash, and the occasional house serf.[84]

The failure of donors to grant estates to their kinfolk was no reflection on their generosity or their financial standing. In this sample, the average ruble value of dowries recorded in 1731 was 2,800 rubles; in 1750, the average had risen to 5,827 rubles.[85] Dowry contracts in Moscow reveal not only that donors parted with jewels, clothing, and other chattel, but also that most dowries included a considerable sum earmarked for the purchase of estates. In a typical contract, Stolnik Koshelev gave his daughter 1,800 rubles "for the purchase of villages" (*na pokupku derevni*) when she married in 1731.[86] In addition to relinquishing a bed, clothing, and linen worth 3,277 rubles, Andrei Saburov added 3,000 rubles to his daughter's portion in 1750, "for the purchase of estates" (*na pokupku votchin*).[87]

Family strategies for the distribution of wealth were markedly different in the provinces, among the less affluent nobility. Of fifty-eight dowries recorded between 1751 and 1868 in Vladimir, Kashin, Tambov, Kursk, and Syzran, twenty-six (45 percent) included a modest amount of land, while thirty-two (55 percent) comprised some combination of chattel, cash, and houseserfs.[88] The contrast between dowries recorded in Moscow and those

83. RGADA, f. 282, op. 1, ch. 1, ed. khr. 583, ll. 440–43.

84. RGADA, f. 282, op. 1, ch. 1, ed. khr. 550 (1731), ll. 2–3, 20–21, 30–31, 42–43, 45–46, 62–64, 70–71, 88–89, 101–3, 105–7, 109–10, 232–33, 321–22, 329–30, 495–96, 501–2, 529–30; f. 282, op. 1, ch. 1, ed. khr. 571 (1750), ll. 8–11, 14–16, 24–25, 37–38, 52–54, 66–69, 76–77, 90–91, 100–101, 302–3, 305–6, 354–55, 360–61, 366–67, 380–81, 388–89, 403–6, 412–13; f. 282, op. 1, ch. 1, ed. khr. 583 (1760), ll. 51–52, 58–59, 77, 79–83, 103–5, 130–31, 430–32, 447–49, 454–55, 476–77, 514–15, 558–65, 668–73; f. 282, op. 1, ch. 1, ed. khr. 610 (1780), ll. 41, 76–77, 237–39, 247–48, 429–30.

85. In 1731, the average value of nineteen dowries was 2,800 rubles. This average does not include one dowry of 17,648 rubles in the sample for 1731. The average for 1750 is also based on a sample of nineteen dowries; a dowry of 70,000 rubles was excluded. In a sample of sixteen dowries for 1760, the average value was 3,584 rubles; one dowry of 30,000 rubles was excluded. Robin Bisha notes that the average value of the dowry among the lesser nobility in the eighteenth century was 3,000 rubles, while dowries among aristocratic families were worth 69,500 rubles. See Bisha (1993), 140–41.

86. RGADA, f. 282, op. 1, ch. 1, ed. khr. 550, ll. 102–3.

87. RGADA, f. 282, op. 1, ch. 1, ed. khr. 571, ll. 90–91.

88. RGADA, f. 615, op. 1, ed. khr. 1996, ll. 1–2, 17, 108–9 (Vladimir, 1751); f. 615, op. 1, ed. khr. 2000, ll. 22, 60 (Vladimir, 1753); f. 615, op. 1, ed. khr. 4220, ll. 1, 38, 42, 70–71, 194, 201–2 (Kashin, 1753); f. 615, op. 1, ed. khr. 11418, ll. 2, 6–7, 22–23 (Tambov, 1753); f. 615, op. 1, ed. khr. 2004, ll. 75–76 (Vladimir, 1755); f. 615, op. 1, ed. khr. 4222, ll. 61–62 (Kashin, 1755); f. 615, op. 1, ed. khr. 4241, l. 82 (Kashin, 1770); f. 615, op. 1, ed. khr. 2042, ll. 16–17, 127–28 (Vladimir, 1775); f. 615, op.

in the provinces underscores the gulf that separated the thin stratum of wealthy aristocratic families from the petty nobility. Many of the latter could offer their daughters nothing more than a single houseserf or a tiny plot of land. After *pomeshchik* Poiarkov failed to come up with a dowry, he finally handed over a peasant woman and her son to his daughter in 1753.[89] The widow Patrekeeva stipulated that the serf family and two single serfs she relinquished in 1776 represented all her daughter could expect from her father's estate.[90] A more affluent widow in Kursk, Puzanova, managed to provide her daughter with much of what she would need after her marriage: in 1778 she registered a lengthy inventory of household goods in her daughter's name, which included a bed and silk scarves, ten pillows, twelve cloth napkins, and nine tablecloths.[91]

At the other extreme, women from wealthy families could anticipate an inheritance in immovable wealth—icons, jewels, clothing, and furniture—as well as villages, houses, and liquid capital. Dowries preserved in the family papers of noble families testify to the means at their disposal: of thirty-five marriage contracts recorded between 1731 and 1868, seventeen (49 percent) included land, while eighteen (51 percent) comprised chattel and cash alone.[92] Even brides who married without an immovable estate began married life with an impressive array of goods. Natalia Piklonskaia married

1, ed. khr. 5565, ll. 1–2, 5, 8, 39–40 (Kursk, 1775); f. 615, op. 1, ed. khr. 2045, ll. 72, 81, 87–88 (Vladimir, 1776); f. 615, op. 1, ed. khr. 11569, ll. 38–39, 51–52, 74–75 (Tambov, 1776); f. 615, op. 1, ed. khr. 11235, ll. 11, 30–31 (Syzran, 1776); f. 615, op. 1, ed. khr. 11577, ll. 14–15, 52–53 (Tambov, 1777); f. 615, op. 1, ed. khr. 11578, ll. 3, 8–10, 21–22 (Tambov, 1777); f. 615, op. 1, ed. khr. 11237, ll. 23–24, 28–29, 32, 36–37, 72, 77 (Syzran, 1777); f. 615, op. 1, ed. khr. 2049, ll. 1–2, 103–4, 122–23 (Vladimir, 1778); f. 615, op. 1, ed. khr. 5587, ll. 13–14, 35 (Kursk, 1778); f. 615, op. 1, ed. khr. 11593, ll. 3–5, 12–14, 20–21, 30–31, 36, 52 (Tambov, 1779); GA Tverskoi oblasti, f. 668 (Kashinskii uezdnyi sud), op. 1, ed. khr. 6444, ll. 33–34, 52–53 (Kashin, 1806, 1808); *Sanktpeterburgskie senatskie ob"iavleniia po sudebnym, . . . i kazennym delam* (14/03/1860), p. 45.

89. RGADA, f. 615, op. 1, ed. khr. 4220, l. 42 (Kashin, 1753).

90. RGADA, f. 615, op. 1, ed. khr. 2045, ll. 72 (Vladimir, 1776).

91. RGADA, f. 615, op. 1, ed. khr. 5587, ll. 13–14.

92. RGIA, f. 994 (Mordvinovy), op. 1, ed. khr. 226 (1731); RGADA, f. 1270 (Musiny-Pushkiny), op. 1, ed. khr. 78 (1733); GIM, f. 47 (Shakhovskie-Glebovy-Streshnevy), ed. khr. 1, ll. 20–21 (1734); RGADA, f. 1258 (Beshentsevy), op. 1, ed. khr. 15, ll. 1–2 (1738); GIM, f. 47, ll. 1–3 (1739); RGIA, f. 840 (Batiushkovy), op. 1, ed. khr. 31, ll. 1, 4 (1742); RGIA, f. 1101, op. 1, ed. khr. 100 (1744); Shchukin (1897), III: 71–72 (1748); RGADA, f. 1263 (Golitsyny), op. 1, ed. khr. 6770 (1751); RGIA, f. 914, op. 1, ed. khr. 122, ll. 1–5 (1751–52); RGIA, f. 840, op. 1, ed. khr. 31, l. 5–6 (1753); RGADA, f. 1265 (Goncharovy), op. 2, ed. khr. 120, l. 1 (1757); RGADA, f. 1263, op. 1, ed. khr. 8464, l. 16 (1758); GIM, f. 60 (Vorontsovy), op. 1, ed. khr. 106, ll. 8, 11, 14, 17 (1758–66); RGADA, f. 1265, op. 2, ed. khr. 156, ll. 1–2 (1767); RGIA, f. 840, op. 1, ed. khr. 31, l. 7 (1771); RGIA, f. 1044 (Saburovy), op. 1, ed. khr. 578 (1771); A. A. Vasil'chikov, *Semeistvo Razumovskikh* (St. Petersburg, 1880), 2: 537–51 (1774); RGADA, f. 1272 (Naryshkiny), op. 1, ed. khr. 101 (1781); GIM, f. 47, ed. khr. 1, l. 7 (1787); RGADA, f. 1274 (Paniny-Bludovy), op. 1, ch. 2, ed. khr. 1082, l. 1 (1790); RGADA, f. 1278 (Stroganovy), op. 1, ed. khr. 579, ll. 1–2 (1800); GIM, f. 47, ed. khr. 1, ll. 11–12 (1808); RGIA, f. 1088, op. 1, ed. khr. 756 (1808); RGADA, f. 1270, op. 1, ed. khr. 1170, ll. 1–2 (1820); RGADA, f. 1278, op. 1, ed. khr. 523 (1821); RGADA, f. 1270, op. 1, ed. khr. 1442 (1823); RGADA, f. 1263, op. 3, ed. khr. 338, l. 1 (1826); GIM, f. 60, op. 1, ed. khr. 434, ll. 1–6 (1845); RGADA, f. 1274, op. 1, ed. khr. 1318 (1868).

Ivan Musin-Pushkin in 1733; upon her marriage, her mother granted her two thousand rubles in movable property, as well as five hundred rubles in cash. Among the items inventoried in Natalia's dowry were jewel-encrusted icons, a Polish fur coat, and lengths of German damask.[93] In some cases, dowry donors stated that they were giving their daughters liquid assets in lieu of their share of the family estate, and stipulated that the dowry comprised their daughters' total inheritance. Thus, when Senator Fedor Ivanovich Glebov relinquished 1,400 serfs and 29,175 rubles in liquid assets to his daughter in 1787, the latter signed a second document, declaring that she would request nothing more from her father's estate.[94] The overwhelming majority of dowry contracts, however, did not bar the recipients from taking part in the partition of family assets after the death of both parents. These documents offer written testimony that for the majority of noble women, the dowry comprised an advance on inheritance, rather than the sum of their portion of the family estate.

Liquid assets in the form of cash and in movable property gave women the means to purchase land of their own, and account for women's prominence as investors in real estate from the mid-eighteenth century. Even dowries composed of jewels and clothing could be exploited as productive assets. Early in the nineteenth century, Sophia Shcherbatova sold the jewels she had received when she married, and with the proceeds purchased land in the fertile southern provinces. "These investments founded the family fortune," her great-granddaughter recalled.[95] Men also made use of their wives' capital; noblewomen as well as merchant wives donated assets to fund their husbands' ventures. The statesman Count S. Iu. Witte recalled how his father invested his mother's considerable dowry, with her permission, in a foundry in the Caucasus. Witte's mother lived to regret her decision after her husband died without paying his debts, leaving his family in extremely reduced circumstances.[96] More often than not, however, Russian noblewomen eschewed "hidden" family investments and used dowry funds to invest in landed estates of their own.

Kinship and Property Transactions

Although noble women and men acquired property at different points in life and by different means, they utilized property in similar ways once it

93. RGADA, f. 1270, op. 1, ed. khr. 78.

94. GIM, f. 47, ed. khr. 1, l. 7.

95. Paul Chavchavadze, *Marie Avinov: Pilgrimage through Hell* (Englewood Cliffs, N. J., 1968), 10. Sharon Kettering argues that jewels were "a source of ready cash" for noblewomen in early-modern France and instrumental to women's economic power. See Kettering, "The Patronage Power of Early Modern French Noblewomen," *Historical Journal* 32, no. 4 (1989): 825–26.

96. S. Iu. Witte, *Vospominaniia: Detstvo. Tsarstvovaniia Aleksandra II i Aleksandra III (1849–1894)* (Berlin, 1923), 38–39.

came into their hands. Given the element of personalism that scholars have identified in the wills of European and American women,[97] however, we might expect to find that women were more likely than their male counterparts to engage in property transactions with kin. Historians of early-modern Britain contend that frequent sales of real estate among kin are associated with family, rather than individual, ownership of property.[98] In Russia, the link between family and land has been assumed to be fragile. Foreign observers in Russia often commented on the ease with which noble men and women alienated family estates, evincing little ancestral loyalty when financial gain was at stake. August von Haxthausen remarked that the Russian nobleman "will dispose of his inheritance immediately if he sees an advantage in doing so."[99] Although the state went to considerable lengths to discourage nobles from parting with family assets, Russian nobles of both sexes sold family property in numbers that astonished visitors from abroad. In this respect, the behavior of female proprietors duplicated that of men; moreover, although women sold a marginally greater percentage of their assets to kin, neither men nor women transferred property to family members in significant numbers.

From the beginning of the eighteenth century until the eve of Emancipation, nobles of both sexes proved reluctant to engage in intrafamilial sales of property.[100] Between 1715 and 1720, only 9 percent of real estate sales by women involved transactions with kin; men sold to kin even more rarely (Table 4.16). Male and female behavior diverged markedly at the end of the eighteenth century, when 20 percent of real estate sales by women were to kin and only 8 percent of sales by men were to relations. In the nineteenth century, however, female sellers again fell in line with their male counterparts: no more than 12 percent of transactions in 1805–10 and 13 percent in 1855–60 accounted for sales to kin. Throughout the period in question, noble women and men were far more likely to sell to a third party.

A second perspective on intrafamilial sales of property is provided by the composition of kin who engaged in property transfers (Table 4.17). Until the mid-nineteenth century, both men and women sold to siblings in preference to any other family member. Only in 1855–60 did sales of property between siblings wane in favor of sales between spouses and between parents and children. Transactions between uncles and aunts and nieces and nephews were prominent until the mid-eighteenth century, after which they rapidly declined. Sales to in-laws were also far from negligible in the

97. See chapter 5.
98. Alan Macfarlane, *The Origins of English Individualism: The Family, Property, and Social Transition* (New York, 1978), 80–101.
99. Haxthausen (1972), 250.
100. The fact that land sold to members of the same clan remained patrimonial may have discouraged transfers of property between kin.

TABLE 4.16 Percentage of Transactions with Kin, by Region, 1715–1860*

	Vladimir		Kashin		Tambov		Kursk		Moscow		All Regions	
	W	M	W	M	W	M	W	M	W	M	W	M
1715–20	0	5	19	11	15	3	0	0	0	5	9	5
	(12)	(19)	(26)	(70)	(13)	(34)	(13)	(91)	(25)	(111)	(79)	(325)
1750–55	13	12	14	17	7	5	50	13	15	12	18	12
	(15)	(17)	(22)	(36)	(27)	(55)	(30)	(69)	(140)	(263)	(234)	(441)
1775–80	35	8	30	14	10	4	49	13	13	8	20	8
	(31)	(38)	(44)	(36)	(59)	(146)	(32)	(47)	(159)	(289)	(325)	(556)
1805–10	9	8	29	35	5	10	—	—	17	15	12	14
	(74)	(126)	(14)	(23)	(40)	(81)			(60)	(81)	(188)	(309)
1855–60	15	14	11	11	13	9	13	9	12	14	13	11
	(66)	(74)	(64)	(63)	(96)	(127)	(87)	(102)	(230)	(245)	(543)	(611)
All periods 1715–1860	16	9	19	15	10	7	25	6	13	11	15	10
	(1,874)	(266)	(170)	(228)	(235)	(443)	(162)	(309)	(614)	(990)	(1,369)	(2,244)

* W = women, M = men. The number of available transactions is in parentheses.
Source: See appendix 1.

TABLE 4.17 Percentage of Transactions with Kin, by Type of Kin, 1715–1860*

	1		2		3		4		5		6		7	
	W	M	W	M	W	M	W	M	W	M	W	M	W	M
1715–20 (W = 6) (M = 15)	0	0	33	33	0	0	33	33	17	27	0	7	17	0
1750–55 (W = 43) (M = 51)	0	0	28	37	7	4	23	18	12	16	0	4	30	21
1775–80 (W = 65) (M = 43)	2	0	38	46	20	5	11	16	6	5	6	2	17	26
1805–10 (W = 23) (M = 38)	13	8	44	55	26	16	9	5	4	5	0	3	4	8
1855–60 (W = 68) (M = 67)	31	46	19	27	44	22	0	2	0	0	2	0	4	3
1715–1860 (W = 205) (M = 214)	12	16	30	39	26	12	10	11	6	7	2	2	14	13

* 1 = spouses;
2 = siblings;
3 = parents or children;
4 = uncles, aunts, nephews, or nieces;
5 = cousins;
6 = grandparents or grandchildren;
7 = in-laws; W = women; M = men. The numbers in parentheses in the left column represent the number of transactions.
Source: See appendix 1.

eighteenth century. The most striking pattern in this survey is the gradual shift from transfers of property between second-degree kin and affines toward sales within the nuclear family. By the mid-nineteenth century, a full 46 percent of men's transactions with family members involved the sale of property to wives. In contrast, 31 percent of intrafamilial sales of property by women were to their husbands and 44 percent were to their children. Overall, although men proved more likely to sell to siblings or wives, while women sold more often to children, the inclination of both sexes who sold to kin was to keep their holdings within the immediate family, with the aim of minimizing the fragmentation of family estates.

———◆———

In the provinces and cities of Imperial Russia, female proprietors were a common sight long before August von Haxthausen remarked on their existence. As Haxthausen observed, the concentration of wealth in female hands provides a new perspective on the economic status of Russian noblewomen. On one level, the prominence of female proprietors from the mid-eighteenth century underscores the impact of the revised rules of inheritance after 1731 on noblewomen's economic standing. At the same time, the activity of women in the market for land from the mid-eighteenth century cannot be explained apart from married women's elevation in the law of property after 1753. The law of separate property encouraged noblewomen to use their dowries as productive assets and to purchase estates in their own names. As a result of greater gender symmetry in the legal realm, noblewomen came to control as much as a third of the land and serfs in private hands on the eve of Emancipation.[101]

If the great majority of female proprietors did not control vast estates, in this respect their financial standing resembled that of their male counterparts. More striking still, regardless of the variable, women engaged in the same variety of property transactions, and on a similar scale, as male proprietors. Unlike women in the West, noblewomen in Russia were neither on the periphery of property ownership, nor were their contributions to the family economy hidden: Russian women's wealth provided a crucial supplement to the fortunes of their husbands.[102] To a far greater degree than historians have suspected, noblewomen played a vital role in the family economy and in the economic life of provincial Russia. How women used the assets they controlled to wield influence over kin, neighbors, and local officials is the subject of the following chapters.

101. Carol Shammas estimates that in the United States in 1900, following reform of married women's property rights, "about one out of every three estates belonged to a woman and women held on the average around a quarter of probated wealth"—an average very similar to my estimate for women of the Russian nobility in the nineteenth century. See Shammas (1994), 16–21.

102. An inventory of the immense estate of Prince Nikolai Iusupov, which comprised more than thirty-three thousand serfs, reveals that Iusupov's grandmothers had contributed dowry villages or purchased more than half the land and 27% of the serfs in Iusupov's hands in 1849. See RGADA, f. 1290 (Iusupovy), op. 3, ed. khr. 1747, ll. 1–10.

CHAPTER FIVE

The Culture of Giving:
Women, Men, and
Testamentary Behavior

As Anna Nelidova approached the end of her life and began to feel—as she expressed it—"weighed down by old age," she carried out a division of her husband's property among her five children. Writing to her daughter, Ekaterina, in 1790, Nelidova assured her that she had protected her interests and that she should not feel slighted by the small amount of property she would receive compared to her brothers. Nelidova pointed out that her daughter's portion of land and serfs was not fragmented but located in one village in Smolensk province, next to her own allotment. "I feel it is my duty to tell you in detail about everything concerning the division, my darling; otherwise you might seek an arrangement more to your advantage," Nelidova wrote. She went on to explain that although Ekaterina would receive only three hundred desiatins (in comparison to the twenty thousand her brothers would inherit), her inheritance consisted of extremely fertile land with abundant forests, while that of her brothers included huge tracts of swampland. Nelidova concluded her letter by asking for her daughter's consent to the property division on her own behalf and on behalf of her sons.[1]

Anna Nelidova's letter is a remarkable document that elucidates, in a few eloquent paragraphs, the conflicting concerns and potential for family discord that accompanied every division of property in Imperial Russia. On one level, Nelidova's letter offers a vivid example of the commitment of

---

1. RGIA, f. 1003 (E. I. Nelidova), op. 1, ed. khr. 67, ll. 1–2. For a biographical sketch of Ekaterina Nelidova (1758–1839), who was maid-of-honor to the Grand Duchess Maria Fedorovna, see *Znamenitye Rossiiane XVIII–XIX vekov: Biografii i portrety. Po izdaniiu velikogo kniazia Nikolaia Mikhailovicha "Russkie portrety XVIII; XIX stoletii* (St. Petersburg, 1996), 315–18.

noble families to minimize the harmful consequences of partible inheritance. Ekaterina Nelidova received no more than the legal entitlement to her father's estate, and her allotment was a consolidated holding. At the same time, Anna Nelidova openly acknowledged the injustice of the law in regard to female inheritance. Nelidova's division of her husband's estate adhered strictly to the rules of intestate inheritance, and her daughter had no legal grounds to expect more; nonetheless, Nelidova was anxious for Ekaterina's approval of the way the division was carried out, and hastened to assure her that the allotment had been chosen with an eye to her advantage. Nelidova's solicitude derived in part from her concern to avoid disputes between her children after her death, as she admitted: if Ekaterina consented to the terms of the division, Nelidova stated, in future she would have no grounds for dissatisfaction with her mother or the right to plague her brothers with legal suits. Nonetheless, the letter voices genuine concern on Nelidova's part for an equitable settlement for her daughter within the constraints of inheritance law. Nelidova's choice of a village for herself contiguous to that of her daughter further suggests that she intended eventually to bequeath her portion to Ekaterina.

Among its many benefits, property ownership presented women with myriad occasions to intervene in the material lives of family members. As property owners and legal personalities in their own right, noblewomen could reward or punish kin by bequeathing or withholding assets. Testamentary behavior thus affords a telling commentary on affective ties within the Russian noble family. As a source for interpreting noble culture, however, wills have been largely ignored by historians of Imperial Russia in favor of memoirs and prescriptive literature.[2] Yet a close reading of these documents provides a unique perspective on noble conceptions of family, kinship, and lineage, and the relation of these to property. As we will see, although Russian nobles placed a high value on lineage and the extended family, property played a negligible role in maintaining such alliances. Extended kinship ties often translated into influence at court and in the political arena, yet neither men nor women demonstrated loyalty to their clan by making multiple bequests of their assets, either real or personal, at the end of their lives. Instead, the nuclear family predominated over the clan in the realm of property relations from at least the seventeenth century.[3] In the absence of children, men and women returned their estates—as well as the less welcome gift of their debts—to their natal families. Even childless testators, however,

2. Tovrov's *The Russian Noble Family* (1987) remains the only study devoted exclusively to this topic. See also Barbara Alpern Engel, *Mothers and Daughters: Women of the Intelligentsia in Nineteenth-Century Russia* (Cambridge, 1983), and Semenova (1982).

3. Valerie Kivelson argues that the nuclear family, rather than the extended-kin group, held first place in the loyalties of the provincial gentry in seventeenth-century Muscovy. See Kivelson (1994).

selected their heirs with great discrimination and distributed their goods among as few legatees as affection, and the law, would allow.

In addition to illuminating family dynamics, testamentary patterns offer tangible evidence of the way property and legal conventions shape gender identity. The final testaments of Russian nobles point to yet another contrast between the culture of property in Russia and the West. Not only did Russian noblewomen exercise greater control over their fortunes during marriage; they also parted company with their European counterparts when deciding the posthumous fate of their assets. On the basis of wills and probate records, numerous historians have identified a discrete female value system with regard to property among Anglo-American and European women. Roughly speaking, they argue that while male testators were constrained by lineal obligations when they bequeathed their fortunes and evinced a clear preference for male legatees, the testaments of women were characterized by personalism and a marked proclivity for female heirs. Moreover, women were far more likely than men to invest movable goods with sentimental meaning and to itemize each of their personal affects. By contrast, in Russia the law of property dictated noblewomen's preoccupations and ensured that women duplicated the behavior of their male equivalents, rather than cultivating a separate female culture in the domain of property relations.

The Perils of Partible Inheritance

Unlike much of the nobility in Western Europe, Russian nobles were avid practitioners of partible inheritance. The Russian elite was not unique in distributing family assets among their offspring: all European systems of inheritance made some provision for younger sons and daughters, even in cases where immovable property was destined solely for the eldest son. In contrast to their counterparts in the West, however, Russian nobles took partible inheritance to an extreme. German nobles also divided their estates among male children, but "used restrictive marriage policies . . . and increasingly favored the eldest son . . . without formally abandoning the system of partible inheritance."[4] Peter I attempted to legislate change in inheritance practice with the Law of Single Inheritance in 1714, but without success; as soon as she took power in 1731, Empress Anna Ivanovna succumbed to noble demands to revoke the law. Peter's successors shared the ambivalence of the nobility on the question of entail. Until 1845 nobles were required to petition the sovereign if they wished to create an entailed estate. Even after

---

4. Judith J. Hurwich, "Inheritance Practices in Early Modern Germany," *Journal of Interdisciplinary History* 23, no. 4 (Spring 1993): 718. The Castilian nobility also used partible inheritance, but testators had the power to give preferential treatment to heirs. Reher (1997), 49.

Nicholas I regularized the practice, the qualifications for entailing property were so high that only the wealthiest nobles could meet them.[5] Devotion to partible inheritance did not preclude acknowledgement of its harmful effects, however, and its implementation remained an exercise in reconciling two incompatible values. Until the eve of the revolution, real tension existed between the nobility's long-held conviction that property should be divided among all sons and daughters, and the conflicting desire to prevent disintegration of the patrimonial estate.[6]

Even when the rules of intestate succession were rigidly followed, the division of family assets was fraught with potential conflict. More prescient members of the nobility tried to maintain family harmony by dictating a precise division of their property in a will and forbidding their children to deviate from the terms of their testament. Testators such as Collegiate Registrar Gnevashin sternly instructed their heirs to divide their estate without quarrels (*bez vsiakago sporu*).[7] When Evgraf Tatishev drew up his will in 1781, he specified which villages should be inherited by each of his four sons. He emphasized that he had made a fair division of his assets, stating that "although each of these estates in terms of numbers of serfs and amount of land are not entirely equal to one another, to the best of my knowledge they are equal in income and profitability."[8] Tatishev also made a smaller bequest to his wife and endowed each of his four daughters with a dowry worth twenty-four thousand rubles.

More often than not, however, noble men and women died intestate, and their heirs were left to draw up agreements on their own. Eighteenth-century notarial records offer hundreds of examples of these contracts, called *razdel'nye zapisi*, or deeds of separation, and they demonstrate how widowed spouses, children, and in-laws managed to settle on a division of the fortune of the deceased. Deeds of separation also exhibit general concern with minimizing the fragmentation of property. In an agreement drawn up between four sisters in 1753, one woman relinquished her share of their father's estate in Ustezhskii and Bezhetskii districts and accepted her sisters' portions in Kashin, in order to consolidate her holdings in the latter district.[9] After her mother's death, Natasia Kolobova signed a contract with her father in 1778, in which she ceded her share of her mother's cloth factory and the

5. See A. M. Anfimov, "Maioratnoe zemlevladenie v tsarskoi Rossii," *Istoriia SSSR*, no. 5 (1962): 151–59; Blum (1961), 378–79; Wagner (1994), 236–38.

6. As William Wagner argues, the persistence of partible inheritance in the late Imperial era derived in part from tradition, but also from the nature of the Russian economy, in which land and serfs were the most secure form of wealth. See Wagner, "Legislative Reform of Inheritance in Russia, 1861–1914," in *Russian Law: Historical and Political Perspectives*, ed. William E. Butler (Leyden, 1977), 154.

7. RGADA, f. 615, op. 1, ed. khr. 2042, ll. 21–22 (Vladimir, 1775).

8. RGADA, f. 1290 (Iusupovy), op. 1, ed. khr. 46, ll. 1–2.

9. RGADA, f. 615, op. 1, ed. khr. 4220, l. 171.

serfs belonging to the establishment in return for a sum of ten thousand rubles. Her father had already expended much of his own capital on training these serfs to work in the factory, she declared, and since the factory could not be divided, she was willing to accept a lump sum in lieu of her share in the business.[10]

Partitioning the family estate was a recurring theme in noble memoirs. In keeping with their idealized portrait of noble life in the pre-reform era, many depicted themselves, or their protagonists, as acting solely in the interests of their siblings. Arkadii Kochubei asserted that he and his brothers were committed to a fair distribution of assets when they divided their father's holdings: "At the beginning of 1826, we finally decided to divide our patrimonial estate, since Mother could no longer administer it, and I had married," he recalled in his memoir. "Disputes about politics often took place in our house over dinner, and for the most part in French, as a result of which our guests believed we were arguing over our inheritance. On the contrary, the division of our property was completed in several hours." Kochubei described the villages that each of his brothers claimed, and went on to say that he was satisfied with a village with a very poor yield at the time, since his wife owned a productive estate.[11]

The authors of other contemporary memoirs praised their fathers for offering the best estates to their siblings and assuming responsibility for estates burdened with debt.[12] Writing to his nephew while in exile, Sergei Volkonskii remembered that "in our family financial affairs," he and his brother "never consulted with the laws." Their division of property was guided instead by "a true feeling of kinship."[13] Not all heirs were so accommodating, however. Disgruntled relations called on legal authorities to intervene if they believed they had received the least productive land or even the laziest serfs. Fekla Chirikova, incensed at the way her father's estate had been divided, submitted a petition to the Land College in 1741 in which she claimed that the official who carried out the division "chose the best houseserfs and peasants and plots of land, and made them over to [my] sister Avdotia Lukina, leaving the worst [serfs and] land to me and my sister Katerina Zhukova."[14]

For all their cognizance of the harmful effects of partible inheritance, individual nobles had few means at their disposal to prevent family holdings

10. RGADA, f. 615, op. 1, ed. khr. 11578, ll. 13–14.

11. Kochubei (1890), 211–12. See also Sergei Nikolaevich Glinka, *Zapiski* (St. Petersburg, 1895), 187, in which Glinka gave his inheritance to his sister, at his mother's request; Iu. N. Karpinskaia, "Iz semeinoi khroniki," *Istoricheskii vestnik* 70, no. 12 (1897): 854; M. V. Tolstoi, "Moi vospominaniia," *Russkii arkhiv*, kn. 1, no. 2 (1881): 253.

12. See, for example, N. N. Mordvinova, "Zapiski grafini N. N. Mordvinovoi," *Russkii arkhiv*, kn. 1, no. 1 (1883): 159.

13. RGIA, f. 914, op. 1, ed. khr. 38, l. 1 (1848).

14. RGADA, f. 1209, op. 83, ed. khr. 142, l. 1.

from disintegrating. Some exploited the flexibility of female inheritance to ensure that their sons would inherit sufficient land. As we have seen, many families elected to award their daughters dowries composed solely of cash and personal goods; others required dowry recipients to relinquish any further claim to the family estate. When his daughter Anna married in 1761, with a dowry of six thousand rubles "for the purchase of villages," Prince Semen Volkonskii stipulated that she enjoyed no further claim on his estate, nor the estates of her mother, brother, and unmarried sisters.[15] The evidence of wills confirms that some fathers awarded their daughters a bare minimum of wealth in chattel and cash. The father of Princess Dashkova, Roman Vorontsov, clearly favored his sons from his first marriage and bequeathed all of his acquired property to them. While Aleksander and Semen Vorontsov inherited thousands of serfs from their father, Vorontsov left instructions that his two younger daughters were to receive dowries of ten thousand rubles—a miserly portion of their father's wealth. Vorontsov was also less than generous with his second wife, leaving her in the care of his two elder sons and instructing them to provide her with an allowance of one thousand rubles a year.[16]

Vorontsov violated no laws when he chose to bestow the greater part of his fortune on his sons. Other parents resorted to more unscrupulous means of favoring one child over another. Recounting the history of her mother's family, N. Bashkirtseva recalled the machinations of her great-grandmother, who conspired with her sons to cheat her daughters out of their inheritance and thus prevent any portion of her husband's estate from passing out of his *rod*. Dividing the estate among her five sons could not be avoided, and in any case the land would remain in the possession of the clan; "to allot portions to daughters," however, "was a real loss for the family name."[17] Writing in the mid-nineteenth century, Elena Khvoshchinskaia described how her grandmother married off each of her six daughters but insisted that they and their families remain on the estate with her.[18] Elizaveta Vodovozova's mother rejected the laws of succession altogether when she partitioned the family fortune in 1861, declaring that "she knew better than all the laws in the world, what each of her children needed."[19] Her wisdom, in this case, prompted her to disinherit four children in favor of her eldest son. The decision to keep family assets intact was not always acrimonious, however, and some children readily made sacrifices to achieve this goal. Maria Nikoleva chronicled the efforts of her father to increase the produc-

15. RGIA, f. 914, op. 1, ed. khr. 122, l. 5.

16. RGADA, f. 1261 (Vorontsovy), op. 1, ed. khr. 8, ll. 1–3.

17. N. D. Bashkirtseva, "Iz Ukrainskoi stariny. Moia rodoslovnaia," *Russkii arkhiv* 1, no. 3 (1900): 331.

18. Khvoshchinskaia, *Vospominaniia* (1898), 3.

19. E. N. Vodovozova, *Na zare zhizni* (Moscow, 1987), 2: 125–26.

tivity of his land, and praised her siblings who prevented fragmentation of the estate by refusing to marry.[20]

Although legislators sometimes deplored the ruinous consequences of partible inheritance, they warned parents that favoritism could also dissipate the family fortune. Members of the 1767 Legislative Commission, in their discussion of parents' responsibilities, advised noble parents to provide for their children equally: "for inequality in maintenance first creates envy, and finally becomes discord, which in time leads to disastrous consequences for the family."[21] And indeed, inheritance disputes often culminated in financial ruin for everyone involved, including the victor in the dispute.

Gender and Testamentary Behavior

The tension inherent in partible inheritance provides the necessary backdrop for a discussion of testamentary behavior. Historians have often maintained that partible inheritance was instrumental in the decline of the Russian nobility.[22] A careful reading of wills, however, leaves no doubt that individual nobles strove to mitigate the effects of fragmenting their estates and that women played a vital role in this dimension of the family economy. Noblewomen of means used their assets to minimize the harm of partible inheritance, granting land to their daughters on the condition that the latter would claim no portion of their fathers' estate, or supplementing the meager inheritance of their sons. Moreover, nobles of both sexes named few beneficiaries in their testaments: when the moment came to divide their earthly goods, men and women defined "family" as narrowly as the law would permit. Even when they had acquired land and personal goods at their disposal, female and male testators adhered with little variation to the rules of intestate succession, ruthlessly excluding other potential legatees and warning their heirs not to violate their final wishes.

A comparative perspective reveals that the behavior of Russian noblewomen, when disposing of their earthly goods, was unusual in a wider European context. An extensive literature concerning the testamentary behavior of women in early-modern France, England, and Italy and in the United States, has arrived at two unanimous conclusions: First, their authors argue that personalism and sentiment, rather than survival of the lineage, motivated women's bequests. Among patrician families in Renaissance Venice, for example, while the bequests of male testators were governed by "a commit-

20. M. C. Nikoleva, "Cherty starinnogo dvorianskogo byta. Vospominaniia," *Russkii arkhiv*, kn. 3, no. 9 (1893): 192.

21. RGADA, f. 342 (Novoulozhennye komissii), op. 1, ed. khr. 220, ch. II, l. 27.

22. For a strong statement of this view, see Pipes (1974), 177. See also Blum (1961), 376–77; Romanovich-Slavatinskii (1870), 166.

ment to the continuing interests of the patrilineage," the bequests of women were more often inspired by affection for kin, both natal and marital.[23] Female testators therefore bestowed property on a wider range of people and divided assets among their children in different ways than their husbands did.[24] Second, these scholars argue that women were more confident than men in the ability of other women to manage property. As a result, women were more inclined to make bequests to female relations and to appoint female kin as executors of their wills.[25] This divergence in the pattern of male and female bequests derived, in part, from discrepancies in the kinds of property the testators possessed. Women were far less likely to have real estate at their disposal; moreover, they enjoyed more flexibility than men in deciding who would inherit their assets, since their children had already been provided for from their father's estate. Without exception, however, these scholars interpret women's choice of heirs as one manifestation of a discrete female value system.[26] In the words of one author, "Women offered a subtle critique of the patriarchal assumptions of the period by giving more authority and power to their daughters than their husbands did."[27]

Any attempt to compare the behavior of Russian women with that of their European equivalents meets immediately with formidable obstacles. If English men and women of all social classes composed wills in considerable numbers, Russian nobles of both sexes were far less likely to draw up a testament before their death. Such reluctance to make provision for kin derived in part from the vagueness of statutory law on the subject of testamentary

23. Stanley Chojnacki, "Dowries and Kinsmen in Early Renaissance Venice," *Journal of Interdisciplinary History* 5, no. 4 (Spring 1975): 594–98. Martha Howell also argues that urban men in late medieval Douai gave property primarily to lineal relations of both sexes, whereas women bestowed gifts individually and to a wider circle of beneficiaries. See Howell, "Fixing Movables: Gifts by Testament in Late Medieval Douai," *Past & Present*, no. 150 (February 1996): 36–38.

24. Erickson (1993), 213; Barbara J. Harris, "Property, Power, and Personal Relations: Elite Mothers and Sons in Yorkist and Early Tudor England," *Signs* 15, no. 3 (1990): 631; Howell (1996), 3–45; Magdalena S. Sánchez, *The Empress, the Queen, and the Nun: Women and Power at the Court of Philip III of Spain* (Baltimore, 1998), 126–27. Susan Amussen observes that women in early-modern England were more likely than men to divide property equally among all their children; Suzanne Lebsock maintains that women in eighteenth- and nineteenth-century Virginia differed from men by discriminating among their offspring. See Amussen, *An Ordered Society: Gender and Class in Early Modern England* (Oxford, 1988), 91, and Lebsock (1984), 135–37.

25. Amussen (1988), 91–92; Erickson (1993), 215; Lebsock (1984), 135; Riemer (1985), 72–73; Carole Shammas, Marylynn Salmon, and Michel Dahlin, *Inheritance in America from Colonial Times to the Present* (New Brunswick, 1987), 44–46.

26. Lebsock (1984), 116, 135; Chojnacki (1975), 596–97. Elsewhere, Chojnacki argues that women in Renaissance Venice were "proponents" of a "more individualized approach to social relations," and that men gradually modified the character of their bequests under their wives' influence. See Chojnacki, "The Power of Love: Wives and Husbands in Late Medieval Venice," in *Women and Power in the Middle Ages*, ed. Mary Erler and Maryanne Kowaleski (Athens, 1988), 139.

27. Amussen (1988), 91–92.

power.[28] Restrictions on testamentary freedom also inhibited the writing of wills in Imperial Russia. Neither men nor women could bequeath patrimonial property to anyone but a lineal heir, and only in extreme circumstances could they disinherit their children. When composing their wills, nobles scrupulously distinguished patrimonial from acquired property and cited the clause in Catherine II's Charter to the Nobility that permitted them to devise the latter as they saw fit. The wills in my sample overwhelmingly concern the division of immovable property and rarely include an inventory of personal goods. These documents also yield little information about the size or value of the testator's estate. For all their shortcomings, however, the wills that survive illustrate how narrowly men and women defined kinship when they distributed their worldly goods and illuminate identical concerns in the testaments of both sexes.

A survey of 133 wills, recorded between 1703 and 1867, reveals that in the realm of testamentary behavior, Russian women had more in common with their male counterparts than with their European sisters.[29] Indeed, the tra-

---

28. See Nevolin (1851), 3: 304; Wagner (1994), 230–31.

29. The wills in this survey are drawn from the following sources: RGADA, f. 282, op. 1, ed. khr. 541, ll. 89–90 (1703); f. 1290, op. 1, ed. khr. 34 (1706); f. 282, op. 1, ed. khr. 543, ll. 49, 152–55, 158, 162–63, 165–67 (1714); f. 9, op. II, kn. 25, ed. khr. 152, l. 544 (1715); f. 615, op. 1, ed. khr. 1956, l. 20 (1717); RGIA, f. 1088, op. 1, ed. khr. 14 (1718); RGADA, f. 615, op. 1, ed. khr. 1958, ll. 8, 49–50, 63 (1719); f. 1280, op. 1, ed. khr. 98 (1719); RGIA, f. 1101, op. 1, ed. khr. 76 (1720); V. A. Borisov, ed., *Opisanie goroda Shui i ego okrestnostei, s prilozheniem starinnykh aktov.* (Moscow, 1851), 420–21 (1720); GIM, f. 60, op. 1, ed. khr. 81, l. 2 (1729); RGADA, f. 1290, op. 1, ed. khr. 37 (1725); RGIA, f. 1101, op. 1, ed. khr. 90, ll. 8–9 (1730); RGADA, f. 1290, op. 1, ed. khr. 39 (1735); f. 1290, op. 1, ed. khr. 40 (1736); f. 282, op. 1, ed. khr. 558, ll. 114–15 (1740); f. 1209, op. 80, ed. khr. 65 (1741); RGIA, f. 1086, op. 1, ed. khr. 1114 (1744); GIM, f. 60, op. 1, ed. khr. 81, l. 6 (1745); RGIA, f. 1086, op. 1, ed. khr. 1115 (1746); RGADA, f. 22, op. 1, ed. khr. 118, ll. 14–16 (1747); f. 1263, op. 1, ed. khr. 8393 (1751); f. 1287, op. 1, ed. khr. 4707 (1753); f. 615, op. 1, ed. khr. 11418, ll. 12–13, 25–27 (1753); f. 615, op. 1, ed. khr. 4220, ll. 109–10 (1753); f. 615, op. 1, ed. khr. 2004, ll. 102–3 (1755); f. 1263, op. 1, ed. khr. 8398 (1756); f. 1209, op. 80, ed. khr. 280 (1763); Shchukin, *Sbornik starinnykh bumag* 2 (1897), 2: 205–6 (1763); RGADA, f. 1263, op. 1, ed. khr. 277 and 300 (1766); f. 1261, op. 1, ed. khr. 8 (1767); f. 615, op. 1, ed. khr. 2042, ll. 21–22, 99–100 (1775); f. 1263, op. 1, ed. khr. 8056 (1775); f. 282, op. 1, ed. khr. 1298, ll. 1–2, 4–8, 12–24, 27–46 (1776); f. 282, op. 1, ed. khr. 1299, ll. 1–4, 6–7, 9–16 (1777); f. 1272, op. 1, ed. khr. 99 (1779); f. 1270, op. 1, ed. khr. 259 (1781); f. 1290, op. 1, ed. khr. 46 (1781); f. 1263, op. 1, ed. khr. 360 (1784); f. 1288, op. 1, ed. khr. 454 (1784); RGIA, f. 942, op. 1, ed. khr. 591, ll. 1–4 (1785); RGADA, f. 1263, op. 1, ed. khr. 7503 (1786); f. 1274, op. 1, ed. khr. 7 (1786); TsGIAM, f. 1871, op. 1, ed. khr. 38 (1786); RGADA, f. 1263, op. 1, ed. khr. 6417 (1789); RGIA, f. 1101, op. 1, ed. khr. 176 (1790); RGADA, f. 1263, op. 3, ed. khr. 126, ll. 7–12 (1796); *PSZ*, 33: 26.432 (1816) (1796); RGIA, f. 1088, op. 1, ed. khr. 714 (1798); GATO, f. 81, op. 3, ed. khr. 1059, l. 4 (1799); RGIA, f. 1346, op. 43, ch. 1, ed. khr. 222 (1799); GIM, f. 60, op. 1, ed. khr. 81, l. 10 (late eighteenth century); RGADA, f. 1258, op. 1, ed. khr. 48 (late eighteenth century); RGIA, f. 1346, op. 43, ch. 1, ed. khr. 295, l. 5 (1801); f. 1088, op. 3, ed. khr. 54, ll. 30–61 (1804); f. 1101, op. 1, ed. khr. 252 (1805); GA Tverskoi oblasti, f. 668, op. 1, ed. khr. 6445, ll. 24–26 (1807); f. 668, op. 1, ed. khr. 6447, ll. 18–19 (1808); RGADA, f. 1274, op. 1, ed. khr. 1123 (1808); RGIA, f. 1101, op. 1, ed. khr. 272 (1809); f. 1048, op. 1, ed. khr. 37 (1812); *PSZ*, 34: 26.678 (05.02.1817); RGADA, f. 1278, op. 1, ed. khr. 266, ll. 14–15 (1820); RGIA, f. 1346, op. 43, ch. 1, ed. khr. 623, ll. 31–32 (1824); f. 942, op. 1, ed. khr. 596 (1826); f. 914, op. 1, ed. khr. 96, ll. 2–6 (1827); f. 1048, op. 1,

dition of partible inheritance profoundly shaped the material preoccupations of both sexes, with the result that gender differences were muted in
this dimension of property relations. Some discrepancies emerge in the testaments: women named daughters more frequently as beneficiaries to
landed property in their wills, and men took greater care to make provision
for their spouses. The overall pattern, however, demonstrates that testators
of both sexes named few beneficiaries to their estates; bequeathed all of their
real property to children, or lacking children, to two or three members of
their natal families; and evinced less concern with the sex of their beneficiaries than with their degree of kinship.

Defining the Family

The most striking feature of noble testaments, both female and male, is the
narrow range of legatees they name. Far from indulging in multiple bequests
as they approached the hour of their death, noble women and men were
anxious to limit their beneficiaries. In this survey, the average number of
beneficiaries to real property in the testaments of women with children was
1.9 (64/33); the average among men was 2.9 (94/32).[30] If men named more
legatees to their estates, however, they also reported a larger number of surviving children; thus, women mentioned an average of 2.5 (87/35) children
in their wills and male testators, an average of 3.5 (111/32) children.[31] When
testators bestowed personal effects, however, they acted with fewer constraints: among the small sample of female testators who made bequests of
personal property alone to individuals, the average number of legatees was
2.9 (29/10); among men, this number reached 4.4 (61/14).[32]

ed. khr. 40 (1830); RGADA, f. 1261, op. 1, ed. khr. 55 (1831); f. 1270, op. 1, ed. khr. 2384 (1831);
RGIA, f. 942, op. 1, ed. khr. 453, ll. 11–19 (1831); f. 1021, op. 1, ed. khr. 13 (1836); RGADA, f.
1274, op. 1, ed. khr. 3241 (1841); RGIA, f. 942, op. 1, ed. khr. 47 (1841); RGADA, f. 1287, op. 1,
ed. khr. 5754 (1844); RGIA, f. 1092, op. 1, ed. khr. 373 (1848); f. 1021, op. 1, ed. khr. 40 (1851);
RGADA, f. 1274, op. 1, ed. khr. 1417 (1852); f. 1274, op. 1, ed. khr. 1418 (1854); RGIA, f. 942,
op. 1, ed. khr. 51, ll. 2–8 (1857); f. 971, op. 1, ed. khr. 162 (1850s); GA Tverskoi oblasti, f. 668,
op. 1, ed. khr. 6279, ll. 3–6 (1860); GIM, f. 60, op. 1, ed. khr. 876, l. 3 (1860); RGIA, f. 942, op.
1, ed. khr. 46, ll. 8–15 (1862); f. 1086, op. 1, ed. khr. 943 (1862); RGADA, f. 1274, op. 1, ed. khr.
1316 (1867); RGIA, f. 1088, op. 1, ed. khr. 879 (nineteenth century); RGADA, f. 1261, op. 1, ed.
khr. 56 (nineteenth century); f. 1274, op. 1, ed. khr. 1150 (nineteenth century); f. 1278, op. 2,
ed. khr. 267 (nineteenth century).

30. The numbers refer to the total number of legatees named in female and male testaments,
divided by the total number of testators.

31. The small number of children that testators name in their wills contradicts evidence from
memoirs, which often describe very large families. No demographic work exists, however, on
female fertility or on infant mortality in Russian noble families.

32. These figures concern bequests of personal property alone—hence, the sample is smaller
than that of testators who bequeathed real estate. Furthermore, the average number of legatees to personal property does not include serfs; inventories of annuities and gifts to house serfs
could comprise dozens of pages in the wills of wealthy nobles.

Such figures speak volumes about the dilemma that noble parents confronted as they divided their assets. The discrepancy between the number of surviving children mentioned in wills and the number of legatees points to a consistent strategy of bequests among noble testators. Clearly, testators of both sexes were compelled to exclude one or more of their children from inheriting their real assets, with the goal of avoiding extreme fragmentation of their property. Contemporaries, both Russian and foreign, often remarked on the absurdity of Russian inheritance practice, which led to single villages being shared by several owners. The nobles in this sample not only were aware of the perils of partible inheritance but also took steps to avoid extreme fragmentation of their holdings. Moreover, these figures suggest that spouses cooperated in their bequests; thus, parents of both sexes were free to exclude children from their inheritance, secure in the knowledge that they would be provided for by the other.

Testators cited a variety of reasons for excluding children from their wills. On occasion, selective behavior derived from long-standing grievances. Maria Bludova bequeathed her possessions in 1776 to her younger daughters and denied any part of her estate to her son, with whom she was engaged in legal dispute.[33] The widow Alfereeva chose to reward one son for good behavior while disinheriting his brothers for disobedience; similarly, Lieutenant Colonel Talerov excluded one of his daughters from his estate in retaliation for her abuse.[34] Russian inheritance law allowed wills to be used as a means to punish neglect or extravagance, and some nobles composed their testaments with retribution as their primary goal.

Overwhelmingly, however, survival of the estate prompted the exclusion of heirs from the assets of one parent. The testaments of noble men and women bring to life the efforts families made to prevent the dissipation of patrimonial wealth, and draw attention to the role of women's property in equalizing their children's allotments. In a typical example, Princess Anna Iusupova followed her husband's instructions when she divided his villages and other goods between their two sons in 1735. She went on to declare that neither she nor their sister would claim their statutory share from the estate; in place of the latter's entitlement, Iusupova bequeathed all of her own villages to her daughter. The daughter also received a substantial dowry in movable property from her father's assets.[35]

Iusupova and her husband were far from atypical in applying the law of partible inheritance to all the property they held between them. Testators such as Iusupova carefully distinguished in their wills between their own fortunes and those of their husbands'; at the same time, they tacitly acknowl-

33. RGADA, f. 282, op. 1, ed. khr. 1298, ll. 15–16.
34. RGADA, f. 282, op. 1, ed. khr. 1298, ll. 12–14, 27–28.
35. RGADA, f. 1290 (Iusupovy), op. 1, ed. khr. 39 (1735).

edged that the interests of their children were better served by passing on consolidated holdings. In 1784 Count Kiril Razumovskii was able to divide his estate among his six sons and to settle a village from his holdings on only one of his daughters, since each of her three sisters would receive two thousand serfs from their mother's estate.[36] Another will, composed jointly by a husband and wife with nine children, demonstrates how men and women worked together to mitigate the worst effects of partible inheritance. In this document, registered in 1776, both parents specified that each child was to receive land "in one place," rather than a portion of each village. Daria Tolstaia added to her husband's bequests to two older sons and granted one of her villages to their youngest son. Tolstaia and her husband, State Counsellor Vasilii Tolstoi, assigned land and serfs to one unmarried daughter while bestowing only movable property on her sisters. By way of compensation, however, both parents stipulated that none of their daughters were responsible for any debts they might leave, and Daria also promised them an estate she would eventually inherit from an aunt.[37]

Among testators with children, members of the nuclear family enjoyed exclusive title to the goods of the deceased. In this sample, 93 percent of noblewomen bequeathed immovable property to their marital families; 96 percent of male testators did the same (Table 5.1). Testators of both sexes who passed over their children conveyed assets instead to their grandchildren. Count Vladimir Orlov divided his acquired estate among six granddaughters, giving villages and one hundred thousand rubles to each. The widow of Sergeant Poznitsyn chose to bequeath her far more modest holdings to her two grandsons, asking her son to be content with only her movable property.[38] After providing for lineal descendants, male testators had nothing to spare for in-laws or friends. A few women deviated from the male norm in this respect: Countess Praskovia Musina-Pushkina displayed rare generosity to her young ward, Praskovia Baranova, when she bequeathed her two hundred serfs from her immense acquired estate, as well as ten thousand rubles.[39] The widow Bulgakova bequeathed her maintenance portion jointly to her daughter and son-in-law in 1720. In 1830 Sofia Stroganova assigned a house in St. Petersburg to her son-in-law.[40] Such gifts, however, were unique. Far from expressing a critique of patriarchy when they distributed immovable property, noblewomen duplicated the testamentary preferences of men and demonstrated the same unambiguous concern with minimizing the fragmentation of estates.

36. RGADA, f. 1263 (Golitsyny), op. 1, ed. khr. 360, l. 2.
37. RGADA, f. 282, op. 1, ed. khr. 1298, ll. 30–34.
38. RGADA, f. 1274, op. 1, ed. khr. 1123 (1808); RGADA, f. 282, op. 1, ed. khr. 1298, ll. 45–46 (1776).
39. RGIA, f. 942 (Zubovy), op. 1, ed. khr. 596 (1826).
40. RGIA, f. 1048 (Saltykovy), op. 1, ed. khr. 40; Borisov (1851), 420–21.

TABLE 5.1 Beneficiaries of Testators with Children*

Types of Beneficiaries	Beneficiaries of Female Testators with Children				Beneficiaries of Male Testators with Children			
	Immovable Property		Personal Property		Immovable Property		Personal Property	
Gender categories								
Total beneficiaries	100	(45)	100	(18)	100	(51)	100	(31)
Male beneficiaries	47	(21)	39	(7)	47	(24)	32	(10)
Female beneficiaries	53	(24)	61	(11)	53	(27)	68	(21)
Marital family categories								
Marital family total	93	(42)	67	(12)	96	(49)	58	(18)
Son	33	(15)	5.5	(1)	45	(23)	6.5	(2)
Daughter	49	(22)	28	(5)	31	(16)	23	(7)
Spouse	2	(1)	5.5	(1)	16	(8)	19	(6)
Grandson	7	(3)	11	(2)	0	(0)	6.5	(2)
Granddaughter	2	(1)	17	(3)	4	(2)	3	(1)
Natal family categories								
Natal family total	0	(0)	27.5	(5)	4	(2)	23	(7)
Brother	0	(0)	0	(0)	0	(0)	3	(1)
Sister	0	(0)	0	(0)	0	(0)	3	(1)
Nephew	0	(0)	5.5	(1)	2	(1)	6.5	(2)
Niece	0	(0)	11	(2)	0	(0)	0	(0)
Other, male	0	(0)	5.5	(1)	0	(0)	3	(1)
Other, female	0	(0)	5.5	(1)	2	(1)	6.5	(2)
In-law categories								
In-law total	4	(2)	5.5	(1)	0	(0)	3	(1)
Male in-laws	4	(2)	5.5	(1)	0	(0)	0	(0)
Female in-laws	0	(0)	0	(0)	0	(0)	3	(1)
Nonkin categories								
Nonkin total	2	(1)	0	(0)	0	(0)	16	(5)
Male nonkin	0	(0)	0	(0)	0	(0)	6	(2)
Female nonkin	2	(1)	0	(0)	0	(0)	10	(3)

* Each value is the percentage of total beneficiaries for the category under consideration. The number of beneficiaries is in parentheses. This table does not include the total number of each type of beneficiary cited in the wills. It measures the distribution of bequests according to relationship. The number of beneficiaries in each column does not include bequests made by a single testator to more than one legatee with the same relationship to the testator. Thus, if testator A bequeathes property to five sons, the category "son" is counted only once.

Source: See footnote 29 in chapter 5 for a description of sources.

Both the rules of inheritance and familial obligation ensured that parents would bequeath land and serfs overwhelmingly to lineal heirs. When making cash bequests, however, or distributing personal goods, testators took greater liberties. By and large, the testaments of nobles of both sexes attended primarily to real estate, and legatees who inherited estates and houses also received their contents. On occasion, however, testators made bequests solely of movable goods, and here the differences between men and women become more apparent. Among female testators with children, marital kin accounted for 67 percent of beneficiaries[41] (see Table 5.1). Male testators, however, proved slightly less inclined to concentrate movable assets in the hands of their wives and children, and cited nonkin in as much as 16 percent of their wills. Legacies of personal property by testators with children, moreover, were composed overwhelmingly of cash. Wealthy proprietors, such as Count Nikolai Sheremetev, could well afford to remember a wide range of kin, as well as trusted servants, with bequests of thousands of rubles.[42] The wife of Assessor Chebyshev left five hundred rubles for the dowry of a kinswoman; her immovable estate was to be sold to pay off her astronomical debts, after which her husband and daughter would inherit anything that remained.[43] Conspicuously absent in these documents, however, are purely sentimental bequests. Prince Pavel Shcherbatov was unusual in specifying that the tutor of his children should inherit a gold watch, as well as two thousand rubles and an annual pension; Shcherbatov also bequeathed his library and prints to his son-in-law and divided his linen among his house serfs.[44]

Although sons were by far the greatest beneficiaries of patrimonial estates, female beneficiaries accounted for 53 percent of bequests of real estate by both men and women; regarding personal property, female legatees represented 68 percent of men's testaments and 61 percent of women's. Thus, such figures indicate that neither men nor women demonstrated a marked preference for same-sex legatees. The conduct of men and women diverged, however, in regard to the kind of property they were willing to bestow on daughters. More than half of the testators in this sample reported surviving children of only one sex. Eleven women mentioned surviving children of both sexes in their wills. Of these, 72 percent (9/11) bequeathed land and serfs to their daughters, whereas 18 percent (2/11) asked them to make due with movable goods. By contrast, 59 percent (10/17) of male testators with children of both sexes left land to their daughters, and 41 percent (7/17) left movable goods alone. Thus, women proved slightly more inclined than men to bequeath real estate to their daughters.

Sadly, noble testaments resist quantification of the generosity of parents toward their daughters. Noble testators rarely specified that bequests to their daughters were in excess of their statutory share—an omission well in keeping with their failure, particularly in the eighteenth century, to note the precise value of their estates. Yet anecdotal evidence suggests that many Russian nobles disregarded the rules of inheritance and bestowed portions

41. Howell observes that although women acted in Douai with considerable liberty when bestowing personal goods, their bequests of immovable property "followed all the conventions." Howell (1996), 38–39.

42. RGIA, f. 1088, op. 3, ed. khr. 54, ll. 33–48.

43. RGADA, f. 282, op. 1, ed. khr. 1299, ll. 6–7 (1777).

44. RGIA, f. 942, op. 1, ed. khr. 453, ll. 11–19.

on their daughters well above their legal entitlement. Natalia Grot referred twice in her memoir to her parents' generosity in bequeathing her not one-fourteenth, but a fifth, of their estates.[45] Delegates to the 1767 Legislative Commission from the Dmitrovskii district deplored the inequity of a law that compelled parents to bequeath almost all of their property to their sons, who might be undeserving, while leaving a miserly one-fourteenth to each daughter.[46] Arguing in favor of the equalization of women's inheritance rights in 1848, Count Bludov observed that parents routinely circumvented the rules of inheritance by selling land and granting the proceeds to their daughters.[47]

When they composed their wills, however, testators proved reluctant to reveal what percentage of their wealth ended up in their daughters' hands. The will of a Muscovite widow, Nadezhda Surovtsova, exemplifies this ambiguous style: Surovtsova bequeathed twenty-seven serfs from "our" estate in Pereslavl' district, as well as a house and its contents, to her son, while assigning her dowry estate of twenty-two serfs to her daughter.[48] Whether the latter represented a portion in excess of her daughter's legal entitlement cannot be determined. Count Nikita Panin was exceptional in citing the number of serfs that belonged to him in three provinces. Of 9,897 serfs, his three daughters received 2,861, divided so that each would receive an annual income of ten thousand rubles in quitrent. In other words, Panin bequeathed roughly 35 percent of his estate to each son and 10 percent to each daughter while also absolving his daughters of any responsibility for his debts.[49] The majority of testators, however, were more vague about the distribution of their wealth.

The survival of children was clearly instrumental in the desire of testators, both female and male, to eliminate superfluous claimants from their wills. If testators with children were cautious with their bequests, however, this pattern was more evident still among testators without children. Although they operated with fewer constraints, childless testators acted with similar reserve when they divided their fortunes. Childless testators of both sexes named 1.8 (44/25, 42/23) beneficiaries to their real estate; when bestowing personal property alone, women named an average of 3.2 (38/12) legatees, while men named 5.3 (37/7). Lacking lineal heirs, testators of both sexes

---

45. Natalia Grot, *Iz semeinoi khroniki. Vospominaniia dlia detei i vnukov*, 7th ed. (St. Petersburg, 1900), 32, 116–17. See also the dowry of Countess Varvara Petrovna Razumovskaia, neé Sheremeteva, in which her father states that her dowry in movable property, worth 141,020 rubles, was given to her in addition to her entitlement from his immovable estate. Vasil'chikov (1880), 2: 547.

46. *SIRIO* (1871), 8: 509.

47. Quoted in A. G. Goikhbarg, *Zakon o rasshirenii prav nasledovaniia po zakonu lits zhenskogo pola i prava zaveshchaniia rodovykh imenii* (St. Petersburg, 1912), 5–6.

48. RGADA, f. 282, op. 1, ed. khr. 1298, ll. 43–44.

49. RGADA, f. 1274 (Paniny-Bludovy), op. 1, ed. khr. 1150 (1814).

bequeathed immovable property to their spouses and natal families; the sole exceptions to this rule appear in regard to urban real estate. In 1798 Maria Sheremeteva left a house in Moscow to a female friend. Sheremeteva was careful to note that she had purchased the house in 1789 and that the Charter to the Nobility of 1785 gave her the right to bequeath this property to whomever she pleased.[50] Prince Dmitrii Golitsyn also bequeathed a house in Vienna to a female friend.[51]

In this sample noblewomen who made bequests of immovable assets displayed a marginal preference for male legatees (53 percent), whereas men selected more female beneficiaries (55 percent) (Table 5.2). Within the natal group, siblings and their children comprised the largest circle of beneficiaries among both sexes. Again, no clear gender bias emerges in this sample. Although women were more likely than men to name nieces as beneficiaries, men left real property more often to sisters. Moreover, men sometimes favored female siblings over brothers. Alesksei Perovskii left his entire estate to his sister, Countess Anna Tolstaia, and her son, while bequeathing nothing to his two brothers, whom he named as his executors. Perovskii's brother, Lev, also bequeathed more than fourteen thousand rubles to another sister, while leaving only furs and gold watches to his brothers.[52] Lieutenant Tolyzin demonstrated particular concern for the material welfare of his sisters when he petitioned the Senate for permission to divide his patrimonial estate of more than two thousand serfs equally between his brother and two sisters.[53]

The care with which childless testators selected their beneficiaries mirrors the pains their more prolific counterparts took to minimize estate fragmentation. In 1776, both Tatiana Saburova and Prince Ivan Bolkhovskii left all their villages, houses, and movable goods to a single nephew.[54] The widow Avdotia Domnina bequeathed all her earthly possessions to her sister in 1755.[55] Maria Kosheleva petitioned the empress in 1781 to exclude her brothers from her will and to leave her estate to her niece, the daughter of a deceased sister.[56] The testament of Praskovia Dashkova was unusual in its range of legatees: in 1747 she divided her villages between two brothers, left a house to her mother, and then cash and personal property to her siblings, aunt, nieces, nephews, and a number of house serfs.[57] With the goal of avoiding legal battles over their estates, testators sternly instructed other

---

50. RGIA, f. 1088, op. 1, ed. khr. 714.
51. RGIA, f. 1088, op. 1, ed. khr. 879 (early nineteenth century).
52. RGIA, f. 1021 (Perovskie), op. 1, ed. khr. 13 (1836); f. 1021, op. 1, ed. khr. 40 (1851).
53. RGIA, f. 1346, op. 43, ch. 1, ed. khr. 295 (1801). His request was granted.
54. RGADA, f. 282, op. 1, ed. khr. 1298, ll. 35, 43.
55. RGADA, f. 615, op. 1, ed. khr. 2004, ll. 102–3.
56. RGADA, f. 1270 (Musiny-Pushkiny), op. 1, ed. khr. 259.
57. RGADA, f. 22, op. 1, ed. khr. 118, ll. 14–16.

TABLE 5.2 Beneficiaries of Childless Testators*

Types of Beneficiaries	Beneficiaries of Childless Female Testators				Beneficiaries of Childless Male Testators			
	Immovable Property		Personal Property		Immovable Property		Personal Property	
Gender categories								
Total beneficiaries	100	(32)	100	(23)	100	(33)	100	(15)
Male beneficiaries	53	(17)	39	(9)	45	(15)	47	(7)
Female beneficiaries	47	(15)	61	(14)	55	(18)	53	(8)
Marital family categories								
Marital family total	16	(5)	4	(1)	30	(10)	7	(1)
Spouse	16	(5)	4	(1)	30	(10)	7	(1)
Natal family categories								
Natal family total	81	(26)	78	(18)	67	(22)	67	(10)
Brother	9	(3)	4	(1)	9	(3)	67	(10)
Sister	9	(3)	4	(1)	15	(5)	13	(2)
Nephew	22	(7)	13	(3)	24	(8)	13	(2)
Niece	22	(7)	22	(5)	6	(2)	7	(1)
Other, male	6	(2)	13	(3)	12	(4)	13	(2)
Other, female	13	(4)	22	(5)	0	(0)	13	(2)
In-law categories								
In-law total	0	(0)	0	(0)	0	(0)	0	(0)
Male in-laws	0	(0)	0	(0)	0	(0)	0	(0)
Female in-laws	0	(0)	0	(0)	0	(0)	0	(0)
Nonkin categories								
Nonkin total	3	(1)	17	(4)	3	(1)	26	(4)
Male nonkin	0	(0)	4	(1)	0	(0)	13	(2)
Female nonkin	3	(1)	13	(3)	3	(1)	13	(2)

* Each value is the percentage of total beneficiaries for the category under consideration. The number of beneficiaries is in parentheses. This table does not include the total number of each type of beneficiary cited in the wills. It measures the distribution of bequests according to relationship. The number of beneficiaries in each column does not include bequests made by a single testator to more than one legatee with the same relationship to the testator. Thus, if testator A bequeathes property to five sons, the category "son" is counted only once.

Source: See footnote 29 in chapter 5 for a description of sources.

potential heirs not to dispute the terms of their will. After naming a niece as the sole heir to her Tula estate, the widow Agrafiia Purgusova threatened her brothers and nephew with retribution in the next world if they acted against her wishes.[58]

Bequests to Spouses

From the beginning of the eighteenth century through the abolition of serfdom, noble testamentary behavior exhibited few variations. By the nine-

58. RGADA, f. 1209, op. 80, ed. khr. 280 (1763).

teenth century, however, the significance of marital ties found tangible expression in men and women's concern for the material well-being of their spouses. Among men with children, wives accounted for 16 percent of the beneficiaries to their husbands' immovable property while husbands represented only 2 percent of the beneficiaries in women's wills. Not surprisingly, this percentage was greater among childless testators. Spouses represented 16 percent of heirs to the real estate of childless women; among childless men, wives accounted for 30 percent their of beneficiaries. It would be rash, however, to conclude on this basis that Russian noblewomen were not fond of their mates: 80 percent of female testators with children in this sample had outlived their husbands. Childless female testators were less likely to be widows—53 percent of the sample—and therefore more likely to make provision for their husbands.

A remarkable number of petitions from nobles of both sexes to leave their spouse a life interest in their estates survive from the first half of the nineteenth century.[59] Many petitioners wrote that their requests derived from the affection they felt for their spouses. When General Major Zherebtsov registered his will in 1799, he explained that "out of love and friendship for my wife," he did not want her to suffer from the loss of income from his estate after his demise. He therefore requested that she administer his property until her own death, after which the estate would revert to his clan. Maria Zherebtsova composed a similar will, leaving her husband a life interest in her estate of two thousand serfs.[60] In 1860 Prince Semen Vorontsov expressed his desire to provide for his wife's future (*zhelaia obespechit' sud'bu suprugi moei*) by awarding her far more than her legal portion of his possessions.[61] Although a widow who accepted a life interest in her husband's property usually relinquished the right to claim her statutory portion of the estate, this did not always hold true: in 1852, Nicholas I granted the request of Privy Councilor Vasilii Sheremetev to leave his wife a life interest in his estate of 2,892 serfs, while permitting her to claim one-seventh of his holdings outright.[62]

Not surprisingly, the generosity of many testators to their spouses derived from the absence of lineal heirs, but this was by no means always true. Prince Pavel Shcherbatov bequeathed his entire patrimonial estate to his only daughter yet also gave two houses to his wife in addition to her statutory share.[63] Men with children also granted their wives a life interest in their

59. *PSZ*, 2nd ser., 21: 20.426 (13.09.1846); 24: 22.948 (21.01.1849); 24: 23.573 (14.10.1849); 25: 23.821 (13.01.1850); 25: 24.061 (07.04.1850); 25: 24.123 (28.04.1850); 25: 24.227 (09.06.1850); 25: 24.394 (11.08.1850); 25: 24.410 (18.08.1850). These petitions are not included in the survey of wills for this chapter. See also RGIA, f. 1086, op. 1, ed. khr. 943 (1862).

60. RGIA, f. 1346, op. 43, ch. 1, ed. khr. 222, ll. 1–2.

61. GIM, f. 60, op. 1, ed. khr. 876, l. 3.

62. RGIA, f. 1088, op. 1, ed. khr. 726.

63. RGIA, f. 942, op. 1, ed. khr. 453, l. 11 (1831).

property, perhaps with the goal of guaranteeing obedience on the part of the couple's sons and daughters. Senator Neliudov left his considerable fortune in his wife's control because he wished to "preserve the union between my wife and our children" after his own demise.[64] Other couples willed their acquired property to each other outright. Makar Mikhailov bequeathed his acquired estate and all his movable property to his wife in 1799, citing their childless state and their love for each other as the reason for his bequest.[65] General Lieutenant Repninskii entrusted his wife Elizaveta with his fortune in perpetuity, for her own maintenance and that of their three children.[66]

Lineage and Property

Whatever role extended relatives played in the lives of Russian noble women and men, they were unlikely to profit from the generosity of kin with immediate heirs. The limited circle of legatees in Russian testaments by no means implies, however, that loyalty to the *rod* was insignificant. David Sabean warns of the danger of assuming that "if kinship had any significance outside of the immediate family, then people would partition their estates according to some system of claim." He goes on to argue that "in any society, the rights and obligations are territorialized in such a way that kin have different purposes for each other, depending on a sort of schema. The rules of property devolution are quite different from the rules of marriage alliance, faction formation, or religious ritual."[67] It should come as no surprise that in light of the limited resources of much of the Russian nobility, the foremost concern of its members should be the financial welfare of their offspring.

The reluctance of testators to make multiple bequests, even of a sentimental nature, clearly demonstrates that although extended kin played a central role in the social and political lives of the Russian nobility, loyalty to the clan was not expressed in their material lives.[68] Memoirs and correspondence offer many examples of how Russian nobles, male and female, used their influence to help kinsmen find a post in government,[69] and while

64. *PSZ*, 34: 26.678 (15.02.1817).

65. GATO, f. 81, op. 3, ed. khr. 1059, l. 4; see also TsGIAM, f. 50, op. 14, ed. khr. 410, ll. 27–29, 52–53 (1834) and *Sanktpeterburgskie senatskie ob"iavleniia*, #8860 (16.03.1859).

66. RGIA, f. 1101, op. 1, ed. khr. 176 (1790).

67. David Warren Sabean, *Property, Production, and Family in Neckarhausen, 1700–1870* (Cambridge, 1990), 203.

68. These findings contradict Tovrov's assertion that "any definition of 'family' would be strengthened by a sharing of wealth," and that wealthy testators named a large number of beneficiaries. See Tovrov (1987), 90.

69. See, for example, a letter from Prince Alexander Golitsyn in 1786 to his sister-in-law, requesting her help in procuring a post for his nephew. RGADA, f. 1263, op. 1, ed. khr. 135, l. 5. Golitsyn also asked Daria Golitsyna to intervene in another family member's legal affairs. RGADA, f. 1263, op. 1, ed. khr. 135, l. 1.

social contacts were by no means limited to visits to and from kin, extended visits from relatives were a routine part of estate life. As one woman wrote of her childhood in the early nineteenth century, "At that time . . . kinship (*rodstvo*) was a sacred word. It often happened that the mother of a family would arrive from a distant province, with children and servants . . . and settle in our home for several months, in order to cure an ailing daughter or find a military post for a son."[70] Nobles of both sexes discharged their obligations to the extended family during their lifetime, however, and not in the posthumous fragmentation of their estates.

Although patrilineality dominated the transmission of wealth and family name, over time the concept of *rodstvo* among the Russian nobility came increasingly to embrace women, regardless of their marital status. Nobles who composed family memoirs devoted equal attention to the forbearers of both father and mother; they also kept genealogies that traced their predecessors through the maternal line.[71] Individual testators cited lineage ties when they bequeathed property to female heirs. In 1766, for example, Count Bestuzhev-Riumin stipulated that his estate should remain within his *rod*, but divided it between his married sister and her son rather than bequeath it to a male relation sharing the family name.[72]

Until the nineteenth century, however, the status of married women vis-à-vis the patrimonial estate was the subject of legal dispute. Late in the eighteenth century, Captain Bakhmetev composed a will in which he attempted to disinherit his brother's sons in favor of their married sister, Princess Golitsyna. The Senate permitted Bakhmetev to withhold his estate from his nephews, as retribution for their "debauched" lifestyle, but refused to allow Golitsyna to inherit Bakhmetev's patrimonial property, which the Senate placed under guardianship.[73] Aleksander Sheremetev also challenged the rules of inheritance when he disinherited his brothers and nephew in favor of his younger sister. The Senate eventually overturned Sheremetev's will, but only after the Moscow Civil Court had confirmed it, on the grounds that the 1714 edict allowed a childless man or woman to will immovable property to any member of his *rod*.[74] According to the interpretation of the latter, Sheremetev's sister was as much a member of the clan as her brothers were. In 1815, however, the Senate declared in no uncertain terms that married women should enjoy one of the key privileges of *rodstvo*: the right to redeem patrimonial property sold into another clan. In their discussion of the controversy that had arisen in local courts on this question, the senators argued

70. T. Tolychova, *Semeinyia zapiski* (Moscow, 1865), 44.
71. See, for example, the genealogy of Ekaterina Liubomirskaia through her mother's line: RGIA, f. 946, op. 1, ed. khr. 6.
72. RGADA, f. 1263, op. 1, ed. khr. 277.
73. *PSZ*, 24: 18.381 (1798).
74. *PSZ*, 31: 24.835 (1811).

that the status of married women vis-à-vis family property had been decided as early as 1770. The only difference between the sexes in regard to kinship, they maintained, was that in descendant lines of inheritance, brothers and their offspring displaced sisters.[75] In short, among the Russian nobility, both the nuclear family and the clan were conceived as dual-gendered.

Russian nobles of both sexes often referred to the claims of *rodstvo* when they made their bequests, and used their testaments overwhelmingly to fulfill lineage obligations. Yet the vagaries of statutory law, combined with the tradition of partible inheritance, left little scope for testators to act as stewards of their patrimony. As a result, few nobles imposed long-term conditions on their descendants. Count Nikolai Sheremetev was exceptional in forbidding his heirs to sell any part of his estate. He further stipulated that if his son and sole heir should die without issue, the estate should not pass to his sister or nephews, all of whom he accused of being spendthrift. Instead, Sheremetev named a male relation and one of his sons as the appropriate successors to his fortune.[76] Count Lev Perovskii attached a series of conditions to his cash bequests to kin, stipulating that their legacies must be placed in interest-generating accounts until they reached a certain age.[77] The overwhelming majority of testators, however, permitted their heirs to carry out further divisions of patrimonial property and imposed no conditions on the use of property by their descendants. Thus, Princess Aleksandra Volkonskaia declared in her will that her father's testament allowed her full license to divide the estate she inherited from him as she saw fit.[78] While nobles were conscious of their role as guardians of the patrimony, they could not use legal channels to prevent their descendants from dissipating the family estate.

Possession and Identity

Historians of women in the West have made much of the differences between male and female testaments, arguing that women were more likely to distribute their goods among a wide circle of beneficiaries, to reward friends and family for loyalty, and to ensure that their fortunes, however modest, would benefit other women. Among the Russian nobility, however, the differences between the sexes in regard to giving were less apparent. Working within the constraints of partible inheritance, noble testators in Russia sacrificed personalism in favor of pragmatism. Testators with children divided their real assets exclusively among children or lineal heirs; those

75. *PSZ*, 33: 25.833 (30.04.1815).
76. RGIA, f. 1088, op. 3, ed. khr. 54, l. 31 (1804).
77. RGIA, f. 1021, op. 1, ed. khr. 40, ll. 2–3 (1851).
78. RGIA, f. 914, op. 1, ed. khr. 96, l. 4 (1827).

without offspring contributed their fortunes to natal kin. Even personal property rarely made its way into the hands of nonkin.

The similarity between men's and women's wills was not limited to their efforts to divide their worldly goods among a small circle of beneficiaries. In the appointment of executors, the behavior of male and female testators fell into identical patterns. Of those women who named executors, 66 percent (23/35) chose men to oversee their last wishes, 23 percent (8/35) appointed women, and the remaining 11 percent (4/35) named executors of both sexes. Men also favored male executors in 64 percent (18/28) of their wills; women executors alone were named in 25 percent (7/28) of the total, with joint male and female executors comprising the remaining 11 percent (3/28). Both sexes evinced confidence in female administrative capabilities, naming female executors in more than one-fourth of the sample to oversee their burial, pay their debts, or make donations to monasteries in their name. Moreover, if we take into account the high percentage of widows who divvied up their husbands' fortunes according to the latter's instructions, it seems that men put no little trust in the ability of their wives to oversee their estates and to provide for the material needs of their children.

In one respect, however, the testaments of men and women parted company. The prominent role noblewomen played in founding religious communities, as well as their philanthropic activities, have been well demonstrated.[79] Women such as Nadezhda Fedorova, who donated forty thousand rubles to a convent in Tambov in 1798, were instrumental in the survival of religious institutions.[80] The testimony of wills confirms that noblewomen were more likely than their male counterparts to donate significant sums to charity. Women made explicit bequests to monasteries or individual serfs in 49 percent (37/75) of this sample; men, however, duplicated their behavior in 38 percent (22/58). Typically, although Prince Ivan Bolkhovskii wished donations to be made to churches after he died, he was content to leave the amount at the discretion of his nephew.[81] The widow of Second Lieutenant Bulanin left a meager estate of a few hundred rubles but donated her icons and ninety rubles to three churches and another one hundred rubles to her

---

79. Adele Lindenmeyr, "Public Life, Private Virtues: Women in Russian Charity, 1762–1914," *Signs* 18, no. 3 (Spring 1993): 567–68; Brenda Meehan, "Popular Piety, Local Initiative, and the Founding of Women's Religious Communities in Russia, 1764–1907," in *Seeking God: The Recovery of Religious Identity in Orthodox Russia, Ukraine, and Georgia*, ed. Stephen K. Batalden (DeKalb, 1993): 83–105; Brenda Mechan-Waters, "Metropolitan Filaret (Drozdov) and the Reform of Russian Women's Monastic Communties," *Russian Review* 50, no. 3 (July 1991): 310–323. On the philanthropic activities of merchant women, see G. N. Ul'ianova, *Blagotvoritel'nost' Moskovskikh predprinimatelei: 1860–1914 gg.* (Moscow, 1999), 271.

80. RGIA, f. 796, op. 79, ed. khr. 502, ll. 1–2 (1798). Letters from the mother superior of Uspenskii convent to Countess Varvara Alekseevna Sheremeteva reveal that the latter was an active patron of the convent. RGIA, f. 1088, op. 1, ed. khr. 37 (1767).

81. RGADA, f. 282, op. 1, ed. khr. 1298, l. 43.

priest, whom she appointed as executor of her will.[82] At another extreme, in 1841 Princess Anastasia Shcherbatova compiled an inventory of pensions and bequests to serfs and impoverished friends, amounting to almost six hundred thousand rubles.[83] Even in women's testaments, however, a lengthy inventory of such bequests was unusual. Most were content with allotting a modest sum for prayers for their soul or manumitting a small number of house serfs.

Gender differences in consumption and in testamentary behavior have become a prominent theme in studies of European and Anglo-American women. These differences point to a marked asymmetry in the relation of the sexes to property. Among the eighteenth-century English gentry, Amanda Vickery argues, "female consumption was repetitive and relatively mundane," whereas "male consumption was by contrast . . . expensive and dynastic."[84] In regard to testamentary behavior, several scholars have noted the care with which women labeled and distributed their personal property, bestowing items of clothing, household goods, and jewels to a wide circle of friends and relations. As Martha Howell observes, these documents express a distinctive quality of female gift-giving, which derived in part from women's diminishing access to immovable property in the early-modern era and from the absence, in practice, of separate accounts in marriage. Since women's claim to property was tenuous, they had all the more reason to "fix" their possessions by naming them as their own.[85]

In short, a consensus has emerged among historians that legal culture in the West produced a system of highly gendered property relations. By contrast, in Russia noblewomen's unusual status in the law of property failed to create similar patterns of gender dimorphism in men's and women's use of property. The realm of consumption remains uncharted territory. In the realm of testamentary behavior, however, the similarities between men and women are unmistakable. A common feature of Russian testaments, whether found in notarial records or in family papers, is their laconic nature. This is not to argue that Russian nobles disdained material goods: in dowry agreements, every icon, corset, and feather pillow was meticulously itemized. Unlike dowries, however, the wills of both men and women focused on the division of land and serfs and gave short shrift to personal property. Here

82. RGADA, f. 282, op. 1, ed. khr. 1298, ll. 28–30.
83. RGIA, f. 942, op. 1, ed. khr. 47.
84. Amanda Vickery, "Women and the World of Goods: A Lancashire Consumer and Her Possessions, 1751–81," in *Consumption and the World of Goods* ed. John Brewer and Roy Porter (London, 1993), 281.
85. Howell (1996), 26, 35. See also Gloria L. Main, "Widows in Rural Massachusetts on the Eve of the Revolution," in *Women in the Age of the American Revolution*, ed. Ronald Hoffmann and Peter J. Albert (Charlottesville, 1989), 88–89, and Davidoff and Hall (1987), 276, 511.

we find no loving description of household goods cherished and handed from mother to daughter.[86] Russian noblewomen, by and large, did not use their wills to give away linens or silver, although they took care to include such goods in their daughters' dowries, nor did they dwell at length on more valuable items. Indeed, it was men who composed wills that lingered on personal effects. As a token of his great affection for his daughter Antonia, Count Dmitrii Bludov bequeathed her his books, paintings, and manuscripts. Prince Ivan Shuvalov specified that his nephew was entitled to any part of his collection of paintings and books that Shuvalov's sister did not claim.[87] On the occasions when female testators wrote in detail of movable goods in their wills, they allocated particular icons or mentioned jewels, rather than furniture, clothing, or books. Even jewels, more often than not, were bequeathed in a summary fashion, rather than carefully itemized. Uliana Putiatina compiled a detailed inventory of the serfs, villages, and fields she left to her nephew and his sons in 1744; as for her personal goods, she was content to record that she bequeathed all her clothing and her pearls to her nephew's two daughters.[88] Only women without immovable estates, such as Fedosia Surmina in 1745, took the trouble to enumerate their household goods and distribute them among their heirs.[89]

One scholar has argued that women in eighteenth-century England used material goods "to create a world of meanings and ultimately to transmit [their] history."[90] The testaments of Russian women tell us little about the role material possessions played in expressing female identity. Instead, women's bequests underscore the extent to which the existence of a discrete female value system in Western Europe grew out of a legal regime that associated men with immovable property and women with personalty. Women of the Russian elite vied with their European counterparts as enthusiastic consumers. Their letters abound with references to clothing, and

86. On the centrality of movable goods in the inheritance of American women, see Laurel Thatcher Ulrich, "Hannah Barnard's Cupboard: Female Property and Identity in Eighteenth-Century New England," in *Through a Glass Darkly: Reflections on Personal Identity in Early America* ed. by Ronald Hoffman, Mechal Sobel, and Fredrika J. Teute (Chapel Hill, 1997): 238–73; on the contrast between men's and women's wills, see Main (1989), 88–89, and Davidoff and Hall (1987), 276, 511.

87. RGADA, f. 1274 (Paniny-Bludovy), op. 1, ed. khr. 1417 (1852); RGADA, f. 1263 (Golitsyny), op. 3, ed. khr. 126, ll. 7–12 (1796).

88. RGIA, f. 1086, op. 1, ed. khr. 1114.

89. Surmina was Princess Dashkova's maternal grandmother. GIM, f. 60, op. 1, ed. khr. 81, l. 6. See also the will of the widow Liapina, who left wooden dishes, a bed, and icons to her nephew and his children. RGADA, f. 282, op. 1, ed. khr. 1299, ll. 15–16 (1777).

90. Vickery (1993), 294.

many were in constant contact with their seamstresses in Paris or other suppliers of fashionable goods.[91] When contemplating posterity, however, Russian nobles of both sexes spared few thoughts for personal artifacts. Their final testaments were an expression of more vital, if conflicting, concerns: the financial well-being of children or close kin, both male and female, through minimizing fragmentation of the family fortune. Thus, the experience of Russian noblewomen confirms the central role of law and property in shaping gender identity. In Europe, sexual assymmetry in the law of property gave rise to a separate female culture. By contrast, although the lives of Russian noble men and women diverged significantly in many respects, in Russia female landownership created a unity of interests between men and women in the material realm.

91. For examples of such letters from noblewomen, see RGIA, f. 1092, op. 1, ed. khr. 140, l. 1 (1799); f. 1117, op. 1, ed. khr. 104, l. 12 (1766); f. 1117, op. 1, ed. khr. 261, ll. 19–24, 52, 59 (1769); P. I. Shchukin, *Shchukinskii sbornik* (Moscow, 1903), 2: 229 (1795).

CHAPTER SIX

The *Pomeshchitsa*, Absent and Present: Women and Estate Management

In his novel of generational conflict, *Fathers and Sons*, Ivan Turgenev touched fleetingly on the diametrically opposed roles available to female property owners in the mid-nineteenth century. Bazarov's mother, Arina Vlaseevna, is portrayed as "a genuine Russian gentlewoman of the olden times; she ought to have lived two centuries before, in the days of old Muscovy. She was very devout and emotional . . . she wrote one, or at the most two letters in a year, but knew what she was about in running the household, preserving and jam making, though she never touched a thing with her own hands." While she oversaw her household, Arina Vlaseevna gladly abdicated responsibility for her estate of twenty-two serfs to her husband, who owned nothing of his own: "She had given up the management of the property to Vassily Ivanovich—and now did not interfere in anything." Turgenev could not resist adding, "Such women are not common nowadays. God knows whether we ought to rejoice!" By contrast, the emancipated, but ridiculous, Avdotia Kukshina declares to Bazarov, "I really am a country lady. . . . I manage my property myself." Yet Turgenev by no means disparaged women's active control of their estates. The freethinking Kukshina is not the only woman we encounter who oversees her property: soon after meeting Anna Odintseva, Bazarov praises the latter for "capitally" managing her estate.[1]

From the mid-eighteenth century, noblewomen's economic standing rose dramatically in Russia. The buying and selling of estates was only one dimension of the control of property, however; after acquiring their holdings, women confronted the choice of managing their fortunes or leaving them

1. Ivan Turgenev, *Fathers and Sons*, 2d ed., ed. Ralph E. Matlaw (New York, 1989), 53, 69, 92, 97–98.

in the hands of male kin. To what extent were either of Turgenev's women "representative" of the *pomeshchitsa* in Imperial Russia? In light of prevailing gender arrangements in Western Europe, we might well assume that Russian women were expected to shun large-scale management and devote themselves to the domestic economy. Historians have argued that economic and political developments from the late eighteenth century undermined female participation in the family business in Europe and deprived women of their public role at court, compelling them to cultivate their identity as wives and mothers.[2] Although the "new domesticity" was primarily a middle-class phenomenon, the emphasis on motherhood as the vital center of female experience was adopted by the aristocracy as well[3] and marked a significant departure from expectations for noblewomen in previous centuries.

At least one historian has proposed that the close of the eighteenth century witnessed a parallel development in the emergence of a Russian form of the cult of domesticity and the exclusion of women from life at court.[4] Scholars have yet to explore in any depth, however, the impact of European gender conventions on traditional Russian notions of gender-appropriate behavior. In the following discussion I will argue that far from succumbing to the new domesticity, Russian noblewomen in the Imperial era ventured on frequent occasions into territory that European contemporaries deemed unsuitable for the female sex. West of the Elbe, the constraints of the law and the ideology of domesticity inhibited married women from making investment decisions, engaging in litigation, and supervising agricultural laborers. In Russia, the demands of domesticity were tempered by the exigencies of property ownership: if contemporaries did not explicitly designate estate management as a feminine occupation, they nonetheless applauded female landowners for overseeing the financial welfare of their dependents and criticized those who neglected their estates.

While historians in nineteenth-century Russia did not examine the experience of Russian women within the interpretive framework of public and private spheres, they offered their own version of the transformation of noblewomen's lives and responsibilities. In her survey of women in Russian history, Elena Shchepkina made a clear distinction between the role of noblewomen in estate management in the seventeenth and early eighteenth centuries and women's activities in the post-Petrine era. Shchepkina painted

2. Davidoff and Hall (1987). See also Joan B. Landes, *Women and the Public Sphere in the Age of the French Revolution* (Ithaca, 1988), and Bonnie G. Smith, *Ladies of the Leisure Class: The Bourgeoises of Northern France in the Nineteenth Century* (Princeton, 1981).

3. Margaret H. Darrow, "French Noblewomen and the New Domesticity, 1750–1850." *Feminist Studies* 5, no. 1 (Spring 1979): 41–65; Judith Schneid Lewis, *In the Family Way: Childbearing in the British Aristocracy, 1760–1860* (New Brunswick, 1986), 57–84.

4. Richard Wortman, "The Russian Empress as Mother," in *The Family in Imperial Russia* ed. David L. Ransel (Urbana, 1978), 60–74.

a vivid picture of the hardships suffered by petty servitors and their wives during colonization of the black-earth district in the Muscovite era. Men were absent for months or years at a time on military expeditions, and in their absence women supervised restless serfs and contended with the threat of Tatar raids. "Entire generations of *pomeshchitsy*, unheard and unnoticed, carried out an immense economic task," Shchepkina declared. These women, she contended, played a critical role in the settlement and cultivation of the black-earth region.[5]

The system of landholding in exchange for military service disappeared in the early eighteenth century, and noblemen drifted back to their estates. As their husbands assumed responsibility for estate management, Shchepkina argued, women were left with the tedious chores of supervising the household, preparing food and clothing, and overseeing the work of their houseserfs. In contrast to the freedom they had once enjoyed, women, especially in petty noble families, could now "display their . . . independence only in command over their serfs."[6] The making of jam was poor compensation for women who had once patrolled the steppes and safeguarded the family estate.

In the Russian version of the story, women's diminishing independence originates with new service patterns rather than changing economic relations; nonetheless, the outcome is the same: women lose control over their productive lives and express their frustration in petty domestic tyranny. Shchepkina's heart-felt account of noblewomen's dwindling participation in estate management has an authentic ring. The liberation of the nobility from compulsory state service in 1762 encouraged noblemen to settle in the provinces; many developed a lively interest in rational estate management and became active administrators of their property.[7] Once their menfolk were free to take charge, there was little reason for noblewomen to take part in estate production.

Two accounts written by foreign observers early in the nineteenth century effectively undermine Shchepkina's conviction that noblewomen were confined to a purely domestic role; moreover, they signal considerable divergence between Russian and Western views of female authority. During their five-year sojourn with Princess Dashkova, Catherine and Martha Wilmot commented repeatedly on the property rights of Russian women, as well as the interest of noblewomen in the affairs on their estates. "I was still more surprised when a Lady was ask'd for who had not yet return'd to Moscow

5. E. Shchepkina, *Iz istorii zhenskoi lichnosti v Rossii* (St. Petersburg, 1914), 62–71.

6. Ibid., 133.

7. On the impact of the Emancipation Manifesto on provincial life, see Leonard (1993), 65–71. I. V. Faizova argues, on the basis of service records from the Heraldry Office, that the rate of retirement did not increase dramatically after 1762. See Faizova, *"Manifest o vol'nosti" i sluzhba dvorianstva v XVIII stoletii* (Moscow, 1999), 107–11.

and her husband replied that she was making some enquiries on her Estate in the Ukraine and that she had some idea of selling it. . . . ; so that when a party of Ladies talk together in a group one is sure of affairs, affairs, affairs being the subject," Catherine wrote to her family in Ireland.[8] On another occasion her sister Martha noted the abilities of an acquaintance who "understands *business* so as to carry on a Distillery of Whiskey for her Brother in Law from which flows all his wealth, and which by the way he spends with his family at Petersburg while she stays with her old Mother and oversees everything in the Country."[9]

In her journal, Martha returned again to this theme, observing that "one so often hears two Ladies perhaps young pretty foolish and coquettish talking to each other about the sale of Lands, purchase of *Souls* (slaves), . . . and then talking of Mme Such a one's affaires at the Senate being in good or bad train, of her oats, her wheat, her barley, etc. being sold to advantage this year."[10]

At the end of the eighteenth century, a French diplomat voiced similar astonishment, as well as distaste, at the conduct of Russian women. According to Charles Masson, during the reign of Catherine II "women had assumed a pre-eminence at Court, which they carried with them into society and into their own houses." Masson was still more appalled by the activities of noblewomen in the provinces. "In the countryside the masculinity of women is even more evident," he wrote. "Women find themselves in a situation, as widows or unmarried women, in which they must take on the management of their estates, whose inhabitants are their property. . . . They then engage in business by no means suitable to their sex."[11]

While acknowledging that noblewomen, on occasion, assumed the role of estate administrator, modern historians have taken their cue from Shchepkina. They maintain that on the estate, women cared for the household and garden while their husbands oversaw investments and large-scale management.[12] In contrast, I will argue that women's property ownership and patterns of landholding compelled women to engage in estate affairs long after their husbands were freed from compulsory service. To be sure,

8. Bradford (1935), 235.

9. Ibid., 268.

10. Ibid., 271–72.

11. [Charles Masson], *Mémoires secrets sur la Russie* (Amsterdam, 1800), 2: 104–8. For an analysis of the Wilmot sisters' and Masson's depiction of Russian women, see Judith Vowles, "Marriage à la Russe," in *Sexuality and the Body in Russian Culture*, ed. Jane T. Costlow, Stephanie Sandler, and Judith Vowles (Stanford, 1993), 53–72.

12. See Tovrov (1987), 118; Priscilla R. Roosevelt, *Life on the Russian Country Estate: A Social and Cultural History* (New Haven, 1995), 179. Mary Cavender argues that estate ownership and profit making were associated with men. See Cavender, "Nests of the Gentry: Family, Estate, and Local Loyalties in Provincial Tver', 1820–1869" (Ph.D. dissertation, University of Michigan, 1997), 132–33, 259–60.

the lengthy absence of noblemen on military service provided one opportunity for women to supervise the estate—an experience they shared with
European counterparts of an earlier era.[13] Yet Shchepkina did not consider
whether women's legal control of property might encourage them to oversee
their holdings, nor did she question whether noblemen freed from the
burden of state service used their freedom to return to the provinces. In
fact, the continued absence of men from their estates, the nature of landholding in Russia, and women's legal status as owners of property in their
own right all conspired to guarantee that noblewomen acted as administrators of their own or their family's estates. Far from treating large-scale management as an exclusively masculine occupation, many Russians in the era
of serfdom perceived supervision of estate business as a logical extension of
managing the household.

The Division of Labor on the Estate

Although gender segregation was a prominent feature of noble family life
in Imperial Russia, running the estate was a joint venture that demanded
the attention of both husband and wife. In many noble households, a traditional division of labor was undoubtedly the rule. Describing life on her
parents' estate, Maria Nikoleva recounted that her father "loved farming and
was a good practitioner of agronomy," while her mother occupied herself
with the "female half of running the household."[14] Yet the most striking
feature of nineteenth-century memoirs of estate life is that they describe
noblewomen making investment decisions and supervising large-scale
management as often as they portray women confined to tasks inside the
home. Necessity dictated that many Russian noblewomen, at some point in
their lives, had to concern themselves as much with the price of wheat and
boundary disputes as with the clothing and education of their children.

As in the case of Arina Vlaseevna, however, the typical noblewoman "never

---

13. A vast literature exists on European noblewomen's responsibilities in the household and
on the estate. Most of these works focus on widows. See, for example, Francis Harris, "Rich and
Poor Widows: Eighteenth-Century Women in the Althorp Papers," *British Library Occasional
Papers* 12 (1990): 124–28; Robert J. Kalas, "The Noble Widow's Place in the Patriarchal House-
hold: The Life and Career of Jeanne de Gontault," *Sixteenth-Century Journal* 24, no. 3 (1993):
519–39; Louise Mirrer, ed., *Upon My Husband's Death: Widows in the Literature and Histories of
Medieval Europe* (Ann Arbor, 1992); Linda Elizabeth Mitchell, "Widowhood in Medieval
England: Baronial Dowagers of the Thirteenth-Century Welsh Marshes" (Ph.D. dissertation,
Indiana University, 1991).

14. Nikoleva, no. 9 (1893), 115. For other examples of women involved exclusively in household management, see Anna Kozminichna Lelong, "Vospominaniia," *Russkii arkhiv* 2, no. 6
(1913): 779–80; E. M. Novoselova, "Vospominaniia 50-kh godov. Pamiati ottsa," *Russkaia starina*
148, no. 10 (1911): 102, 104.

touched a thing with her own hands." For all but the most impoverished noblewomen, household management meant overseeing the work of her domestic serfs rather than engaging in the work of the household itself. More than one nineteenth-century memoirist recalled that an efficient manager carried out the real work of the household. Nikoleva admitted that running the "female half" of the household meant in practice delegating most of the work to their energetic housekeeper, Fedora: "In her hands were the storerooms, provisions, and preparations for the house; everything depended on her," Nikoleva remembered. Despite all these responsibilities, Fedora also managed to raise Nikoleva and her sisters.[15] Another memoirist wrote that his mother took no interest in either household or estate management and that she entrusted her bailiff, gardener, and housekeeper with all her affairs.[16]

The lengthy absences of men from their estates left other women no choice but to take on the additional burden of supervising their husbands' holdings. Even after the abolition of compulsory lifelong service in 1762, noblemen continued to serve the state and were absent from their estates for months, if not years, at a time.[17] Frequent written exchanges between husband and wife attest to the vital role of noblewomen in maintaining the economic viability of the family.[18] These letters recount the hardships of military service; they also reveal that noblemen required income from their estates to supplement inadequate salaries, and looked to their wives for practical support.[19] In the late seventeenth century, the wife of Prince Khovanskii oversaw his affairs in Moscow and submitted frequent petitions concerning the terms of his military service.[20] Women also raised funds for their husbands when proceeds from the estate fell short. Thus, in 1717 Stefanida Khoneneva mortgaged her dowry, consisting of seven households of serfs and their land, for three hundred rubles. In the deed she declared that she was sending the money to her husband for the purchase of provisions and horses.[21]

The letters of Ekaterina Rumiansteva provide rare insight into the day-to-day activities of Russian noblewomen and the frustration many must have

15. Nikoleva, no. 9 (1893), 115–16.

16. N. V. Davydov, "Iz pomeshchich'ei zhizni 40–50 gg.," *Golos minuvshego*, no. 2 (February 1916): 196.

17. See footnote 7.

18. Marc Raeff acknowledges that "an energetic wife" might assume management of the estate in her husband's absence, but does not characterize this phenomenon as typical. See Raeff, *Origins of the Russian Intelligentsia* (New York, 1966), 90. More recently, Valerie Kivelson [(1996), 97–99] has drawn attention to women's role in fostering stable communities in the provinces.

19. See the letters of Prince Nikolai Osipovich Shcherbatov to his wife in 1757, describing the trials of military service and giving her instructions on the sale of land and other estate affairs. RGADA, f. 1395 (Iankovy), op. 1, ed. khr. 206, ll. 1–7.

20. *Starina i novizna* (Moscow, 1905), 10: 301–12.

21. RGADA, f. 615, op. 1, ed. khr. 1956, ll. 93–94.

experienced when burdened with sole responsibility for their family's affairs. During the reign of Catherine II, Count Rumianstev relied completely on his wife to stave off financial ruin during his lengthy military service. Perhaps Countess Rumiansteva was more dissatisfied than most—her love for her husband was not reciprocated and he refused to live with her for many years—but the problems she faced were not atypical. In letter after letter she reproached him for leaving her to cope on her own. "I swear that if you leave without making up your mind," she wrote regarding their future life together, "that I will gather all the documents and letters in the house, and hand them over to your family, because I no longer want . . . everything to be in my hands. You go about with your lover and amuse yourself, while I weep here . . . and go further into debt."[22] She responded to his demands for money by pointing out that she had nothing left to mortgage,[23] and warned that he would deprive her and their children of their last crust of bread if she sacrificed her only remaining village.[24] Her letters refer to the poor yield from their holdings and to attempts to increase their income by investing in cloth production. On several occasions she discussed a factory in one of their villages. "I do not despair of it making a profit in the future. . . . First, we need a [good] manager, and second, we need to build a separate factory, for which I have already ordered timber to be brought."[25] The expense of maintaining separate households and the difficulty of managing their estates without adequate help was another recurring theme. "Our household is a candle that burns at both ends—we live in two houses, there are endless expenses, and no one to watch over our expenditures."[26] In addition to the problem of paying their debts, Rumiansteva complained to her husband of conflicts with their serfs, who refused to accept orders he sent through her.[27] When Rumianstev wanted to allow one village of serfs to pay *obrok* rather than fulfill their labor obligations, his wife advised him against it. She argued that not only would it be difficult to collect payments, but also the village economy would be ruined and they would harvest even less grain.[28]

Many noblewomen, such as Rumiansteva, looked on property management as a hardship and were all too happy to pass the responsibility for collecting rent and making investment decisions to their male kin. Rather than dealing with greedy bailiffs and recalcitrant serfs on their own, estate owners of both sexes would grant another family member a power of attorney, or

22. *Pis'ma Grafini E. M. Rumianstevu k ee muzhu, fel'dmarshalu grafu P. A. Rumianstevu-Zadunaiskomu, 1762–1779* (St. Petersburg, 1888), 7.

23. Ibid., 11.

24. Ibid., 9.

25. Ibid., 83.

26. Ibid., 104.

27. Ibid., 107.

28. Ibid., 103.

doverennost', with the power to administer and even alienate their property. Married women often transferred control of their estates to their husbands, as did Princess Gargarina in 1819 when she inherited three thousand serfs from her father, Count Orlov.[29] Anna Lelong praised an aunt for placing her estate in the capable hands of Lelong's father.[30] It was not unusual, however, for women to discover that faith in their menfolk had been misplaced. After her husband left her to serve in the Crimean War, Princess Urusova became involved in the affairs of her estate for the first time and was horrified at the results of her husband's management.[31] In such cases a disillusioned wife could revoke the power of attorney she had granted her husband: after going through the proper legal channels, Fedos'ia Ogolevsteva placed an announcement in *Moskovskie vedomosti* in 1854 and declared that her husband could no longer contract business for her.[32] Although women enjoyed the legal right to resume control of their estates, men did not relinquish their power without a struggle. In *A Family Chronicle*, Sergei Aksakov recounted the story of his grandfather's cousin, a young woman who married foolishly and handed over her extensive holdings to her husband. While the latter "did wonders in the way of improving his wife's property," it soon transpired that he was a cruel master who abused her serfs and alienated the neighboring landowners. It was only with the help of her cousin that the young woman escaped her husband and resumed control of her estate.[33]

If some noblewomen waived the right to supervise their affairs, others took on administrative responsibilities. Aleksei Tomilov granted his wife a power of attorney over his estate when he went to war in 1812, with the right to sell any part of his holdings if she deemed it necessary.[34] Antonia Bludova entrusted her estates in Volynskii and Smolensk provinces to other women.[35] Moreover, even wives who gave their husbands a power of attorney by no means relinquished all responsibility and concern for their estates. Although Dmitrii Buturlin managed the extensive holdings of his wife, Elizaveta, the latter received elaborate reports from Mikhail Filepenko, their estate manager, once a week. Filepenko acquainted Buturlina with all the details of agricultural production on the estate and consulted with her about hiring a doctor who would tend to her serfs on a full-time basis.[36]

---

29. RGADA, f. 1262 (Gagariny), op. 1, ed. khr. 914, l. 1.
30. Lelong, no. 6 (1913), 779.
31. RGIA, f. 1330, op. 6, ed. khr. 1635, ll. 2–22.
32. *Pribavleniia k no. 9-mu Moskovskikh Vedomostei* (January 21, 1854), 63.
33. Aksakov (1982), 44–66.
34. RGIA, f. 1086, op. 1, ed. khr. 881.
35. RGADA, f. 1274, op. 1, ed. khr. 1432, ll. 1, 6 and ed. khr. 1436 (1872–76).
36. GNB, f. 116 (Buturliny), op. 1, ed. khr. 289, ll. 3–4, 17–20. Filepenko wrote regularly both to Elizaveta Mikhailovna (ed. khr. 288–293 {1850–55}) and to Dmitrii Petrovich (ed. khr. 271–286).

Among Anglo-American women, married women's legal incapacity as property owners, as well as their provisional tenure in many types of property, inhibited women from taking an active interest in the affairs of their estates. In England, "The characteristics of women's property reinforced their propensity to turn attention away from economic activity. A clergyman's widow living on the rent from an Essex farm, when pressed to make improvements in the buildings, replied that as she only had the benefit of the income during her lifetime, she should not be expected to bear the costs."[37] Gender conventions restricted women in the antebellum South to the management of affairs within the big house, and no southern lady would be seen supervising the work of slaves in the fields.[38] The wife of a plantation owner might look after the garden and the poultry yards, but in the words of one contemporary, "Ladies do not look after the farming interest of the country."[39]

By contrast, Russian women enjoyed full rights of ownership in their holdings, which encouraged them to take a lively interest in agricultural production on their estates. One noblewoman, A. Butkovskaia, described how, after her husband retired from military service, they decided to use her dowry to purchase an estate. "I dreamed with pleasure about the tasks of farming, which, by the way, was nothing like it is now," she wrote, explaining how Emancipation had forced the gentry to reorganize their estates. "At that time everything was based on the size of the work force, on expanding arable land, and the 'Economic Journal', of which I have kept forty volumes in my library to this day, was the code that guided landlords who wished to improve their estates. . . . I also subscribed to the 'Farming Gazette.'" Butkovskaia recounted how she arrived in her village in 1824 as a young proprietress, bursting with "various plans for building and agricultural improvements." Observing that there were far too few serfs to farm the land effectively, she purchased an entire village—thirty serfs—in Penza province and resettled them on her estate in Novgorod, near St. Petersburg. "Today this would seem barbaric," she confessed, "but at that time it never occurred to anyone to pity these people, forced to abandon their homeland and their cottages," uprooted from the rich soil of the black-earth region to eke out a scanty existence from the poor land in the north. Butkovskaia's interest in estate affairs was shared by other female proprietors she encountered. Her closest neighbor was an elderly woman who regaled Butkovskaia and her husband with stories of life in the time

---

37. Davidoff and Hall (1987), 277.

38. During the American Civil War, women took on the supervision of slaves with little enthusiasm. See Drew Gilpin Faust, *Mothers of Invention: Women of the Slaveholding South in the American Civil War* (New York, 1997), 53–79.

39. Elizabeth Fox-Genovese, *Within the Plantation Household: Black and White Women of the Old South* (Chapel Hill, 1988), 117.

of Catherine the Great and who taught them "all the wisdom of local agriculture."[40]

Whereas Butkovskaia's personal involvement in estate affairs derived in part from her modest means, concern for agricultural productivity extended as well to much wealthier *pomeshchitsy*. Princess Varvara Golitsyna abandoned her beloved estate in Saratov after she inherited an estate in Ukraine from her uncle, Prince Potemkin. Once the domain of Polish landowners, the estate had been let to various tenants and for years had generated very little income. Golitsyna believed her personal supervision was necessary if productivity on her new estate was to improve, and went to live there, forfeiting happiness for financial gain.[41]

Anecdotal evidence from memoirs, in and of itself, clearly does not prove that Russian noblewomen routinely assumed the role of estate administrator nor that they were actively encouraged to do so. The historian will search in vain for advice aimed at women on managing their estates—with the notable exception of the feminist Maria Vernadskaia, who wrote in one essay, "If a young woman can count on possessing land at some point, why should she not study basic agronomy?"[42] The testimony of contemporaries, however, reveals that the boundaries of permissible conduct for elite women were highly flexible in the realm of estate administration. Sofia Skalon spoke of household and estate management in one breath when she wrote of her mother's life at the end of the eighteenth century: "My mother . . . saw to our upbringing, and also managed the household, and later the entire village as well."[43] Anastasia Musina-Pushkina included estate management among the tasks she expected her daughter to assume after she married and

40. A. Ia. Butkovskaia, "Rasskazy babushki," *Istoricheskii vestnik* 18, no. 12 (1884): 618–21.

41. F. F. Vigel, *Zapiski* (Moscow, 1928), 76 [reprinted by Oriental Research Partners (Cambridge, 1974)].

42. Maria Nikolaevna Vernadskaia, *Sobranie sochinenii* (St. Petersburg, 1862), 121. In the forward to a publication for children, "The Young People's Friend," the author wrote that his journal would include essays on a variety of subjects, including the study of domestic and large-scale administration, "appropriate for both sexes" (. . . *domashnim i khozaiistvennym upravleniiam, obemu polu prilichnym*). See *Drug iunoshestva* (Moscow, 1807), xi. The author of several popular cookbooks and works on household management, Ekaterina Avdeeva also published a work on farming, *Rukovodstvo k ustroistvu ferm i vedeniiu na nikh khoziaistva* (St. Petersburg, 1863). Avdeeva touched briefly on the topic of land cultivation; the bulk of the work, however, consists of recipes and instructions on tending the garden and livestock. Alison Smith notes that by the mid-nineteenth century, journals such as the *Farming Gazette* (*Zemledel'cheskaia gazeta*) included articles on "women's work," which occasionally touched on agriculture. Yet she also observes that Avdeeva's least successful publications were her works on farming, which were poorly reviewed and never reissued—a suggestion that "readers were less likely to accept a woman's voice in agricultural matters than in the kitchen." See Smith, "Cabbage and Cuisine: Diet in Kostroma and Kazan Provinces before the Great Reforms" (Ph.D. dissertation, University of Chicago, 2000), 146–48.

43. S. V. Skalon, "Vospominaniia," *Istoricheskii vestnik* 44, no. 5 (May 1891): 345.

set up her new household. In her frequent letters, Musina-Pushkina reproached her daughter for failing to study French and for her indifference to estate affairs. Her letters express her conviction that the responsibilities of the *pomeshchitsa* were not limited to supervising her houseserfs. "My friend, between guests you should see to the housekeeping," she wrote in 1825. "Have you gone out to the fields, have you seen the crops?"[44] Musina-Pushkina's admonishments demonstrate that far from being an unwomanly occupation, large-scale management was a natural extension of the domestic economy.

To Russians of both sexes, noblewomen's activities as managers of property—which brought them into frequent contact with local and central authorities and with the legal process—in no way impinged on male prerogatives in the public sphere, specifically, the domain of state service. Antonia Bludova highlighted this distinction when she recalled that while her father was occupied with his post in government, he delegated full responsibility for estate affairs to her mother.[45] Thus, the authors of memoirs drew attention to the energy and business acumen of female proprietors yet never commented on their behavior as unusual or inappropriate for their sex. Writing early in the nineteenth century, the memoirist F. F. Vigel all but prescribed an active role for women in estate administration when he criticized Princess Gargarina: "Like all the nobility in our country, not only women, but also men, she did not think about her business affairs (*khoziaistvennye dela*), which were in a sorry state."[46] In a curious passage in her memoir, Elizaveta Vodovozova remembered her mother saying, "After our marriage, Nikolai Grigorievich assigned roles in the household to each of us: I was to look after the children, and supervise the housekeeping, the livestock, and the servants, and I was not to interfere in his management of the serfs and farming."[47] The revelation that Vodovozova's father believed it necessary to inform his young wife that she should confine her activities to the domestic economy is highly suggestive. A traditional division of labor may have been the rule on most estates, but it clearly was not a foregone conclusion.

44. Shchukin (1912), 10: 115.

45. Bludova, no. 7/8 (1872), 1218. Princess Dashkova also distinguished between public affairs—referring to matters of state—and her domestic life, which included detailed attention to affairs on her estate. See Dashkova (1995), 99.

46. Vigel (1974), 26. See also the short story, "Pomeshchitsa," in which a young widow inspires admiration among her neighbors for her competent estate management. Elizaveta Nikolaevna Akhmatova, "Pomeshchitsa," in *Sbornik literaturnykh statei, posviashchennykh russkimi pisateliami pamiati pokoinogo knigoprodavtsa-izdatelia Aleksandra Filipovicha Smirdina* (St. Petersburg, 1858), 3: 3–190.

47. Vodovozova (1987), 1: 61–62.

Marital Status and Estate Administration

The picture that emerges from memoir literature, published primarily after Emancipation, as well as archival records is of noblewomen actively engaged in managing the interests of their own estates or those of their husbands and children. For some women, widowhood marked the natural starting point of their responsibility for estate affairs. In many noble families, however, frequent separations led married women to take charge of the family holdings. Martha Wilmot remarked that Russian couples often lived apart, and told of an acquaintance who lived "separated from her Husband *in the Russian way*, that is keeping different establishments but on very good terms and writing Letters to each other by every post."[48] The pattern of noble landholding contributed further to the likelihood that women could not confine their tasks to the "female half" of the household. Each of these factors explains why so many memoirists depicted noblewomen moving with ease between domestic tasks and large-scale management, ruling over each part of their domain with a firm hand. "In the winter she would lie in bed and from her pillow she supervised her affairs," Anna Kern wrote of her formidable grandmother, "but in the summer she would oversee work in the fields."[49]

Unmarried women who had lost their parents could, in principle, live apart from their families. As early as 1714, Peter I decreed that when an unmarried girl reached her majority, she had the right to claim her portion of the family estate and to leave her brother's house, "in the presence of witnesses."[50] Noblewomen who used their legal prerogatives to set up house on their own, however, clearly acted in defiance of social convention. When Anna Orlova refused to leave her father's estate after his death, her uncle, Count Vladimir Orlov, warned that she ran a grave risk to her reputation by living alone, without a parent's supervision, until she chose to marry.[51] On the other hand, unmarried women who assumed responsibility for the family estate and cared for their orphaned siblings were the object of approbation.[52]

Not surprisingly, widowhood often compelled women to take their place as the head of the family and to assume responsibility for the family's financial

---

48. Bradford (1935), 286–87.

49. A. P. Kern, "Iz vospominanii o moem detstve," in *Vospominaniia, dnevniki, perepiska* (Moscow, 1974), 112.

50. *PSZ*, 5: 2.789 (23.03.1714). Unmarried daughters with living parents, however, were strictly subordinated to their authority. See William G. Wagner, "The Trojan Mare: Women's Rights and Civil Rights in Late Imperial Russia," in *Civil Rights in Imperial Russia* ed. Olga Crisp and Linda Edmondson (Oxford, 1989), 68.

51. Vladimir Orlov-Davydov, *Biograficheskii ocherk grafa Vladimira Grigor'evicha Orlova* (St. Petersburg, 1878), 2: 181–97.

52. A. Lachinova, "Neskol'ko slov o P. Letneve," in *Sobranie sochinenii P. Letneva* (Kiev, 1892), 1: ii–iv.

interests. Some women experienced widowhood as liberation from a strict or abusive husband, as well as an opportunity to distribute family assets as they saw fit. I. A. Raevskii's grandmother lived in fear of her husband, who frequently beat her. When he died, however, leaving a heavily mortgaged estate, she devoted herself to raising her small children and to putting her husband's affairs in order. Raevskii's grandfather had left some property, but the author stated that it was his grandmother's business sense and her "extreme caution" which provided the inheritance she bequeathed her children. "She bought inexpensive, but fertile, unsettled land, and settled it with serfs from her infertile land," Raevskii wrote, and added that she would sell timber from her unproductive estates. She lived modestly, spending the winter in Moscow and the summer on her estate, and as a result "acquired an enormous fortune in a very short time." Raevskii's grandmother later divided the property she had acquired among her four children, three sons and a daughter, distributing an equal portion of the estate to each child. It was said, Raevskii commented, that she favored her daughter above her three sons, and this may explain why the former received far more than her legal portion.[53]

Estate records also reveal the extent to which bereaved families depended on the energy and business sense of the *pomeshchitsa*. Late in the seventeenth century, the widow of Prince Vorotynskii labored to restore order to her husband's estate. After recovering her dowry and obtaining title to her maintenance portion in numerous villages, Princess Vorotynskaia bought parcels of land, exchanged property with other proprietors, and resettled serfs from one estate to another. Her death in 1692, observed one scholar, was a "catastrophe for her household."[54] Count Boris Sheremetev entrusted his enormous estate to the care of his wife, Anna, in a will composed before his death in 1718.[55] Since Sheremetev owned villages in provinces all over northern Russia, his widow kept up an unflagging correspondence with bailiffs. Her correspondence demonstrates her concern with preserving her children's inheritance as well as the intensive labor involved in supervising estates in several provinces. "One can only think that the talent for administration (*khoziaistvennaia zhilka*) so apparent in her eldest son was a characteristic inherited from Anna Petrovna," her daughter's biographer exclaimed.[56] He offered numerous examples of how Sheremeteva labored to clear the estate of debt and pointed out that until her death in 1728, bailiffs rarely left her service.[57]

53. I. A. Raevskii, "Iz vospominanii I. A. Raevskogo" *Istoricheskii vestnik* 101, no. 8 (1905): 391–92. See also Elizaveta Mengden, "Iz dnevnika vnuchki," *Russkaia starina* 153, no. 1 (1913): 126.

54. A. I. Zaozerskii, "Boiarskii dvor," *Russkii istoricheskii zhurnal* kn. 8 (1922): 106.

55. RGIA, f. 1088, op. 1, ed. khr. 14, l. 3.

56. *Skhimonakhinia Nektariia: Kniaginia Natalia Borisovna Dolgorukova, doch'fel'dmarshala Sheremeteva* (Moscow, 1909), 76.

57. Ibid., 77, 79–178.

The motif of family fortunes prospering under a widow's care runs through many nineteenth-century memoirs. When Arkadii Kochubei's father died, his mother "indefatigably looked after our estate. She improved every part of it and acquired still more land, erected new buildings and wine distilleries, . . . [she] saw to the upbringing of her daughter and took care of her elderly mother-in-law, who could not get along without her."[58] Sofia Meshcherskaia's grandmother helped her husband administer an estate of more than two thousand serfs in Tver' province, and after his death, she assumed his position as head of the family and estate manager.[59] Semenov-Tian-Shanskii lost his father in infancy but wrote at length of how his mother managed to pay off his father's debts and free their heavily mortgaged estate by selling wheat at a good profit. "In addition to superb administrative and management abilities, my mother possessed financial acumen as well . . . which my father did not have," he observed.[60]

Once they acquired power in the form of property, women proved as capable as men of behaving like tyrants and terrorizing their families with the threat of withholding their inheritance. Many writers had vivid recollections of their grandmothers' capricious behavior, regardless of whether they benefited or suffered from their whims. Anna Kern's grandmother, who jealously supervised her estate of four thousand serfs in Tver' province, no sooner granted Anna two villages for her dowry than she mortgaged them to provide enough money for the education of Kern's brothers and sisters.[61] In order to spite her son-in-law, the grandmother of M. Vatatsi persuaded her daughter to renounce her claim to her father's estate, and gave her one of her own smaller villages in its place.[62] Sofia Meshcherskaia's memories of her grandmother were happier: before her death the old woman made sure that each of her granddaughters would receive a dowry of five thousand rubles, which was well above what they could expect as a portion of their parents' estate.[63]

Although these memoirists portrayed their mothers and grandmothers as making the transition to widowhood with minimal difficulty, one woman remembered this change in her own life as a complicated one. "At first it was very difficult for me to force myself to take over the business of

58. Kochubei (1890), 136.

59. Sofia Vasil'evna Meshcherskaia, *Vospominaniia kniagini Sofii Vasil'evnoi Meshcherskoi* (Tver', 1902), 14.

60. P. P. Semenov-Tian-Shanskii, *Memuary P. P. Semenova-Tian-Shanskogo. Tom I. Detstvo i iunost' (1827–1855 gg.)*, 7th ed. (Petrograd, 1917), 88–9. See also A. E. Labzina, *Vospominaniia, 1763–1819* (St. Petersburg, 1914), 9 [Republished by Oriental Research Partners (Cambridge, 1974)]; E. Mengden (1913), 104; E. D. Subbotina, *Na revoliutsionnom puti* (Moscow, 1928), 8, 16–17.

61. Kern (1974), 113.

62. M. P. Vatatsi, "Byl' minuvshego," *Istoricheskii vestnik* 131, no. 3 (1913): 772.

63. Meshcherskaia (1902), 17.

managing our estates," Elizaveta Iankova admitted. "Concerning all important matters Dmitrii Aleksandrovich always consulted with me and we decided everything together, but I never became familiar with all the details of managing our estate."[64] And indeed, when Iankova purchased an estate of her own in 1799, she granted her husband full discretion to manage the property and to sell or mortgage any part of it as he saw fit.[65] Only after his death did she take responsibility for her own property, as well as his.

The experience of Ekaterina Alekseevna Musina-Pushkina suggests one model of how the transition to widowhood, with its attendant responsibilities, could take place, transforming a relatively idle life into an active one. In 1815 Aleksei Ivanovich Musin-Pushkin wrote to his wife, "I am not surprised that you are bored with nothing to do, while it is very pleasant and merry for me here since I am occupied with business from morning till night. I am only sad to be apart from you." Musin-Pushkin did not conceal the details of estate business from Ekaterina, nor did he spare her his concern about the poor yield from their villages. Still, he urged her not to worry about the state of their finances and assured her that he would cope with the problem of their expenses.[66] When Musin-Pushkin passed away in 1816, however, Ekaterina assumed the responsibilities that had been her husband's. Both of her sons entrusted their mother with the property they had inherited from their father, since they were obliged to leave Moscow during their military service.[67] An inventory of the income Vladimir Alekseevich received annually from his mother indicates that Ekaterina managed her sons' estates for at least five years.[68]

Documents demonstrate that Ekaterina Musina-Pushkina was an active administrator of her own and her family's estates for more than a decade; it is unlikely that she could have assumed such a complicated task without some experience of estate management during her husband's lifetime. Correspondence between Musina-Pushkina and her bailiff reveals the many dimensions of her work: she was concerned not only with collecting *obrok* payments on time but also with carrying out repairs on the estate, conducting land surveys, and marrying peasants when they came of age.[69] Ekaterina also corresponded with the wives of her bailiffs. In one letter, Elena Lenina reported to the countess that when she returned to her village, she "found [her] husband in good health," and informed her that "butter is plentiful," and that more breeding stock had been purchased. Desiring to be "useful

64. D. Blagovo, *Rasskazy babushki iz vospominanii piati pokolenii* (Leningrad, 1989), 200–1.
65. RGADA, f. 1395 (Iankovy), op. 1, ed. khr. 240, l. 1.
66. RGADA, f. 1270 (Musiny-Pushkiny), op. 1, ed. khr. 803, ll. 6–8, 18.
67. RGADA, f. 1270, op. 1, ed. khr. 942, l. 1 (1817); f. 1270, op. 1, ed. khr. 1072, l. 1 (1819).
68. RGADA, f. 1270, op. 1, ed. khr. 1323, ll. 1–2 (1817–22).
69. RGADA, f. 1270, op. 1, ed. khr. 1058, ll. 1–19 (1818); f. 1270, op. 1, ed. khr. 1510, ll. 1–15 (1824).

and helpful" to her husband, Lenina continued, upon her arrival she "immediately surveyed the livestock . . . and found everything in order."[70] Although Musina-Pushkina left an unusually rich record of her activities on the estate, her role was not exceptional: heirs of both sexes saw fit to leave their property in their mothers' hands while they were abroad or otherwise occupied, and sometimes resumed control only when the latter died or grew too frail to cope with the burden of estate administration.[71]

Widowhood provided the first opportunity for many women to display their business acumen. Other noblewomen not only assisted their husbands but also acted as estate managers in their place. Thus, marriage by no means prevented women from exercising their administrative talents. The most famous prototype of the *pomeshchitsa* in Russian literature, Saltykov-Shchedrin's Arina Golovlyova, "gave herself a free hand in running the huge Golovlyov estates,"[72] with no help whatsoever from her ineffectual spouse. Far from being a figment of the author's imagination, Golovlyova was based on Saltykov's mother, Olga Mikhailovna, who began to manage her husband's estate when she was nineteen. Thirty years later, on the eve of Emancipation, the Saltykov estates had expanded from 275 to almost 3,000 serfs—350 of whom were registered in the name of Saltykov's father and 2,527 in Olga Mikhailovna's name.[73]

The theme of the young bride who puts her husband's affairs in order and saves the family estate from ruin appeared in more than one family chronicle in the nineteenth century. A. Meshcherskii recounted how his grandfather's sister-in-law repurchased the estate his grandfather had mortgaged, after which the latter, having lost all faith in his own business abilities, handed over the estate to his wife and took no further part in its management.[74] Varin'ka Tolstaia persuaded her extravagant husband to leave St. Petersburg to live in his village, where she supervised his affairs and settled all of his debts.[75] In his memoir featuring several formidable women, F. Vigel spoke highly of Countess Branitskaia, who, having married a man twice her age, "saved him several times from ruin and . . . doubled his enormous fortune." Although renowned as a miser, Branitskaia hired a French chef to prepare fabulous meals that would distract her

70. RGADA, f. 1270, op. 1, ed. khr. 1876, ll. 1–4 (1827).

71. See, for example, GIM, f. 175 (Shatilovy), op. 1, ed. khr. 4, l. 16 (1851); RGADA, f. 1274 (Paniny-Bludovy), op. 1, ed. khr. 3240, ll. 1–2 (*Doverennost'* from Count A. N. Panin to his mother, 1841).

72. Saltykov-Shchedrin (1988), 21.

73. S. Makashin, *Saltykov-Shchedrin*, 2d ed. (Moscow, 1951), 1: 36–38.

74. A. V. Meshcherskii, "Iz moei stariny. Vospominaniia," *Russkii arkhiv* 2, no. 6 (1900): 262–63. An aunt of Meshcherskii's also took over her husband's estate when he fell into debt, and with the help of one bailiff, put his affairs in order and left each one of their sons an inheritance of no less than one million rubles. Ibid., no. 7 (1900): 381.

75. Tolstoi no. 3 (1881), 103.

husband, who otherwise might be tempted to interfere in their business affairs.[76]

Married women among the lesser nobility also took on the task of manager when their husbands displayed little talent or inclination for estate administration. Natalia Grot wrote that her mother was a much better manager than her father and helped him keep his affairs in order.[77] Another woman recalled that even after her mother remarried, she remained "constantly occupied with estate affairs."[78] The mother of Ekaterina Zhukovskaia continued to build up the family fortune after her husband lost interest in the estate. "She tirelessly saw to the sale of this estate, the purchase of another, the building of a house, and so on," Zhukovskaia wrote. Like many other women with her responsibilities, "she had no time to raise children."[79] Sergei Aksakov wrote of a neighboring proprietor, "Chichagov, [who,] like my mother, knew nothing and cared nothing about the management of a house and estate. All that he left to his wife and her mother."[80] Similarly, when Privy Councilor Zakhar found himself mired in debt, he chose his wife as guardian, entrusting her with responsibility to manage his estate, pay off his creditors, and provide for their young son.[81]

Even when they did not manage the family estate single-handedly, noblewomen were involved in their husbands' affairs as well as their own. Indeed, the fact that women did not lose their legal personalities when they married could work to their husbands' advantage, and allowed women to raise money for their spouses when they were absent, to sell or purchase property,[82] or to pursue property disputes. During her husband's illness, Princess Kherkheulidzeva continued his suit in the Senate to recover an estate he had mortgaged thirty years earlier.[83] Creditors were also aware that repayment

76. Vigel (1974), 52, 70.

77. Grot (1900), 18.

78. E. Ia. Polivanova, "Strumilovskaia kolobroda (Iz semeinoi khroniki)," *Istoricheskii vestnik* 112, no. 6 (1908): 850. See also Semenov-Tian-Shanskii (1917), 88, and E. Mengden (1913), 104. See also a detailed account of a *pomeshchitsa* in Tver' province, who administered the family estate (her dowry and inheritance) before and after her husband's death. V. V. Gur'ianova, "Tverskaia pomeshchitsa vtoroi poloviny XVIII veka Praskov'ia Il'inichna Manzei," in *Zhenshchiny v sotsial'noi istorii Rossii: Sbornik nauchnykh trudov* (Tver', 1997), 20–31. The poet G. R. Derzhavin delegated all responsibility for estate affairs to his capable second wife, Daria Alekseevna. I. P. Khrushchov, "Milena, vtoraia zhena Derzhavina," *Russkii vestnik* 283, kn. 2 (1903): 562–63, 572.

79. Ekaterina Zhukovskaia, *Zapiski* (Leningrad, 1930), 19. See also Bludova, no. 7/8 (1872), 1217.

80. Sergei Aksakov, *Years of Childhood*, trans. J. D. Duff (Oxford, 1983), 228.

81. *PSZ*, 2d ser., 41: 43.460 (05.07.1868).

82. For some examples of women transacting business for their husbands, see RGADA, f. 1270, op. 1, ed. khr. 416; f. 615, op. 1, ed. khr. 4190, ll. 119–20 (Kashin 1718); f. 1270, op. 1, ed. khr. 2045, l. 65 (Vladimir 1776); f. 282, op. 1, ed. khr. 394, ll. 227–31 (Moscow 1755); GAVO, f. 92, op. 5, ed. khr. 21, ll. 50–1 (Vladimir 1806).

83. RGIA, f. 1330, op. 3, ed. khr. 55 (1805).

might be forthcoming from a noblewoman of means when her husband failed to pay his debts. Anastasia Naryshkina received a letter in 1831 from a merchant's daughter when her husband failed to repay nine thousand rubles he had borrowed from the merchant's wife. Praskov'ia Volnenkova explained that Naryshkin's failure to settle his debt had left her mother bankrupt,[84] but it seems unlikely that Anastasia was able to satisfy her husband's creditors, in light of letters to her bailiff indicating that she too lived beyond her means. "I owe a great deal of money and everyone is demanding payment from me," she wrote to him in frustration.[85]

Financial as well as legal autonomy permitted Russian noblewomen to live separately from their husbands and to manage family holdings in different provinces. Princess Tatiana Vasilievna Iusupova despised her second husband, but she was deeply involved in the administration of his estates. Her letters to their estate manager indicate that she oversaw their villages in Romanovskii district, near her residence in St. Petersburg, and that peasants from this area would appeal to her in person. "Today a woman serf from my husband's estate in Pskov came to me and requested, because of her poor health, to be freed to go to the almshouse in Pskov; I, seeing her inability to work . . . and that she is without kin . . . ask that you inform the Prince of these circumstances and request her manumission," she wrote in 1817. On another occasion she asked the estate manager to find a place in one of their factories for one of the princess's women, who was skilled at dying yarn but "without occupation is forgetting her needlework." Iusupova also reported on the sale of various products from their estates—amounting to 2,001 rubles in June 1817—and on the collection of 7,000 rubles in *obrok*.[86] Clearly, marital discord did not prevent the prince from turning to his wife as well as his bailiffs for the smooth functioning of his vast domain. Iusupova's son from her first marriage also trusted his mother's abilities, leaving his estates in four provinces in her keeping while he was abroad.

The letters of the estate manager A. Kaznacheev to Anna Raevskaia between 1838 and 1855 confirm that married couples not only owned but sometimes managed their property independently of one another. Kaznacheev recounted in detail the progress of lawsuits concerning Raevskaia's estates and consulted with her about selling a house in Simferopol'. Significantly, in one communication he requested that Raevskaia pass on some news to her spouse, "since your husband does not read my letters."[87]

---

84. RGADA, f. 1272 (Naryshkiny), op. 2, ed. khr. 139, l. 38.

85. RGADA, f. 1272, op. 2, ed. khr. 139, l. 12.

86. RGADA, f. 1290 (Iusupovy), op. 3, ed. khr. 294, ll. 1–14. For a biographical sketch of Tatiana Iusupova (1769–1841), see *Znamenitye Rossiiane* (1996), 642–45.

87. *Shchukinskii sbornik* 5 (1906), 215–18, 224–40. The letters of the manager of a sugar refinery to Princess Maria Aleksandrovna Dolgorukaia also suggest that he communicated separately with the princess and her husband about estate affairs. RGIA, f. 931, op. 1, ed. khr. 52 and ed. khr. 141 (1859–60).

Apparently Raevskaia administered her own estates with minimal recourse to her husband—a practice that could not have been so unusual, given the propensity of noble couples to spend long periods of time in separation. Far from discouraging women from taking decisions and making business investments, circumstances compelled the *pomeshchitsa* to see to her own affairs.

Labor Management on the Estate

No matter how great their involvement in estate administration, estate owners of both sexes relied to a large extent on their bailiffs. This held true in particular for proprietors whose holdings were scattered in different provinces. In contrast to landholding patterns in Western Europe, in Russia the estates of the nobility were rarely contiguous and sometimes never visited by their proprietor. Wealthier nobles often spent most of the year in Moscow or St. Petersburg, or divided the year between the capital and one of their estates. Thus, much of what falls under the rubric of estate administration consisted not of the personal supervision of the proprietor, but of regular correspondence with various overseers and meetings with estate managers who would report from the estate.

The authors of memoirs rarely dwelled on the details of day-to-day estate management, but archival evidence helps complete the picture of landowners' concerns and the activities of their representatives. The sheer abundance of correspondence in estate records underscores the importance of regular exchanges between landlord and bailiff: no matter was too trivial for the attention of the effective proprietor. This held true for even the wealthiest estate owners. The instructions of tsaritsa Praskovia Fedorovna to her bailiffs in Kozlov volost' express typical concerns. In one letter written in 1717, the tsaritsa directs her bailiff to send a *starosta* and a clerk who had fallen into disfavor to her residence in St. Petersburg; in another communication she tells him to gather rent on the proceeds from a mill. Praskovia Fedorovna also intervened in land disputes. Her daughter, Praskovia Ioanovna, another significant landowner, demanded accounts from her bailiff of how much revenue was generated from the sale of grain on her estates, as well as a reckoning of how many eggs were collected and how many lambs, geese, and chickens had been produced. Peasants appealed directly to their *pomeshchitsa*, as in the case of several serfs who requested not to pay rent in 1738 because their homes had burned down.[88]

Monitoring the yield of their estates was only one of the tasks conscientious proprietors confronted. When filing suit against his sister, who claimed to have purchased a village from their mother before her death in 1812,

88. SPbFIRI, kol. 154, op. 1, ed. khr. 9, ll. 1–88.

Captain Kologrivov enumerated some of the duties estate ownership implied: "My mother managed the village of Ponikarpova, in which she spent much of her time, in her own right; in her name alone she paid the poll-tax, sent [serf] recruits to the army, collected labor dues from the peasants, and so forth; at her discretion (*po svoei vole*) she married peasant women and girls to serfs in her other villages."[89] As we will see, landowners of both sexes also devoted considerable energy to waging legal battles with neighbors and kin, particularly over the vexed question of estate boundaries. Prudent proprietors tried to avoid endless lawsuits by commissioning proper land surveys: early in the nineteenth century, Princess Repnina wrote to her mother and explained the necessity of commissioning a survey of the village they owned jointly as soon as possible. Repnina also suggested that it would be to their mutual benefit, and to the benefit of their peasants, if her mother would allow her to reorganize the administration of their estates and place the entire village under the supervision of one steward.[90]

The instructions and correspondence of noblewomen throughout the eighteenth and nineteenth centuries depict recurring problems and concerns, regardless of the size of the estate. The letters of *pomeshchitsy* frequently express impatience with their bailiffs' failure to carry out orders or with their habit of concealing the true state of affairs in their domain. "I am extremely surprised at your management, that you have written nothing about . . . why the rent has not been collected. I know that you have been drinking and that you have not been tending to affairs," Anna Sheremeteva sharply reprimanded one bailiff in 1719.[91] When Elizaveta Polianskaia wrote to the land office for her estates a century later, she echoed Sheremeteva's exasperation: "Having heard your complaints about the bailiff Agafon Danilov and discovering that he drinks, I find it fair that you fire him, and in his place I am sending you the peasant Vladimir, who is an honest and abstinent man."[92] One estate manager responded to the accusations of his proprietress with outrage: "Whether I have managed [your estate] badly or well, I have managed it as I was able, and as if it were my own property," A. Popov wrote in 1813, and in his own defense, he went on to cite the considerable revenue of the estate during the years he had been in charge.[93]

Above and beyond corresponding with their bailiffs, proprietors of both sexes drafted lengthy documents that explained how their representatives should manage affairs in their absence. Scholars have devoted detailed studies

89. RGIA, f. 1330, op. 4, ed. khr. 938, ll. 3–5.
90. RGIA, f. 1035 (Repniny), op. 1, ed. khr. 861, ll. 1–2.
91. RGADA, f. 1287 (Sheremetevy), op. 1, ed. khr. 4689, l. 5.
92. RGADA, f. 1276 (Polianskie), op. 1, ed. khr. 1212, l. 2.
93. RGADA, f. 1277 (Samariny), op. 1, ed. khr. 221, ll. 1–2.

to the instructions of eighteenth-century *pomeshchiki*.[94] The authors of these works do not note, however, that noblewomen issued similar directives to their stewards and were as concerned as their male counterparts with regulating estate affairs. These instructions also reveal that many *pomeshchitsy* were deeply concerned with day-to-day activities on their estates. In 1781 Natalia Mordvinova issued instructions to the steward of her estate in Belorus'. She gave him directions on every dimension of estate management, from when wheat should be sown and livestock purchased, to his responsibility for improving the condition of indigent peasants on the estate. Far from merely affixing her signature to the document, Mordvinova obviously composed the instruction herself: half of the document is written in her own hand.[95]

Sofia Vladimirevna Stroganova's interest in the welfare and productivity of her serfs extended to establishing a school on her estate, for which she issued a handbook to instruct them in "morals and agriculture."[96] Stroganova's school attracted the attention of Count Nikolai Semenovich Mordvinov, a prominent member of the Free Economic Society and the son of Natalia Mordvinova: he cited the school as an example to other proprietors and offered Stroganova financial help on behalf of the society.[97] Stroganova also expressed her concern with the organization of her villages in a treatise entitled "Instruction on village administration, established on the estates of Countess Stroganova, compiled by the proprietress herself in 1820 . . .". This instruction laid down rules for the topics to be discussed at meetings of the village commune and for how elections to the commune should be conducted. It also specified the responsibilities of the village elder, as well as his term of office.[98] Sofia Stroganova's labors to improve her holdings and the productivity of her serfs demonstrate that rational estate administration was not a purely male concern. She was, moreover, one of several women who joined the Free Economic Society after Count Mordvinov became president of the organization in 1823.[99]

Power and Property Ownership

As landowners and estate managers, noblewomen asserted their authority within their families, over their dependents, and beyond the boundaries of

94. See in particular V. A. Aleksandrov, *Sel'skaia obshchina v Rossii (XVII–nachalo XIX v.)* (Moscow, 1976); Michael Confino, *Domaines et seigneurs en Russie vers la fin du XVIII siècle* (Paris, 1963); Peter Kolchin, *Unfree Labor: American Slavery and Russian Serfdom* (Cambridge, 1987), 68–78.

95. RGIA, f. 994 (Mordvinovy), op. 1, ed. khr. 252, ll. 1–5.

96. RGADA, f. 1278, op. 1, ed. khr. 657.

97. *Arkhiv grafov Mordvinovykh*, ed. V. A. Bil'basov (St. Petersburg, 1903), 9: 433, 503, 507–8.

98. RGADA, f. 1278, op. 1, ed. khr. 660.

99. Mordvinova (1883), 180.

their estates in provincial society. The extent to which the estate was a social organism has been the subject of considerable debate. One scholar observed, "The estate was not just a producer of income, and perhaps not primarily that; it was a social organism as well, and its owner enjoyed the power, authority, and dignity of ruling over a small self-contained world."[100] Peter Kolchin argues, by contrast, that the extended absence of noble proprietors from their estates inhibited paternalistic concern among owners for their dependents, and precluded "the development of warm personal relations between master and serf."[101] In fact, habitual absenteeism was a luxury only the wealthiest nobles could afford. Most proprietors made the rounds of their estates on an annual basis, traveling vast distances to survey their holdings, while others spent at least part of the year in residence.[102] Whether absent or present, the *pomeshchitsa*'s responsibilities extended well beyond overseeing estate productivity to caring for the welfare of her numerous dependents.

Noble memoirs convey a vivid picture of the estate as a social organism while offering an idealized portrait of relations between female proprietors and their serfs. They also demonstrate that by focusing on the absentee proprietor, historians have barely begun to consider the role of the proprietor's wife, who was frequently in residence while her husband was away. Sofia Mengden wrote that her grandmother lived year-round on her estate in Kostroma province, where she supervised cloth production, treated her serfs when they were ill, and "looked after all their needs."[103] Semenov-Tian-Shanskii praised his mother's solicitude for her peasants during the famine of 1837 and reported that she made regular trips from their estate in Riazan to oversee production on a second estate in Tambov.[104] Ekaterina Khvostova remembered her mother's frequent excursions through their village, where she would talk with their peasants and bring them medicine, sugar, and tea.[105]

---

100. Augustine (1970), 408.

101. Kolchin (1987), 148–49. For a dissenting view, see Edgar Melton, "Enlightened Seigniorialism and Its Dilemmas in Serf Russia, 1750–1830," *Journal of Modern History* 62 (December 1990): 675–708.

102. Estimates on absenteeism vary: Carol Leonard [(1993), 68] argues that after 1762 over half of adult male nobles lived on their estates. An inventory compiled in 1817 for Ruzskii district listed ninety-two female proprietors, of whom one-third were in residence. See TsGIAM, f. 394, op. 1, ed. khr. 93, ll. 1–7. Memoirs and other anecdotal evidence suggest that petty landowners were in permanent residence and that noble men and women across the economic spectrum spent most of the year on their estates. For some examples, see *Krest'ianskoe dvizhenie v Rossii v 1796–1825 gg.* (1961), 635; E. N. Moller, "Pamiatnye zametki E. N. Moller, rozhdennoi Murav'evoi, 1820–1872," *Russkaia starina* 66, no. 5 (1890): 341; E. I. Raevskaia, "Iz pamiatnoi knigi E. I. Raevskoi," *Russkii arkhiv*, kn. 1, no. 2 (1883): 298.

103. Sofia Mengden, "Otryvki semeinoi khroniki," *Russkaia starina* 134, no. 4 (1908): 99.

104. Semenov-Tian-Shanskii (1917), 89–90, 125.

105. E. A. Khvostova, *Zapiski, 1812–1841* (Leningrad, 1928), 38. See also O. I. Kornilova, *Byl' iz vremeni krepostnichestva (Vospominaniia o moei materi i ee okruzhaiushchem)* (St. Petersburg, 1890).

Within the estate, the *pomeshchita*'s power was almost unlimited, and the temptation to abuse her power proved irresistible to some. The authors of memoirs dwelled at length on their mothers' good deeds; nineteenth-century historians, however, regarded women serf owners more unkindly. If memoirists exaggerated their mothers' virtues, historians went to the opposite extreme, portraying the *pomeshchitsa* as tyrannical and abusive. Shchepkina explained that women's cruelty derived from their "perpetual dependence, first on their kin, then on their husbands," and believed that women felt "strong and powerful" only vis-à-vis their serfs.[106] Mikhnevich noted that female serf owners rivaled their male counterparts in regard to abuse of their peasants, and at times surpassed them.[107] The historian Ilinskii also waxed eloquent on mean-spirited widows whose tyranny was unchecked by the moderating influence of education. Adding a quantitative flourish to his argument, the scholar observed that women were more likely than men to sell serf children separately from their parents.[108]

The personal records of noblewomen offer a third perspective on the relationship between serf and proprietress, providing some middle ground between the two extremes of maternalism and abuse. These documents underscore the familiarity of many estate owners, both male and female, with affairs on their estates, and the obligation many felt toward their dependents. In a letter to Elizaveta Shishkina in 1796, Ekaterina Tiashkova acknowledged her dependence on her peasants when she asked for news of a serf woman who had fallen ill. "I am very concerned about her, for if she dies, then what remains of my estate will be done for."[109] Absentee proprietors knew many of their peasants by name and were aware of their individual problems. When Antonia Bludova asked her bailiff to find out if her peasants' plea to reduce their tax burden was justified, she enjoined him to pay particular attention to Semen Mikhailov, who had recently lost all his livestock.[110] Ekaterina Ermolova wrote to the bailiff of her estate in 1856 and asked him to explain to her why the peasant Stepan Nikiforov did not have the use of land his father had purchased; she also asked his advice when Avdotia Kondrat'eva requested permission for her sons to set up their own households. "Should I allow this or not?" Ermolova inquired. "You know better than I how they live."[111] Another noblewoman recorded mediating in

106. Shchepkina (1914), 133.

107. Mikhnevich (1895), 221.

108. P. A. Ilinskii, "K voprosu o polozhenii zhenshchiny v 18 stoletii v Kostromskoi oblasti, po arkhivnym dannym," in *Trudy tret'ego oblastnogo istoriko-arkheologicheskogo s"ezda* (Vladimir, 1909), 5, 8.

109. GIM, f. 182 (Shishkiny), op. 1, ed. khr. 7, l. 195.

110. RGADA, f. 1274 (Paniny-Bludovy), op. 1, ch. 3, ed. khr. 3248, l. 14 (1855).

111. RGADA, f. 1406 (Ermolovy), op. 1, ed. khr. 47, ll. 2, 32.

the family quarrels of her serfs.[112] The poverty of their laborers was also a recurring theme in the correspondence of noblewomen. Writing to her brother, Antiokh, in 1734, Princess Maria Kantemir expressed sympathy for her serfs, who were suffering from three years of bad harvests; she also noted that their sorry economic state had forced her to borrow money far beyond her means.[113] When her bailiff complained that her peasants could not pay their *obrok*, Ekaterina Tomilova responded that she had no desire to ruin her peasants but that he must distinguish between those who had not the means to pay and those who simply refused.[114]

Maintaining order on the estate could be trying for proprietors of both sexes. In this respect, however, noblewomen showed themselves capable of responding to insubordination through legal channels, or when necessary, with a display of firmness. The widow Chikhacheva petitioned the Senate in 1805 to take action against a merchant who had set up a tavern in one of her villages without her consent. Chikhacheva feared, with good reason, that her peasants would take advantage of the tavern to drink and carouse: since the tavern had opened, there had been two fires on her estate, which "reduced thirty-six peasant households and their property to ash."[115] When the serfs of Elena Khvoshchinskaia's mother refused to harvest her grain, she went out to confront them; while her steward stood by, trembling, Ekaterina Golitsyna forced the peasants to hand over those who initiated the disorder and sent the rest back to work.[116]

On the occasions when noblewomen confronted outright rebellion on the part of their serfs, their authority was challenged on the basis of ill treatment rather than on the grounds of their sex. By and large, peasants were gender blind in their petitions. One exception to this rule was their interpretation of noble laws of inheritance, which they perceived through the lens of their own customs. Thus, after the death of one nobleman in Smolensk province, the serfs of his estate refused to submit to his widow, observing that since their proprietor had left no offspring, they could not understand how his widow claimed them.[117] Peasants on the estate of Dashkova's daughter, Countess Shcherbinina, alleged that Shcherbinina had no right to inherit them from her mother and brother, and stated that they wished to be returned to Dashkova's family, the Vorontsovs.[118] Peasants by

112. Ekaterina Petrovna Kvashnina-Samarina, "Dnevnik," in *K istorii sotsial'no-bytovykh otnoshenii v nachale XIX stoletiia*, by S. M. Smirnov, (Novgorod, 1928), 7.

113. I. I. Shimko, *Novye dannye k biografii kn. Antiokha Dmitrievicha Kantemira i ego blizhaishikh rodstvennikov* (St. Petersburg, 1891), 28.

114. RGIA, f. 1086, op. 1, ed. khr. 834, l. 1 (1807).

115. RGIA, f. 1330, op. 3, ed. khr. 98, l. 7.

116. Elena Iur'evna Khvoshchinskaia, "Vospominaniia," *Russkaia starina*, no. 3 (1898): 569–70.

117. *Krest'ianskoe dvizhenie v Rossii v 1796–1825 gg.* (1961), 148–49.

118. Ibid., 282–83. See also 36–38.

no means discriminated against women estate owners in this regard: the claims of male proprietors were also scrutinized.[119] Only a few serfs employed this strategy to justify disobedience, however; most were content with complaining of abusive overseers and excessive labor dues.[120]

Property ownership not only allowed women the scope to exercise authority on their estates but also brought with it conflicts, privileges, and responsibilities in the wider sphere of provincial society. As Wilson Augustine has noted, for the Russian nobility landownership was "at the very heart of the business of life; ownership of an estate involved a nobleman in certain relations with central and local governments, and it also connected him with the serf society which formed the broad foundation of the Russian polity. The underdeveloped state of the law . . . put him in close and sometimes uncomfortable contact with his neighbors, while his sons or relations were drawn to him by the expectancy of inheritance. In these ways social relations centered around landownership."[121] Augustine discusses landownership as an exclusively male phenomenon, but in their role as proprietors, noblewomen also found themselves at the center of a social network involving local authorities, neighboring landowners, and serfs. Women estate owners confronted the same problems that plagued their male counterparts and enjoyed similar opportunities to exert influence on authorities within their district.

Encounters with neighbors and local authorities often took place in the context of perpetual disputes over boundaries and resources. With the goal of defending every last desiatin of their holdings, noblewomen engaged in incessant litigation with other landowners and state peasants. An inventory compiled in 1807 for Ekaterina Bariatinskaia listed seventy-eight current disputes involving the countess and her neighbors over runaway serfs and theft of land and other property.[122] Peasants also had the temerity to challenge noble proprietors over their land rights. The *pomeshchitsa* Sheshkovskaia struggled with state peasants in the village of Rozhestvena over the boundaries of her estate after a land survey in 1795.[123] Conflicts erupted when Russian nobles—such as Aksakov's grandfather—moved east and purchased land in areas already settled by non-Russians. Thus, Bashkirs in Orenburg province lodged a complaint against the widow of Titular Counselor Turganinov: not content with the land her husband had acquired from the Bashkirs for a miserly sum in 1776, she proceeded to seize land in 1792

119. See a similar case involving Prince Mikhail Golitsyn: RGIA, f. 1286, op. 7 (1838), ed. khr. 12, ll. 1–5, 24.

120. *Krest'ianskoe dvizhenie v Rossii v 1796–1825 gg.* (1961), 474–77, 631–38; *Krest'ianskoe dvizhenie v Rossii v 1826–1849 gg.: Sbornik dokumentov*, ed. A. V. Predtechenskii (Moscow, 1961), 67–70, 106–9, 341–42.

121. Augustine (1970), 387.

122. RGADA, f. 1255 (Bariatinskie), op. 4, ed. khr. 374.

123. RGIA, f. 1330, op. 1, ed. khr. 5, l. 3.

above and beyond what he had purchased.[124] The greatest obstacle to obtaining justice in such disputes was not the gender of the participants but the chronic inefficiency of the legal system in the era of serfdom.

When the justice of a primitive legal system did not satisfy them, noblewomen proved capable of resorting to violence to reclaim land and serfs. Some women were the victims of such attacks, as was a *pomeshchitsa* in Smolensk province who was driven from her estate by an aggressive neighbor in 1742.[125] Yet, as serf owners, bellicose noblewomen could rally their peasants and retaliate in kind. A dispute between grenadier Friazin and the *pomeshchitsa* Pobedinskaia ended in violence when Friazin and another neighbor rode into the fields of her estate and began beating her serfs. Summoned by one who escaped, Pobedinskaia rallied her peasants and went to confront her neighbors, who fired on her when she arrived. Pobedinskaia claimed she was wounded in one hand and went home; her peasants testified, however, that she urged them on, crying, "Beat them to death! And I will answer for it."[126] During a legal wrangle over property in 1780 between Irina Ushakova and Natasia Annenkova, the latter gathered a force of three hundred armed serfs from her villages and wrought havoc on the disputed estate.[127] Ensign Ivan Voiekov told a similar tale of how his stepmother descended on his estate with her peasants, purportedly to claim her portion of his father's property. After killing a number of serfs, Voiekova made off with much of her stepson's property, as well as the documents proving his title to the estate. Voiekov complained in his petition that he could not even retrieve the bodies of his serfs, since his stepmother's peasants continued to occupy the roads around his village and terrorize passersby.[128]

Voiekov's petition also reveals that women landowners could influence local authorities to obtain—or obstruct—justice. The authorities in Vladimir would not respond to his petition, he claimed, because his stepmother was protected by the town governor, Shishkov. Nor was Voiekov the only petitioner to allege complicity between a proprietress and the authorities. Tatiana Bazhenova wrote that her husband's stepmother had carried out the division of her husband's estate with the help of a representative from the Land College. "Knowing that my husband was not at home," the official notarized the division "in the night . . . in the home of Pelagia," Bazhenova's stepmother.[129]

124. RGIA, f. 1330, op. 5, ed. khr. 1950, ll. 66, 105 (1846).
125. M. M. Bogoslovskii, *Byt i nravy russkogo dvorianstvo v pervoi polovine XVIII veka*, 2d. ed. (Petrograd, 1918), 34.
126. Soloviev (1964), 12: 235. Pobedinskaia was sentenced to a monastery for life. See also Soloviev (1964), 12: 19.
127. RGADA, f. 1209, op. 79, ed. khr. 523, l. 1.
128. RGADA, f. 1255, op. 4, ed. khr. 125, l. 2.
129. RGADA, f. 1209, op. 79, ed. khr. 56, l. 223.

The anecdotes of memoirists substantiate the fragmentary testimony of petitioners' tales and hint at the potential influence of women proprietors in provincial society. Writing about Olga Mikhailovna Saltykova, her niece recalled that Saltykova "commanded the obedience of her husband and children, and even the entire district. Everyone came to her for advice and help concerning public and private matters (*v delakh obshchestvennykh i semeinykh*)."[130] Vigel related the unhappiness Princess Varvara Golitsyna suffered in the social universe of Moscow and St. Petersburg. By contrast, in her Saratov estate she ruled absolutely over the neighboring landowners, who were eager to curry her favor.[131]

Clearly, women wielded influence primarily through informal channels. As landowners, they shared the prerogative of men to vote in district elections; unlike men, however, they could not participate in person in noble assemblies but sent representatives in their stead.[132] This principle was established during elections to the Legislative Commission of 1767 and remained in place until the close of the Imperial era.[133] And yet, in light of the limited efficacy of local government before 1861, disqualification from noble assemblies may not have hindered noblewomen from bringing pressure to bear on local authorities. In Russia, landownership was not the source of political rights, as was the case in Western Europe[134]; nonetheless, wealth and the control of property were deciding factors in the contest for authority in provincial society. As estate owners, noblewomen, like their male counterparts, were positioned to exercise influence over their neighbors and local officials.

Domesticity and the Transformation of Gender Conventions

By far the most striking feature of this survey of archival and memoir literature is the wide spectrum of roles available to women who owned property. Neither Arina Vlaseevna nor Anna Odintseva represented the "typical" *pomeshchitsa* in Imperial Russia. If young girls were not explicitly encouraged to become active estate managers, in everyday life they witnessed the vital

130. Makashin (1951), 30.

131. Vigel (1974), 76.

132. Vera Mikhailova, *Russkie zakony o zhenshchine* (Moscow, 1913), 1–5.

133. During the elections to the Legislative Commission, 204 women landowners in eleven districts registered their votes, as compared with 1,097 men. A. V. Florovskii, *Sostav zakonodatel'noi kommissii, 1767–74 gg.* (Odessa, 1915), 263–66. Married women usually asked their husbands to register their votes for them. For one example, see TsGIAM, f. 4, op. 3, ed. khr. 11, l. 1 (1858).

134. A. D. Gradovskii, *Istoriia mestnogo upravleniia v Rossii* (St. Petersburg, 1868), 1: 23.

role women could assume as administrators of family property. There is no suggestion in nineteenth-century memoirs that noblewomen who managed estates and looked after their own financial interests violated any norms for womanly behavior, nor that the men in their families were diminished by displays of feminine competence. Noble proprietors of both sexes are praised equally for acting as custodians of family fortunes, for saving the ancestral estate, and for passing on a sound inheritance to their children. Similarly, women who neglected their estates or managed them poorly were not forgiven on the grounds of their sex.

The question remains, however, whether the expectations that governed women's behavior varied over time, and if they did not, what accounted for their stability. Among European historians, the paradigm of separate spheres—and the revision of that paradigm—has dominated accounts of women's experience. Scholars have roundly criticized the notion of public and private as an analytic tool, and extensively documented how the behavior of European women failed to conform to the "new domesticity."[135] For all its limitations as a description of women's lives, however, separate-spheres ideology generated a vast body of prescriptive literature, which educated Russians avidly consumed.[136] Simply stated, domestic ideology held that woman's participation in public life should be limited and that her proper sphere of influence was the home. Educators and authors of advice manuals transformed the domestic realm into an object of reverence and placed women firmly at its center. While the association between women and domestic life was hardly an innovation in late-eighteenth-century Europe, this theory of gender arrangements articulated the tasks and significance of

135. Historians argue that women failed to conform to the ideals of domesticity in their daily lives; they also have demonstrated that women made use of separate-spheres ideology to take part in activities that fell within the realm of the public. The conviction that the new accent on domesticity forced upper-class women from productive and public life has also come under attack. Inevitably, these studies focus primarily on Anglo-American women. See, for example, Linda Colley, *Britons: Forging the Nation 1707–1837* (New Haven, 1992), 237–81; M. Jeanne Peterson, "No Angels in the House: The Victorian Myth and the Paget Women," *American Historical Review* 89, no. 3 (1984): 677–708; Amanda Vickery, *The Gentleman's Daughter: Women's Lives in Georgian England* (New Haven, 1998). One author notes, however, that the opportunity for aristocratic Englishwomen to take active part in political life disappeared at the end of the eighteenth century, and that a hundred years would pass before women "ventured boldly into street politics." See Amanda Foreman, *Georgiana, Duchess of Devonshire* (London, 1998), 159. Others maintain that the notion of public and private spheres cannot be applied without considerable modification to societies outside the Anglo-American world. See Susan M. Reverby and Dorothy O. Helly, "Introduction: Converging on History," in *Gendered Domains: Rethinking Public and Private in Women's History* ed. Dorothy O. Helly and Susan M. Reverby (Ithaca, 1992), 6–7.

136. On the impact of prescriptive literature in Russia, see Diana Greene, "Mid-Nineteenth-Century Domestic Ideology in Russia," in *Women and Russian Culture: Projections and Self-Perceptions*, ed. Rosalind Marsh (New York, 1998), 78–97, and Catriona Kelly, *Refining Russia: Advice Literature, Polite Culture, and Gender from Catherine to Yeltsin* (Oxford, 2001).

motherhood to a novel degree,[137] and to the exclusion of alternative sources of female identity.

The impact of separate-spheres ideology on Russian gender conventions was manifested in part by heightened sensitivity to the appropriate scope and setting of female authority. One scholar has identified a shift at the very top of the social pyramid, in the role of the Russian empress. By eliminating the threat of female rule with a new law of succession in 1801, Paul I initiated a new order for his consort, in which "her principal sphere was to become the home, rather than the court or the state."[138] Moreover, if the succession of women rulers in the eighteenth century had not presented "a special problem" for Russians,[139] by the nineteenth century contemporaries proved more inclined to assess authority in strictly gendered terms. Looking back at the reign of Catherine II, the daughter of the poet Tiutchev stated, "Catherine II was not so much an intelligent woman as a man of genius; it was her calling to influence people, to direct them, rule them." Tiutcheva went on to admit that despite the gentle nature of the new empress, Maria Feodorovna, she felt more reticence in her company than she experienced with the emperor himself. "In relation to women, I feel the difference in rank, while in relation to men I feel only the difference of sex," she observed.[140]

Within the smaller universe of the family, change proceeded at a more leisurely pace. From the late eighteenth century, Russian writers and educators followed the lead of their European counterparts in exhorting women to spend less time enjoying life at court and in society and to devote themselves to tending their children. An article that appeared in the journal *Patriot* in 1804 stated, "There is not, and will not be, any hope of improving morals as long as women will not return to domestic life."[141] Exhortations to noblewomen to focus on motherhood fell largely on deaf ears, however, if memoir literature can be believed. Indeed, both men and women writing after Emancipation portrayed indifferent childrearing as typical of an earlier era. Many of these authors recounted that estate management occupied their mothers from morning to night.[142] "For a long time, we did not know who our real mother was," wrote Nadezhda Sokhanskaia. "Mama was constantly absent, seeing to estate affairs, and our aunts, it seems, quarreled

137. Elisabeth Badinter, *L'amour en plus: Histoire de l'amour maternel (XVIIe–XXe siècle)* (Paris, 1980).

138. Wortman (1978), 60–63.

139. Brenda Meehan-Waters, "Catherine the Great and the Problem of Female Rule," *Russian Review* 34, no. 3 (July 1975): 302.

140. A. F. Tiutcheva, *Pri dvore dvukh imperatorov. Vospominaniia. Dnevnik. 1853–1855* (Moscow, 1928), 109, 169.

141. Quoted in Shashkov (1879), 235.

142. Labzina (1974), 9; Zhukovskaia (1930), 1; Vodovozova (1987), I: 103.

about who could best replace her."[143] A. Kupreianova's grandmother took no part in raising her offspring, seven of whom died. Kupreianova wrote that her grandmother was unperturbed by the death of her children, and "calmly returned to her duty. And her duty was to please her husband and to uphold the honor of the noble family."[144] While Ekaterina Khvostova spoke of her mother's love for her, the latter abandoned Khvostova at the age of three months to follow her husband for two years during his military service.[145]

These accounts highlight the uneven implementation of domestic ideology in pre-reform Russia. In other families, the transformation of family life and the significance of affective ties were already apparent early in the nineteenth century. For noblewomen such as Varvara Tomilova, the tasks of motherhood extended to the physical care of her daughter. Writing to her husband, Alexei, in 1812, Tomilova informed him that she herself bathed their daughter every day; she went on to explain that Katia's nanny was less than observant of the rules of hygiene and that these daily baths strengthened Katia's attachment to her.[146] Four years later, Tomilova kept a daily journal in which she recorded her daughter's progress in Russian and French, as well as her frequent tantrums, in exhaustive detail.[147] Varvara Tomilova personally supervised the education of her daughter and that of a female relative who lived with her, yet managed to find time for estate management as well.[148]

Although discontinuity before and after 1861 should not be overstated, the evidence from memoirs points to a marked shift in gender conventions and family patterns in the post-Emancipation era. Elements of separate-spheres ideology became part of the larger discourse on gender arrangements in the final decades of serfdom.[149] Yet the testimony of memoirs

143. N. S. Sokhanskaia, "Avtobiografiia," *Russkoe obozrenie*, no. 6 (1896): 483.

144. Kupreianova (1914), 651.

145. Khvostova (1928), 26. See also A-va [A. N. Kazina], "Zhenskaia zhizn'," *Otechestvennye zapiski* 219, no. 3 (March 1875): 211. As Barbara Engel argues, until the mid-nineteenth century, in the noble family a mother's "relationship with her daughter was mediated by other female figures," such as the nurse and governess. See Engel, "Mothers and Daughters: Family Patterns and the Female Intelligentsia," in *The Family in Imperial Russia* ed. David L. Ransel (Urbana, 1978), 49.

146. RGIA, f. 1086, op. 1, ed. khr. 203a, l. 213.

147. RGIA, f. 1086, op. 1, ed. khr. 703 (1816).

148. RGIA, f. 1086, op. 1, ed. khr. 203a, l. 39 (1812); f. 1086, op. 1, ed. khr. 881 (1812). The letters of Varvara's husband, Aleksei Tomilov, also express a close bond with his mother. He wrote frequently to her while beginning his military service, addressing her as "*matushka kormilitsa*" (mother-wet-nurse). See RGIA, f. 1086, op. 1, ed. khr. 50, ll. 4, 5, 55, 73 (1797).

149. Separate-spheres ideology appeared full blown in a housekeeping manual by Raida Varlamova in 1856. In her introduction, Varlamova wrote that the wife and mother should be the "peaceful angel in the house." Varlamova also frowned on the practice of hiring wet nurses. If a woman proved unable to breast-feed, however, she might hire a wet nurse, the choice of which "should be entrusted without fail to the doctor." Varlamova, *Semeinyi magazin* (Moscow, 1856), i, 146–47.

demonstrates that among eighteenth- and early-nineteenth-century contemporaries, no particular opprobrium attached to noblewomen who abdicated responsibility for their children to servants and maiden aunts. At the
same time, these memoirs, written, by and large, after 1861, betray new
expectations for maternal behavior. The abolition of serfdom did away with
the free labor that had comprised the traditional mainstay of the noble
household; as a result, the deluge of childrearing literature and manuals on
housekeeping intensified in the 1860s, signaling a heightened preoccupation with the tasks of household management and the responsibilities of
motherhood.[150]

Prescriptive literature did not explicitly ban women from assuming the role
of estate administrator. Nonetheless, in the latter part of the century, the
clash between European expectations for feminine propriety and traditional
Russian gender arrangements was expressed in a more critical view of female
proprietors. Whereas Vigel had urged women to see to the prosperity of their
estates, the attitude of later contemporaries toward competent female proprietors proved more ambivalent. In his account of estate life on the eve of
Emancipation, D. Sverbeev related the story of a neighboring landowner
whose wife had saved his estate from ruin, commenting that the latter's talent
for estate affairs was distinctly "unfeminine (. . . *ona . . . sposobnaia na vsiakoe
delo ne po-zhenski . . . vzialas' za ustroistvo imenii muzha*)."[151] When Sofia
Subbotina was arrested in 1874 for opening a school on her estate for peasants and workers, one clerk testified against her and accused her of conducting her life in a way unbefitting a wealthy proprietress: "[She] got up
early, conversed with workers, and ran the estate herself (*vela sama khoziaistvo*)."[152] Many writers of fiction depicted competent female administrators
as grasping or unnatural[153]; in the work of others, such as Chekhov and Ostrovsky, women's mismanagement of property represented yet another symptom
of the decline of the Russian nobility. In Ostrovsky's "The Forest," one character asserts, "But really, we've had so many of our noble estates completely
ruined by old women. If a man throws his money away, there's usually some
sort of reason in his extravagance. But there's no limit to an old woman's stu-
pidity."[154] The significance of such examples should not be overstated.
Nonetheless, they illustrate some modification, at least at the level of repre-
sentation, of Russian attitudes toward women's economic authority.

150. Engel (1978), 59.
151. D. N. Sverbeev, "Zapiski," in *Pomeshchich'ia Rossiia po zapiskam sovremennikov* (Moscow,
1911), 154, 161.
152. Subbotina (1928), 17.
153. Nikolai Gogol, "Ivan Fyodorovich Shponka and His Aunt," in *Diary of a Madman and
Other Stories*, trans. Ronald Wilks (London, 1972), 171–72.
154. Alexander Ostrovsky, "The Forest," in *Five Plays of Alexander Ostrovsky*, trans. Eugene K.
Bristow (New York, 1969), 451.

In practice, however, the traditional association between household and estate management ensured that noblewomen continued to take an active part in estate administration. Significantly, Russian noblewomen's increased attention to childrearing in the post-Emancipation era did not preclude their attention to large-scale management. Describing his childhood in Ukraine on the eve of the revolution, Vladimir Korostovets devoted part of his account to his mother's work in modernizing their estate and introducing "industrial methods," despite the objections of his grandmother, who owned the estate.[155] After Prince Tenishev bestowed property on his wife, rather than supervising it himself he asked his wife's closest friend, Princess Sviatopolk-Chetvertinskaia, to help Maria Tenisheva put the estate in order.[156] Although the number of estates in the hands of nobles declined sharply in the decades after Emancipation, the prominent role of noblewomen in estate management endured throughout the nineteenth century.

With few alternative models available to her, the Russian noblewoman, both before and after Emancipation, derived her identity in large part from the twin roles of wife and mother. It was the substance of those roles, rather than the roles themselves, that was subtly revised in the course of the nineteenth century. For the Russian noblewoman of the pre-Emancipation era, a good mother was one who, above all, looked after the financial interests of her children even if she neglected their physical care. Princess Dashkova articulated this approach to motherhood when she recounted her efforts to ensure her children's inheritance: "I wanted to be as good a steward of my children's property as I was their governess and sick-nurse, and no price was too high."[157] Maternal solicitude for their children's affairs prompted other women to more heroic acts. Recounting the progress of a serf revolt in 1857, the military governor Koliubakin wrote with admiration of a local *pomeshchitsa*: "Inspired by the sentiments and obligations of a mother and proprietor (*materi-pravitel'nitsy*) who must preserve her children's inheritance," she mounted her horse and rode off to confront her rebellious peasants.[158] As

155. Vladimir Korostovets, *Seed and Harvest* (London, 1931), 73–87. Korostovets's father was alive for much of this period, but he remained in St. Petersburg even after his retirement and plays a very minor role in the memoir.

156. Princess M. K. Tenisheva, *Vpechatleniia moei zhizni* (Leningrad, 1991), 92–95. See also a letter from the district marshal of the nobility to Evgenia Borisovna Kavelina in 1893, asking that she, as a landowner "familiar with all the branches of agriculture," complete a detailed questionnaire. In her response, Kavelina noted the difficulty of finding laborers, and that the peasants in her region came to work "reluctantly." See RGIA, f. 947, op. 1, ed. khr. 114, ll. 1, 3.

157. Dashkova (1995), 114. See also the example of Elena Gan (1814–42), who asserted that she wrote fiction in order to provide for her children. Gan's daughter later complained that their mother left them in the care of nurses and governesses. See Engel (1983), 32–33.

158. *Krest'ianskoe dvizhenie v Rossii v 1857–mae 1861 gg.: Sbornik dokumentov*, ed. S. B. Okun' (Moscow, 1963), 50.

good wives, noblewomen not only supervised activity within the household but also looked after the administration and financial well-being of the estate. While some women, such as Countess Rumiantseva, experienced these responsibilities as burdensome, others took pleasure in putting matters to rights on their holdings, or at least in the authority they wielded over other family members. Again, Dashkova offered the most eloquent testimony on skilled estate management as a source of pleasure and identity for many Russian women. Her memoirs are replete with discussions of her labor to put her estate in order, and her pride in the affluence of her peasants is evident throughout the work.[159]

Russian noblewomen's active engagement in estate management, as well as favorable commentary on feminine business abilities, underscores the resistance of Russian gender conventions to European notions of feminine propriety. The divergence between Russian and Western gender arrangements epitomized the contrast between noble tradition and the new culture of the middle class. European noblewomen of the old regime enjoyed greater liberty in the "public" sphere than did their middle-class successors: they acted as arbiters of manners at court and assumed responsibility for estate management when necessity dictated—a practice that continued into the nineteenth century.[160] Yet, even under the ancien régime, the law of property in the West inhibited married women of all social classes from transacting business on their own behalf. For all its incongruity with the reality of European women's lives, domestic ideology in the West was reinforced by a legal system that limited married women's legal personalities and ensured that their contributions to the family enterprise remained "hidden" from view.

Like their European counterparts, Russian noblewomen were admonished to be modest, chaste, and submissive to their husbands,[161] while men were encouraged to look on their wives as fragile beings in need of their protection.[162] The ideal of the frail and dependent wife, however, was very much at odds with a legal regime that held married women accountable for their affairs. Moreover, it contradicted the everyday experience of

159. Dashkova (1995), 194, 248.

160. For examples of early-modern French noblewomen administering the family's financial affairs, see Diefendorf [(1995), 183], although she does not claim that this role was typical. On aristocratic women and estate management in the nineteenth century, see David Higgs, *Nobles in Nineteenth-Century France: The Practice of Inegalitarianism* (Baltimore, 1987), 196, and K. D. Reynolds, *Aristocratic Women and Political Society in Victorian Britain* (Oxford, 1998), 26–70. On the role of eighteenth-century Polish noblewomen in family politics and financial affairs, see Lynn Lubamersky, "Women and Political Patronage in the Politics of the Polish-Lithuanian Commonwealth," *Polish Review* 44, no. 3 (1999): 259–75.

161. *Zhenskaia filosofiia* (Moscow, 1793), 33–34.

162. See the advice of Count Andrei Petrovich Shuvalov to his sons: "Nravouchitel'noe zaveshchanie synov'iam" (1780s). RGIA, f. 1092, op. 1, ed. khr. 136, l. 19.

noblewomen who supervised their estates and dealt competently with matters of property and of the law—all with minimal assistance from their menfolk.

More than one historian has identified Emancipation as a watershed in the history of the noble family. One scholar observes that when Russian noblewomen faced a shortage of servants and reduced circumstances after 1861, they began to "get involved in raising their children, often tending their infants personally for the first time."[163] Be that as it may, noblewomen's legal status muted the impact of separate-spheres ideology in Russia: in matters of property, Western European ideals of womanhood did not displace but coexisted with traditional gender arrangements in Imperial Russia. Although Russian authors in the first half of the nineteenth century adopted the rhetoric of sentimentalism and admonished women to confine their influence to the domestic sphere, their veneration of European models did not extend to absolving women of responsibility for their own, and their children's, financial affairs. For their part, Russian noblewomen embraced the ideology of domesticity only when the material circumstances of their lives changed after Emancipation.

163. Roberta Thompson Manning, *The Crisis of the Old Order in Russia: Gentry and Government* (Princeton, 1982), 40. See also B. N. Mironov, *Sotsial'naia istoriia Rossii perioda imperii (XVIII–nachalo XX v.) Genezis lichnosti, demokraticheskoi sem'i, grazhdanskogo obshchestva i pravovogo gosudarstva* (St. Petersburg, 1999), 1: 264.

Women and the Legal Process

Of all the tasks that confronted estate owners in Imperial Russia, litigation was perhaps the most burdensome. Russian nobles were notoriously litigious: nineteenth-century memoirs depict landowners as perpetually embroiled in boundary conflicts with neighbors or entangled in inheritance suits with family members and, as often as not, neither party to such legal wrangles was satisfied with the outcome. Nobles who brought their grievances to court routinely lamented the arbitrary administration of justice in Russia. Property disputes could drag on for years, if not decades; as a result, it was not uncommon for litigants to face financial ruin while waiting for the courts to decide their case. For their part, historians agree that nobles rarely benefited from their litigiousness. They maintain that knowledge of the law in the provinces was fragmentary at best and that justice remained a highly elusive goal until the legal reforms of the 1860s.[1] Indeed, for both contemporaries and modern scholars, the legal system embodied the very ills that lay at the heart of Russian backwardness: inefficiency, corruption, the arbitrary exercise of power, and disregard for the rule of law.

This chapter moves beyond the estate to examine the fortunes of female proprietors in the wider context of the legal process. Noblewomen's recourse to litigation, and their successful defense of their property rights, have been recurring themes of this study. Property disputes offer ample testimony to women's engagement with the legal process. They document noblewomen's visibility both as plaintiffs and as defendants and chronicle the development of women's access to and control of their fortunes. Scholars of comparative property rights have found that "legal provisions

1. Wortman (1976), 20; LeDonne (1984), 145–46.

may exist for [women's] protection, yet they fail to bring their grievances forward."[2] In Russia, however, authorities expected noblewomen to assume responsibility for their legal affairs, and women displayed a lively sense of their rights in regard to property.

Property conflicts also document change over time: they testify to the role gender played in dictating the kinds of conflicts in which women took part, and the degree of protection officials offered female litigants. For all the insights they provide, however, property disputes reveal little about the interaction between female plaintiffs and legal authorities. Although petitioners often complained that the courts failed to rule in accordance with the law, the resolutions that survive maintain a brave pretense of legality. Decisions recorded in the Land College and the Senate brim with references to decrees and rulings, and leave the impression that the rules of property were practiced consistently. As a result, the role of patronage, not to mention the rank or gender of the litigants, in determining the outcome of a suit is rarely detected.

With an eye to studying the interaction between *pomeshchitsy* and the local and central authorities, this discussion will take a closer look at noblewomen's participation in the legal process. What follows will attend, first, to noblewomen's role in handling their legal affairs. Second, the problem of whether women confronted particular obstacles in obtaining justice will be addressed. Here I will consider the fate of women's property in a particular legal context—namely, that of estate sequestration in the first half of the nineteenth century. Unlike inheritance disputes, cases involving the sequestration of noble property for serf abuse and poor estate management provide detailed accounts of encounters between noble proprietors and local officials. Such cases highlight new expectations on the part of the government for noble behavior; they also provide an elaborate record of how civil authorities collected and evaluated evidence, and how they applied the law to proprietors of both sexes.

While weighing the significance of gender in the dealings of noble proprietors with judicial-administrative institutions, I will also consider the broader implications of women's successful negotiation through the courts. The presence of noblewomen in the legal order depended on the willingness of male officials to accept their claims and to rule strictly according to the laws of property and judicial procedure. Appeals that reached the Senate demonstrate that local officials often fell short of this goal. The story of women's legal battles thus provides one perspective on the evolution of legal norms before the mid-nineteenth century, as well as the central government's struggle to impose those norms on the provinces. The record of

2. Renée Hirschon, "Introduction: Property, Power, and Gender Relations," in *Women and Property—Women as Property* ed. Renée Hirschon (New York, 1984), 17.

female litigation reveals that noblewomen were adept at securing protection through patronage networks and, like their male counterparts, exploited the element of personal authority that characterized the dispensing of justice in Imperial Russia. It also demonstrates, however, that noblewomen benefited from the growing aspiration to legal order among officials and bureaucrats from the late eighteenth century.

The Female Petitioner: Literacy and Legal Knowledge

The spectacle of noblewomen defending their rights before legal authorities in Russia was not an eighteenth-century innovation but a tradition of long standing. If the presence of the female petitioner in the courts and chancelleries has been acknowledged, however, many dimensions of her participation in the legal process have yet to be explored. In particular, noblewomen's knowledge of the law and their role in composing petitions demands consideration. Contemporaries often portrayed noblewomen as ignorant of the law and incapable of dealing with their legal affairs. The petitions and correspondence of women tell a conflicting story: they present female petitioners as competent litigants who were familiar with the fundamental rules of inheritance.

The most striking characteristic of the female litigant from the opening decades of the eighteenth century is her sheer visibility. A survey of property suits heard in the Land College and in the Senate reveals that in the eighteenth century, 57.5 percent of the recorded suits involved litigants of both sexes. Women alone took part in a further 9 percent of these cases, whereas 33.4 percent consisted of conflicts between male disputants.[3] This trend persisted, with some variation, into the nineteenth century. Between 1807 and 1863, the proportion of cases in which both men and women took part decreased by almost 10 percent, to 48.5 percent, in favor of conflicts between same-sex litigants: thus, the proportion of disputes in which women alone took part increased to 13.3 percent, whereas that of male disputes grew to 38.3 percent.[4] Although men predominated in same-sex suits, noblewomen were consistently active in legal conflicts from the beginning of the eighteenth century, both as plaintiffs and as defendants.[5]

3. See chapter 1, footnote 43.

4. See the inventories in RGIA, f. 1330 (Obshchie sobraniia departamentov Senata), op. 4 (1807–27), op. 5 (1828–47), and op. 6 (1848–63). All of these cases (392 in total) concerned conflicts over inheritance or property disputes between nonkin.

5. Comparable figures for noblewomen in Western Europe do not exist. However, in her study of women's property rights in early-modern England, Amy Erickson found that women of all social classes filed suit in the Court of Chancery, accounting for 26% of the cases heard in the seventeenth and early eighteenth centuries. See Erickson (1993), 114–15.

Documenting the rise of noblewomen's participation in property litigation is a straightforward task. The greater challenge lies in determining whether women themselves took part in the disputes they instigated. During debates on legal reform in the nineteenth century, the ability of women to manage their legal affairs became the subject of discussion in a number of popular journals. Proponents of the reforms argued that legal knowledge was indispensable for women who owned estates or who were the guardians of their children. These same authors were unanimous, however, in their conviction that women were ignorant of the most fundamental principles of Russian law.

In an attempt to rectify this state of affairs, many of the thick journals that targeted a female audience published articles on the state of women's legal rights and women's need for a basic education in jurisprudence. Writing in *Rassvet* in 1859, one author pointed out that Russian law made no distinctions between men and women, and that women needed to defend their interests, particularly in their capacity as mothers. In response to those who would argue that the family is woman's proper domain, this author asserted that even if she never ventured beyond the domestic sphere, a woman needed to protect the interests of her dependents. "A large number of settled estates in Russia belong to women," he observed. "Female proprietors are often called upon to enter into various contracts and agreements, and to defend not only their own interests, but those of their peasants."[6] Another author not only deplored women's ignorance of the law but contended that most disputes initiated by women were unnecessary and derived from female ignorance. To make matters worse, women contributed to the length of their suits because of their natural inability to focus on the matter at hand. Instead of presenting their case in a straightforward fashion, female litigants wasted the time of the courts by recounting family quarrels and domestic trivia before arriving at the purpose of their suit.[7]

In keeping with this negative assessment of women's legal knowledge, the historian Ilinskii maintained that the existence of petitions from women in archives of provincial courts should not lead us to believe that they acted on their own behalf. Describing women and the legal process in eighteenth-century Russia, Ilinskii portrayed women as the ignorant dupes of clerks and officials, who composed their petitions and pursued their affairs for them. "Reading these documents, written in cunning bureaucratese, we may safely conclude that this was entirely the affair of officials," Ilinskii asserted, and argued that women played no part in their disputes. The officials, moreover,

6. T. Shishkin, "Neskol'ko slov o neobkhodimosti iuridicheskikh poznanii dlia zhenshchin," *Rassvet* 3 (1859): 126.

7. N. Sokolovskii, "Sovremennyi byt russkoi zhenshchiny i sudebnaia reforma (Iuridicheskie zametki)," *Zhenskii vestnik*, no. 9 (1867): 60–61.

had no interest in working in their clients' interests but were ready to settle as quickly as possible in order to maximize their profits.

Ilinskii's assumption that illiterate women were at the mercy of government officials is underscored by his portrayal of one remarkable woman who, he believed, managed her own legal affairs. Natasia Vitovtova not only was literate but also managed to acquire some knowledge of the law. "This can be explained by the fact that her grandfather and uncle were scrivners," Ilinskii wrote. He went on to argue that her petitions demonstrated that "she was familiar with the laws and the formulas of petitions, and she understood the legal red tape of that time." From the quantity and character of petitions written by Vitovtova, including one in which she reproached her sisters for neglecting their affairs in Moscow, Ilinskii concluded that this "lawyer in skirts" was respected by her neighbors and that she also ruled over her husband.[8] Regrettably, Ilinskii made no mention of how Vitovtova's petitions differed from those of other female proprietors, nor did he elaborate on his assertion that Vitovtova herself, rather than a clerk or official, was responsible for the content of her petitions.

Literary depictions of female acuity in the legal domain were no more optimistic. The playwright Ostrovsky revealed similar assumptions about feminine impotence when he portrayed a petty noblewoman on the verge of losing her small estate in a property dispute. "Now, they say, I must make a complaint to the Senate," she says to her daughter. "But who is going to write it? . . . I don't know A from B. If Maksim Dorofeich doesn't take charge, then you know we'll turn out beggars."[9]

The commentary of historians and legal reformers suggests that noblewomen understood little of the intricacies of the legal process. Yet, given the state of legal knowledge until the mid-nineteenth century, neither sex was likely to be conversant with more than the fundamentals of property law.[10] Petitions were silent on the mediating role of clerks and officials in deciding how to present a suit. Indeed, the very access of noble proprietors to information about the law of property in the eighteenth and early nineteenth centuries is still debated. Contemporaries bemoaned the rudimentary state of legal culture outside the capitals. Thus, after assuming his post as governor of Tambov province in 1786, the poet Derzhavin wrote to a friend in Moscow, "In Tambov province there is a great lack of laws. What is unknown is whether or not they have ever been in use here."[11] Such accounts

8. Ilinskii (1909), 13–14.

9. "The Poor Bride," in Ostrovsky (1969), 164.

10. Delegates to the Legislative Commission in 1767 complained that ignorance of the law led to ruinous lawsuits for nobles of both sexes. *SIRIO* (1869), 4: 379.

11. Quoted in Wortman (1976), 107. For conflicting evidence on the circulation of legal texts, see Gary Marker, *Publishing, Printing, and the Origins of Intellectual Life in Russia, 1700–1800* (Princeton, 1985), 198. Marker points out that five thousand copies of the *Ulozhenie* were published between 1780 and 1796.

have prompted historians to argue that even local officials were hard-pressed to obtain copies of the laws, although decrees were supposed to be circulated to provincial courts.

If ignorance of the law was widespread, however, it was not universal. Frequent exchanges between central authorities and provincial chancelleries, as well as directives from the former, provided at least some local officials with the means to make informed rulings.[12] Individual nobles were not unaware of the benefits of legal knowledge: wealthy members of the nobility included works on the law among necessary purchases when they traveled abroad.[13] Some provincial proprietors attempted to keep abreast of rulings in St. Petersburg. In his diary, written in the mid-eighteenth century, a wealthy landowner in Kursk province reported the publication of decrees from the Senate in his notebook, as well as recording production on his estate and trips to Kiev and Moscow.[14] Moreover, litigants of both sexes referred explicitly to legal rulings in their petitions when they appealed for justice. Eighteenth-century petitioners often cited "the points," or the articles of the Law of Single Inheritance of 1714, as well as subsequent legal rulings, such as Catherine I's addendum to the laws of inheritance in 1725.[15] The sluggish pace of litigation left many no choice but to become familiar with the decrees that were relevant to their case.[16]

The absence of a coherent legal code and the primitive state of education in jurisprudence did little to foster Russian familiarity with the law. Every eighteenth-century monarch took up, and subsequently abandoned, the task of legal codification; at last, in 1830, Nicholas I appointed a commission to collect all of the decrees issued after the *Ulozhenie* of 1649.[17] As a result, works

12. From the second half of the eighteenth century, the Senate made a concerted effort to monitor the legal process in the provinces, and received reports from local institutions on the receipt and implementation of decrees. See, for example, RGADA, f. 264 (VI Departament Senata), op. 2, ed. khr. 53 (1767); f. 264, op. 2, ed. khr. 178 (1773–74); f. 264, op. 2, ed. khr. 253 (1782); f. 264, op. 2, ed. khr. 367 (1799).

13. See an inventory, compiled early in the eighteenth century, concerning items "which must be purchased in Holland and in other cities" from the papers of the Sheremetev family. RGIA, f. 1088, op. 3, ed. khr. 1292, l. 5.

14. I. P. Annenkov, "Dnevnik kurskogo pomeshchika I. P. Annenkova, 1745–1766," in *Materialy po istorii SSSR* (Moscow, 1957), 5: 708–9, 714–15.

15. For some of these, see RGADA, f. 1209, op. 79, ed. khr. 4, l. 41 (1722): ". . . A v ukaze i v punktakh . . . napisano imianno . . ."; f. 1209, op. 79, ed. khr. 9, l. 3 (1724); f. 1209, op. 79, ed. khr. 51, l. 32 (1758); f. 1209, op. 79, ed. khr. 365, l. 20 (1752).

16. In a petition to the tsar, the widow Chesmenskaia recounted the progress of her suit through the lower courts to the Senate, and cited specific *ukazy*, or rulings, to support her suit; she alleged that none of the courts had ruled according to the law. See "Proshenie na Vysochaishee imia vdovy General-Maiora Chesmenskogo," in *Chteniia v Imperatorskom obshchestve istorii i drevnosti Rossiiskikh pri Moskovskom universitete* (January–March, 1873): 263–65.

17. For a history of these attempts, see S. V. Pakhman, *Istoriia kodifikatsii grazhdanskogo prava*, 2 vols. (St. Petersburg, 1876).

explaining the law and the execution of contracts were also absent until the late eighteenth century. Catherine II was the first Russian monarch to attend to the legal education of noblemen, despite the fact that noble men and women dispensed justice on their estates and were frequently engaged in disputes with neighbors over boundaries, runaway serfs, and the control of local resources. In her campaign to disseminate legal knowledge among the nobility, Catherine was assisted by S. E. Desnitskii, the first professor of Russian law. Familiarity with the law was imperative for the noble proprietor, Desnitskii informed a gathering of the nobility in 1778: basic jurisprudence "would show the nobleman how to effect sales and mortgage of his estates, how to fulfill his role as judge over his peasants, and how to conduct suits against his neighbors."[18]

If learning how to dispense justice played no part in the education of noblemen, how likely were women to be aware of the fundamental principles of the law? In Western Europe, an abundant literature explaining the legal process was available to literate laymen by the eighteenth century. Remarkably, some of these handbooks were addressed specifically to a female audience and offered advice to women on the best means of devising a marriage settlement. At least four manuals devoted to married women's property rights appeared in England in the eighteenth century alone. One such manual, *The Lady's Law*, published in 1732, proclaimed that "the fair Sex are here inform'd, how to preserve their Land, Goods, and the most valuable Effects, from the encroachments of anyone."[19]

Russian women did not enjoy the same benefit of legal advice as some of their European counterparts. The first manuals on the writing of letters and legal documents appeared in Russia only in the late eighteenth century and were not directed at women. The author of a treatise published in 1791 advised his readers to compose petitions themselves, since they could state their case with greater "liveliness and sensitivity" than an outsider who was paid to do so. If necessary, he added, the petitioner should seek the advice of someone honest and well versed in the law, to help with the composition of the petition.[20] Such manuals were not addressed specifically to women. During the compilation of the Digest of Russian Laws (*Svod zakonov*), however, Ilarion Vasil'ev published a short work dedicated to women, in which he set forth their rights in marriage and as Russian citizens.[21] An article in the *Ladies' Journal* (*Damskii zhurnal*), titled "Feelings and Thoughts upon Reading a Handbook about the Rights of Women in Russia," appeared

18. Wortman (1976), 26–27.

19. Amy Louise Erickson, "Common Law versus Common Practice: The Use of Marriage Settlements in Early Modern England," *Economic History Review* 42, no. 1 (1990): 26.

20. Petr Bogdanovich, *Novyi i polnyi pis'movnik* (St. Petersburg, 1791), 13–14.

21. I. V. Vasil'ev, *Femida, ili nachertanie prav, preimushchestv i obiazannostei zhenskogo pola v Rossii* (Moscow, 1827).

soon afterward. The author, Anna Krestinskaia, expressed her gratitude to Vasil'ev for explaining women's political and legal status in Russia; for outlining their obligations as wives, mothers, and citizens; and for acquainting women with their right to engage in property transactions. She observed that until this time legal knowledge had been virtually inaccessible to a female audience, since women's first responsibility was to their families and they could not devote the necessary time to perusing enormous tomes of decrees and regulations. With the publication of Vasil'ev's work, she admonished her readers, "every woman should, without fail, take upon herself the responsibility to learn all the resolutions concerning her."[22]

Despite the dearth of legal advice within the reach of Russian women, it does not follow that they were the helpless dupes of officialdom, as Ilinskii and Ostrovsky assumed. To be sure, it is possible to find examples of noblewomen who were perplexed by the workings of the legal system and preferred to delegate responsibility to male kin. On some occasions husbands or male relations clearly provoked disagreements and composed petitions for their wives. Pelagia Ochkina sued her uncle in 1799 for ownership of a factory he had held in common with his brother; in his petition to the Senate, her uncle claimed that it was in fact the uncle of his niece's husband who had incited her to dispute the terms of their original agreement.[23] When Mikhail Tarkhov submitted a petition in 1741 disputing the right of his sister-in-law and nephew to inherit his brother's estate, he complained that her petition had been signed and the affair pursued by his sister-in-law's brother.[24] According to more than one memoir, noblewomen relied on male protection to bring their suits to a successful conclusion. Andrei Bolotov recounted how neighbors took advantage of his father's death to prosecute his mother for harboring a fugitive serf. The poet Derzhavin wrote that the humiliation of his mother at the hands of dishonest officials inspired him to seek justice for "widows and orphans" when he obtained his post in government.[25] The sister of A. Del'vig enlisted her brother's help when she became involved in an inheritance dispute with her stepchildren after her husband's death.[26] Martha Wilmot related the stories of two young noblewomen ruined in the course of property disputes, but she attributed their misfortune to the corrupt legal system in Russia rather than to the inability of women to grasp the principles of the law.[27]

22. Anna Krestinskaia, "Chuvstva i mysli pri chtenii ruchnoi knizhki o pravakh zhenshchin v Rossii," *Damskii zhurnal*, no. 24 (1827): 234–38.

23. RGIA, f. 1330, op. 2, ed. khr. 6, l. 4.

24. RGADA, f. 1209, op. 79, ed. khr. 68, l. 2.

25. Andrei Bolotov, *Zhizn' i prikliucheniia Andreia Bolotova. Tom I, 1738–1759* (Moscow, 1931), 150–55 [republished by Oriental Research Partners (Cambridge, 1973)]; Garil Romanovich Derzhavin, *Sochineniia Derzhavina* (St. Petersburg, 1871), 6: 404–5.

26. A. M. Del'vig, *Polveka russkoi zhizni. Vospominaniia A. I. Del'viga, 1820–1870* (Moscow, 1930), 1: 353–55, 375–79.

27. Bradford (1935), 290, 308–9.

These tales of vulnerable female supplicants are matched, however, by examples of noblewomen braving the legal labyrinth without their menfolk. In 1779, the widow Avdotia Barykova warned Il'ia Chulkov that she was prepared to take their disagreement over the terms of a land sale to the local oral court (*slovesnyi sud*).[28] Catherine and Martha Wilmot were astonished by the acumen of Princess Dashkova in settling her daughter's myriad suits; they also expressed surprise at Russian noblewomen's familiarity and interest in legal matters as they listened to their acquaintances "talking of Mme Such a one's affaires at the Senate being in good or bad train."[29] Alexandra Smirnova recalled that following her father's death in 1814, "mother was occupied with affairs on the estate and with lawsuits. The word lawsuit even today rings in my ears, as it was so often repeated in my presence."[30] Aside from overseeing their own affairs, women also took on responsibility for legal matters when they received a power of attorney over the estates of their children or husbands. Alexander Panin was hardly unique in entrusting his mother with continuing or initiating any lawsuits concerning his estate when he went abroad in 1841.[31]

Of necessity, Dashkova, Panina, and the mother of Smirnova must have gleaned some working knowledge of the law, if not to be swindled by self-seeking bureaucrats. Some women learned the essentials of jurisprudence through extensive reading. Describing the education of his sister in the 1730s, the memoirist Danilov wrote that she read many works about religion and history, and as a result she knew a great deal about the law (*znala mnogoe kasaiushcheesia do zakona*).[32] In *The Idiot*, Dostoevsky also attributed knowledge of legal matters to his tormented heroine, Natasia Filippovna. Women such as Princess Dashkova were certainly exceptional by virtue of their status and education; nonetheless, it is highly probable that more humble noblewomen—such as Ilinskii's Vitovtova—understood the basic rules governing the law of property and were perfectly capable of asserting their rights when they were threatened with dispossession.

Illiteracy comprised one conspicuous constraint for women who wished to conduct business or legal matters on their own behalf. The illiteracy—not to mention ignorance—of eighteenth-century noblewomen remains an article of faith among historians of Russia.[33] While noblemen acquired at

28. *Pamiatniki Moskovskoi delovoi pis'mennosti XVIII veka* (Moscow, 1981), 20.
29. Bradford (1935), 271–72.
30. Alexandra Osipovna Smirnova, "Zapiski," *Russkii arkhiv* 5, no. 2 (1895): 25.
31. RGADA, f. 1274 (Paniny-Bludovy), op. 1, ed. khr. 3240, ll. 1–2.
32. Danilov (1883), 13. In the mid-nineteenth century, E. A. Frederiks (née Saburova) included legal history among the subjects she studied. See her notebooks in RGIA, f. 1044, op. 1, ed. khr. 40.
33. N. D. Chechulin, *Russkoe provintsial'noe obshchestvo vo vtoroi polovine XVIII veka* (St. Petersburg, 1889), 37; Ilinskii (1909), 13; Levshin (1887), 158–59; Shashkov (1879), 317. No systematic research on women's literacy in the eighteenth century exists for Russia. Boris Mironov's work addresses this question only for the mid-nineteenth century. See Mironov, *Istoriia v tsifrakh: Matematika v istoricheskikh issledovaniiakh* (Leningrad, 1991), 73, 85–86.

TABLE 7.1 Literacy Rates (in Percentages) among Noble Women and Men, 1750–1860*

	Vladimir		Kashin		Tambov		Moscow		All Regions	
	W	M	W	M	W	M	W	M	W	M
1750–55	26	100	20	100	4	77	50	94	41	92
	(19)	(10)	(25)	(4)	(28)	(26)	(228)	(192)	(300)	(232)
1775–80	72	88	40	100	45	88	81	98	67	97
	(25)	(16)	(62)	(15)	(76)	(50)	(240)	(302)	(403)	(383)
1805–10	88	97	88	93	100	100	97	100	92	98
	(69)	(38)	(26)	(14)	(5)	(3)	(73)	(44)	(172)	(99)
1855–60	100	100	—	—	—	—	—	—	100	100
	(55)	(22)							(55)	(22)
All periods	83	97	47	97	37	85	70	89	65	96
1715–1860	(167)	(86)	(113)	(33)	(109)	(79)	(541)	(538)	(930)	(736)

* W = women, M = men. The number of women or men present at estate sales is in parentheses.
Source: See appendix 1.

least the rudiments of literacy in government service, women relied exclusively on instruction received at home from indifferent tutors and governesses.[34] The extremely low literacy rates of women in the provinces (4 to 26 percent) in the mid-eighteenth century therefore come as no surprise[35] (Table 7.1). The revelation that 50 percent of noblewomen in Moscow who participated in sales of property could at least witness deeds and sign their names is, however, more encouraging. Clearly, opportunities for instruction were more prevalent in the capital, and, among the higher strata of the nobility, women's education had assumed increasing importance. The significance of female education among wealthy nobles is further borne out by the correspondence of the daughters of noblemen. Responding in 1759 to her father's reproaches about her failure to write to him in French, ten-year-old Elizaveta Streshneva asked him to pay less attention to her mistakes.[36]

34. On the history of women's education in Russia, see E. O. Likhacheva, *Materialy dlia istorii zhenskogo obrazovaniia v Rossii*, 2 vols. (St. Petersburg, 1899–1901). While members of the nobility in Ukraine wrote of the need for schools for women in their petitions to the Legislative Commission in 1767, provincial nobles in Russia expressed little interest in female education. See V. Bochkarev, "Kul'turnye zaprosy russkogo obshchestva nachala tsarstvovaniia Ekateriny II po materialam zakonodatel'noi komissii 1767 goda," *Russkaia starina* 162 (May 1915): 319–20, 322.

35. Here, literacy is defined simply as the ability to sign a document with one's full name. In a comparative perspective, Russian noblewomen lagged behind their European counterparts. In a survey of female deponents from 1640 to 1750 in northern England, for example, only 19% of gentry women were unable to sign their names when they appeared in court. See R. A. Houston, "The Development of Literacy: Northern England, 1640–1750," *Economic History Review*, 2d ser., 35, no. 2 (May 1982): 207–8.

36. RGIA, f. 923 (Glebovy), op. 1, ed. khr. 43, l. 1. See also a letter from Prince Nikolai Shcherbatov to his wife in 1757, in which he requests that his daughter write more often to him and that she pay attention to her spelling, "since in her last letter, there was not a single line without misspellings." RGADA, f. 1395, op. 1, ed. khr. 206, l. 4.

Ekaterina Tolstaia wrote to a friend in far more grammatical French in 1799, informing her that she had begun reading a history of Russia with her mother: she was particularly enthralled by the story of Princess Olga, who brought Christianity to Russia yet also was capable of wreaking a most unchristian revenge on her enemies.[37] Russian noblewomen enjoyed few opportunities for formal education; nonetheless, female correspondence from the mid-eighteenth century reveals that a growing number of noble families provided at least basic instruction in literacy and languages for their daughters.

Both in Moscow and in the provinces, women's literacy rates rose dramatically in the second half of the eighteenth century. Approximately 92 percent of female witnesses to deeds could sign their own names by the beginning of the nineteenth century. The illiterate noblewoman was an anomaly by the mid-nineteenth century. Burgeoning literacy rates shed new light on the feasibility of feminine involvement in legal affairs: women gained a clear advantage if they could at least read and witness their own documents. Thus, Praskovia Rtishcheva submitted a petition to the Land College in 1758, disputing the claim of her brother, Ivan Somov, that she had sold him her estate in Kozlov. Rtishcheva informed the college that she had not sold the estate to her brother, and pointed out that the deed had been signed, allegedly at her request, by a Major Shcherbachev. She had never asked Shcherbachev to witness a sale for her, Rtishcheva continued, nor would she have needed to, since if she sold the estate she would have signed the document herself (*ezheli by ona onoe . . . imenie prodala ona by sama k toi kupchei ruku prilozhila*). Whether on the basis of this reasoning or some other evidence, the Land College ruled in Rtishcheva's favor.[38]

Evidence in court documents also points indisputably to the active participation of women in composing their petitions to the courts. Take, for example, the case of Alexandra Voeikova, who incurred the wrath of the Senate in 1789 when she attempted to put a stop to her husband's adultery and extravagance. Writing from St. Petersburg, her representative in the capital instructed her to hurry and compose her petition without delay, but admonished her not to write anything superfluous.[39] Voeikova failed to heed his advice. Her petitions to the Senate were lengthy and convoluted but the defense she offered was indisputably her own. Happily, by the nineteenth century, petitioners took greater care to record who had composed and copied the documents they presented to the authorities. When Senator Kurut came to Tambov province in 1843 to inspect the local courts, Varvara Pushchina indicated that she had composed and copied out the petition in

37. RGIA, f. 946 (Liubomirskie), op. 1, ed. khr. 15, l. 30.
38. RGADA, f. 1209, op. 79, ed. khr. 241, ll. 5–6.
39. RGADA, f. 7 (Razriad VII), op. 2, ed. khr. 2749, l. 32.

which she complained of the illegal activities of the local marshal of the nobility. Lidiia Zhukova also wrote her own appeal later the same year.[40] Princess Elizaveta Golitsyna attempted to settle an inheritance dispute between her children by turning to the Senate in 1850. A clerk had recopied her petition, but Golitsyna herself had composed the document.[41] Clerks who wrote petitions for illiterate women noted that the document had been composed "from the words of petitioner."[42]

Historians' contention that women were helpless when confronted with legal matters stands in sharp contrast to the experience of female proprietors in Imperial Russia, many of whom were perfectly capable of shepherding lawsuits through the courts. From the opening decades of the eighteenth century noblewomen proved as litigious as their male counterparts and appeared before the authorities on a regular basis to sue for a larger part of the family fortune, for repayment of debt, and to resist encroachments from neighboring landowners. Male assumption of female impotence, read against the backdrop of women's participation in property disputes, reveals more about changing gender conventions in Russia than it does about women's experience of the legal system. Vulnerable they may have been, when faced with the corruption and inefficiency for which Russia's legal institutions were legendary. Still, noblewomen as a group made ample use of the courts for their own ends and stood as fair a chance as their male counterparts of obtaining a satisfactory verdict.

Women and Patronage Networks

For all that proceedings in the Senate evinced real concern for decisions based on the consistent application of statutory law, the role of patronage networks in the outcome of disputes was considerable in the pre-reform era. Legal records provide myriad examples of noblewomen as successful litigants: in conflicts over inheritance, noblewomen suffered no particular liabilities by virtue of their sex and benefited from the Senate's determination to uphold their property rights. Correspondence and the complaints of petitioners reveal, however, that the outcome of civil cases could hinge on the influence of a powerful figure in government. The securing of patronage was instrumental both in gaining access to the courts and to the outcome

40. RGIA, f. 1383 (Reviziia senatora Kuruty I. E. Tambovskoi gubernii), op. 1, ed. khr. 175, ll. 37–8; f. 1383, op. 1, ed. khr. 195, l. 2.

41. RGIA, f. 1330, op. 6, ed. khr. 406, l. 6. For other examples of women composing their own petitions, see RGIA, f. 1286, op. 8 (1843), ed. khr. 509, ll. 2–3; f. 1330, op. 6, ed. khr. 1891, l. 6 (1862).

42. RGIA, f. 796, op. 50 (1769), ed. khr. 124, l. 4; TsGIAM, f. 394, op. 1, ed. khr. 131, l. 3 (1819).

of a suit. Banned from civil service, noblewomen enjoyed few opportunities to influence the Senate or other judicial institutions on behalf of others. They proved successful, however, in securing protection for themselves when they engaged in litigation on their own behalf.

While few traces survive of the role of patronage in noblewomen's legal suits, impressionistic sources demonstrate that noblewomen relied on social superiors to obtain access or to influence the courts in their favor. On occasion, women's petitions reveal that they were aware of how personal contacts could improve the outcome of their disputes or bias authorities against them. When Agafiia Shechkova petitioned to repurchase an estate sold by her sister in 1740, she asked that the case be moved to a neighboring court, since she was already involved in a conflict with the governor of Rylskii province—and hence could not receive a fair hearing there.[43] In her petitions to the Senate against her husband, Alexandra Voeikova complained repeatedly that his powerful friends controlled the outcome of her suit and would decide the case in his favor.[44] Personal contacts also could work in women's favor, however: in his sweeping indictment of the Russian court in the eighteenth century, Prince Shcherbatov accused several noblewomen of using their connections to win property disputes, and further implicated Catherine II in arbitrarily deciding cases to the advantage of her favorites.[45] M. Adam recalled that provincial authorities defied the law by permitting her aunt to live apart from her abusive husband and ignoring the latter's petitions.[46]

Nobles of both sexes appealed to family members and acquaintances who enjoyed influence with the Senate to intercede for them and guarantee that rivals did not obstruct the course of justice. Praskovia Zheltukina turned to a member of the Senate to act as her "defender and mediator" in an inheritance suit in 1798; she assured him that regardless of the outcome, she trusted him to act in accordance with "the voice of truth and justice."[47] In 1831 Princess Alexandra Volkonskaia appealed to Senator Sumarokov to oversee the interests of her daughter, who had administered the estate of Princess Kriukova and had been unfairly charged by the latter of withholding income from her villages.[48] And while noble petitioners generally sought male defenders in their legal battles, this was not always the case: Elizaveta Iankova spoke warmly in her memoir of Ekaterina Gerard, who traveled on

43. RGADA, f. 1209, op. 79, ed. khr. 65, l. 17. "... bila chelom ... ob otkaze poslat' ukaz v Sevskuiu Pravinstyalnuiu kantseliariiu ponezhe imeetsa y neiu prikaznaia ssora s Rylskim voevodoiu."
44. RGADA, f. 7, op. 2, ed. khr. 2749.
45. Shcherbatov (1969), 219, 247.
46. M. Adam, "Iz semeinoi khroniki," *Istoricheskii vestnik* 94, no. 12 (1903): 826.
47. RGIA, f. 878 (Tatishchevy), op. 2, ed. khr. 302, l. 8.
48. RGIA, f. 914 (Volkonskie), op. 1, ed. khr. 10, l. 1.

many occasions to St. Petersburg and used her influential connections on behalf of friends.[49] If the role of patronage in female litigation cannot be quantified, such anecdotes demonstrate that noblewomen, like their male counterparts, made ample use of patronage ties to facilitate the course of justice.

Morality and the Limits of Proprietary Power

Throughout the Imperial era, noblewomen engaged in the full spectrum of conflicts over property, involving kin, neighbors, tradesmen, and state peasants. The role of gender in shaping the outcome of legal conflicts depended in large part on the configuration of litigants. Thus, while the sex of litigants was of little significance in suits with neighbors or over inheritance, in suits between spouses, gender moved to the forefront. The law of property took female vulnerability into account only when women transacted business with their husbands, and even this limited protection was withdrawn early in the nineteenth century. Although patronage also played an important role in civil suits, status and wealth, rather than sex, determined the successful manipulation of personal influence.

The tenuous nature of noble status, as well as noble property rights, in Imperial Russia has become a truism among historians. Russian nobles not only confirmed their position by "acting" noble; they also risked forfeiting their status, with its attendant privileges, through unbecoming behavior.[50] Chief among those privileges was the exclusive right to control settled estates. Catherine II's Charter to the Nobility guaranteed noble proprietors protection from the arbitrary confiscation of property; at the same time, the charter included a "broad legal basis for loss of nobility."[51] Confiscation of property was rare, however; it was reserved in large part for nobles guilty of treason to the sovereign, however loosely defined.[52] Much more common than confiscation was the sequestration of noble estates, which may not have

49. Blagovo (1989), 316.

50. See in particular, Iurii M. Lotman, "The Poetics of Everyday Behavior in Eighteenth-Century Russian Culture," in *The Semiotics of Russian Cultural History* ed. Alexander D. Nakhimovsky and Alice Stone Nakhimovsky (Ithaca, 1985): 67–94; Priscilla R. Roosevelt, "Emerald Thrones and Living Statues: Theater and Theatricality on the Russian Estate," *Russian Review* 50, no. 1 (January 1991): 18; Tovrov (1987), 3.

51. Meehan-Waters (1983), 300.

52. As we have seen (chapter 2), nobles who went abroad without the sovereign's permission risked confiscation of their property. An Englishwoman who lived in Russia in the mid-nineteenth century noted, "Should a Russian contrive to leave his country by stratagem, he is forbidden to return and all his property is confiscated." See *At Home with the Gentry: A Victorian English Lady's Diary of Russian Country Life*, attrib. to Amelia Lyons; ed. John McNair (Nottingham, 1998), 22.

deprived proprietors of ownership or the income of their holdings, but restricted their administration and use of their estates in a variety of ways.

In the opening decades of the nineteenth century, the significance of "acting" noble took on new meaning in the context of estate administration. The power of noble proprietors over their serf dependents had been, in practice, almost absolute until the end of the eighteenth century. Under Catherine II's successors, however, the central government took greater care to regulate the relationship between master and serf, and instructed local authorities to watch out for abusive proprietors. As noble assemblies in the provinces began to monitor the administration of serfs and estates, proprietors suspected of abuse, or of squandering their fortunes, were called on to account for management of their holdings. If they were found guilty, their estates were taken under guardianship in short order. The sequestration of estates thus illustrates the limitations of noble proprietary rights, which culminated in the abolition of serfdom, and provides a detailed record of the interaction between noble women and men, and legal authorities.

These cases also draw attention to the changing relationship between gender, behavior, and the control of property. Traditionally, women had been more likely than men to sacrifice control of their fortunes when they were convicted of adultery or immorality.[53] With the renewed accent on conservative values during the reign of Nicholas I, Russian noblemen found themselves equally at risk of losing control of their estates when they were charged with immorality, serf abuse, or poor estate management. Although female proprietors were also the target of such accusations, this trend often worked to the advantage of women, who could now take steps both to defend their own fortunes from wastrel husbands and to prevent their husbands from squandering the inheritance destined for their children. Whereas noblewomen who tried to restrain their husbands' extravagance in the eighteenth century were severely reprimanded, exasperated wives in the last decades of serfdom found greater satisfaction at the hands of the courts.

The institutional framework necessary for monitoring the conduct of provincial nobles took shape in 1775 and 1785, during Catherine II's reform of provincial administration. With the establishment of noble assemblies on the district and provincial level, presided over by a marshal of the nobility, the provincial elite enjoyed its first experience of corporate organizations and limited self-government. Among the institutions that Catherine created was the *Dvorianskaia opeka*, or the Noble Board of Guardians. The roots of the *opeka* went back as far as 1755, when Empress Elizabeth established a temporary wardship in the Provincial Surveying Office (*Gubernskaia Mezhevaia Kantseliariia*) for widows, orphans, and other powerless persons

53. See chapter 3.

(*bezglasnye litsa*) during the implementation of land surveys.[54] Representatives to the Legislative Commission requested the creation of such an institution on a permanent basis in 1767. The Noble Board of Guardians was formally established in 1775 and placed under the auspices of the newly created higher land court (*verkhnyi zemskii sud*) or the district court (*uezdnyi sud*). Officials on the board were entrusted with regulating the trusteeships of estates belonging to widows and orphans, as well as with overseeing the education of the latter.[55]

According to contemporaries, the quality of administration in the provinces left much to be desired, and in this respect the *Dvorianskaia opeka* was no exception. During his inspection of Kursk province in 1805, Prince Aleksei Kurakin wrote that the local trusteeships failed to meet their obligations to the nobility: although they managed to appoint guardians to the estates of orphans, they rarely supervised their actual administration of estates.[56] Careless bookkeeping was also rampant in district offices. The marshal of the nobility in Shchigrovskii district, Kursk province, reported in 1826 that the local *opeka* had no records concerning the income and expenditure of estates held in trusteeship for the current year. Moreover, records from previous years were still unbound and many were illegible.[57] The shortcomings of the *Dvorianskaia opeka* should come as no surprise, however, in light of the limited number of officials who staffed the institution. The marshal of the nobility served as head of the *opeka*, and he was assisted by two or three members of the district or higher land court. Several clerks completed the staff of the body.[58]

At the time of its creation, the work of the Noble Board of Guardians was confined initially to administering the property of orphans, the chronically insolvent, and on occasion, the feeble-minded. By the second quarter of the nineteenth century, however, noble assemblies began to sequester estates for a wider range of offenses, effectively transforming the *Dvorianskaia opeka* into an institution of moral regulation. Authorities responded with alacrity to the complaints of family members and neighbors about the activities of noble proprietors, and sometimes on the slenderest of pretenses sought to wrest control of settled estates from nobles suspected of conduct unbefitting their station. The power of the noble assemblies was far from unlimited: their decision to place estates in trusteeship required the approval of the minister of internal affairs, who then passed on his decision for confirmation in the

54. *PSZ*, 14: 10.410 (20.05.1755).

55. S. A. Korf, *Dvorianstvo i ego soslovnoe upravlenie za stoletie 1762–1855 godov* (St. Petersburg, 1906), 105–8; Madariaga (1981), 286.

56. I. Blinov, "Senatorskie revizii," *Zhurnal Ministerstva Iustitsii* 19, no. 2 (February 1913): 286.

57. RGIA, f. 1555, op. 1, ed. khr. 133, l. 4.

58. A list of the members may be found in RGIA, f. 1379, op. 1, ed. khr. 57b, l. 54 (1839) and in f. 1558, op. 1, ed. khr. 34, ll. 21, 60 (1828). See also Korf (1906), 105–8.

Senate. Even these bureaucratic limitations, however, left the marshal of the nobility considerable latitude to interfere in the affairs of the local nobility.

An examination of cases concerning estates taken into guardianship provides a glimpse into encounters between noble proprietors and local authorities. It also offers a novel perspective on the significance of gender in the legal process. From the beginning of the eighteenth century, gender did not comprise a serious obstacle for women who engaged in litigation with neighbors or kin. Questions of morality played no role in property conflicts—with the notable exception of battles between husbands and wives—and legal authorities proved willing to uphold the rights of female litigants. Disputes heard by the noble assemblies, however, focused overwhelmingly on the character of the accused proprietor and his or her ability to administer family property competently. As a result, debates over the sequestration of estates reveal far more about contemporary expectations of male and female behavior, and the meaning of nobility, than do disputes over boundaries or inheritance.

As institutions of local government became active in the provinces in the opening decades of the nineteenth century, authorities began to monitor the conduct of the nobility more closely and to define the obligations of estate administrators more explicitly. Their jurisdiction was by no means limited to conflicts over property: the marshal of the nobility was often called on to intervene in family quarrels, to reconcile husbands and wives, and to confront parents suspected of neglecting their children.[59] While keeping order among the provincial nobility, the district marshal was also charged with scrutinizing the morals of local proprietors and identifying those failings that might interfere with their ability to manage property. This new preoccupation manifested itself in unexpected ways. In 1856, for example, an official in the Ministry of Internal Affairs received a request from Countess Anna Tolstaia for permission to leave her husband a life interest in her estate. Bequests to spouses were common practice by the mid-nineteenth century; nonetheless, the official required the district marshal to investigate the "moral qualities and way of life" of the petitioner and her husband before permission was granted.[60]

It was the administration of property during a proprietor's lifetime, however, that proved the dominant concern of the state. Several categories of misbehavior on the part of the nobility drew the attention of local authorities and called into question the administrative talents of the suspect. One of these was immoral conduct, which included offenses ranging from drunk-

59. TsGIAM, f. 4 (Kantseliariia moskovskogo dvorianskogo deputatskogo sobraniia), op. 2, ed. khr. 30 (1829); f. 4, op. 2, ed. khr. 41; f. 4, op. 2, ed. khr. 42; f. 4, op. 2, ed. khr. 49 (1832); f. 380 (Kantseliariia moskovskogo gubernskogo predvoditelia dvorianstva), ed. khr. 11-a (1849); f. 380, ed. khr. 84 (1871). See also Cavender (1997), 302–12.

60. TsGIAM, f. 380, op. 2, ed. khr. 53, l. 1.

enness and card playing to the rape of serf women. Another was the mistreatment of serfs, which was defined not only by physical abuse but also by the inability to provide peasants with adequate land for their support. Insolvency and careless estate management proved the downfall of estate owners of both sexes: their holdings were turned over to guardians who, ironically, were often no more capable of running a productive estate than the original owners. Regardless of the offense, complaints originated overwhelmingly with the kin of the offender, who witnessed his or her misdeeds with increasing disquiet and finally took steps to halt the dissipation of family wealth. On other occasions, neighbors expressed distress at unconventional or flagrantly dissolute behavior of other proprietors. In both cases, proprietors on nearby estates were questioned about the justice of the complaints and their testimony often proved decisive.

The attention of the state to the rational administration of noble estates and the preservation of family fortunes had ample precedent. Peter the Great imposed the Law of Single Inheritance on the nobility with the goal of preventing the fragmentation of family holdings. Later in the eighteenth century, Anna Ivanovna eased military service requirements so that one son in every family might take on the responsibility of managing the estate. Following the emancipation of the nobility from obligatory service to the state, noble proprietors displayed considerable interest in increasing the profitability of their estates—a pastime that the state strongly supported.[61] Eighteenth-century monarchs appointed guardians to the estates of the mentally incompetent and to those of proprietors who allowed themselves to be swindled.[62] Although contemporaries singled out serfdom as one of the root causes of national poverty in the decades preceding Emancipation, in the eyes of many, noble extravagance and neglect of the affairs on their estates shared the onus of blame. The association between morality and prudent estate management, however, marked a new era in official concern for the consequences of noble extravagance and incompetent estate administration.

In contrast to previous campaigns to encourage productivity on noble estates, in the nineteenth century allegations of poor administration were closely linked with criticism of the character of the accused. Careless management alone rarely prompted the interference of local officials in the property affairs of the nobility. Discussions of proprietors suspected of

---

61. For an in-depth study of the Free Economic Society and the introduction of rational agriculture in Russia, see Confino (1963). For a more recent discussion of scientific agriculture in Tver' province, see Cavender (1997), 198–270.

62. Catherine II appointed two guardians to the estate of the widow Maria Pavlovna Naryshkina after she was swindled out of her estate of more than one thousand serfs. In the suit between Naryshkina and Privy Councillor Talyzin, Catherine decided in Naryshkina's favor but forbade her to sell or mortgage any part of her estate without the guardians' permission. See *PSZ*, 22: 16.000 (23.05.1784) and *Arkhiv kniazia Vorontsova* (1888), 34: 437–42.

incompetent administration of their estates and human property were couched in language that underscored the obligation of men and women of noble birth to distinguish themselves from other social groups by conduct befitting their station. In keeping with their general concern to elevate the level of culture among their fellow nobles, local officials focused as much on the propensity of many proprietors to drink to excess and carouse with their peasants as they did on the actual administration of their estates. For their part, accusers quickly adopted official rhetoric and were rarely satisfied with allegations of poor estate management or even serf abuse. They buttressed their claims by casting aspersions on the personal life of the accused, although misdeeds such as habitual drunkenness did not provide legal grounds for stripping proprietors of their property rights. While authorities strove to consider only admissible evidence, their decisions were influenced by allegations of debauchery, especially when the fortunes and well-being of children were at stake.

The portrait of the provincial nobility that emerges from cases heard by the local assemblies is, to say the least, an unflattering one. In a town near Moscow, neighbors complained to the marshal of the nobility of the widow of a titular councillor, Anna Ruzskaia, who wandered the streets in a drunken state, hailing passersby with rude words and gestures. Her behavior had become so unbearable, the governor stated in his report, that people made every effort to avoid passing in front of her house.[63] Natalia Brattsova and her children lived in a peasant hut after her husband threw her out of their house and refused to provide them with food. The marshal of Volokolamskii district recounted in 1801 how he went to reprimand Ensign Brattsov, and found him drunk and living in a house full of broken furniture and glass shattered from the windows.[64] When the wife of Captain Bazhin complained to the marshal of Moscow district of her husband's wild behavior, the marshal informed the governor of the province that both the captain and his wife drank to excess and fought so violently that the local police refused to answer for their lives.[65]

Although some cases originated with the complaints of neighbors, the large majority of petitions reviewed by the district marshals derived from conflict within families—particularly between husbands and wives—over rational property management. Provincial authorities listened with considerable sympathy to the complaints of wives whose husbands frittered away their estates. Indeed, husbands and wives attempted to depose each other from estate management with surprising frequency in the first half of the

63. TsGIAM, f. 394 (Kantseliariia ruzskogo uezdnogo predvoditelia dvorianstva, 1790–1897), op. 1, ed. khr. 271, l. 1. Report from the Moscow civil governor to the Ruzskii district marshall of the nobility, 1841.

64. TsGIAM, f. 4, op. 2, ed. khr. 3, ll. 1–2.

65. TsGIAM, f. 4, op. 2, ed. khr. 241, ll. 1–3 (1829).

nineteenth century. In other cases, children and other potential heirs tried to put a stop to unseemly behavior on the part of their elders as they frittered away their assets. A close reading of the evidence presented to the minister of internal affairs and the Senate, as well as the deliberations of the latter, reveals that women were by no means disadvantaged by virtue of their sex when male kin leveled charges of mismanagement against them. Proprietors of both sexes were held to the same standard when the financial welfare of their families and proper care of their serfs and estates were in question. Although the local marshal was often inclined to act on the basis of hearsay when his constituents were suspected of wrongdoing, his superiors in St. Petersburg insisted on careful and unbiased investigation of the charges, frequently requesting additional investigations and further testimony before making a final decision to deprive the accused of their property rights.

Thanks to the efforts of central authorities, women proved no more vulnerable than men when their conduct came under scrutiny. Thus, Lieutenant Feoktistov was disappointed in his effort to persuade the authorities to take his wife's estate into trusteeship in 1841. He maintained that his wife had proved herself irresponsible when she granted a power of attorney to Collegiate Assessor Batashev with what he alleged were unlimited rights over her property. When the marshal of the nobility in Tula went to confront Varvara Feoktistova with her husband's complaints, she responded that her husband was not in his right mind and that he had been in the hospital after inflicting wounds on himself several months before. The marshal nonetheless recommended that the noble assembly review the case; he stated in his report that although he had no positive evidence that cast suspicion on Varvara Feoktistova's way of life, he had heard rumors that substantiated her husband's charges. For their part, however, the members of the Senate found insufficient evidence that Feoktistova was either squandering money or leading an immoral life, and they instructed the civil and military governors to carry out a more detailed investigation before taking any action against her.[66] On other occasions, local officials dismissed men's allegations against their wives before they could ever reach the Senate. When Ensign Kostomarov appealed to the military governor of Moscow province to sequester his wife's estate, which he alleged she was running into the ground, the marshal of the nobility informed the governor that he had no reason to believe Kostomarov's charges and that it was far more likely that the latter was abusing his wife.[67]

66. RGIA, f. 1286 (Departament politsii ispolnitel'noi), op. 8 (1842), ed. khr. 284, ll. 7–13, 29–30.

67. TsGIAM, f. 380, op. 2, ed. khr. 26, ll. 2, 16 (1851). For similar cases, see RGIA, f. 1286, op. 6 (1836), ed. khr. 286; TsGIAM, f. 380, op. 2, ed. khr. 2 (1847); f. 380, op. 2, ed. khr. 26 (1851); f. 380, op. 4, ed. khr. 54 (1850); RGIA, f. 1286, op. 15 (1854), ed. khr. 1002, ll. 16–17.

Even when women failed to adhere to accepted gender conventions, their property remained in their hands as long as they were not guilty of blatant mistreatment of serfs or burdening their estates with debt. The daughter and son-in-law of one Ozerova of Tver' province complained that the latter drank in the company of her peasants, had manumitted several of her serfs, and mortgaged part of her estate. Ozerova's daughter feared that she and her two young children would be deprived of their inheritance if her mother continued to indulge in such behavior. Members of the noble assembly decided it was imperative that Ozerova's estate be taken into trusteeship— an opinion they underscored by pointing out that Ozerova had appeared before them incoherent and apparently in a drunken state. The Senate, however, rejected their verdict: although there was little doubt that Ozerova was inclined to drink, they observed, there was no evidence whatsoever that she mistreated her serfs or that her estate was poorly administered. On the contrary, she was paying her debts on a regular basis and she had in no way trespassed the law by manumitting her serfs. In short, the Senate concluded, taking Ozerova's estate into trusteeship "with the goal of preserving her estate in her clan, and in order not to weaken noble estates, would not be in keeping with the law."[68] The senators may have witnessed the dissipation of noble fortunes with disapproval; nonetheless, they perceived their first responsibility as preventing abuse of the law, rather than checking the baser impulses of individual proprietors.

Noblewomen perpetrated a variety of misdeeds that the local assemblies found abhorrent, and tension often erupted between provincial officials and central authorities over the proper response to the betrayal of their sex and their station in life. Indeed, exchanges between members of the Senate, the minister of internal affairs, and district marshals highlight the divergence in their interests: while authorities in St. Petersburg aspired to promote a rational legal culture in the provinces, many officials on the local level were more concerned with preventing the debasement of the nobility.[69] The nobles of Orenburg province were appalled by the marriage of widowed noblewoman Baryshnikova to a peasant in 1843, and promptly conceded to the demand of her former brother-in-law to take her estate into custody, on the grounds that her second marriage proved her incapable of managing her estate for the benefit of her two underaged children. In their review of the case, Senator Peshchurov and the minister of internal affairs agreed that although marriage between a noblewoman and peasant was unseemly, no law forbade such unions, nor could women be deprived of their property

68. RGIA, f. 1286, op. 6 (1835), ed. khr. 374, ll. 3–9.

69. For an account of the conflict between central and local authorities over the importance of *zakonnost'* (the rule of law), see Paul W. Werth, "Baptism, Authority, and the Problem of *Zakonnost'* in Orenburg Diocese: The Induction of Over 800 'Pagans' into the Christian Faith," *Slavic Review* 56, no. 3 (Fall 1997): 472, 480.

rights on these grounds. Unless the noble assembly could produce real evidence of extravagance and poor administration on the part of Baryshnikova, they had no right to forbid her to exercise her property rights or to take her estate into guardianship.[70]

If local authorities appeared too inclined to accept gossip as grounds for restricting a proprietor's property rights in the case of women, the same held true for men. In 1841 Lieutenant Colonel Bel'skii was charged with raping a ten-year-old peasant girl on his estate. Although the Smolenskii Criminal Court (*ugolovnaia palata*) acquitted Bel'skii on the grounds of insufficient evidence, members of the court nonetheless raised the question of whether Bel'skii should be permitted to manage his estate, since the investigation had brought to light incidents that cast doubt on his character. Acting, perhaps, on the principle that where there is smoke, there is fire, the civil governor of Smolensk province suggested in turn that Bel'skii's estate should be taken into trusteeship for three years: the suspicion of his crime still remained and he should be reminded that such misdeeds do not go unpunished. The minister of internal affairs and the Senate objected that an estate could not be placed under guardianship for a predetermined period of time; both, however, seemed inclined to agree that Bel'skii had forfeited his rights to administer his estate by the very suspicion that he had raped a young girl.[71]

Although these cases indicate too much eagerness on the part of provincial authorities to intervene in the affairs of the local nobility, other provincial governors and marshals of the nobility carried out their investigations with care and acted primarily with the interests of the dependents of proprietors in mind. One of the most common charges that they confronted was the complaint on the part of women that their husbands were running their estates into the ground. Petitions from long-suffering wives not only share common grievances against their husbands—extravagance, physical abuse and mistreatment of serfs, excessive drinking—but also display similar strategies for presenting their case. These women emphasized that they came forward only after years of tolerating their husbands' behavior; they also routinely stated that the behavior of their spouses endangered the financial welfare, if not the survival, of their children. Ekaterina Koltovskaia wrote in her petition to the military governor of Moscow province that although it went against her nature "and the rules for women" to bring her husband's misdeeds to the attention of the authorities, concern for her children forced her to act.[72] Both husbands and wives were acutely aware of their audience and used the rhetoric of family interest to great effect. Petitioners invariably

70. RGIA, f. 1286, op. 8 (1843), ed. khr. 453, ll. 2–6.
71. RGIA, f. 1286, op. 8 (1841), ed. khr. 232, ll. 4–8.
72. TsGIAM, f. 380, op. 2, ed. khr. 11, l. 1 (1849).

denied any self-interest when they lodged complaints against their spouses. In a typical example, Collegiate Assessor Karinskii claimed in 1846 that his wife's extravagance would soon leave the family without so much as a crust of bread. Appealing to the marshal of the nobility, Karinskii insisted that he had taken action against his wife only out of concern for his four daughters and that he had no interest in administering his wife's property himself.[73] For their part, district marshals and other authorities attempted to reconcile quarrelling couples and encourage errant proprietors to mend their ways before resorting to legal action.

The willingness of authorities to listen to women's charges against their husbands and to take action against them presents a real contrast to the response of officials, both civil and ecclesiastical, in the eighteenth century. Officials no longer automatically suspected women of a perverse desire to undermine their husbands' authority, but took pains to establish the legitimacy of their charges. In Kursk province, the wife of Andrei Besedin turned to the Dmitrievskii district marshal when she could no longer tolerate her husband's drunkenness and cruel treatment of his peasants. The marshal reported that he went twice to visit Besedin and urged him to put a stop to his excesses. When this failed, he brought the matter to the Kursk Noble Assembly, which voted in favor of taking Besedin's estate into trusteeship. Many of Besedin's neighbors, as well as his relatives, testified that Besedin was a competent manager and not guilty of unseemly behavior; moreover, they pointed out that the accusations against him had originated with his wife, who, eager to take over the estate herself, resorted to slandering her husband before the government. When the Senate finally ruled on the case in 1846, however, they agreed with the original recommendation of the assembly in Kursk: twelve neighboring land owners testified against Besedin, and his own mother had chosen to bequeath her estate to Besedin's wife, rather than see it squandered by her son. The marshal emphasized in his report that his actions had not been prompted by "any desire personally to [create] unpleasantness for Besedin, but by good-will towards his family" and with the goal of uncovering the truth.[74]

Noblewomen made use of the *Dvorianskaia opeka* to prevent the dissipation of their husbands' property. They also placed their own holdings under its protection when they feared their husbands' extravagance. Thus, in 1843 Princess Ekaterina Dolgorukaia petitioned the emperor to place her considerable estate in trusteeship and named her brother as the appropriate

73. TsGIAM, f. 380, op. 2, ed. khr. 7, l. 24 (1848).
74. RGIA, f. 1286, op. 8 (1841), ed. khr. 221, ll. 5–8, 28–30. For other cases in which men's estates were sequestered at the request of their wives, see RGIA, f. 1286, op. 6 (1835), ed. khr. 363; TsGIAM, f. 4, op. 2, ed. khr. 75 (1838); RGIA, f. 1286, op. 8 (1841), ed. khr. 212; f. 1286, op. 8 (1842), ed. khr. 286; f. 1286, op. 8 (1843), ed. khr. 445; f. 1286, op. 12 (1850), ed. khr. 660.

guardian for her property. Her husband, she recounted, was a notorious spendthrift, and since she was currently living abroad, she could not attend to her affairs and prevent him from ruining her estate in her absence. Dolgorukaia's request was quickly granted; after the death of her husband in 1852, she returned to Russia and her estate was subsequently returned to her management.[75] Similarly, according to an inventory of estates under the supervision of the Kirsanovskii Trusteeship in 1814, the estate of Tatiana Arbeneva had been sequestered because of "lack of self-restraint" on the part of her husband, Ensign Arbenev.[76]

Another sign of changing gender conventions in the context of property law was the increased skepticism with which legal authorities greeted male petitioners' tales of their wives' adultery. Whereas eighteenth-century noblemen used charges of marital infidelity against their wives with considerable success, by the nineteenth century authorities were far less likely to take such charges at face value. General Lieutenant Kuprianov made a valiant attempt to wrest his wife's estate of 850 serfs out of her control, accusing her of conducting an affair with a local merchant and lavishing expensive presents on him. Kuprianova's version of the story differed radically from that of her husband. She declined even to acknowledge his allegations of adultery and cited example after example of his inability to manage his financial affairs, adding that she alone was financing their daughter's education. In the end, Kuprianova's defense won the day: only a few months after her estate had been taken into trusteeship, the emperor instructed the minister of internal affairs to release Kuprianova's holdings from the *opeka* and return them to her possession.[77]

On the other hand, flagrantly dissolute behavior prejudiced the authorities against propertied women with young children and considerably weakened their defense. The marshal of Moscow district, Chertkov, admitted that he could find no evidence that the wife of Collegiate Assessor Modzalevskii either abused her peasants or spent excessive sums of money, as her husband maintained. Yet, when he went to confront her with these charges, he found her apartment in complete disorder, with various items and even cash scattered around the room. To make matters worse, Modzalevskaia refused to live with her husband and take care of their son. In her own defense, Modzalevskaia claimed that her husband had abandoned her and then initiated the suit because she refused to transfer her estate to his possession. The minister of internal affairs wrote in his report to the Senate that although the charges of serf abuse could not be proved conclusively,

75. RGIA, f. 1286, op. 8 (1843), ed. khr. 509, ll. 2–3, 26.

76. RGIA, f. 1549 (Reviziia senatora L'vova A. L. Tambovskoi gubernii, 1814–1815 gg.), op. 1, ed. khr. 202, l. 5.

77. RGIA, f. 1286, op. 6 (1836), ed. khr. 286, ll. 1, 26–30. See also RGIA, f. 1537, op. 1, ed. khr. 69, ll. 9–11, 15 (1800).

he nonetheless agreed that Modzalevskaia's unseemly conduct and her disregard for her property, not to mention her father's damning testimony, more than justified taking her estate into trusteeship for the sake of her son.[78]

Proprietors and Serf Abuse

By far the most common motive for relieving proprietors of control of their estates were charges of repeated serf abuse. In the first half of the nineteenth century, local and central authorities developed a veritable obsession with preventing the mistreatment of peasants—and thus minimizing the possibility of peasant revolt. Time and again, officials in St. Petersburg instructed provincial authorities to warn the local nobility that they bore responsibility for their peasant dependents and that they would forfeit control of their estates if they abused their authority. Under the rubric of mistreatment came not only physical abuse and excessive labor requirements but also the failure to provide serfs with adequate land to supply their own needs. As a result, provincial marshals and governors obsessively gathered information about the number of nobles in their jurisdiction who owned fewer than twenty serfs and allotted their peasants less than four and a half desiatins of land, which comprised the bare minimum for subsistence.[79] They also monitored their jurisdictions for other signs of serf abuse. In 1832, the minister of internal affairs instructed the marshal of the nobility for Moscow province to keep a close eye on nobles suspected of mistreating their peasants, and warned of the "murmuring" among serfs when the proper measures were not observed during their resettlement. While the minister downplayed the scale of the problem—he assured the marshal that such incidents were rare and were generally the fault of bailiffs—he nonetheless urged the district marshals to monitor the local nobility more closely. Ten years later, the Ministry of Internal Affairs shed all pretense of believing that the mistreatment of serfs was an uncommon occurrence. This time the minister stated that incidents of cruel handling of peasants were far from rare, and he took the district marshals to task for not putting a stop to mistreatment.[80]

An astonishing number of cases involving abusive proprietors survive, scattered throughout the records of the office of the marshals of the nobility, as well as in collections of the police and the Senate. During the eigh-

---

78. RGIA, f. 1286, op. 8 (1841), ed. khr. 213, ll. 3–9, 26–27, 33–35. Husbands who could prove that their wives had given birth to illegitimate children were also in luck: see RGIA, f. 1286, op. 12 (1850), ed. khr. 755, ll. 10–16.

79. TsGIAM, f. 394, op. 1, ed. khr. 425, ll. 1–2; RGIA, f. 958, op. 1, ed. khr. 726, ll. 2–6 (1844).

80. TsGIAM, f. 4, op. 2, ed. khr. 256, ll. 1–2, 8; RGIA, f. 1384 (Reviziia senatora kn. Davydova S. I. Kaluzhskoi gubernii, 1849–1851 gg.), op. 1, ed. khr. 614, ll. 75–76.

teenth century, it was not unheard of for proprietors to be punished for ill-using their peasants:[81] in 1768 the infamous Saltychika stepped well over the line when she flogged her house serfs for minor or imagined offenses and then ordered them to carry off the bodies of the peasants who died from her abuse.[82] By and large, however, even serfs who were badly abused had little recourse, since the law actively discouraged them from lodging complaints against their proprietors when they were mistreated.[83] Yet peasants made use of another strategy to take revenge on owners they despised, by accusing them of maligning the sovereign "by word and deed" (*slovo i delo*)—while, incidentally, noting that their treatment of their dependents left a great deal to be desired. Thus, in 1764 Nikolai Ivanov alleged that his mistress, Ustinia Sokolova, returned from the coronation of Catherine II and said that the new empress was unworthy to rule Russia, since she was a foreigner by birth. For his pains, Ivanov was severely punished, as were virtually all peasants who told scurrilous tales about their owners.[84]

When Emperor Paul modified the law in 1797 and permitted serfs to petition the sovereign when they suffered ill treatment, he was immediately deluged with appeals from disgruntled peasants. The testimony of these serfs was not accepted as evidence against their proprietors; the guilt of the offending proprietor could be established, however, if neighboring landowners and peasants who did not belong to the accused stepped forth with supporting testimony. In the years immediately following the new decree, proprietors were convicted of ill treatment only on the rare occasions.[85] By the second decade of the nineteenth century, however, authorities acted in defense of discontented serfs with greater enthusiasm.

A range of punishments were inflicted on those indicted of beating and starving their peasants. In extreme cases, abusive proprietors were stripped of noble status and exiled or incarcerated in monasteries for life, where they

81. As early as 1719, Peter the Great decreed that the property of serf owners who mistreated their peasants should be placed under guardianship. During the eighteenth century, however, this provision was largely ignored. See Blum (1961), 435–39. V. I. Semevskii found eighteen cases of proprietors charged with serf abuse in the eighteenth century, and noted great inconsistency in the sentences they received. See Semevskii, *Krest'iane v tsarstvovanie Imperatritsy Ekateriny II* (St. Petersburg, 1881), I: 189–96. For the earliest incidents of proprietors suspected of beating their peasants to death, see *PSZ* 15: 11.291 (10.06.1761) and 11.450 (25.02.1762).

82. *PSZ*, 18: 13.211 (10.12.1768). The testimony of Saltykova's serfs may be found in RGADA, f. 7, op. 2, ed. khr. 2078, ll. 17–18.

83. On the ambiguities in Russian law concerning the right of serfs to petition against their proprietors, see Isabel de Madariaga, "Catherine II and the Serfs: A Reconsideration of Some Problems," *Slavonic and East European Review* 52, no. 126 (January 1974): 47–54.

84. RGADA, f. 7, op. 2, ed. khr. 2135, ll. 9, 13. See also f. 7, op. 1, ed. khr. 1751 (1756) and ed. khr. 1752 (1756).

85. It should come as no surprise that authorities generally pronounced accusations on the part of serfs as unfounded. See the sample of cases in RGADA, f. 7, op. 2, ed. khr. 2985, ch. 1 (1797).

would have time to reflect on their sins.[86] This was the fate of the notorious Saltychika, as well as of Anna Lopukhina, whose house serfs reported that she beat their children and stuck pins into the chests and tongues of her serf women.[87] After Lieutenant Fedor Tarbeev murdered his serf woman in 1769, the Senate sentenced him to six months in a monastery and then to the lowest ranks of military service.[88] In Simbirsk province, the wife of Major Nagatkin forfeited her noble status in 1801 when an eleven-year-old house serf died after a severe beating.[89] As convictions for serf abuse rose in the nineteenth century, the Senate no longer elected to exile guilty proprietors to the nearest monastery but chose to restrict their property rights in a variety of ways: in some cases, abusive proprietors were forbidden to manage their estates, while in others they were prohibited from entering into any contracts concerning their property. More often than not, these proprietors were forbidden to set foot on their estates altogether.

Allegations of serf abuse provide a unique perspective on the significance of gender in the interaction between noble proprietors and legal authorities. Despite evidence to the contrary, many nineteenth-century historians generalized wildly on the basis of a few notorious incidents and conjectured that women were prone by nature to tyrannize their dependents.[90] More difficult to establish is the attitude of government authorities toward female proprietors: is there reason to believe that they were inclined to take charges against noblewomen more seriously than complaints about noblemen? Were women more likely than men to encounter resistance on the part of recalcitrant serfs? And when *pomeshchitsy* were taken to task for punishing their peasants without cause, was the source of the complaint the serfs themselves, or kin of the proprietress who hoped to take the estate out of her hands?

A rough comparison of the numbers of cases involving men and women reveals that the proportion of women accused of mistreating their serfs was well in keeping with the percentage of estates in female hands in the first half of the nineteenth century. The secret department that Paul established to deal with serf petitions heard forty-five cases in 1797–98, of which only five featured female proprietors.[91] In the records of the Moscow Noble Assembly, 109 complaints against abusive owners survive, of which 65 (60 percent) were lodged against men and 44 (40 percent) against women

---

86. A small number of nobles were exiled to Siberia for mistreating their serfs during the reign of Catherine II. See Madariaga (1974), 53.

87. RGADA, f. 7, op. 2, ed. khr. 3567, ll. 3, 5–6 (1800).

88. RGIA, f. 796, op. 50, ed. khr. 323 (1769), l. 1.

89. RGIA, f. 1345, op. 98, ed. khr. 667, ll. 27–29, 32–33.

90. See V. A. Gol'tsev, *Zakonodatel'stvo i nravy v Rossii XVIII veka*, 2d ed. (St. Petersburg, 1896), 80; Ilinskii (1909), 5, 8; Shchepkina (1914), 133; S. M. Soloviev, *Istoriia Rossii v tsarstvovanie Imperatritsy Ekateriny II* (Moscow, 1879), 5: 137.

91. RGADA, f. 7, op. 2, ed. khr. 2985, ch. 1 and 2.

between 1794 and 1846.[92] While sadism on the part of the fair sex proved more titillating to nineteenth-century contemporaries, unkindness and neglect of peasants was distributed equally among men and women.

Officials in the decades before Emancipation may have shared historians' pessimistic view of female nature. In his report on the state of the peasantry on the eve of Emancipation, A. V. Golovnin observed that female proprietors were "more obstinate . . . and, unfortunately, . . . more heartless";[93] another official remarked that "women surpass men in their cruelty and are distinguished by the inventiveness of their punishments."[94] When peasants carried tales of abuse and starvation to the district courts, however, officials drew no distinction between men and women. In order to gauge the veracity of the accusations, the marshal of the nobility would visit the estate of the accused on several occasions and look out for signs of physical mistreatment; he would also gather testimony from neighboring landowners and their peasants concerning the conduct of the suspect. If the evidence indicated that the landowner under surveillance had indeed abused his peasants, then his or her estate was taken into guardianship in short order. Many of these proprietors were forbidden to administer their holdings or to visit them, although they received an allowance from the proceeds of their estates.

Such punishments seem mild in comparison to the lifetime of exile inflicted on noblewomen in the eighteenth century. Even proprietors who had a hand in the death of their peasants as a result of excessive beatings were not stripped of their noble status, much less dispatched to a monastery.[95] Thus, one Denisov and his wife in Kursk province were con-

92. See the inventory in TsGIAM, f. 4, op. 2. Of 165 estates taken under guardianship for extravagance and serf abuse between 1850 and 1859, 28 belonged to women: M. A. Rakhmatullin, *Krest'ianskoe dvizhenie v velikorusskikh guberniiakh v 1826–1857 gg.* (Moscow, 1990), 181.

93. RGIA, f. 958 (Kiselev P. D.), op. 1, ed. khr. 666, l. 5.

94. Quoted in Rakhmatullin (1990), 181.

95. A survey of nineteen cases of female proprietors accused of serf abuse yielded the following results: four women were sentenced to spend one to five years in a monastery (the last of these dates from 1802); the estates of ten were sequestered; another four women were merely reprimanded. Only one woman was stripped of her status and exiled to hard labor in Siberia, after she beat a serf girl to death; her husband was reprimanded only for allowing his wife to indulge in abusive behavior. See RGIA, f. 1345, op. 98, ed. khr. 231, ll. 18, 21 (1798); f. 1345, op. 98, ed. khr. 546, ll. 8, 13 (1801); f. 1345, op. 98, ed. khr. 610, ll. 24–27, 30–31 (1801); f. 1345, op. 98, ed. khr. 634, ll. 1–2, 32, 55 (1802); TsGIAM, f. 383, op. 1, ed. khr. 55 (1827); RGIA, f. 1286, op. 7 (1838), ed. khr. 24; f. 1286, op. 8 (1841), ed. khr. 211; f. 1286, op. 8 (1841), ed. khr. 216, ll. 2, 7; f. 1286, op. 8 (1841), ed. khr. 231; f. 1286, op. 8 (1841), ed. khr. 272, ll. 1–5, 10; f. 1286, op. 8 (1842), ed. khr. 256; f. 1286, op. 8 (1842), ed. khr. 269, ll. 2–5; f. 1286, op. 8 (1843), ed. khr. 515, ll. 2–3, 5; f. 1286, op. 8 (1843), ed. khr. 536, ll. 2–5, 30–33, 43; TsGIAM, f. 380, op. 2, ed. khr. 191 (1850); RGIA, f. 1286, op. 15 (1854), ed. khr. 909, ll. 1–3; f. 1330, op. 6, ed. khr. 1291 (1858); f. 1330, op. 6, ed. khr. 1891 (1862). In eight cases involving male proprietors, one was exiled to Siberia with his wife (1797), another was sentenced to five years in a monastery, the estates of three were sequestered, and three cases were unresolved or dismissed for insufficient evidence. See RGIA, f. 1345, op. 98, ed. khr. 12, ll. 1–4, 40–43

victed of causing the death of one of their serfs in 1826, yet neither suffered punishment more severe than exile from their estate.[96] A similar penalty was imposed on a female proprietor called Mistrova in Tver' province in 1841: after severely beating a serf woman who died soon afterward, she was forbidden to live on her estate and sentenced to two months in prison. She did not, however, lose her nobility.[97]

The discussions in noble assemblies and by central authorities on the crimes of errant nobles leave no doubt that the dominant preoccupation of Imperial officials on the lookout for signs of serf abuse (*zhestokoe obrashchenie so krest'ianami*), extravagance (*motostvo, rastochitel'nost'*), or immoral conduct (*neprilichnoe povedenie, neblagovidnaia* or *razvratvnaia zhizn'*) was not the sex of the offender, but his or her noble status. This motif was echoed in petitions to the authorities. Time and again, the essence of the charges presented in petitions and in official correspondence between central and local authorities is that the accused was guilty of conduct unbefitting a member of the nobility. The Noble Assembly in Syzran debated whether to sequester the estate of Lieutenant Shil'nikov in 1839, for his drunkenness and his conduct "unbecoming noble rank."[98] In his report on the appalling conduct of Aleksandra Tiutcheva, the marshal of the nobility in Volokolamskii district wrote that Tiutcheva had gone through her inheritance so quickly that she was now left without a roof over her head. Despite her noble descent, he went on, she had lost all sense of shame and was now reduced to doing the work of peasants in order to survive.[99] The authorities took the *pomeshchitsa* Naryshkina to task for mismanaging her daughter's affairs when she acted as guardian of her estate. The marshal who commented on the case remarked that Naryshkina enjoyed a reputation "demeaning to her noble status."[100] Indeed, the refrain that surfaces in many of these cases is that the accused was guilty not of conduct unbefitting their sex, but of conduct inappropriate for anyone of noble rank. For betraying their social estate, proprietors were consequently deprived of one of the most significant prerogatives of noble status: the right to administer their estates and human property.

(1797); f. 1345, op. 98, ed. khr. 288, ll. 32, 38, 42 (1799); f. 1286, op. 6 (1835), ed. khr. 383; f. 1286, op. 6 (1836), ed. khr. 293; f. 1286, op. 7 (1838), ed. khr. 37; TsGIAM, f. 380, op. 2, ed. khr. 192 (1850); RGIA, f. 1330, op. 6, ed. khr. 1277 (1858).

96. RGIA, f. 1555 (Reviziia senatora Kn. Dolgorukova A. A. Voronezhskoi, Kurskoi, Penzenskoi, Saratovskoi, Simbirskoi i Tambovskoi gubernii, 1826 g.), op. 1, ed. khr. 183, ll. 12–15.

97. RGIA, f. 1286, op. 8 (1841), ed. khr. 231, ll. 2–4.

98. RGIA, f. 1286, op. 6 (1836), ed. khr. 297, l. 22.

99. TsGIAM, f. 380, op. 2, ed. khr. 99, l. 1 (1850).

100. TsGIAM, f. 4, op. 2, ed. khr. 187, l. 23 (1844). See also RGIA, f. 1549, op. 1, ed. khr. 51 (1814), l. 29; f. 1286, op. 8 (1842), ed. khr. 269, ll. 2–5; TsGIAM, f. 380, op. 2, ed. khr. 81 (1868); f. 4, op. 2, ed. khr. 191, l. 15 (1845); f. 380, op. 4, ed. khr. 44, l. 14 (1849); f. 4, op. 2, ed. khr. 59, l. 16 (1835); RGIA, f. 1286, op. 7 (1838), ed. khr. 17, l. 2; TsGIAM, f. 4, op. 2, ed. khr. 116, l. 2 (1846).

Once an estate was taken into trusteeship, the guardians appointed were responsible for administering the estate and presenting accounts of income and expenditures to the *Dvorianskaia opeka*. As often as not, these estates proved no more productive in the hands of guardians than they had been under their proprietors; nobles deprived of the right to manage their holdings complained bitterly about the management skills of guardians. For their part, peasants often preferred the management of their proprietor to that of anonymous guardians.[101] The peasants of Kamenok village in Bogorodskii district petitioned the local marshal of the nobility to release the estate of their proprietor, Korol'kov, from trusteeship. They presented numerous examples of the high quality of life they had enjoyed under Korol'kov, who built houses for his serfs at his own expense when part of the village was destroyed by fire; he constructed a factory on his estate, which gave them opportunities to earn more money; during the famine of 1839, he had distributed grain to those in need. Curiously, Korol'kov's misdemeanors are not mentioned in the exchange between the marshal and the military governor. Although the marshal saw no reason not to concede to the request, noting that "a guardian can never act as freely as a genuine proprietor in the peasants' interest," the governor of Moscow province responded that he could not remove the estate from trusteeship.[102] The peasants belonging to Ekaterina Grigor'eva came forward with a similar petition in 1852. As the peasants of Kamenok village had done, Grigor'eva's serfs praised their owner for coming to their aid during poor harvests and purchasing livestock for them; by contrast, the guardian was not "the real owner of the estate" and did not have the same right to come to their aid. On these grounds the sympathetic marshal recommended that Grigor'eva's estate be released from trusteeship, even though he found her holdings in great disrepair.[103]

———

The records of provincial noble assemblies and officials are replete with investigations into the character and competence of noble proprietors of both sexes yet the impact of this campaign on the conduct of the provincial nobility is ambiguous. Both Imperial and Soviet historians maintained that the marshals of the nobility were more than willing to ignore the suffering of abused serfs in the interest of upholding the privileges of their fellow nobles.[104] Records of the *Dvorianskaia opeka* in Tambov and Moscow

---

101. As one historian observed, peasants belonging to estates taken under guardianship may have escaped abuse but suffered a further decline in their standard of living. A. D. Povalishin, *Riazanskie pomeshchiki i ikh krepostnye* (Riazan', 1903), 151.

102. TsGIAM, f. 380, op. 4, ed. khr. 85, ll. 7–8, 16–17 (1853).

103. TsGIAM, f. 380, op. 4, ed. khr. 73, ll. 6–16, 47.

104. Inna Ivanovna Ignatovich, *Pomeshchich'i krest'iane nakanune osvobozhdeniia*, 3rd ed. (Leningrad, 1925), 59–60; Povalishin (1903), 109.

provinces suggest that the number of accusations far exceeded the actual number of estates held in guardianship. In 1844, the Noble Board of Guardians in Tambov inventoried eighty-seven estates in trusteeship, the majority of which required guardians simply because their owners were children.[105] The marshal of the nobility for Moscow province reported that only three estates had been taken under guardianship in 1851, all of which belonged to women and all for abusive or immoral behavior.[106] If accusations were abundant, conviction rates were modest: between 1834 and 1845, almost 3,000 proprietors were tried for serf abuse, but only 660 (22 percent) were convicted.[107] Nonetheless, in 1838 alone, 140 estates were sequestered as a result of convictions for mistreatment; this number reached 215 by 1859.[108] Thus, the percentage of noble estates in trusteeship was far from insignificant,[109] and these figures point to the conclusion that surveillance on the part of the marshals of the nobility checked the worst impulses of proprietors inclined to mistreat their peasants.[110]

The establishment of institutions of self-government on a local level permitted authorities to patrol the provinces and intervene in the private lives of the nobility to a degree only dreamed of by Peter the Great. From the point of view of corporate privilege, the sequestering of estates highlighted the instability of the nobility's proprietary rights in the last decades of serfdom.[111] Sequestration was an effective means of checking the mistreat-

105. RGIA, f. 1383, op. 2, ed. khr. 250, ll. 36–69. After serfdom was abolished, estates continued to be taken under guardianship because their proprietors were insolvent. The historian Anfimov, in his work on the landholding nobility in the late Imperial era, pronounced the *Dvorianskaia opeka* a "reactionary establishment," designed to preserve the power of great landholders by protecting them from their creditors. See Anfimov (1969), 342.

106. TsGIAM, f. 380, op. 4, ed. khr. 60, ll. 1–3. The Ministry of Internal Affairs reported that in 1841, 98 estates were held in guardianship for serf abuse, another 80 had been sequestered because their proprietors were spendthrifts but the majority—916—were in guardianship because of debt. See *Materialy dlia istorii krepostnogo prava v Rossii. Izvlecheniia iz sekretnykh otchetov Ministerstva Vnutrennikh Del za 1836–1856 g.* (Berlin, 1873), 56.

107. See Rakhmatullin (1990), 179, and Boris N. Mironov, "Local Government in Russia in the First Half of the Nineteenth Century: Provincial Government and Estate Self-Government," *Jahrbücher für Geschichte Osteuropas* 42 (1994): 193. Mironov offers an optimistic interpretation of the data on noble convictions, pointing out that the conviction rates for landlords in some provinces were as high as those for peasants accused of crimes.

108. Blum (1961), 440.

109. Mironov contends that 20% of noble estates were under trusteeship in 1836. See Mironov (1994), 193.

110. Rakhmatillin argues that the percentage of estates taken under trusteeship for serf abuse declined in the 1850s as a result of stricter measures against abusive proprietors. See Rakhmatullin (1990), 180. In 1847 an official in the Ministry of Internal Affairs attributed the sharp decline in accusations of serf abuse to increased surveillance on the part of the marshals of the nobility. See *Materialy dlia istorii krepostnogo prava v Rossii* (1873), 169–70.

111. During the public debate that preceded the Emancipation Manifesto in 1861, many nobles perceived the proposed land settlement, as well as the loss of their human labor, as a violation of their property rights. See Daniel Field, *The End of Serfdom: Nobility and Bureaucracy in Russia, 1855–1861* (Cambridge, 1976), 108.

ment of serfs and the dissipation of noble fortunes; at the same time, it was subject to abuse. Thus, in 1842, the heirs of Count Kiril Gudovich persuaded the emperor to sequester his estate, on the grounds that Gudovich was losing his powers of reason and he intended to mortgage his property. The moment Gudovich agreed to divide the estate among his children, the sequestration was lifted.[112] In other cases, nobles convincingly argued that their kin had requested sequestration of their estates with the sole intention of limiting their property rights.[113] Moreover, although the Charter to the Nobility in 1785 specified that the property of an estate owner convicted of a crime should devolve upon his heirs, in practice this guarantee proved more tenuous.[114] The heirs of the convicted proprietor could count on eventually taking possession of the estate. During the proprietor's lifetime, however, the fate of this property was uncertain. The daughters of Ekaterina Grushetskaia petitioned the Senate in desperation in 1858, after their mother's estate had been sequestered for serf abuse and they were left penniless. In response, the Senate ruled that Grushetskaia's estate must remain in trusteeship until she died; on the subject of providing for her daughters, the Senate was silent.[115]

From the perspective of gender, the disputes heard in the noble assemblies highlight the even-handed treatment of women proprietors by judicial and administrative authorities. Clearly, noblewomen suffered as much as their male counterparts from restrictions on their corporate rights. Nonetheless, they benefited from official promotion of the link between virtue and noble status, as well as from the efforts of the central administration to enforce legal norms in the provinces. Exchanges between central and local authorities on the sequestration of estates betray little regard for the sex of the offender: the same means of collecting evidence were employed for proprietors of both sexes, and authorities made a point of weighing all evidence according to the guidelines laid out in the *Svod zakonov*. Officials may not have approved of noblewomen who drank or married beneath their station, but they refused to deprive them of their property rights on these grounds, unless their character flaws were accompanied by real evidence of incompetent estate management. This dispassionate approach was a marked improvement over that of eighteenth-century officials, who were more inclined to restrict the property rights of women who transgressed accepted moral boundaries and gender conventions. At the same time, male pro-

112. RGIA, f. 1286, op. 8 (1843), ed. khr. 460, ll. 4–5, 16–17, 24.

113. See TsGIAM, f. 4, op. 2, ed. khr. 116 (1846) and f. 380, op. 4, ed. khr. 64 (1851).

114. Robert E. Jones, *The Emancipation of the Russian Nobility, 1762–1785* (Princeton, 1973), 282. Nobles who were stripped of their status and exiled were deprived only of settled estates; they retained the right to their chattel, houses, and ownership of property not dependent on noble status. See *SZ*, 10 (1876), art. 332.

115. RGIA, f. 1330, op. 6, ed. khr. 1291, l. 16.

prietors found they were treated with less leniency at the hands of legal institutions. The charges of their wives were no longer dismissed out of hand, their accusations of adultery met with greater skepticism, and noblemen found that they too were expected to adhere to a higher standard of behavior and estate administration.

For all its shortcomings, the legal process in Imperial Russia offered many noblewomen the opportunity to pursue their own interests and to defend themselves and their children against dispossession. To be sure, successful negotiation through the courts depended on a variety of intangible factors: the ability to persuade authorities to hear one's case, the support of family members, and even strength of personality. One scholar has commented that the difficulty of taking cases to court "discouraged litigation and led to . . . abstention from the defense of the individual's interests."[116] In light of this assessment, the rough equality in male and female participation in property litigation is all the more striking. Despite the obstacles to obtaining justice, noblewomen experienced no greater disadvantages than their male counterparts. At least in the realm of property law, when noblewomen persisted in their suits, they found that their confidence in the courts was not misplaced.

116. Wortman (1976), 240.

Conclusion

In gender relations, as in so many other dimensions of historical development, Russia had fallen out of step with her neighbors in the West by the nineteenth century. The divergence between Russia and Western Europe rarely worked in Russia's favor: as industrialization and revolution transformed European society, Russian backwardness vis-à-vis the West became more pronounced. Yet, throughout Europe, the spoils of economic and political progress were not shared equally by men and women. The prominence of the middle class was grounded in large part on an order that prescribed increasingly rigid gender roles for both sexes and intensified male domination in the family.[1] Married women's control of property in Russia appeared all the more remarkable when viewed against the restrictive provisions of the Napoleonic Code that governed marital property relations in much of the West.

Nineteenth-century Russian scholars issued extravagant pronouncements about the legal status of women in their country, declaring them the most fortunate women in Europe with regard to control of property but the most disadvantaged in the realm of inheritance.[2] Both generalizations were overstated. It cannot be denied, however, that from the eighteenth century the evolution of women's property rights in Russia diverged significantly from that of their European counterparts. In Western Europe, differential control and use of property sharply distinguished the sexes, as many legal codes

1. Isabel V. Hull, *Sexuality, State, and Civil Society in Germany, 1700–1815* (Ithaca, 1996).
2. Gessen (1908), col. 2837; Anna Evreinova, "Ob uravnenii prav zhenshchin pri nasledovanii," *Drug zhenshchin*, no. 11 (November 1883): 62; A. Liubavskii, "Ob uravnenii nasledstvennykh prav muzhchin i zhenshchin," *Zhurnal Ministerstva Iustitsii* 20, kn. 2 (May 1864): 412; *Zamechaniia o nedostatakh deistvuiushchikh grazhdanskikh zakonov* (1891), no. 573.

treated men's and women's property as separate entities, governed by different rules.[3] If Russian legislators stopped short of establishing complete parity between the sexes in property law, they ventured further than their European counterparts in eliminating the distinguishing features of women's property. As a result, by the end of the eighteenth century, Russian law guaranteed women's entitlement to a fixed share of family assets and did away with gender tutelage in regard to property.

Greater equality under the law translated, in practice, into striking similarities between men and women in regard to use of their assets. The discrete female value system that historians have identified among propertied women in Western Europe was largely absent in Russia. In the realm of property use, Russian noble women and men displayed a remarkable identity of interests. Women as a group engaged in the same range of property transactions as men, and the scale of individual women's holdings was commensurate with that of their male counterparts. Married women were present at property transactions and carried out business in their own names. Regardless of marital status, women assumed responsibility for managing the family estate and augmenting their children's inheritance. When making bequests, women and men were equally concerned with limiting the number of beneficiaries and resisting fragmentation of the family estate. Although partible inheritance could stir up conflict among kin, it also created a unity of interests between husband and wife concerning the financial welfare of their survivors.

The advancement of noblewomen's legal prerogatives in Russia was an integral part of the evolution of noble property rights in the eighteenth century. As the nobility struggled to secure their corporate privileges and clarify their property rights, the relation of women to property also came under scrutiny. The extension of married women's control of their fortunes transpired as officials invested greater rights of property in (noble) individuals and shored up the institution of private property vis-à-vis the claims of the larger kin group and the state. Once noblewomen acquired these privileges, the aspiration to legality on the part of the state's representatives ensured that noblewomen's rights were not a mere formality. For the defense of their prerogatives, noblewomen depended on legal authorities who were often corrupt and ill-informed. Yet, at the center of government, the efforts of officials to create a more rational legal culture worked in favor of the realization of women's property rights.

By the nineteenth century, noblewomen's control of their fortunes was an established principle of Russian property law, which had become the subject of both scholarly debate and popular misconception. When Senator N. S. Mordvinov argued that women's assets should not be subject to their

3. See, in particular, Staves (1990), 194.

husbands' creditors, he observed that the law of property in Russia had not distinguished between men's and women's rights "for centuries," although married women gained full control of their fortunes only in 1753. Many educated Russians shared Mordvinov's misconception and seized on this "peculiarity" of property law as yet another manifestation of Russia's unique historical development.[4] Noblewomen's control of property acquired cultural significance within the larger debate over Russian national identity: conservative authors viewed women's property rights as evidence of Russia's innate superiority to the West, while Westernizing authors employed women's legal status as a metaphor for the potential for progressive change in their country. The subject of Russian women's legal status, past and present, inspired more than one author to wax eloquent on Russia's superiority in regard to equality of the sexes.[5] "The laws of several countries respect the sensitivity and weakness of women to such a degree, that they forbid them to act as witnesses," observed I. Vasil'ev, tongue in cheek, in 1827. He went on to point out that Russian courts honored the testimony of both men and women.[6] Anatole Leroy-Beaulieu observed that Russians refused to use the word *emancipation* in regard to the struggle for women's independence: "They will tell you that, with them, woman *is* emancipated, since the law allows her to manage her own property in wedlock."[7] The slavophile protagonist of Herzen's story "The Magpie-Thief" insists that as far as human rights are concerned, Russia's women were far more fortunate than their European counterparts. "From ancient times," he informs his readers, a woman's "estate has not been joined with that of her husband; she has the right to take part in elections, as well as the right to manage her serfs."[8] On the subject of women's equality, these authors maintained, Russia had nothing to learn from the West.

The abolition of serfdom in 1861 transformed the lives of noble estate owners of both sexes. Like their male counterparts, female proprietors were far from united in their response to the news of Emancipation. Antonia

---

4. *Arkhiv grafov Mordvinovykh* (1903), 8: 102. See also Marie Tsebrikova, "Russia," in *The Woman Question in Europe*, ed. Theodore Stanton (New York, 1884), 394. Vladimirskii-Budanov wrote that the "recognition of equal rights for men and women" was "the distinguishing feature of Russian law." See Vladimirskii-Budanov (1909), 374.

5. One author maintained that in regard to property rights, women in medieval Russia had far outstripped their counterparts in the West—"that West," she added, "with which we now cannot keep pace." M. N. Ditrikh, *Russkaia zhenshchina velikokniazheskogo vremeni* (St. Petersburg, 1904), 38.

6. I. V. Vasil'ev, "O preimushchestvakh zhenshchin v Rossii po delam ugolovnym," *Damskii zhurnal*, no. 13 (1827): 7. Yet Vasil'ev also singled out for praise the provisions of criminal law that made allowances for the "sensitivity" of the female sex, in particular, statutes that exempted noblewomen from corporal punishment and that postponed corporal punishment in the case of nursing mothers. See Vasil'ev (1827), no. 11: 242–43.

7. Leroy-Beaulieu (1898), 1: 218–19.

8. A. I. Herzen, "Soroka-Vorovka," in *Povesti i rasskazy* (Moscow, 1962), 266.

Bludova welcomed the abolition of serfdom with "gratitude" and noted with approval the calm reception of the Emancipation Manifesto among the serfs on her estate in Kursk.[9] The reaction of an anonymous *pomeshchitsa* was, perhaps, more typical, when she called on the "wives and mothers of Russian nobles" to protest this violation of noble property rights and what amounted to outright confiscation of half their property.[10] Scholars have posited that noble families were no longer able to provide adequately for their daughters after 1861 and that unmarried women had no option but to seek their own means of support.[11] In the late nineteenth century, the nobility turned from landholding and relied increasingly on state service, industry, and professional careers to provide for their families.[12] The economic fortunes of noblewomen in this new environment remain uncharted territory.

Variations in women's legal prerogatives in the late Imperial era have garnered greater interest. In the law of property, noblewomen's standing remained secure. Lawmakers continued to uphold women's control of their fortunes against the encroachments of husbands, insisting that "not only does the property of a wife not become the property of her husband, but he does not even acquire through marriage the right to use or manage it."[13] Women of all social classes also managed to obtain legal separation from their husbands in growing numbers after 1861. Yet, in other respects, the position of women failed to improve, or even deteriorated. Reformers fell short of granting women equal inheritance rights in the revised law of succession in 1912.[14] Moreover, the progressive legal order that emerged after Emancipation emphasized female dependence and vulnerability to a degree unprecedented in Russian law. As Laura Engelstein argues in regard to criminal law, as late as 1903 "women remained the objects of . . . custodial solicitude. . . . Like children and the mentally incompetent, women continued to be marked by special disabilities in relation to the law."[15]

The figure of the formidable woman and her powerless counterpart in Russian culture was paralleled in the legal realm by conflicting representations of gender relations. As we have seen, Russian women's status in the legal order was fraught with contradictions. Family law presupposed the domination of men over women and demanded the complete subordination of wives to their husbands. By contrast, the law of property projected

9. RGADA, f. 1274, op. 1, ed. khr. 928 (1861).

10. "Somneniia i dumy russkoi pomeshchitsy po sluchaiu predpolozhennogo preobrazovaniia," *Chteniia v imperatorskom obshchestve istorii i drevnostei rossiiskikh pri Moskovskom universitete* (January–March 1873), 271–72.

11. Edmondson (1984), 12.

12. Becker (1985).

13. Decision of the Civil Cassation Department, 1870. Quoted in Wagner (1994), 207.

14. See Wagner (1994).

15. Laura Engelstein, *The Keys to Happiness: Sex and the Search for Modernity in Fin-de-Siècle Russia* (Ithaca, 1992), 71.

an image of women, regardless of marital status, as competent administrators of property, requiring neither protection nor supervision. The authors of the law of property downplayed sexual difference by abolishing concessions to feminine weakness and assuming that women were capable of acting in their own economic interests—an assumption borne out by noblewomen's visibility as litigants in property disputes and by the active role many assumed in estate management.

These conflicting notions of womanhood shaped both the formidable heroines of Turgenev's novels and the downtrodden victims of Ostrovsky's plays. Far from being figments of the authors' imagination, their historical counterparts appear in petitions, land disputes, deeds of sale, and instructions to bailiffs. Of these documents, some testify to female vulnerability in the patriarchal order of Imperial Russia; others, however, relate how noblewomen parlayed their control of estates and human labor into influence within the family and provincial society. While family law upheld the patriarchal ideal, the law of property provided a competing vision of feminine autonomy, along with the possibility of realizing that vision.

Appendix 1

A Note on Sources:
The *Krepostnye Knigi*

With the exception of the tables in appendix 2 and chapter 5, the statistical tables in this study are based exclusively on approximately eight thousand notarial transactions. Until 1775, property transfers were recorded in the local notarial office in the provinces and in the Justice College in Moscow. These documents may be found in fond 615 (Krepostnye knigi mestnykh uchrezhdenii XVI–XVIII vv.) and fond 282 (Iustits-kollegiia) in the Archive of Ancient Acts (Rossiiskii gosudarstvennyi arkhiv drevnikh aktov). After 1775, property transfers were registered in courts at the district or provincial level—namely, the Provincial Chambers of Civil Law (Palata grazhdanskogo suda) or the district court (*uezdnyi sud*).

Fonds 615 and 282 contain thousands of property transactions, involving every type of conveyance: the sale of estates, both settled and unsettled; the sale of serfs without land; manumission of serfs; mortgages of land and serfs; rental of land; the sale of gardens, shops, houses, and allotments of land in town; dowries; wills; deeds of separation. While each category of transaction was supposed to be recorded in its own register, in many districts various categories were recorded in a general (*obshchaia*) inventory. The collection also includes inventories of letters granting power of attorney to representatives.[1]

To trace the pattern of noblewomen's participation in the market for land and serfs between 1700 and 1861, I drew my sample from transactions recorded in notarial offices in four districts and in the Justice College in Moscow, at five points in time. Within each five-year period, I collected up to three years of data, when the records were available. The choice of districts was dictated by availability. Although notarial records exist for as many

---

1. A description of the collection may be found in RGADA, f. 615, op. 1, ch. 1.

as 226 towns in fond 615, very few of these contain a continuous run of data. Transactions for 1805–10 were gathered from collections in archives in Tambov, Tver', and Vladimir, and those for 1855–60 were drawn primarily from the supplement to the *St. Petersburg Senate Gazette*, in which property transactions from all provincial and district offices were published monthly. For each transaction, I recorded the following variables:

- sex and rank of buyer and seller
- marital status for female transactors
- the type of property sold
- the ruble value of the property[2]
- the amount of land, in *desiatiny*
- the number of serfs sold with the estate
- how the property sold was originally acquired
- kinship of transactors
- whether or not each participant was present at the transaction
- the literacy of each participant

A complete list of the sources used for the tables, by district, follows.

VLADIMIR

(1715) RGADA, f. 615, op. 1, ed. khr. 1954 (*obshchaia*) (entire).
(1717) RGADA, f. 615, op. 1, ed. khr. 1956 (*obshchaia*) (entire)
(1719) RGADA, f. 615, op. 1, ed. khr. 1958 (*obshchaia*) (entire)
(1751) RGADA, f. 615, op. 1, ed. khr. 1996 (*obshchaia*) (entire)
(1753) RGADA, f. 615, op. 1, ed. khr. 2000 (*obshchaia*) (entire)
(1755) RGADA, f. 615, op. 1, ed. khr. 2004 (*obshchaia*) (entire)
(1775) RGADA, f. 615, op. 1, ed. khr. 2042 (*obshchaia*) (entire)
(1775) RGADA, f. 615, op. 1, ed. khr. 2043 (*obshchaia*) (entire)
(1776) RGADA, f. 615, op. 1, ed. khr. 2045 (*obshchaia*) (entire)
(1778) RGADA, f. 615, op. 1, ed. khr. 2049 (*obshchaia*) (entire)
(1806) GAVO, f. 92, op. 5, ed. khr. 21 (*kniga na zapisku kupchikh krepostei*) (entire)
(1809) GAVO, f. 92, op. 2, ed. khr. 96 (entire)
(1856) GAVO, f. 92, op. 5, ed. khr. 286 (entire)
(1858) GAVO, f. 92, op. 2, ed. khr. 659 (entire)
(1860) GAVO, f. 92, op. 2, ed. khr. 682 (entire)

KASHIN

(1715) RGADA, f. 615, op. 1, ed. khr. 4186 (*obshchaia*) (entire)
(1718) RGADA, f. 615, op. 1, ed. khr. 4190 (*obshchaia*) (entire)

2. Transactions for 1805–10 usually were valued in assignants, although this was not always specified. Transactions for 1855–60 were valued in silver rubles.

(1719) RGADA, f. 615, op. 1, ed. khr. 4191 (*obshchaia*) (entire)
(1750) RGADA, f. 615, op. 1, ed. khr. 4217 (*obshchaia*) (entire)
(1753) RGADA, f. 615, op. 1, ed. khr. 4220 (*obshchaia*) (entire)
(1755) RGADA, f. 615, op. 1, ed. khr. 4222 (*obshchaia*) (entire)
(1770) RGADA, f. 615, op. 1, ed. khr. 4241 (*obshchaia*) (entire)
(1771) RGADA, f. 615, op. 1, ed. khr. 4240 (*obshchaia*) (entire)
(1772) RGADA, f. 615, op. 1, ed. khr. 4242 (*obshchaia*) (entire)
(1773) RGADA, f. 615, op. 1, ed. khr. 4243 (*obshchaia*) (entire)
(1806) GA Tverskoi oblasti, f. 668, op. 1, ed. khr. 6444 (*kupchie kreposti*) (entire)
(1807) GA Tverskoi oblasti, f. 668, op. 1, ed. khr. 6446 (*otpusknye*) (entire)
(1807) GA Tverskoi oblasti, f. 668, op. 1, ed. khr. 6445 (*kupchie kreposti*) (entire)
(1808) GA Tverskoi oblasti, f. 668, op. 1, ed. khr. 6447 (*kupchie kreposti*) (entire)
(1858) GA Tverskoi oblasti, f. 668, op. 1, ed. khr. 6469 (*kupchie, otpusknye*) (entire)
(1860–63) GA Tverskoi oblasti, f. 668, op. 1, ed. khr. 6279 (*kupchie kreposti*) (entire)
(1860) *Sanktpeterburgskie senatskie ob"iavleniia po sudebnym . . . delam* (entire)

Tambov

(1715–16) RGADA, f. 615, op. 1, ed. khr. 11250 (*obshchaia*) (entire)
(1717) RGADA, f. 615, op. 1, ed. khr. 11252 (*obshchaia*) (entire)
(1718) RGADA, f. 615, op. 1, ed. khr. 11254 (*obshchaia*) (entire)
(1750) RGADA, f. 615, op. 1, ed. khr. 11395 (*votchinnaia*) (entire)
(1751) RGADA, f. 615, op. 1, ed. khr. 11404 (*votchinnaia*) (entire)
(1753) RGADA, f. 615, op. 1, ed. khr. 11415 (*votchinnaia*) (entire)
(1753) RGADA, f. 615, op. 1, ed. khr. 11417 (*krest'ianskaia*) (entire)
(1753) RGADA, f. 615, op. 1, ed. khr. 11418 (*na dvorovykh liudei*) (entire)
(1754) RGADA, f. 615, op. 1, ed. khr. 11427 (*krest'ianskaia*) (entire)
(1754) RGADA, f. 615, op. 1, ed. khr. 11428 (*na dvorovykh liudei*) (entire)
(1754) RGADA, f. 615, op. 1, ed. khr. 11431 (*zaemnaia*) (entire)
(1755) RGADA, f. 615, op. 1, ed. khr. 11436 (*votchinnaia*) (entire)
(1755) RGADA, f. 615, op. 1, ed. khr. 11438 (*krest'ianskaia*) (entire)
(1775) RGADA, f. 615, op. 1, ed. khr. 11558 (*votchinnaia*) (entire)
(1776) RGADA, f. 615, op. 1, ed. khr. 11566 (*votchinnaia*) (entire)
(1776) RGADA, f. 615, op. 1, ed. khr. 11568 (*krest'ianskaia*) (entire)
(1776) RGADA, f. 615, op. 1, ed. khr. 11569 (*na dvorovykh liudei*) (entire)
(1776) RGADA, f. 615, op. 1, ed. khr. 11571 (*zaemnaia*) (entire)
(1777) RGADA, f. 615, op. 1, ed. khr. 11575 (*dvorovaia*) (entire)
(1777) RGADA, f. 615, op. 1, ed. khr. 11576 (*krest'ianskaia*) (entire)
(1777) RGADA, f. 615, op. 1, ed. khr. 11577 (*na dvorovykh liudei*) (entire)
(1777) RGADA, f. 615, op. 1, ed. khr. 11578 (*sdelochnaia*) (entire)
(1777) RGADA, f. 615, op. 1, ed. khr. 11579 (*naemnaia*) (entire)
(1778) RGADA, f. 615, op. 1, ed. khr. 11581 (*votchinnaia*) (entire)
(1779) RGADA, f. 615, op. 1, ed. khr. 11589 (*votchinnaia*) (entire)
(1779) RGADA, f. 615, op. 1, ed. khr. 11591 (*krest'ianskaia*) (entire)
(1779) RGADA, f. 615, op. 1, ed. khr. 11592 (*na dvorovykh liudei*) (entire)
(1779) RGADA, f. 615, op. 1, ed. khr. 11593 (*sdelochnaia*) (entire)
(1805) GATO, f. 67, op. 1, ed. khr. 27a (*votchinnaia*) (entire)
(1806–9) RGADA, f. 264, op. 8, ed. khr. 139 (ll. 716–24, 794–98, 864–900)
(1857) (1859–60) *Sanktpeterburgskie senatskie ob"iavleniia po sudebnym . . . delam*

KURSK

(1719) RGADA, f. 615, op. 1, ed. khr. 5281 (*obshchaia*) (entire)
(1720) RGADA, f. 615, op. 1, ed. khr. 5283 (*obshchaia*) (entire)
(1750) RGADA, f. 615, op. 1, ed. khr. 5394 (*votchinnaia*) (entire)
(1752) RGADA, f. 615, op. 1, ed. khr. 5410 (*votchinnaia*) (entire)
(1775) RGADA, f. 615, op. 1, ed. khr. 5562 (*votchinnaia*) (entire)
(1778) RGADA, f. 615, op. 1, ed. khr. 5584 (*votchinnaia*) (entire)
(1857) (1859–60) *Sanktpeterburgskie senatskie ob"iavleniia po sudebnym . . . delam*

MOSCOW

(1716) RGADA, f. 282, op. 1, ed. khr. 337 (*votchinnaia*) (ll. 1–177)
(1720) RGADA, f. 282, op. 1, ed. khr. 341 (*votchinnaia*) (ll. 1–175)
(1751) RGADA, f. 282, op. 1, ed. khr. 394 (*votchinnaia*) (pp. 1–585)
(1753) RGADA, f. 282, op. 1, ed. khr. 497 (*na dvory, dvorovye mesta, i zavody*) (pp. 1–355, 754–853)
(1754) RGADA, f. 282, op. 1, ed. khr. 399 (*votchinnaia*) (pp. 237–415)
(1754) RGADA, f. 282, op. 1, ed. khr. 400 (*votchinnaia*) (pp. 1840–2008)
(1775) RGADA, f. 282, op. 1, ed. khr. 426 (*votchinnaia*) (pp. 605–773)
(1776) RGADA, f. 282, op. 1, ed. khr. 524 (*na dvory, dvorovye mesta, i zavody*) (pp. 200–487)
(1777) RGADA, f. 282, op. 1, ed. khr. 429 (*votchinnaia*) (pp. 859–1475)
(1778) RGADA, f. 282, op. 1, ed. khr. 529 (*na dvory, dvorovye mesta, i zavody*) (entire)
(1810) TsGIAM, f. 50, op. 14, ed. khr. 1262 (ll. 1–203)
(1857) (1859–60) *Sanktpeterburgskie senatskie ob"iavleniia po sudebnym . . . delam*

Kinship of Litigants in Inheritance Disputes Involving Noblewomen, 1700–1861*

Kinship of Litigants	18th Century		19th Century		1700–1861	
Husbands vs. wives	4	(2)	16	(11)	11	(13)
Mothers vs. sons	2	(1)	4	(3)	3	(4)
Fathers vs. daughters	0	(0)	3	(2)	2	(2)
Sisters vs. brothers	7	(3)	14	(10)	11	(13)
Sisters vs. sisters	16	(7)	3	(2)	8	(9)
Women vs. sisters-in-law	4	(2)	8	(6)	7	(8)
Women vs. brothers-in-law	11	(5)	8	(6)	9	(11)
Other relatives by marriage	9	(4)	13	(9)	11	(13)
Aunts vs. nieces/nephews	20	(9)	3	(2)	9	(11)
Uncles vs. nieces/nephews	2	(1)	10	(7)	7	(8)
Cousins vs. cousins	11	(5)	7	(5)	9	(10)
Women vs. stepchildren	7	(3)	7	(5)	7	(8)
Miscellaneous	7	(3)	4	(3)	5	(6)
Total	100	(45)	100	(71)	100	(116)

* Each value is the percentage of the total number of cases. The number of cases is given in parentheses.

Sources: RGADA, f. 1209, op. 79 and op. 84, ch. 14; RGIA, f. 1330, op. 1–6 and f. 1346, op. 43, ch. 1–2.

Bibliography

Manuscript Sources

Moscow

Gosudarstvennyi arkhiv Rossiiskoi federatsii (GARF)
(State Archive of the Russian Federation)

fond 109   III otdelenie Sobstvennoi ego imperatorskogo velichestva kantseliarii. 2-aia
            ekspeditsiia.

Gosudarstvennyi istoricheskii muzei (GIM)
Otdel pis'mennykh istochnikov
(State Historical Museum)

fond 47   Shakovskie-Glebovy-Streshnevy
fond 52   Demidovy
fond 60   Vorontsovy
fond 175   Shatilovy
fond 182   Shishkiny

Rossiiskii gosudarstvennyi arkhiv drevnikh aktov (RGADA)
(Russian State Archive of Ancient Acts)

fond 7   Razriad VII (Dela tainoi ekspeditsii)
fond 8   Kalinkin dom (Kalinkin House and Files on Crimes against Morality)
fond 9   Kabinet Petra I
fond 22   Dela sudnye
fond 181   Rukopisnoe sobranie biblioteki MGAMID
fond 248   Senate i ego uchrezhdenii
fond 264   Shestoi Departament Senata
fond 282   Iustits-kollegiia

fond 342   Novoulozhennye komissii (1700–1796)
fond 615   Krepostnye knigi mestnykh uchrezhdenii XVI–XVIII vv.
fond 1209   Arkhiv prezhnikh votchinnykh del
fond 1255   Bariatinskie
fond 1256   Bakhmetevy
fond 1258   Beshentsevy
fond 1261   Vorontsovy
fond 1262   Gagariny
fond 1263   Golitsyny
fond 1265   Goncharovy
fond 1270   Musiny-Pushkiny
fond 1272   Naryshkiny
fond 1274   Paniny-Bludovy
fond 1276   Polianskie
fond 1277   Samariny
fond 1278   Stroganovy
fond 1280   Sukhotiny
fond 1287   Sheremetevy
fond 1288   Shuvalovy
fond 1290   Iusupovy
fond 1355   Ekonomicheskie primechaniia k general'nomu mezhevaniiu
fond 1395   Iankovy
fond 1406   Ermolovy

Tsentral'nyi gosudarstvennyi istoricheskii arkhiv Moskvy (TsGIAM)
(Central State Historical Archive of the City of Moscow)

fond 4   Kantseliariia moskovskogo dvorianskogo deputatskogo sobraniia
fond 50   Moskovskaia palata grazhdanskogo suda
fond 380   Kantseliariia moskovskogo gubernskogo predvoditelia dvorianstva
fond 383   Kantseliariia moskovskogo uezdnogo predvoditelia dvorianstva
fond 394   Kantseliariia ruzskogo uezdnogo predvoditelia dvorianstva
fond 1614   Glebovy-Streshnevy
fond 1871   Apukhtiny

St. Petersburg

Rossiiskii gosudarstvennyi istoricheskii arkhiv (RGIA)
(Russian State Historical Archive)

fond 796   Kantseliariia Sinoda (1721–1918 gg.)
fond 840   Batiushkovy
fond 878   Tatishchevy
fond 914   Volkonskie
fond 923   Glebovy
fond 931   Dolgorukie
fond 942   Zubovy
fond 946   Liubomirskie
fond 947   Kaveliny

fond 948   Kaznakovy
fond 958   Kiselev P. D.
fond 971   Kochubei
fond 994   Mordvinovy
fond 1003   Nelidova, Ekaterina Ivanova
fond 1021   Perovskie
fond 1035   Repniny
fond 1044   Saburovy
fond 1048   Saltykovy
fond 1068   Tutolminy i Tylub'evy
fond 1086   Tomilovy i Shvartsy
fond 1088   Sheremetevy
fond 1092   Shuvalovy
fond 1101   Dokumenty lichnogo proiskhozhdeniia, ne sostavliaiushchie otdel'nykh fondov
fond 1117   Saltykov I. P. i Miatleva P. I.
fond 1286   Departament politsii ispolnitel'noi (1803–1880 gg.)
fond 1330   Obshchie sobraniia departamentov Senata (1796–1917 gg.)
fond 1343   Departament gerol'dii Senata
fond 1345   Piatyi (ugolovnyi) departament Senata
fond 1346   Vtoroi (apelliatsionyi) departament Senata
fond 1350   Tretii departament Senata
fond 1379   Reviziia senatora Kniazhnina B. Ia. Novgorodskoi gubernii (1838–1839 gg.)
fond 1381   Reviziia senatora Begicheva D. N. Kaluzhskoi i Orlovskoi gubernii (1842–1843 gg.)
fond 1383   Reviziia senatora Kuruty I. E. Tambovskoi gubernii (1843–1845 gg.)
fond 1384   Reviziia senatora kn. Davydova S. I. Kaluzhskoi gubernii (1849–1851 gg.)
fond 1537   Reviziia senatorov Spiridova M. G. I Lopukhina I. V. Viatskoi, Kazanskoi i Orenburgskoi gubernii (1799–1800 gg.)
fond 1549   Reviziia senatora L'vova A. L. Tambovskoi gubernii (1814–1815 gg.)
fond 1554   Reviziia senatorov kn. Dolgorukova A. A. i Durasova E. A. Kazanskoi gubernii (1824–1825 gg.)
fond 1555   Reviziia senatora kn. Dolgorukova A. A. Voronezhskoi, Kurskoi, Penzenskoi, Saratovskoi, Simbirskoi i Tambovskoi gubernii (1826 g.)
fond 1556   Reviziia senatora Brozina V. I. Slabodsko-Ukrainskoi gubernii (1826–1827 gg.)
fond 1557   Reviziia senatora Ogareva N. I. Saratovskoi gubernii (1826–1827 gg.)
fond 1558   Reviziia senatora Ogareva N. I. Tul'skoi gubernii (1828 g.)

Gosudarstvennaia natsional'naia biblioteka (GNB) Otdel rukopisei.
(State National Library. Manuscript Division)

fond Ermitazhnoe sobranie
fond 116   Buturliny

Sankt-Peterburgskii filial Instituta rossiiskoi istorii RAN (SPbFIRI) (St. Petersburg Branch of the Institute of Russian History of the Russian Academy of Sciences)

kol. 154   Kollektsiia I. Ia. Shliapkina
kol. 238   Kollektsiia N. P. Likhacheva

Tambov

Gosudarstvennyi arkhiv Tambovskoi oblasti (GATO) (State Archive of Tambov oblast)

fond 67   Tambovskaia palata grazhdanskogo suda
fond 81   Morshanskii uezdnyi sud

Tver'

Gosudarstvennyi arkhiv Tverskoi oblasti (GA Tverskoi oblasti) (State Archive of Tver' oblast)

fond 668   Kashinskii uezdnyi sud
fond 674   Tverskoi uezdnyi sud

Vladimir

Gosudarstvennyi arkhiv Vladimirskoi oblasti (GAVO) (State Archive of Vladimir oblast)

fond 92   Vladimirskaia palata grazhdanskogo suda

MEMOIRS AND OTHER PUBLISHED PRIMARY SOURCES

Adam, Juliette Edmond [Juliette Lamber]. *Impressions Françaises en Russie.* Paris, 1912.
Adam, M. "Iz semeinoi khroniki." *Istoricheskii vestnik* 94, no. 12 (1903): 816–27.
Akhmatova, Elizaveta Nikolaevna. "Pomeshchitsa." In *Sbornik literaturnykh statei, posviashchennykh russkimi pisateliami pamiati pokoinogo knigoprodavtsa-izdatelia Aleksandra Filipovicha Smirdina,* vol. 3, 3–190. St. Petersburg, 1858.
Aksakov, Sergei. *A Russian Gentleman.* Translated by J. D. Duff. Oxford: Oxford University Press, 1982.
——. *Years of Childhood.* Translated by J. D. Duff. Oxford: Oxford University Press, 1983.
Akty iuridicheskie, ili sobranie form starinnogo deloproizvodstva. St. Petersburg, 1838.
Akty, otnosiashchiesia do iuridicheskogo byta drevnei Rossii. 4 vols. St. Petersburg, 1857–84.
Annenkov, I. P. "Dnevnik kurskogo pomeshchika I. P. Annenkova, 1745–1766." In *Materialy po istorii SSSR* 5, 677–823. Moscow: Izdatel'stvo Akademii Nauk SSSR, 1957.
Arkhiv grafov Mordvinovykh. 10 vols. Edited by V. A. Bil'basov. St. Petersburg, 1901–3.
Arkhiv kniazia F. A. Kurakina. 10 vols. Edited by M. I. Semevskii. St. Petersburg, 1890–1902.
Arkhiv kniazia Vorontsova. 40 vols. Edited by P. I. Bartenev. Moscow, 1870–95.
At Home with the Gentry: A Victorian English Lady's Diary of Russian Country Life. Attributed to Amelia Lyons. Edited by John McNair. Nottingham: Bramcote Press, 1998.
A-va [A. N. Kazina]. "Zhenskaia zhizn'." *Otechestvennye zapiski* 219, no. 3 (March 1875): 203–58.
Avdeeva, Ekaterina. *Rukovodstvo k ustroistvu ferm i vedeniiu na nikh khoziaistva.* St. Petersburg, 1863.
Baranov, P. N., ed. *Opis' vysochaishim ukazam i poveleniiam, khraniashchimsia v Sankt-Peterburgskom Senatskom archive za XVIII vek.* 3 vols. St. Petersburg, 1872–78.
Bardakova, M. M. (M. Marina). "Iz vospominanii o Tsarskom sele." *Russkaia starina* 148, no. 11 (1911): 327–37.
Bashkirtseva, N. D. "Iz Ukrainskoi stariny. Moia rodoslovnaia." *Russkii arkhiv* 1, no. 3 (1900): 321–54.
Bespiatykh, Iu. N. *Peterburg Anny Ioannovny v inostrannykh opisaniiakh.* St. Petersburg, 1997.

Blagovo, D. *Rasskazy babushki iz vospominanii piati pokolenii.* Leningrad, 1989.

Bludova, A. D. "Zapiski grafini Antoniny Dmitrievny Bludovoi." *Russkii arkhiv* kn. 1, no. 7/8 (1872): 1217–1310; kn. 1, no. 4 (1874): 833–83.

Bogdanovich, Petr. *Novyi i polnyi pis'movnik.* St. Petersburg, 1791.

Bolotov, Andrei. *Zhizn' i prikliucheniia Andreia Bolotova.* 3 vols. Moscow-Leningrad, 1931.

Boretskoi, A. P. "Zakhudaloe dvorianstvo." *Russkia mysl'* 12 (1882): 339–53.

Borisov, V. A., ed. *Opisanie goroda Shui i ego okrestnostei, s prilozheniem starinnykh aktov.* Moscow, 1851.

Bradford, Martha Wilmot. *The Russian Journals of Martha and Catherine Wilmot, 1803-1808.* Edited by the Marchioness of Londonderry and H. M. Hyde. London: Macmillan and Co., 1935.

Butkovskaia, A. Ia. "Rasskazy babushki." *Istoricheskii vestnik* 18, no. 12 (1884): 594–631.

Chekhov, Anton. *Plays.* Translated by Ronald Wilks. London: Penguin Books, 1951.

——. *A Woman's Kingdom and Other Stories.* Translated by Ronald Hingley. Oxford: Oxford University Press, 1989.

Collins, Samuel. *The Present State of Russia.* London, 1671.

Custine, Marquis de. *La Russie en 1839.* 2d ed. 3 vols. Paris, 1843.

Danilov, M. V. "Zapiski." *Russkii arkhiv,* kn. 2, no. 3 (1883): 1–67.

Dashkova, Ekaterina Romanovna. *The Memoirs of Princess Dashkova.* Translated and edited by Kyril Fitzlyon, with an introduction by Jehanne M. Gheith. Durham: Duke University Press, 1995.

Davydov, N. V. "Iz pomeshchich'ei zhizni 40–50 gg." *Golos minuvshego,* no. 2 (February 1916): 164–200.

Del'vig, A. I. *Polveka russkoi zhizni. Vospominaniia A. I. Del'viga, 1820–1870.* 2 vols. Moscow, 1930.

Derzhavin, Gavril Romanovich. *Sochineniia Derzhavina.* 2d ed. 7 vols. Edited by Ia. Grot. St. Petersburg, 1864–1878.

Doklady i prigovory sostoiavshiesia v pravitel'stvuiushchem Senate v tsarstvovanie Petra Velikogo. 6 vols. in 5. St. Petersburg, 1880–1901.

The Domostroi: Rules for Russian Households in the Time of Ivan the Terrible. Edited and translated by Carolyn Johnston Pouncy. Ithaca: Cornell University Press, 1994.

Dostoevsky, Fyodor. *Uncle's Dream and Other Stories.* Translated by David McDuff. London: Penguin Books, 1989.

Drug iunoshestva. Moscow, 1807.

Glinka, Sergei Nikolaevich. *Zapiski.* St. Petersburg, 1895.

Gogol, Nikolai. *Diary of a Madman and Other Stories.* Translated by Ronald Wilks. London: Penguin Books, 1972.

Grasserie, Raoul de la. *Les Codes Suédois de 1734.* Paris: A. Pedone, 1895.

Grazhdanskie zakony gubernii tsarstva Pol'skogo. Tom I: Grazhdanskoe ulozhenie 1825 goda. St. Petersburg, 1875.

Grot, Natalia. *Iz semeinoi khroniki. Vospominaniia dlia detei i vnukov.* 7th ed. St. Petersburg, 1900.

Haxthausen, August von. *Studies on the Interior of Russia.* Edited by S. Frederick Starr. Translated by E. Schmidt. Chicago: University of Chicago Press, 1972.

Karpinskaia, Iu. N. "Iz semeinoi khroniki." *Istoricheskii vestnik* 70, no. 12 (1897): 853–70.

Kern, A. P. (Markova-Vinogradskaia). "Iz vospominanii o moem detstve." In *Vospominaniia, dnevniki, perepiska,* 101–22. Moscow, 1974.

Khrushchov, I. P. "Milena, vtoraia zhena Derzhavina." *Russkii vestnik* 283, kn. 2 (1903): 549–80.

Khvoshchinskaia, Elena Iur'evna. *Vospominaniia.* St. Petersburg, 1898.

——. "Vospominaniia." *Russkaia starina,* no. 3 (1898): 559–85.

Khvostova, E. A. [Ekaterina Sushkova]. *Zapiski, 1812–1841.* Leningrad, 1928.

Kochubei, Arkadii Vasil'evich. *Semeinaia khronika. Zapiski, 1790–1873.* St. Petersburg, 1890.

Korb, Johann Georg. *Diary of an Austrian Secretary of Legation at the Court of Czar Peter the Great.* 2 vols. Translated by Count MacDonnell. London, 1863.

Kornilova, O. I. *Byl' iz vremeni krepostnichestva (Vospominaniia o moei materi i ee okruzhaiushchem).* St. Petersburg, 1890.

Korostovets, Vladimir. *Seed and Harvest.* London: Faber and Faber, 1931.

Krest'ianskoe dvizhenie v Rossii v 1796–1825 gg.: Sbornik dokumentov. Edited by S. N. Valk. Moscow, 1961.

Krest'ianskoe dvizhenie v Rossii v 1826–1849 gg.: Sbornik dokumentov. Edited by A. V. Predtechenskii. Moscow, 1961.

Krest'ianskoe dvizhenie v Rossii v 1857–mae 1861 gg.: Sbornik dokumentov. Edited by S. B. Okun'. Moscow, 1963.

Krestinskaia, Anna. "Chuvstva i mysli pri chtenii ruchnoi knizhki o pravakh zhenshchin v Rossii." *Damskii zhurnal,* no. 24 (1827): 234–38.

Kupreianova, A. N. "Iz semeinykh vospominanii." *Bogoslovskii vestnik* 1, no. 4 (1914): 650–63.

Kvashnina-Samarina, Ekaterina Petrovna. "Dnevnik." In *K istorii sotsial'no-bytovykh otnoshenii v nachale XIX stoletiia,* 1–11. Edited by S. M. Smirnov. Novgorod, 1928.

Labzina, A. E. *Vospominaniia, 1763–1819.* St. Petersburg, 1914. Reprinted by Oriental Research Partners, Cambridge, Mass., 1974.

Lachinova, A. "Neskol'ko slov o P. Letneve." In *Sobranie sochinenii P. Letneva,* vol. 1, i–xxx. Kiev, 1892.

Lelong, Anna Kozminichna. "Vospominaniia." *Russkii arkhiv* 2, no. 6 (1913): 778–808; no. 7 (1913): 52–103.

Leroy-Beaulieu, Anatole. *The Empire of the Tsars and the Russians.* 3 vols. Translated by Zenaide A. Ragozin. New York: G. P. Putnam, 1898.

[Masson, Charles]. *Mémoires secrets sur la Russie, et particuliérement sur la fin du regne de Catherine II et le commencement de celui de Paul I.* 2 vols. Amsterdam, 1800.

Materialy dlia istorii krepostnogo prava v Rossii. Izvlecheniia iz sekretnykh otchetov Ministerstva Vnutrennikh Del za 1836–1856 g. Berlin, 1873.

Mengden, Elizaveta. "Iz dnevnika vnuchki." *Russkaia starina* 153, no. 1 (1913): 103–31.

Mengden, Sofia. "Otryvki semeinoi khroniki." *Russkaia starina* 134, no. 4 (1908): 97–116.

Meshcherskaia, Sofia Vasil'evna. *Vospominaniia kniagini Sofii Vasil'evnoi Meshcherskoi.* Tver', 1902.

Meshcherskii, A. V. "Iz moei stariny. Vospominaniia." *Russkii arkhiv* 2, no. 6 (1900): 239–63; no. 7 (1900): 355–82.

Moller, E. N. "Pamiatnye zametki E. N. Moller, rozhdennoi Murav'evoi, 1820–1872." *Russkaia starina* 66, no. 5 (1890): 325–42.

Montagu, Mary Wortley. *The Complete Letters of Lady Mary Wortley Montagu. Vol. I: 1708–1720.* Oxford: Clarendon Press, 1965.

Mordvinova, N. N. "Zapiski grafini N. N. Mordvinovoi." *Russkii arkhiv,* kn. 1, no. 1 (1883): 145–99.

The Muscovite Law Code (Ulozhenie) of 1649. Part I: Text and Translation. Translated and edited by Richard Hellie. Irvine, Calif.: Charles Schlacks Jr. Publisher, 1988.

Nikoleva, M. S. "Cherty starinnogo dvorianskogo byta. Vospominaniia." *Russkii arkhiv,* kn. 3, no. 9 (1893): 107–20; no. 10 (1893): 129–96.

Novoselova, E. M. "Vospominaniia 50-kh godov. Pamiati ottsa." *Russkaia starina* 148, no. 10 (1911): 98–111.

Olearius, Adam. *The Travels of Olearius in Seventeenth-Century Russia.* Translated and edited by Samuel H. Baron. Stanford: Stanford University Press, 1967.

Opisanie dokumentov i del, khraniashchikhsia v arkhive sviateishego pravitel'stvuiushchego Sinoda (*OAS*). 30 vols. St. Petersburg, 1868–1916.

Orlov-Davydov, V. P. *Biograficheskii ocherk grafa Vladimira Grigor'evicha Orlova.* 2 vols. St. Petersburg, 1878.

Os'mnadtsatyi vek. Istoricheskii sbornik. 4 vols. Edited by Petr Bartenev. Moscow, 1868–69.

Ostrovsky, Alexander. *Five Plays of Alexander Ostrovsky.* Translated by Eugene K. Bristow. New York: Pegasus, 1969.

Pamiatniki Moskovskoi delovoi pis'mennosti XVIII veka. Moscow, 1981.

Perry, John. "Extracts from the State of Russia under the Present Czar." In *Seven Britons in Imperial Russia, 1698–1812,* 21–63. Edited by Peter Putnam. Princeton: Princeton University Press, 1952.

Polivanova, E. Ia. "Strumilovskaia kolobroda (Iz semeinoi khroniki)." *Istoricheskii vestnik* 112, no. 6 (1908): 846–63.

Polnoe sobranie zakonov Rossiiskoi imperii (*PSZ*). 1st series (1649–1825). 45 vols. St. Petersburg, 1830; 2d series (1825–1881). 55 vols. St. Petersburg, 1830–84.

"Poslednie dni tsarstvovaniia Ekateriny II (Pis'ma kniagini Anny Aleksandrovny Golistynoi)." *Istoricheskii vestnik* 30 (October 1887): 82–109.

Proekty Ugolovnogo ulozheniia 1754–1766 godov: novoulozhennoi knigi chast' vtoraia. O rozysknykh delakh i kakie za raznye zlodeistva i prestupleniia kazni, nakazaniia i shtrafy polozheny. St. Petersburg, 1882.

Raeff, Marc, ed. *Plans for Political Reform in Imperial Russia, 1730–1905.* Englewood Cliffs, N.J.: Prentice-Hall, 1966.

Raevskaia, E. I. "Iz pamiatnoi knigi E. I. Raevskoi." *Russkii arkhiv,* kn. 1, no. 2 (1883): 291–302.

Raevskii, I. A. "Iz vospominanii I. A. Raevskogo." *Istoricheskii vestnik* 101, no. 8 (1905): 391–409.

Real Estate Transfer Deeds in Novgorod, 1609–1616. Text and commentary by Ingegerd Norlander. Stockholm: Almqvist and Wiksell International, 1987.

Rondeau, Mme. *Pis'ma ledi Rondo, suprugi angliiskogo ministra pri Rossiiskom dvore, v tsarstvovanie Imperatritsy Anny Ioannovny.* St. Petersburg, 1836. (Translation of Mme. Rondeau, *Letters from a Lady, Who Resided Some Years in Russia, to Her Friend in England.* London, 1775.)

Rozanov, N. P. *Istoriia Moskovskogo eparkhial'nogo upravleniia so vremeni uchrezhdeniia Sviateishego Sinoda.* 3 vols. in 2. Moscow, 1869–71.

Rumiantsova, E. M. *Pis'ma grafini E. M. Rumiantsevoi k ee muzhu, fel'dmarshalu grafu P. A. Rumiantsovu-Zadunaiskomu, 1762–1779.* St. Petersburg, 1888.

Saltykov-Shchedrin, Mikhail. *The Golovlyov Family.* Translated by Ronald Wilks. New York: Penguin, 1988.

Sanktpeterburgskie senatskie ob"iavleniia po sudebnym, rasporiaditel'nym, politseiskim i kazennym delam. St. Petersburg, 1825–92.

Sbornik imperatorskogo russkogo istoricheskogo obshchestva (*SIRIO*). 148 vols. St. Petersburg, 1867–1916.

Semenov-Tian-Shanskii, P. P. *Memuary P. P. Semenova-Tian-Shanskogo. Tom I. Detstvo i iunost' (1827–1855 gg.).* 7th ed. Petrograd, 1917.

Senatskii arkhiv. 15 vols. St. Petersburg, 1888–1913.

Shcherbatov, Prince M. M. *On the Corruption of Morals in Russia.* Edited and translated by A. Lentin. Cambridge: Cambridge University Press, 1969.

Shchukin, Petr Ivanovich. *Sbornik starinnykh bumag.* 10 vols. Moscow, 1896–1902.

——. *Shchukinskii sbornik.* 10 vols. Moscow, 1902–12.

Skalon, S. V. "Vospominaniia S. V. Skalon (urozhdennoi Kapnist)." *Istoricheskii vestnik* 44, no. 5 (May 1891): 338–67.

Skhimonakhinia Nektariia: Kniaginia Natalia Borisovna Dolgorukova, doch' fel'dmarshala Sheremeteva. Moscow, 1909.

Smirnova, Aleksandra Osipovna. "Zapiski." *Russkii arkhiv* 5, no. 2 (1895): 17–27.

Sokhanskaia, N. S. "Avtobiografiia." *Russkoe obozrenie,* no. 6 (1896): 480–88.

Starina i novizna. 22 vols. Moscow, 1897–1917.

Subbotina, E. D. *Na revoliutsionnom puti.* Moscow, 1928.

Sverbeev, D. N. "Zapiski." In *Pomeshchich'ia Rossia po zapiskam sovremennikov,* 151–76. Moscow, 1911.

Svod zakonov Rossiiskoi imperii (SZ). 10 vols. St. Petersburg, 1876, 1900, 1913.

Tenisheva, M. K. *Vpechatleniia moei zhizni.* Leningrad, 1991.

Tiutcheva, A. F. *Pri dvore dvukh imperatorov. Vospominaniia. Dnevnik. 1853–1855.* Moscow, 1928.

Tolstoi, M. V. "Moi vospominaniia." *Russkii arkhiv,* kn. 1, no. 2 (1881): 245–313; no. 3 (1881): 42–131.

Tolychova, T. *Semeinyia zapiski.* Moscow, 1865.

Turgenev, Ivan. *Fathers and Sons.* 2d ed. Edited with a revised translation by Ralph E. Matlaw. New York: W. W. Norton, 1989.

Varlamova, Raida. *Semeinyi magazin.* Moscow, 1856.

Vasil'chikov, A. A. *Semeistvo Razumovskikh.* 5 vols. St. Petersburg, 1880–94.

Vasil'ev, I. V. *Femida, ili nachertanie prav, preimushchestv i obiazannostei zhenskogo pola v Rossii.* Moscow, 1827.

——. "O preimushchestvakh zhenshchin v Rossii po delam ugolovnym." *Damskii zhurnal,* no. 11 (1827): 242–44; no. 13 (1827): 6–11.

Vatatsi, M. P. "Byl' minuvshego." *Istoricheskii vestnik* 131, no. 3 (1913): 765–77.

Vernadskaia, Maria Nikolaevna. *Sobranie sochinenii.* St. Petersburg, 1862.

Vigel, F. F. *Zapiski.* Moscow, 1928. Republished by Oriental Research Partners, Cambridge, Mass., 1974.

Vodovozova, E. N. *Na zare zhizni.* 2 vols. Moscow: Khudozhestvennaia literatura, 1987.

Volkhovskii, F. V. "Otryvki odnoi chelovecheskoi zhizni." *Sovremennik* 4, no. 4 (1911): 254–67.

Volkonskii, S. M. *O dekabristakh (po semeinym vospominaniiam).* St. Petersburg, 1998. First published in 1922.

Weber, Friedrich Christian. *The Present State of Russia.* 2 vols. London: Frank Cass, 1968.

Witte, S. Iu. *Vospominaniia: Detstvo. Tsartsvovaniia Aleksandra II i Aleksandra III (1849–1894).* Berlin: "Slovo," 1923.

Zamechaniia o nedostatkakh deistvuiushchikh grazhdanskikh zakonov. Izdanie redaktsionnoi kommissii po sostavleniiu proekta grazhdanskogo ulozheniia. St. Petersburg, 1891.

Zhenskaia filosofiia. Moscow, 1793.

Zhukovskaia, Ekaterina. *Zapiski.* Leningrad, 1930.

Secondary Sources

Abensour, Leon. *La femme et le féminisme, avant la Revolution.* Paris: Ernest Leroux, 1923.

Aleksandrov, V. A. *Sel'skaia obshchina v Rossii (XVII–nachalo XIX v.)* Moscow, 1976.

Alekseev, V. P. *Dvoriane Salovy iz Sosnovki.* Briansk, 1993.

Amussen, Susan Dwyer. *An Ordered Society: Gender and Class in Early Modern England.* Oxford: Basil Blackwell, 1988.

Anfimov, A. M. *Krupnoe pomeshchich'e khoziaistvo evropeiskoi Rossii (konets XIX–nachalo XX veka).* Moscow, 1969.

——. "Maioratnoe zemlevladenie v tsarskoi Rossii." *Istoriia SSSR,* no. 5 (1962): 151–60.

Anisimov, Evgenii V. "Empress Anna Ivanovna, 1730–1740." In *The Emperors and Empresses of Russia: Rediscovering the Romanovs*, 37–65. Edited by Donald J. Raleigh. Armonk, N.Y.: M. E. Sharpe, 1996.

———. *The Reforms of Peter the Great: Progress through Coercion in Russia*. Translated by John T. Alexander. Armonk, N.Y.: M. E. Sharpe, 1993.

Archer, Rowena A. "'How Ladies…who live on their manors ought to manage their households and estates': Women as Landholders and Administrators in the Later Middle Ages." In *Woman Is a Worthy Wight: Women in English Society, c. 1200–1500*, 149–81. Edited by P. J. P. Goldberg. Far Thrupp, Stroud, Gloucestershire: Alan Sutton, 1992.

Artemova, E. Iu. "Zapiski frantsuzskikh puteshestvennikov o kul'ture Rossii poslednei treti XVIII veka." *Istoriia SSSR*, no. 3 (1988): 165–73.

Atkinson, Dorothy. "Society and the Sexes in the Russian Past." In *Women in Russia*, 3–38. Edited by D. Atkinson, A. Dallin, and G. Lapidus. Stanford: Stanford University Press, 1977.

Augustine, Wilson R. "Notes toward a Portrait of the Eighteenth-Century Russian Nobility." *Canadian Slavic Studies* 4, no. 3 (Fall 1970): 373–425.

Badinter, Elisabeth. *L'amour en plus: Histoire de l'amour maternel (XVIIe–XXe siècle)*. Paris: Flammarion, 1980.

Barker-Benfield, G. J. *The Culture of Sensibility: Sex and Society in Eighteenth-Century Britain*. Chicago: University of Chicago Press, 1992.

Barnes, Sandra T. "Women, Property, and Power." In *Beyond the Second Sex: New Directions in the Anthropology of Gender*, 255–280. Edited by Peggy Reeves Sanday and Ruth Gallagher Goodenough. Philadelphia: University of Pennsylvania Press, 1990.

Basch, Norma. *In the Eyes of the Law: Women, Marriage, and Property in Nineteenth-Century New York*. Ithaca: Cornell University Press, 1982.

Becker, Seymour. *Nobility and Privilege in Late Imperial Russia*. DeKalb: Northern Illinois University Press, 1985.

Bernhardt, Kathryn. *Women and Property in China, 960–1949*. Stanford: Stanford University Press, 1999.

Biemer, Linda Briggs. *Women and Property in Colonial New York: The Transition from Dutch to English Law, 1643–1727*. Ann Arbor: UMI Research Press, 1983.

Birkett, Jennifer. "'A Mere Matter of Business': Marriage, Divorce and the French Revolution." In *Marriage and Property: Women and Marital Customs in History*, 119–37. Edited by Elizabeth Craik. Aberdeen: Aberdeen University Press, 1984.

Bisha, Robin. "The Promise of Patriarchy: Marriage in Eighteenth-Century Russia." Ph.D. dissertation. Indiana University, 1993.

Blinov, I. "Senatorskie revizii." *Zhurnal Ministerstva Iustitsii* 19, no. 2 (February 1913): 257–302.

Blum, Jerome. *Lord and Peasant in Russia from the Ninth to the Nineteenth Century*. Princeton: Princeton University Press, 1961.

Bochkarev, V. "Kul'turnye zaprosy russkogo obshchestva nachala tsarstvovaniia Ekateriny II po materialam zakonodatel'noi komissii 1767 goda." *Russkaia starina* 162 (May 1915): 312–25.

Bogoslovskii, M. M. *Byt i nravy russkogo dvorianstvo v pervoi polovine XVIII veka*. 2d ed. Petrograd, 1918.

———. *Oblastnaia reforma Petra Velikago. Provintsiia 1719–27gg*. Moscow, 1902.

Boskovska, Nada. "Muscovite Women during the Seventeenth Century: At the Peak of the Deprivation of Their Rights or on the Road towards New Freedom?" In *Von Moskau nach St. Petersburg: Das russische Reich im 17. Jahrhundert*, 47–62. Edited by Hans-Joachim Torke. Wiesbaden: Harrassowitz Verlag, 2000.

Buckler, Georgina. "Women in Byzantine Law about 1100 A.D." *Byzantion: Revue Internationale des Études Byzantines* 11 (1936): 391–416.

Burbank, Jane. "Legal Culture, Citizenship, and Peasant Jurisprudence: Perspectives from the Early Twentieth Century." In *Reforming Justice in Russia, 1864–1996: Power, Culture, and the Limits of Legal Order,* 82–106. Edited by Peter H. Solomon Jr. Amonk, N.Y.: M. E. Sharpe, 1997.

Carswell, John. *The South Sea Bubble.* London: Cresset Press, 1960.

Cavender, Mary Wells. "Nests of the Gentry: Family, Estate, and Local Loyalties in Provincial Tver', 1820–1869." Ph.D. dissertation. University of Michigan, 1997.

Chavchavadze, Paul. *Marie Avinov: Pilgrimage through Hell.* Englewood Cliffs, N.J.: Prentice-Hall, 1968.

Chechulin, N. D. *Russkoe provintsial'noe obshchestvo vo vtoroi polovine XVIII veka.* St. Petersburg, 1889.

Chernikova, T. V. "Gosudarevo slovo i delo vo vremena Anny Ioannovny." *Istoriia SSSR,* no. 5 (1989): 155–63.

Chojnacki, Stanley. "Dowries and Kinsmen in Early Renaissance Venice." *Journal of Interdisciplinary History* 5, no. 4 (Spring 1975): 571–600.

——. "The Power of Love: Wives and Husbands in Late Medieval Venice." In *Women and Power in the Middle Ages,* 126–48. Edited by Mary Erler and Maryanne Kowaleski. Athens: University of Georgia Press, 1988.

Colley, Linda. *Britons: Forging the Nation 1707–1837.* New Haven: Yale University Press, 1992.

Confino, Michael. *Domaines et seigneurs en Russie vers la fin du XVIII siècle.* Paris: Institut d'Études Slaves, 1963.

——. "Histoire et psychologie: Á propos de la noblese russe au XVIIIe siècle." *Annales: Économies, sociétés, civilisations* 22, no. 6 (November–December 1967): 1163–205.

Cooper, J. P. "Patterns of Inheritance and Settlement by Great Landowners from the Fifteenth to the Eighteenth Centuries." In *Family and Inheritance: Rural Society in Western Europe, 1200–1800,* 192–305. Edited by Jack Goody, Joan Thirsk, and E. P. Thompson. Cambridge: Cambridge University Press, 1976.

Crisp, Olga. "Russian Financial Policy and the Gold Standard at the End of the Nineteenth Century." In *Studies in the Russian Economy before 1914,* 96–110. London: Macmillan Press, 1976.

Crummey, Robert O. *Aristocrats and Servitors: The Boyar Elite in Russia, 1613–1689.* Princeton: Princeton University Press, 1983.

Darrow, Margaret H. "French Noblewomen and the New Domesticity, 1750–1850." *Feminist Studies* 5, no. 1 (Spring 1979): 41–65.

Davidoff, Leonore and Catherine Hall. *Family Fortunes: Men and Women of the English Middle Class, 1780–1850.* Chicago: University of Chicago Press, 1987.

Debol'skii, N. N. *Grazhdanskaia deesposobnost' po russkomu pravu do kontsa XVII veka.* St. Petersburg, 1903.

DeJean, Joan. *Tender Geographies: Women and the Origins of the Novel in France.* New York: Columbia University Press, 1991.

D'Eszlary, Charles. "Le Statut de la femme dans le droit Hongrois." *Recueils de la Société Jean Bodin pour l'histoire comparative des institutions* 12 (1962): 421–45.

Diefendorf, Barbara B. *Paris City Councillors in the Sixteenth Century: The Politics of Patrimony.* Princeton: Princeton University Press, 1983.

——. "Widowhood and Remarriage in Sixteenth-Century Paris." *Journal of Family History* 7, no. 4 (Winter 1982): 379–95.

——. "Women and Property in Ancien Regime France: Theory and Practice in Dauphine and Paris." In *Early Modern Conceptions of Property,* 170–93. Edited by John Brewer and Susan Staves. London: Routledge, 1995.

Ditrikh, Maria Nikolaevna. *Russkaia zhenshchina velikokniazheskogo vremeni.* St. Petersburg, 1904.

Dmokhovskii. "O pravakh zhenshchiny v Rossii." *Biblioteka dlia chteniia* 172 (July 1862): 67–97.

Dobriakov, Aleksandr. *Russkaia zhenshchina v do-mongol'skii period.* St. Petersburg, 1864.

Dolin, Tim. *Mistress of the House: Women of Property in the Victorian Novel.* Aldershot: Ashgate, 1997.

Donicht, Gaby. "The Idea of Morality in the Russian Noble Family of Late Imperial Russia, 1870–1914." Paper presented at the Third Carleton Conference on the History of the Family, Ottawa, Ontario, May 15–17, 1997.

Dubakin, D. N. *Vliianie khristianstva na semeinyi byt russkogo obshchestva.* St. Petersburg, 1880.

Dukes, Paul. *Catherine the Great and the Russian Nobility: A Study Based on the Materials of the Legislative Commission of 1767.* Cambridge: Cambridge University Press, 1967.

Dunham, Vera Sandomirsky. "The Strong-Woman Motif." In *The Transformation of Russian Society,* 459–83. Edited by Cyril Black. Cambridge: Harvard University Press, 1960.

Ebrey, Patricia Buckley. *The Inner Quarters: Marriage and the Lives of Chinese Women in the Sung Period.* Berkeley: University of California Press, 1993.

Eck, Alexandre. "La Situation juridique de la femme russe au moyen âge." *Recueils de la Société Jean Bodin pour l'histoire comparative des institutions* 12 (1962): 405–20.

Edmondson, Linda Harriet. *Feminism in Russia, 1900–1917.* Stanford: Stanford University Press, 1984.

El'iashevich, V. B. *Istoriia prava pozemel'noi sobstvennosti v Rossii.* 2 vols. Paris, 1948–51.

Engel, Barbara Alpern. "Mothers and Daughters: Family Patterns and the Female Intelligentsia." In *The Family in Imperial Russia,* 44–59. Edited by David L. Ransel. Urbana: University of Illinois Press, 1978.

——. *Mothers and Daughters: Women of the Intelligentsia in Nineteenth-Century Russia.* Cambridge: Cambridge University Press, 1983.

Engelstein, Laura. *The Keys to Happiness: Sex and the Search for Modernity in Fin-de-Siècle Russia.* Ithaca: Cornell University Press, 1992.

English, Barbara. *The Great Landowners of East Yorkshire, 1530–1910.* New York: Harvester Wheatsheaf, 1990.

Erickson, Amy Louise. "Common Law versus Common Practice: The Use of Marriage Settlements in Early Modern England." *Economic History Review* 42, no. 1 (1990): 21–39.

——. *Women and Property in Early Modern England.* London: Routledge, 1993.

Evreinova, Anna. "Ob uravnenii prav zhenshchin pri nasledovanii." *Drug zhenshchin,* no. 11 (November 1883): 62–90.

Faizova, I. V. *"Manifest o vol'nosti" i sluzhba dvorianstva v XVIII stoletii.* Moscow: "Nauka," 1999.

Farrow, Lee A. "Inheritance, Status, and Security: Noble Life in Eighteenth-Century Russia." Unpublished manuscript, 2000.

——. "Peter the Great's Law of Single Inheritance: State Imperatives and Noble Resistance." *Russian Review* 55, no. 3 (July 1996): 430–47.

Faust, Drew Gilpin. *Mothers of Invention: Women of the Slaveholding South in the American Civil War.* New York: Vintage Books, 1997.

Field, Daniel. *The End of Serfdom: Nobility and Bureaucracy in Russia, 1855–1861.* Cambridge: Harvard University Press, 1976.

Florovskii, A. V. *Sostav zakonodatel'noi kommissii, 1767–74 gg.* Odessa, 1915.

Foreman, Amanda. *Georgiana, Duchess of Devonshire.* London: HarperCollins, 1998.

Forster, Robert. *The Nobility of Toulouse in the Eighteenth Century: A Social and Economic Study.* Baltimore: Johns Hopkins University Press, 1960.

Fox-Genovese, Elizabeth. *Within the Plantation Household: Black and White Women of the Old South.* Chapel Hill: University of North Carolina Press, 1988.

Freeze, Gregory L. "Bringing Order to the Russian Family: Marriage and Divorce in Imperial Russia, 1760–1860." *Journal of Modern History* 62, no. 4 (December 1990): 709–46.

Fügedi, Erik. "Some Characteristics of the Medieval Hungarian Noble Family." *Journal of Family History* 7, no. 1 (Spring 1982): 27–39.

Gates-Coon, Rebecca. *The Landed Estates of the Esterházy Princes: Hungary during the Reforms of Maria Theresia and Joseph II.* Baltimore: The Johns Hopkins University Press, 1994.

Gatrell, Peter. *The Tsarist Economy, 1850–1917.* New York: St. Martin's Press, 1986.

Gessen, I. V. "Vliianie zakonodatel'stva na polozhenie zhenshchin." *Pravo,* no. 51 (1908): cols. 2833–40.

Glasse, Antonia. "The Formidable Woman: Portrait and Original." *Russian Literature Triquarterly,* no. 9 (Spring 1974): 433–53.

Glasson, E. *Histoire du droit et des institutions de la France.* 8 vols. Paris, 1887–1903.

Goikhbarg, A. G. *Zakon o rasshirenii prav nasledovaniia po zakonu lits zhenskogo pola i prava zaveshchaniia rodovykh imenii.* St. Petersburg, 1912.

Gold, Penny Schine. *The Lady and the Virgin: Image, Attitude, and Experience in Twelfth-Century France.* Chicago: University of Chicago Press, 1985.

Golikova, N. B. "Rostovshchichestvo v Rossii nachala XVIII v. i ego nekotorye osobennosti." In *Problemy genezisa kapitalizma,* 242–90. Moscow: Nauka, 1970.

Gol'tsev, V. A. *Zakonodatel'stvo i nravy v Rossii XVIII veka.* 2d ed. St. Petersburg, 1896.

Goody, Jack. "Inheritance, Property, and Women: Some Comparative Considerations." In *Family and Inheritance: Rural Society in Western Europe, 1200–1800,* 10–36. Edited by Jack Goody, Joan Thirsk, and E. P. Thompson. Cambridge: Cambridge University Press, 1976.

Got'e, Iu. V. *Istoriia oblastnogo upravleniia v Rossii ot Petra I do Ekateriny II.* Moscow, 1913.

——. *Ocherk istorii zemlevladeniia v Rossii.* Sergiev Posad, 1915.

Gradovskii, A. D. *Istoriia mestnogo upravleniia v Rossii.* St. Petersburg, 1868.

Greene, Diana. "Mid-Nineteenth-Century Domestic Ideology in Russia." In *Women and Russian Culture: Projections and Self-Perceptions,* 78–97. Edited by Rosalind Marsh. New York: Berghahn Books, 1998.

Gur'ianova, V. V. "Tverskaia pomeshchitsa vtoroi poloviny XVIII veka Praskov'ia Il'inichna Manzei." In *Zhenshchiny v sotsial'noi istorii Rossii: Sbornik nauchnykh trudov,* 20–31. Tver': Tverskoi gosudarstvennyi universitet, 1997.

Habakkuk, John. *Marriage, Debt, and the Estates System: English Landownership, 1650–1950.* Oxford: Clarendon Press, 1994.

Halperin, Charles. "Sixteenth-Century Foreign Travel Accounts to Muscovy: A Methodological Excursus." *Sixteenth Century Journal* 6, no. 2 (October 1975): 89–110.

Hamburg, Gary M. *Politics of the Russian Nobility, 1881–1905.* New Brunswick: Rutgers University Press, 1984.

Harris, Barbara J. "Property, Power, and Personal Relations: Elite Mothers and Sons in Yorkist and Early Tudor England." *Signs* 15, no. 3 (Spring 1990): 606–32.

Harris, Frances. "Rich and Poor Widows: Eighteenth-Century Women in the Althorp Papers." *British Library Occasional Papers* 12 (1990): 124–28.

Heldt, Barbara. *Terrible Perfection: Women and Russian Literature.* Bloomington: Indiana University Press, 1987.

Hellie, Richard. *Enserfment and Military Change in Muscovy.* Chicago: University of Chicago Press, 1971.

——. *Slavery in Russia, 1450–1725.* Chicago: University of Chicago Press, 1982.

——. "Women and Slavery in Muscovy." *Russian History,* 10, pt. 2 (1983): 213–29.

Herlihy, David. "Land, Family and Women in Continental Europe, 701–1200." *Traditio* 18 (1962): 89–120.

Higgs, David. *Nobles in Nineteenth-Century France: The Practice of Inegalitarianism.* Baltimore: Johns Hopkins University Press, 1987.

Hirschon, Renée. "Introduction: Property, Power, and Gender Relations." In *Women and Property—Women as Property*, 1–22. Edited by Renée Hirschon. New York: St. Martin's Press, 1984.

Holcombe, Lee. *Wives and Property: Reform of the Married Women's Property Law in Nineteenth-Century England.* Toronto: University of Toronto Press, 1983.

Houston, R. A. "The Development of Literacy: Northern England, 1640–1750." *Economic History Review.* 2d series, 35, no. 2 (May 1982): 199–216.

Hovde, B. J. *The Scandinavian Countries, 1720–1865: The Rise of the Middle Classes.* 2 vols. Boston: Chapman and Grimes, 1943.

Howell, Martha C. "Fixing Movables: Gifts by Testament in Late Medieval Douai." *Past & Present,* no. 150 (February 1996): 3–45.

——. *The Marriage Exchange: Property, Social Place, and Gender in Cities of the Low Countries, 1300–1550.* Chicago: University of Chicago Press, 1998.

Hubbs, Joanna. *Mother Russia: The Feminine Myth in Russian Culture.* Bloomington: Indiana University Press, 1988.

Hughes, Diane Owen. "From Brideprice to Dowry in Mediterranean Europe." *Women and History,* no. 10 (1985): 13–8. First published in *Journal of Family History* 3, no. 3 (Fall 1978): 262–96.

Hughes, Lindsey. "Between Two Worlds: Tsarevna Natal'ia Alekseevna and the 'Emancipation' of Petrine Women." In *A Window on Russia: Papers from the Fifth International Conference of the Study Group on Eighteenth-Century Russia, Gargnano, 1994,* 29–36. Edited by Maria di Salvo and Lindsey Hughes. Rome, 1996.

——. "Peter the Great's Two Weddings: Changing Images of Women in a Transitional Age." In *Women in Russia and Ukraine,* edited by Rosalind Marsh. Cambridge: Cambridge University Press, 1996.

——. *Russia in the Age of Peter the Great.* New Haven: Yale University Press, 1998.

——. *Sophia, Regent of Russia, 1657–1704.* New Haven: Yale University Press, 1990.

Hull, Isabel V. *Sexuality, State, and Civil Society in Germany, 1700–1815.* Ithaca: Cornell University Press, 1996.

Hurwich, Judith J. "Inheritance Practices in Early Modern Germany." *Journal of Interdisciplinary History* 23, no. 4 (Spring 1993): 699–718.

Ignatovich, Inna Ivanovna. *Pomeshchich'i krest'iane nakanune osvobozhdeniia.* 3rd ed. Leningrad, 1925.

Ilinskii, P. A. "K voprosu o polozhenii zhenshchiny v 18 stoletii v Kostromskoi oblasti, po arkhivnym dannym." In *Trudy tret'ego oblastnogo istoriko-arkheologicheskogo s"ezda,* 1–17. Vladimir, 1909.

Indova, E. I. *Dvortsovoe khoziaistvo v Rossii: Pervaia polovina XVIII veka.* Moscow, 1964.

Ingrassia, Catherine. "The Pleasure of Business and the Business of Pleasure: Gender, Credit, and the South Sea Bubble." *Studies in Eighteenth-Century Culture* 24 (1995): 191–210.

Ioksimovich, Ch. M. *Manufakturnaia promyshlennost' v proshlom i nastoiashchem.* Moscow, 1915.

Joffe, Muriel and Adele Lindenmeyr. "Daughters, Wives, and Partners: Women of the Moscow Merchant Elite." In *Merchant Moscow: Images of Russia's Vanished Bourgeoisie,* 95–108. Edited by James L. West and Iurii A. Petrov. Princeton: Princeton University Press, 1998.

Jones, Robert E. *The Emancipation of the Russian Nobility, 1762–1785.* Princeton: Princeton University Press, 1973.

——. "Urban Planning and the Development of Provincial Towns in Russia, 1762–1796." In *The Eighteenth Century in Russia,* 321–44. Edited by J. G. Garrard. Oxford: Clarendon Press, 1973.

Jordan, William Chester. *Women and Credit in Pre-Industrial and Developing Societies.* Philadelphia: University of Pennsylvania Press, 1993.

Kahan, Arcadius. "The Costs of 'Westernization' in Russia: The Gentry and the Economy in the Eighteenth Century." *Slavic Review* 25, no. 1 (March 1966): 40–66.

——. *The Plow, the Hammer, and the Knout: An Economic History of Eighteenth-Century Russia.* Chicago: University of Chicago Press, 1985.

Kaiser, Daniel H. "'Forgive Us Our Debts . . .': Debts and Debtors in Early Modern Russia." In *Forschungen zur osteuropäischen Geschichte,* 155–183. Berlin: Harrassowitz Verlag, 1995.

——. "Women, Property, and the Law in Early Modern Russia." Paper presented at Indiana University, 1988.

——. "Women's Property in Muscovite Families, 1500–1725." Paper presented at Kent State University, 1988.

Kalas, Robert J. "The Noble Widow's Place in the Patriarchal Household: The Life and Career of Jeanne de Gontault." *Sixteenth Century Journal* 24, no. 3 (1993): 519–39.

Kapustina, G. D. "Zapisnye knigi Moskovskoi krepostnoi kontory kak istoricheskii istochnik (Pervaia chetvert' XVIII v.)." In *Problemy istochnikovedeniia,* vol. 7, 216–73. Moscow, 1959.

Karnovich, E. P. *Zamechatel'nye bogatstva chastnykh lits v Rossii.* St. Petersburg, 1874.

Kavelin, K. D. *Sobranie sochinenii.* 4 vols. St. Petersburg, 1900.

Kelly, Catriona. *Refining Russia: Advice Literature, Polite Culture, and Gender from Catherine II to Yeltsin.* Oxford: Oxford University Press, 2001.

——. "Teacups and Coffins: The Culture of Russian Merchant Women, 1850–1917. In *Women in Russia and Ukraine,* 55–77. Edited by Rosalind Marsh. Cambridge: Cambridge University Press, 1996.

Kettering, Sharon. "The Patronage Power of Early Modern French Noblewomen." *Historical Journal* 32, no. 4 (1989): 817–41.

Khvostov, V. M. *Zhenshchina nakanune novoi epokhi.* Moscow, 1905.

Kivelson, Valerie A. *Autocracy in the Provinces: The Muscovite Gentry and Political Culture in the Seventeenth Century.* Stanford: Stanford University Press, 1996.

——. "The Effects of Partible Inheritance: Gentry Families and the State in Muscovy." *Russian Review* 53, no. 2 (April 1994): 197–212.

Klapisch-Zuber, Christiane. *Women, Family, and Ritual in Renaissance Italy.* Translated by Lydia Cochrane. Chicago: University of Chicago Press, 1985.

Kleimola, Ann M. "'In Accordance with the Canons of the Holy Apostles': Muscovite Dowries and Women's Property Rights." *Russian Review* 51, no. 2 (April 1992): 204–29.

Kliuchevskii, Vasili. *Peter the Great.* Translated by Liliana Archibald. London: Macmillan, 1958.

Kolchin, Peter. *Unfree Labor: American Slavery and Russian Serfdom.* Cambridge: Belknap Press of Harvard University Press, 1987.

Kollmann, Nancy Shields. "Women's Honor in Early Modern Russia." In *Russia's Women: Accommodation, Resistance, Transformation,* 60–73. Edited by Barbara Evans Clements, Barbara Alpern Engel, and Christine D. Worobec. Berkeley: University of California Press, 1991.

Korf, S. A. *Dvorianstvo i ego soslovnoe upravlenie za stoletie 1762–1855 godov.* St. Petersburg, 1906.

Kuehn, Thomas. "Some Ambiguities of Female Inheritance Ideology in the Renaissance." *Continuity and Change* 2, no. 1 (May 1987): 11–36.

Landes, Joan B. *Women and the Public Sphere in the Age of the French Revolution.* Ithaca: Cornell University Press, 1988.

Latkin, V. N. *Zakonodatel'nye kommissii v Rossii v XVIII st.* St. Petersburg, 1887.

Lebedev, A. "O brachnykh razvodakh po arkhivnym dokumentam Khar'kovskoi i Kurskoi dukhovnykh konsistorii." In *Chteniia Imperatorskom obshchestve istorii i drevnostei rossiiskikh*, vol. 2, 1–30. Moscow, 1887.

Lebsock, Suzanne. *The Free Women of Petersburg: Status and Culture in a Southern Town, 1784–1860.* New York: W. W. Norton, 1984.

LeDonne, John P. *Absolutism and Ruling Class: The Formation of the Russian Political Order, 1700–1825.* Oxford: Oxford University Press, 1991.

——. *Ruling Russia: Politics and Administration in the Age of Absolutism, 1762–1796.* Princeton: Princeton University Press, 1984.

Leonard, Carol S. *Reform and Regicide: The Reign of Peter III of Russia.* Bloomington: Indiana University Press, 1993.

Levin, Eve. "Women and Property in Medieval Novgorod: Dependence and Independence." *Russian History*, 10, pt. 2 (1983): 154–69.

Levshin, A. "Zhenskie nravy i vospitanie proshlogo veka (Istoricheskie kartiny)." *Kolos'ia: Zhurnal nauchno-literaturnyi*, no. 1 (January 1887): 155–80.

Levy, Sandra. "Women and the Control of Property in Sixteenth-Century Muscovy." *Russian History*, 10, pt. 2 (1983): 201–12.

Lewis, Judith Schneid. *In the Family Way: Childbearing in the British Aristocracy, 1760–1860.* New Brunswick: Rutgers University Press, 1986.

Liddington, Jill. *Female Fortune: Land, Gender, and Authority: The Anne Lister Diaries and Other Writings, 1833–36.* London: Rivers Oram Press, 1998.

Lieven, Dominic. *The Aristocracy in Europe, 1815–1914.* New York: Columbia University Press, 1992.

Likhacheva, E. O. *Materialy dlia istorii zhenskogo obrazovaniia v Rossii (1086–1856).* 2 vols. St. Petersburg, 1899–1901.

Lindenmeyr, Adele. "Public Life, Private Virtues: Women in Russian Charity, 1762–1914." *Signs* 18, no. 3 (Spring 1993): 562–91.

Liubavskii, A. "Ob uravnenii nasledstvennykh prav muzhchin i zhenshchin." *Zhurnal Ministerstva Iustitsii* 20, kn. 2 (May 1864): 399–424.

Lorence-Kot, Bogna. *Child-Rearing and Reform: A Study of the Nobility in Eighteenth-Century Poland.* Westport, Conn.: Greenwood Press, 1985.

Lotman, Iurii M. "The Poetics of Everyday Behavior in Eighteenth-Century Russian Culture." In *The Semiotics of Russian Cultural History*, 67–94. Edited by Alexander D. Nakhimovsky and Alice Stone Nakhimovsky. Ithaca: Cornell University Press, 1985.

Lubamersky, Lynn. "Women and Political Patronage in the Politics of the Polish-Lithuanian Commonwealth." *Polish Review* 44, no. 3 (1999): 259–75.

Macfarlane, Alan. *The Origins of English Individualism: The Family, Property, and Social Transition.* Oxford: Basil Blackwell, 1978.

Macrides, Ruth. "The Transmission of Property in the Patriarchal Register." In *La transmission du patrimoine: Byzance et l'aire méditerranéenne*, 179–88. Edited by Joëlle Beaucamp and Gilbert Dagron. Paris: De Boccard, 1998.

Madariaga, Isabel de. "Catherine II and the Serfs: A Reconsideration of Some Problems." *Slavonic and East European Review* 52, no. 126 (January 1974): 34–62.

——. *Russia in the Age of Catherine the Great.* New Haven: Yale University Press, 1981.

Main, Gloria L. "Widows in Rural Massachusetts on the Eve of the Revolution." In *Women in the Age of the American Revolution*, 67–90. Edited by Ronald Hoffman and Peter J. Albert. Charlottesville: University Press of Virginia, 1989.

Makashin, S. *Saltykov-Shchedrin.* 2d ed. 2 vols. Moscow, 1951.

Manning, Roberta Thompson. *The Crisis of the Old Order in Russia: Gentry and Government.* Princeton: Princeton University Press, 1982.

Marcus, Abraham. "Men, Women, and Property: Dealers in Real Estate in 18th Century Aleppo." *Journal of the Economic and Social History of the Orient* 26, part II (1983): 137–63.

Marker, Gary. *Publishing, Printing, and the Origins of Intellectual Life in Russia, 1700–1800.* Princeton: Princeton University Press, 1985.

Marrese, Michelle Lamarche. "The Enigma of Married Women's Control of Property in Eighteenth-Century Russia." *Russian Review* 58, no. 3 (July 1999): 380–95.

——. "Women and Westernization in Petrine Russia." *Study Group on Eighteenth-Century Russia Newsletter.* Cambridge (1998): 105–17.

Marshall, Sherrin. *The Dutch Gentry, 1500–1650: Family, Faith, and Fortune.* Westport, Conn.: Greenwood Press, 1987.

McCaffray, Susan P. "What Should Russia Be? Patriotism and Political Economy in the Thought of N. S. Mordvinov." *Slavic Review* 59, no. 3 (Fall 2000): 572–96.

McNally, Susanne Janosik. "From Public Person to Private Prisoner: The Changing Place of Women in Medieval Russia." Ph.D. dissertation. State University of New York at Binghamton, 1976.

Meehan, Brenda. "Popular Piety, Local Initiative, and the Founding of Women's Religious Communities in Russia, 1764–1907." In *Seeking God: The Recovery of Religious Identity in Orthodox Russia, Ukraine, and Georgia,* 83–105. Edited by Stephen K. Batalden. DeKalb: Northern Illinois University Press, 1993.

Meehan-Waters, Brenda. *Autocracy and Aristocracy: The Russian Service Elite of 1730.* New Brunswick: Rutgers University Press, 1982.

——. "Catherine the Great and the Problem of Female Rule." *Russian Review* 34, no. 3 (July 1975): 293–307.

——. "The Development and the Limits of Security of Noble Status, Person, and Property in Eighteenth-Century Russia." In *Russia and the West in the Eighteenth Century,* 294–305. Edited by A. G. Cross. Newtonville, Mass.: Oriental Research Partners, 1983.

——. "Metropolitan Filaret (Drozdov) and the Reform of Russian Women's Monastic Communities." *Russian Review* 50, no. 3 (July 1991): 310–23.

Meier, D. I. *Russkoe grazhdanskoe pravo.* 2 vols. St. Petersburg, 1861.

Melton, Edgar. "Enlightened Seigniorialism and Its Dilemmas in Serf Russia, 1750–1830." *Journal of Modern History* 62 (December 1990): 675–708.

Meriweather, Margaret L. "Women and *Waqf* Revisited: The Case of Aleppo, 1770–1840." In *Women in the Ottoman Empire: Middle Eastern Women in the Early Modern Era,* 128–52. Edited by Madeline C. Zilfi. New York: Brill, 1997.

Metcalf, Alida C. "Women and Means: Women and Family Property in Colonial Brazil." *Journal of Social History* 24, no. 3 (Spring 1991): 277–98.

Meyer, Donald. *Sex and Power: The Rise of Women in America, Russia, Sweden, and Italy.* Middletown, Conn.: Wesleyan University Press, 1987.

Mikhailova, Vera. *Russkie zakony o zhenshchine.* Moscow, 1913.

Mikhnevich, V. O. *Russkaia zhenshchina XVIII stoletiia.* Kiev, 1895.

Milov, L. V. *Issledovanie ob "ekonomicheskikh primechaniiakh" k general'nomu mezhevaniiu (k istorii russkogo krest'ianstva i sel'skogo khoziaistva vtoroi poloviny XVIII v.).* Moscow, 1965.

Milov, L. V. and I. M. Garskova. "A Typology of Feudal Estates in Russia in the First Half of the Seventeenth Century (Factor Analysis)." *Russian Review* 47, no. 4 (October 1988): 375–90.

Mironov, Boris N. "Consequences of the Price Revolution in Eighteenth-Century Russia." *Economic History Review* 45, no. 3 (1992): 457–78.

——. *Istoriia v tsifrakh: Matematika v istoricheskikh issledovaniiakh.* Leningrad, 1991.

——. "Local Government in Russia in the First Half of the Nineteenth Century: Provincial Government and Estate Self-Government." *Jahrbücher für Geschichte Osteuropas* 42 (1994): 161–201.

——. *Sotsial'naia istoriia Rossii perioda imperii (XVIII–nachalo XX v.) Genezis lichnosti, demokraticheskoi sem'i, grazhdanskogo obshchestva i pravovogo gosudarstva.* 2 vols. St. Petersburg, 1999.

Mirrer, Louise, ed. *Upon My Husband's Death: Widows in the Literature and Histories of Medieval Europe.* Ann Arbor: University of Michigan Press, 1992.

Mitchell, Linda Elizabeth. "Widowhood in Medieval England: Baronial Dowagers of the Thirteenth-Century Welsh Marches." Ph.D. dissertation. Indiana University, 1991.

Moses, Claire Goldberg. *French Feminism in the Nineteenth Century.* Albany: State University of New York Press, 1984.

Murray, Mary. *The Law of the Father? Patriarchy in the Transition from Feudalism to Capitalism.* London: Routledge, 1995.

Narrett, David E. *Inheritance and Family Life in Colonial New York City.* Ithaca: Cornell University Press, 1992.

Nazzari, Muriel. *Disappearance of the Dowry: Women, Families, and Social Change in São Paulo, Brazil (1600–1900).* Stanford: Stanford University Press, 1991.

Nevolin, Konstantin. *Istoriia rossiiskikh grazhdanskikh zakonov.* 3 vols. St. Petersburg, 1851.

Nevzorov, A. S. *Russkaia zhenshchina v deistvuiushchem zakonodatel'stve i deistvitel'noi zhizni.* Revel', 1892.

Nicholls, Kenneth. "Irishwomen and Property in the Sixteenth Century." In *Women in Early Modern Ireland,* 17–31. Edited by Margaret MacCurtain and Mary O'Dowd. Edinburgh: Edinburgh University Press, 1991.

Okin, Susan Moller. "Patriarchy and Married Women's Property in England: Questions on Some Current Views." *Eighteenth-Century Studies* 17, no. 2 (Winter 1983/84): 121–38.

Orovich, Ia. *Zhenshchina v prave.* 2d ed. St. Petersburg, 1896.

Orshanskii, I. G. *Issledovaniia po russkomu pravu semeinomu i nasledstvennomu.* St. Petersburg, 1877.

——. "Nasledstvennye prava russkoi zhenshchiny." *Zhurnal grazhdanskogo i ugolovnogo prava,* no. 2 (1876): 1–38.

——. "O pridanom." *Zhurnal grazhdanskogo i torgovogo prava,* no. 12 (1872): 985–1045.

Ostrogorski, M. Ia. *The Rights of Women: A Comparative Study in History and Legislation.* London: Swan Sonnenschein, 1893.

Ourliac, Paul and Jean-Louis Gazzaniga. *Histoire du droit privé français de l'an mil au Code Civil.* Paris: Albin Michel, 1985.

Pakhman, S. V. *Istoriia kodifikatsii grazhdanskogo prava.* 2 vols. St. Petersburg, 1876.

Paramonov, A. S. *O zakonodatel'stve Anny Ioannovny.* St. Petersburg, 1904.

Pavlenko, N. I. "O rostovshchichestve dvorian v XVIII v. (K postanovke voprosa)." In *Dvorianstvo i krepostnoi stroi Rossii XVI–XVIII vv.,* 265–71. Moscow, 1975.

Pavlov, A. S. *Kurs tserkovnogo prava.* St. Petesburg, 1902.

Pavlova, Elena. "Private Land Ownership in Northeastern Rus' and Mongol Land Laws." *Russian History* 26, no. 2 (Summer 1999): 125–44.

Pavlov-Sil'vanskii, N. *Proekty reform v zapiskakh sovremennikov Petra Velikogo.* St. Petersburg, 1897.

Pedlow, Gregory W. "Marriage, Family Size, and Inheritance among Hessian Nobles, 1650–1900." *Journal of Family History* 7, no. 4 (Winter 1982): 333–52.

Perkin, Joan. *Women and Marriage in Nineteenth-Century England.* London: Routledge, 1989.

Peterson, M. Jeanne. "No Angels in the House: The Victorian Myth and the Paget Women." *American Historical Review* 89, no. 3 (1984): 677–708.

Pipes, Richard. *Russia under the Old Regime.* New York: Scribner's, 1974.

Pisarev, S. N. *Uchrezhdenie po priniatiiu i napravleniiu proshenii i zhalob, prinosimykh na Vysochaishee Imia, 1810–1910 gg.* St. Petersburg, 1909.

Pobedonostsev, K. *Kurs grazhdanskogo prava.* 3 vols. St. Petersburg, 1871.

Poovey, Mary. *Uneven Developments: The Ideological Work of Gender in Mid-Victorian England.* Chicago: University of Chicago Press, 1988.

Portemer, Jean. "Le Statut de la femme en France depuis la reformation des coutumes jusqu'à la redaction du Code Civil." *Recueils de la Société Jean Bodin pour l'histoire comparative des institutions* 12 (1962): 447–97.

Povalishin, A. D. *Riazanskie pomeshchiki i ikh krepostnye.* Riazan', 1903.

Pushkareva, N. L. *Chastnaia zhizn' russkoi zhenshchiny: nevesta, zhena, liubovnitsa (X-nachalo XIX v.)* Moscow: Nauchno-izdatel'skii tsentr "Ladomir," 1997.

———. "Imushchestvennye prava zhenshchin na Rusi (X–XV vv.)." *Istoricheskie zapiski* 114 (1986): 180–224.

———. *Women in Russian History: From the Tenth to the Twentieth Century.* Translated and edited by Eve Levin. Armonk, N.Y.: M. E. Sharpe, 1997.

———. *Zhenshchiny drevnei Rusi.* Moscow: "Mysl'," 1989.

Raeff, Marc. *Origins of the Russian Intelligentsia.* New York: Harcourt, Brace, and World, 1966.

Rakhmatullin, M. A. *Krest'ianskoe dvizhenie v velikorusskikh guberniiakh v 1826–1857 gg.* Moscow: Nauka, 1990.

Reher, David S. *Perspectives on the Family in Spain, Past and Present.* Oxford: Clarendon Press, 1997.

Reingardt, N. V. *O lichnykh i imushchestvennykh pravakh zhenshchin po russkomu zakonu.* Kazan, 1885.

Reverby, Susan M. and Dorothy O. Helly. "Introduction: Converging on History." In *Gendered Domains: Rethinking Public and Private in Women's History,* 1–24. Edited by Dorothy O. Helly and Susan M. Reverby. Ithaca: Cornell University Press, 1992.

Reynolds, K. D. *Aristocratic Women and Political Society in Victorian Britain.* Oxford: Clarendon Press, 1998.

Rieber, Alfred J. *Merchants and Entrepreneurs in Imperial Russia.* Chapel Hill: University of North Carolina Press, 1982.

Riemer, Eleanor S. "Women, Dowries, and Capital Investment in Thirteenth-Century Siena." *Women and History* 10 (1985): 59–79.

Roman, Stanislaw. "Le Statut de la femme dans l'Europe orientale (Pologne et Russie) au moyen âge et aux temps modernes." *Recueils de la Société Jean Bodin pour l'histoire comparative des institutions* 12 (1962): 389–403.

Romanovich-Slavatinskii, A. *Dvorianstvo v Rossii ot nachala XVIII veka do otmeny krepostnogo prava.* St. Petersburg, 1870.

Roosevelt, Priscilla R. "Emerald Thrones and Living Statues: Theater and Theatricality on the Russian Estate." *Russian Review* 50, no. 1 (January 1991): 1–23.

———. *Life on the Russian Country Estate: A Social and Cultural History.* New Haven: Yale University Press, 1995.

Rossiiskoe zakonadatel'stvo X–XX vekov. 10 vols. Edited by A. G. Mankov. Moscow, 1984–91.

Rozhdestvenskii, Nikolai Fedorovich. *Istoricheskoe izlozhenie russkogo zakonodatel'stva o nasledstve.* St. Petersburg, 1839.

Sabean, David Warren. *Property, Production, and Family in Neckarhausen, 1700–1870.* New York: Cambridge University Press, 1990.

Salmon, Marylynn. *Women and the Law of Property in Early America.* Chapel Hill: University of North Carolina Press, 1986.

———. "Women and the Law of Property in South Carolina: The Evidence from Marriage Settlements, 1730 to 1830." *William and Mary Quarterly,* 3rd series, 39 (1982): 655–85.

Sánchez, Magdalena S. *The Empress, the Queen, and the Nun: Women and Power at the Court of Philip III of Spain.* Baltimore: Johns Hopkins University Press, 1998.

Semenova, L. N. *Ocherki istorii byta i kul'turnoi zhizni Rossii: Pervaia polovina XVIII v.* Leningrad, 1982.

Semevskii, V. I. *Krest'iane v tsarstvovanie Imperatritsy Ekateriny II.* 2 vols. St. Petersburg, 1881–1901.

Sergeevich, V. I. *Lektsii i issledovaniia po drevnei istorii russkogo prava.* 2d ed. St. Petersburg, 1899.

Shammas, Carol. "Re-assessing the Married Women's Property Acts." *Journal of Women's History* 6, no. 1 (Spring 1994): 9–30.

Shammas, Carol, Marylynn Salmon, and Michel Dahlin. *Inheritance in America from Colonial Times to the Present.* New Brunswick: Rutgers University Press, 1987.

Shashkov, S. S. *Istoriia russkoi zhenshchiny.* St. Petersburg, 1879.

Shcheglov, V. G. *Polozhenie i prava zhenshchiny v sem'e i obshchestve v drevnosti, srednie veka i novoe vremia.* Iaroslavl', 1898.

Shchepkina, E. *Iz istorii zhenskoi lichnosti v Rossii.* St. Petersburg, 1914.

———. *Starinnye pomeshchiki na sluzhbe i doma.* St. Petersburg, 1890.

Shepukova, N. M. "Ob izmenenii razmerov dushevladeniia pomeshchikov evropeiskoi Rossii v pervoi chetverti XVIII–pervoi polovine XIX v." In *Ezhegodnik po agrarnoi istorii vostochnoi Evropy. 1963 g.*, 388–419. Vilnius, 1964.

Shimko, I. I. *Novye dannye k biografii kn. Antiokha Dmitrievicha Kantemira i ego blizhaishikh rodstvennikov.* St. Petersburg, 1891.

Shishkin, T. "Neskol'ko slov o neobkhodimosti iuridicheskikh poznanii dlia zhenshchin." *Rassvet* 3 (1859): 117–30.

Shul'gin, Vitalii. *O sostoianii zhenshchin v Rossii do Petra Velikogo.* Kiev, 1850.

Sinaiskii, V. I. *Lichnoe i imushchestvennoe polozhenie zamuzhnei zhenshchiny v grazhdanskom prave.* Iur'ev, 1910.

Smith, Alison K. "Cabbage and Cuisine: Diet in Kostroma and Kazan Provinces before the Great Reforms." Ph.D. dissertation. University of Chicago, 2000.

Smith, Bonnie G. *Ladies of the Leisure Class: The Bourgeoises of Northern France in the Nineteenth Century.* Princeton: Princeton University Press, 1981.

Sokolovskii, N. "Sovremennyi byt russkoi zhenshchiny i sudebnaia reforma (Iuridicheskie zametki)." *Zhenskii vestnik*, no. 9 (1867): 57–83.

Soloviev, S. M. *Istoriia Rossii.* 29 vols. in 15. Moscow, 1959–66.

Spring, Eileen. *Law, Land, and Family: Aristocratic Inheritance in England, 1300–1800.* Chapel Hill: University of North Carolina Press, 1993.

Staves, Susan. *Married Women's Separate Property in England, 1660–1833.* Cambridge: Harvard University Press, 1990.

———. "Pin Money." In *Studies in Eighteenth-Century Culture*, vol. 14, 47–77. Edited by O. M. Brack Jr. Published for the American Society for Eighteenth-Century Studies. Madison: University of Wisconsin Press, 1985.

———. "Resentment or Resignation? Dividing the Spoils among Daughters and Younger Sons." In *Early Modern Conceptions of Property*, 194–218. Edited by John Brewer and Susan Staves. London: Routledge, 1995.

Stone, Lawrence. *Broken Lives: Separation and Divorce in England, 1660–1857.* Oxford: Oxford University Press, 1993.

Thirsk, Joan. "The European Debate on Customs of Inheritance, 1500–1700." In *Family and Inheritance: Rural Society in Western Europe, 1200–1800*, 177–91. Edited by Jack Goody, Joan Thirsk, and E. P. Thompson. Cambridge: Cambridge University Press, 1976.

Tishkin, G. A. *Zhenskii vopros v Rossii 50-60-e gody XIX v.* Leningrad, 1984.

Tovrov, Jessica. *The Russian Noble Family: Structure and Change.* New York: Garland Publishing, 1987.

Troitskii, S. M. *Russkii absoliutizm i dvorianstvo v XVIII v.* Moscow, 1974.

Tsebrikova, Marie. "Russia." In *The Woman Question in Europe*, 390–423. Edited by Theodore Stanton. New York: G. P. Putnam's Sons, 1884.

Tugan-Baranovskii, M. *Russkaia fabrika.* 6th ed. Moscow, 1934.

Ul'ianova, G. N. *Blagotvoritel'nost' Moskovskikh predprinimatelei: 1860–1914 gg.* Moscow: "Mosgorarkhiv," 1999.

Ulrich, Laurel Thatcher. *Good Wives: Image and Reality in the Lives of Women in Northern New England, 1650–1750.* New York: Oxford University Press, 1982.

———. "Hannah Barnard's Cupboard: Female Property and Identity in Eighteenth-Century New England." In *Through a Glass Darkly: Reflections on Personal Identity in Early America*, 238–73. Edited by Ronald Hoffman, Mechal Sobel, and Fredrika J. Teute. Chapel Hill: University of North Carolina Press, 1997.

Vernadsky, George. "Studies in the History of Moscovian Private Law of the 16th and 17th Centuries. Inheritance: The Case of the Childless Wife." In *Studi in Memoria di Aldo Albertoni*, vol. 3, 433–454. (Padua, 1938)

Veselovskii, S. B. *Feodal'noe zemlevladenie v severo-vostochnoi Rusi.* 2 vols. Moscow, 1947.

Vickery, Amanda. *The Gentleman's Daughter: Women's Lives in Georgian England.* New Haven: Yale University Press, 1998.

———. "Women and the World of Goods: A Lancashire Consumer and Her Possessions, 1751–81." In *Consumption and the World of Goods*, 274–301. Edited by John Brewer and Roy Porter. London: Routledge, 1993.

Viollet, Paul. *Histoire du droit civil français.* 2d ed. Paris, 1893.

Vladimirskii-Budanov, M. F. *Obzor istorii russkogo prava.* 6th ed. St. Petersburg, 1909.

Vowles, Judith. "Marriage à la Russe." In *Sexuality and the Body in Russian Culture*, 53–72, 300–303. Edited by Jane T. Costlow, Stephanie Sandler, and Judith Vowles. Stanford: Stanford University Press, 1993.

Wagner, William G. "Legislative Reform of Inheritance in Russia, 1861–1914." In *Russian Law: Historical and Political Perspectives*, 143–78. Edited by William E. Butler. Leyden: A. W. Sijthoff, 1977.

———. *Marriage, Property, and Law in Late Imperial Russia.* Oxford: Clarendon Press, 1994.

———. "The Trojan Mare: Women's Rights and Civil Rights in Late Imperial Russia." In *Civil Rights in Imperial Russia*, 65–84. Edited by Olga Crisp and Linda Edmondson. Oxford: Clarendon Press, 1989.

Weickhardt, George G. "Legal Rights of Women in Russia, 1100–1750." *Slavic Review* 55, no. 1 (Spring 1996): 1–23.

———. "The Pre-Petrine Law of Property." *Slavic Review* 52, no. 4 (Winter 1993): 663–79.

———. "Was There Private Property in Muscovite Russia?" *Slavic Review* 53, no. 2 (Summer 1994): 531–38.

Wemple, Suzanne Fonay. *Women in Frankish Society: Marriage and the Cloister, 500 to 900.* Philadelphia: University of Pennsylvania Press, 1981.

Werth, Paul W. "Baptism, Authority, and the Problem of *Zakonnost'* in Orenburg Diocese: The Induction of Over 800 'Pagans' into the Christian Faith." *Slavic Review* 56, no. 3 (Fall 1997): 456–80.

Wortman, Richard. *The Development of a Russian Legal Consciousness.* Chicago: University of Chicago Press, 1976.

———. "Property Rights, Populism, and Russian Political Culture." In *Civil Rights in Imperial Russia*, 13–32. Edited by Olga Crisp and Linda Edmondson. Oxford: Clarendon Press, 1989.

———. "The Russian Empress as Mother." In *The Family in Imperial Russia*, 60–74. Edited by David L. Ransel. Urbana: University of Illinois Press, 1978.

Wyntjes, Sherrin Marshall. "Survivors and Status: Widowhood and Family in the Early Modern Netherlands." *Journal of Family History* 7, no. 4 (Winter 1982): 396–405.

Zagorovskii, A. "Lichnye i imushchestvennye otnosheniia mezhdu suprugami." *Russkaia mysl'*, no. 4 (1897): 45–68.

Zaozerskii, A. I. "Boiarskii dvor." *Russkii istoricheskii zhurnal*, kn. 8 (1922): 88–114.

Zarinebaf-Shahr, Fariba. "Ottoman Women and the Tradition of Seeking Justice in the Eighteenth Century." In *Women in the Ottoman Empire: Middle Eastern Women in the Early Modern Era*, 253–63. Edited by Madeline C. Zilfi. New York: Brill, 1997.

Zirin, Mary Fleming. "Introduction." In *The Cavalry Maiden: Journals of a Russian Officer in the Napoleonic Wars*, ix–xxxvii. By Nadezhda Durova. Bloomington: Indiana University Press, 1989.

Znamenitye Rossiiane XVIII–XIX vekov: Biografii i portrety. Po izdaniiu velikogo kniazia Nikolaia Mikhailovicha "Russkie portrety XVIII i XIX stoletii." St. Petersburg: Lenizdat, 1996.

Zweigert, Konrad and Hein Kötz. *An Introduction to Comparative Law*. 2 vols. Translated by Tony Weir. Amsterdam: North-Holland, 1977.

Index